It Seemed
Like A Good Idea
At The Time

MICHAEL GRADE

It Seemed Like A Good Idea At The Time

PAN BOOKS

First published 1999 by Macmillan

This edition published 2000 by Pan Books
an imprint of Macmillan Publishers Ltd
25 Eccleston Place, London SW1W 9NF
Basingstoke and Oxford
Associated companies throughout the world
www.macmillan.com

ISBN 0 330 36770 6

Copyright © Michael Grade 1999

The right of Michael Grade to be identified as the
author of this work has been asserted by him in accordance
with the Copyright, Designs and Patents Act 1988.

All rights reserved. No part of this publication may be
reproduced, stored in or introduced into a retrieval system, or
transmitted, in any form, or by any means (electronic, mechanical,
photocopying, recording or otherwise) without the prior written
permission of the publisher. Any person who does any unauthorized
act in relation to this publication may be liable to criminal
prosecution and civil claims for damages.

1 3 5 7 9 8 6 4 2

A CIP catalogue record for this book is available from
the British Library.

Typeset by SetSystems Ltd, Saffron Walden, Essex
Printed and bound in Great Britain by
Mackays of Chatham plc, Chatham, Kent

This book is sold subject to the condition that it shall not,
by way of trade or otherwise, be lent, re-sold, hired out,
or otherwise circulated without the publisher's prior consent
in any form of binding or cover other than that in which
it is published and without a similar condition including this
condition being imposed on the subsequent purchaser.

FOR ALISON, JONATHAN AND SAMUEL

ACKNOWLEDGEMENTS

This book is intended as an entirely personal memoir. It is therefore only a contribution to the public record, not in any way to be construed as a definitive account of events described. I have ignored the usual strict rules of impartiality, which I slavishly endeavoured to apply throughout my broadcasting career, and very liberating it has been. I have tried to be true to my own recall and my own feelings. I once asked a celebrated television writer, noted for exquisite and faithful small-screen adaptations of classics, how he ever decided what to leave in and what to leave out. He replied that, just before setting pen to paper, he would reread the work to be adapted. He then cast it aside and anything he remembered from the original he included. Anything he forgot, he assumed, safely it usually turned out, did not matter. I wish I shared his confidence.

That said, facts are facts and dates are dates, and wherever possible I have, I hope, been accurate about the unarguable. To this end, I am indebted to the amount of time a number of colleagues, both past and present, have devoted to the cause of keeping my narrative on the straight and narrow path of factual accuracy. In particular, I must thank Ros Sloboda, Jan Bates, Sue Robertson, Martin Young, Pat Coward and the 'Farmtackle' archives for their contribution. At the risk of sounding like one of those predictable Oscar Awards acceptance speeches, I really *would* like to thank my agent Georgina Capel and my ever patient editor Georgina Morley, without whom I would never have embarked on the book, let alone completed it.

Contents

LIST OF ILLUSTRATIONS

ELI WALLACH: 'What I don't understand is why a man like you took the job in the first place.'

YUL BRYNNER: 'I wonder myself.'

ELI WALLACH: 'No, come on: tell me why.'

STEVE McQUEEN: 'Like a fellow I knew in El Paso. One day he just took his clothes off and jumped into a mess of cactus. I asked him the same question, *Why?*'

ELI WALLACH: 'And?'

STEVE McQUEEN: 'He said it seemed a good idea at the time.'

The Magnificent Seven, United Artists, 1960.

Chapter One

LIFE WITH OLGA – OR
WAS IT GOLDA?

WHEN I WAS LIVING in the States, I had just one very expensive session with a Hollywood shrink. After he'd heard me tell the story of my life, Dr Perlman delivered his verdict: 'You should either be gay or an alcoholic . . .' He paused. 'Probably both.'

Well . . . Jewish boys can always blame their mothers for the way they turn out in later life. In my case, it was my grandmother who was the mother figure in my life, so that's where my story must begin, with my grandparents, Olga (or, if the whim took her, Golda) and Isaac Winogradski talking quietly in bed one night and finally deciding that turn-of-the-century Russia was no place for a Jewish family to bring up their children. This was 1911, and under the Tsar's pogroms, anti-Semitism was rife – not outright extermination on the Nazi pattern but certainly social humiliation and physical intimidation. Bravely, they decided to get out.

Their home town was Tokmak near Odessa, in what is now known as the Ukraine. Showbusiness has very deep roots in our family. Isaac's father ran what must have been one of the very first cinema houses showing single-reel silent films, and after a short acting career, Isaac, too, took over the management of a small cinema. Olga had been a semi-professional singer and actress, but the birth of their first two children Louis (Lew) in 1906 and Boris (Bernie) in 1909 put a stop to her career.

When the Winogradski family fled the Ukraine, it was just another of those unnumbered exoduses on which the Jews have had to embark throughout their history. My grandfather came over to Britain first, to the East End of London where one of my grandmother's brothers was living. Olga followed some months later, and at her husband's insistence spent the waiting time learning not English but Yiddish so that she would be able to communicate with the rest of the Jewish population when she eventually arrived in the East End. She never forgot the horrors of the endless train journey through Russia to Berlin, the struggle to get temporary lodgings there, then a visa to enter Britain as a stateless alien, then pawning her rings to pay for boat tickets. She had her two small children, Lew and Bernie, to cope with and she spoke not a word of German. Eventually, she got passage on an onion boat to Tilbury.

They settled in two rooms above a shoe shop in Brick Lane and Isaac tried his hand at running a cinema in the Mile End Road, but the outbreak of the First World War put an end to that venture. They had two more children: my father Leslie, who was born in 1916, and in 1925, my aunt Rita. Life was grim. Though a clever man in his own way, Isaac didn't have a head for business and he was fond of a flutter, so money was always short. He ended up as a semi-skilled worker in the rag trade. Never strong, he died young from Hodgkin's disease, leaving my grandmother with four children to support on no income. This was years before the welfare state. My grandmother often recalled how she took in washing, borrowed and scrimped and somehow managed to keep a crust on the table for the children.

The first real money Olga saw was when her eldest son, Lew, who must have inherited her talent for dancing, proved to have a natural aptitude for the Charleston and began to win cash prizes in dance competitions. On one occasion he won twenty-four bottles of brandy and my grandmother sold them to a wedding party, realizing enough cash to clear her debts and pay the rent. His speciality was performing the Charleston in double-quick time on a table. Bernie started work in the china trade but was inspired by Lew's example and also took up professional dancing. To avoid being confused with his brother, he changed his professional name to Delfont, and with his Japanese partner, Toko, he toured the music halls for seven years before he started organizing shows instead of appearing in them.

Lew became the family's father-figure: he had natural authority and he was a keen disciplinarian; Bernie always said the other children were a little in awe of him. He was also very bright academically, especially at maths. Bernie wasn't as sharp a scholar but he was a natural entrepreneur, always up to schemes and scams. Leslie, my father, was born after they had settled in Britain. He was apparently quite wild in his teens and seemed to have inherited Isaac's gambling instincts. Somehow, he put it all behind him, because by the time I appeared, he was rather quiet and self-effacing and turned out to be the least flamboyant of the Grade brothers. Unlike Lew and Bernie, he wasn't seduced by the smell of greasepaint, there was nothing of the showman about him. He kept well out of the public eye; I don't think he ever gave a press interview, but by common consent he was probably the cleverest of the three and the first to enjoy commercial success.

In 1935, Lew quit his career as a professional dancer and went into partnership as a theatrical agent with Joan Collins's father, Joe. Initially Bernie joined his elder brother as a part-time talent-spotter before launching his own business and taking the first tentative steps towards becoming an impresario. My father became an office boy for Miss Leddington, who ran a group of music halls.

Once he had learned enough, my father in turn started his own agency, though unlike his brothers he had never been on the stage so didn't have their range of professional contacts. Nevertheless, he soon proved to have a genius for talent-spotting and negotiating, and when war broke out he was beginning to do quite well.

All the Grade brothers enlisted for military service. Bernie was turned down; Lew went into the Army but was discharged because of a knee injury; so my father was the only war hero in the family. He joined the RAF and his first posting was to Hendon, which wasn't a disaster because he could still keep an eye on his Shaftesbury Avenue office, though of course the Air Ministry didn't know *that*. He made his double life official when he assured his CO that he could lay on shows with all the big stars for the RAF Benevolent Fund – Vera Lynn, Billy Cotton, you name them, he promised to have them on parade, but of course, he'd have to go up to London during the week to arrange the shows. The CO agreed, and Leslie, resplendent in RAF blue, spent all week in his West End office, managing both to keep his own business afloat and help the war effort. Fly-posters of the time displayed a bizarre contrast between the great and the lowly. They advertised some of the biggest names in showbusiness as 'Presented by Leading Aircraftman Grade, by kind permission of the Air Ministry'.

Then an unknown whistle-blower told the RAF's top brass about my father's double life and within hours he was on a plane to Tripoli. But the luck of the Grades held. At a military airport in the Middle East he bumped into George Formby, at that time a huge star doing his bit keeping up the morale of the troops. 'Hello, Leslie,' he said. 'What are you doing here?' In no time they'd struck a deal and Formby used his influence to get Dad a job organizing the shows the stars were putting on for the troops.

He either got unlucky or lucky – depends how you look at it. Unlucky, because he was struck down by typhoid fever in Cairo; lucky, because of eight who went down with the disease, only two survived. One was my father, the other, the man who told me the story, a journalist who, years later, came to interview me on behalf of a trade magazine. He recalled Leslie in hospital when he was convalescing, sitting up in bed, sending telegrams and making bookings, keeping his business going on the other side of the globe.

Meanwhile, after his short spell of military service, Lew was back in Civvy Street. He quarrelled with Joe Collins and joined my father. The firm's name was changed from West End Varieties to 'Lew and Leslie Grade Ltd – Variety Agents Licensed by the LCC'. In those days, apparently, you needed a licence from the local council to make money. After the war, they became a formidable partnership, the extrovert Lew flying round the world glad-handing clients and talent-spotting while my father remained quietly in the office, doing his dealing by telephone. In time, the firm they started grew into a huge business, handling many big names, Paul Scofield, Albert Finney, Roger Moore, Vanessa Redgrave, Cliff Richard, Des O'Connor, Roy Castle, Arthur Askey, Arthur Haynes. After the start of commercial television, Leslie began to represent film directors and writers and just about anyone saleable in the entertainment business. By then the firm was known as the Grade Organisation.

There couldn't have been a greater contrast than that between my father's quiet behind-the-scenes style and Lew's energetic salesmanship. When they first launched the agency, Val Parnell's Moss Empires had control of the top British theatres; if the agency was to get its artists into the big time, the Grade brothers had to establish a relationship with Val Parnell. Harry Foster, their great rival agent, was the British end of the business supplying all the American stars to Val Parnell. Foster and Parnell were very close and regularly played golf together. Lew decided he would nobble Val on the golf course. One of the agency's staff was a former comedian turned agent called Johnny Riscoe. He was a member of the Coombe Hill golf club where Val Parnell and Harry Foster played. Lew sent for Johnny and announced that he had decided to take up golf. Riscoe was dispatched to arrange a game for him.

On the due day, Lew turned up clad in expensive golfing gear, plus-fours, set of Henry Cotton clubs, the best of everything money could buy. He had never been on a golf course in his life but, ever impatient, he spurned the professional's offer of a trial lesson on the practice tee. He had, after all, been the world professional Charleston champion and he was sure that one sport was much like another. They went straight to the first tee where Lew made numerous and ever wilder attempts to hit the ball, his swing possibly hampered by the huge cigar in his mouth. He missed every time and finally threw down the clubs in disgust, announcing that he was abandoning his golfing career. According to Johnny Riscoe, though, Lew was determined to turn defeat into victory, so as soon as he got back into the office he rang Val Parnell and told him he was sending over a present, a brand new set of Henry Cotton clubs.

Dad's strategy was different: he hardly left his desk but spent the time on the telephone, ringing someone who knew someone who knew someone who knew Val Parnell, negotiating in ever narrower circles until he got close to his quarry. In the event, the arrival of 'recording stars' changed the balance of power in the American agencies. This led to the Grade agency displacing Harry Foster as the chief supplier of stars to Moss Empires – Frank Sinatra, Johnnie Ray, Nat King Cole, Frankie Laine, Guy Mitchell, Lena Horne and the rest. Between them, the Grade brothers eventually had the entertainment business pretty well sewn up. Later, it wasn't uncommon to have a variety show in which Leslie supplied the artists, Bernie provided the theatre and Lew's ATV televised it.

My father, although the youngest of the brothers, had been the first to marry – in 1940, to my mother, Winifred Smith, the sister of George Smith, who later kept the firm's accounts. She was already pregnant with my eldest sister Lynda when they tied the knot. An orthodox Jew, my grandmother would have been horrified on two counts had she known: the bride was pregnant and she wasn't Jewish; I'm not sure which she would have seen as the greater calamity. Luckily, Olga and Rita had been evacuated from London because of the Blitz so my father was able to live a kind of double life for the first year of his marriage, oscillating between a flat in Hackney with his wife and baby daughter and visits to my grandmother where he behaved as if he were still single. There was hell to pay when he eventually had to confess all to her, but Olga couldn't resist the joy of being a grandmother and bouncing the baby on her knee. She quickly became reconciled to her favourite son, though she never accepted Winifred as a member of the family.

I came along in 1943 but the odds had been stacked against the marriage from the start. My mother was older than my father, they got married at the outbreak of war when Leslie was away in the RAF and Winifred had entered the strange, close-knit world of a Jewish family, dominated by the formidable Olga, who had strong views about most things and especially the catastrophe of her son introducing a *shiksa* into the family – in fact, all her sons did.

I doubt it was a true love match, more likely one of those many ill-starred unions forged in the hothouse of war, and when my mother fell in love with a Canadian airman called Kenneth Walton Beckett, she was faced with an impossible choice: she could stay in a family where she knew she would never be welcome, or she could leave her children and share the life of the man she loved. She decided to go.

I was only a year and three months old so I remember none of this. Curiously, Winifred's second husband, by then professionally known as Kent Walton, ended up working for me at London Weekend Television (LWT) as a wrestling commentator. I always knew vaguely what my mother looked like because Lynda and I had a photograph of her in an album we carefully kept hidden and looked at occasionally. Many years later, I think I spotted her at a football match in Leicester. Before she'd married my father, she and her brother George were in a bad car accident in which both of them sustained leg injuries, and I saw a lady in the crowd with Kent Walton. When they walked away I noticed that she had a slight limp.

I never discussed any of this with my father, and I've never made any attempt to get in touch with my mother, or vice versa. I feel neither guilt nor regret about this. I have no memory of her, she played no part in my life and she caused my father great pain. Even had I wished to, I could only have sought her out at the price of alienating my father and grandmother. I didn't know her so I didn't miss her.

My mother might have gone but, thanks to my grandmother, I never felt deprived of maternal love, and I simply adored my father. I was a very biddable child, anxious to please and always eager to avoid any confrontation. It took a long time and a number of failed relationships for me to learn that I needed to act and behave in tune with my deepest feelings instead of trying always to do what was expected of me.

My father was the kindest, most generous and self-effacing man I have ever known, but much of my childhood was spent away from him. He worked all hours, battling to establish his business, and he couldn't have coped with two small children. However, I was never conscious of being deprived of his love. We drew much closer as I moved through childhood into adolescence and his life became more settled. Because I was then old enough to appreciate his many sterling qualities, this made the bond between us all the stronger. He was a very good man, fluent in business talk but rather inarticulate when it came to saying what he really felt about personal matters, yet he always managed to show his love for me. He was in a cut-throat business and had many fierce competitors, but so far as I know, he never turned any into enemies. He was universally popular, even loved.

Dad went about life in a disciplined way, quietly and systematically building up the business. He was different from his two brothers, not just in temperament but in physical characteristics. My earliest memories are of his fine blond hair, much like a baby's, vivid blue eyes and delicate hands. He had long, slender fingers, always in movement. He was as eloquent in gesture as he was tongue-tied in speech, except when he was talking business on the telephone when he was positively voluble.

He was driven by a sense of time, perhaps because after his narrow escape from death when he caught typhoid he knew subconsciously that his lifespan was precious. He kept his watch ten minutes fast so that he'd never be late for an appointment. I'd meet him for lunch at a prearranged time and pitch up on the dot, to find him already ten minutes into his first course.

'You're almost late,' was his invariable comment. If I arranged to be at his flat at a certain time, as I walked along the road I would see him at the window, anxiously looking out for me. He arrived in the office at half past six in the morning to open the post, and he would always leave for home at six in the evening; you could set your watch by him. He might be in the middle of a meeting, but on the stroke of six, he'd say, 'I'm off now,' and away he'd go. When he got home he didn't leave the business behind: he'd spend most of the evening on the telephone, dealing, gossiping and gathering intelligence.

Every artist has his chosen instrument, Menuhin his violin and Rubinstein his piano: my father was a veritable virtuoso of the telephone. The comedian Jack Benny was often booked by Dad to play the London Palladium, and Jack used to love to sit in my father's office watching him work two or three telephones at once, carrying on multiple conversations, doing multiple deals.

Showbiz personalities tend to be chronically insecure, dependent not only on the applause of an audience but also on the reassurance of their agent that they are loved and valued. Leslie was offering telephonic counsel to his clients long before Chad Varah founded the Samaritans. He'd work his way through a long list of telephone numbers of artists and managers subtly infiltrating advice and criticism into apparently rambling, gossipy chat. The more neurotic would note the time at which he phoned them, convinced that the earlier it was, the higher they stood in his estimation. To receive his first phone call meant as much as top billing at the Palladium. The process became known as Leslie's Hit Parade.

He got so taken up in the careers of his clients that he almost lived his life vicariously through them, agonizing over their setbacks, glorying in their triumphs and talking about them incessantly, so much so that my stepmother Audrey (whom Dad married in 1948) and I decided to teach him a lesson. One of his clients was Dickie Valentine, a great vocal star in the fifties. Dad would rant on and on about Dickie Valentine until we were sick of the sound of the poor guy's name. So Audrey bought a budgerigar and we spent hours teaching it to say, 'Dickie Valentine? Bah!'

I cannot recall ever having a row with him. He was very reserved and gave the impression of being rather prudish, so he never attempted one of those 'Let me tell you the facts of life' conversations with either Lynda or me. Indeed, no one in the family ever taught me the facts of life. I learned them, as it were, behind the proverbial bicycle sheds.

There was an unspoken agreement between us that we never talked about my mother, which was a relief to me because I knew he must have found the whole episode deeply painful. And in any case, I wouldn't have known what to say. Some of his close friends would playfully exploit his horror of intimacy, especially his distaste for sexually explicit conversation. A dear colleague of his was Robert Fox, the father of the film and TV stars Edward and James and their impresario brother William. Robert was a suave Old Harrovian who specialized in the legitimate theatre, what was then called the Once Nightly Department. My dad and he shared great ambitions to revive the ailing British film industry; together, they produced Cliff Richard's hit movies, they found the backing for Joe Losey's film *The Servant*, which was one of Dirk Bogarde's first serious roles, and set up *Alfie*, which made a star of Michael Caine.

Robert had sized up my father as a real puritan, and loved to tease him. I called into Dad's office one day and there was Robert sitting in an armchair puffing his pipe. 'Why, Michael,' he said, with mock solicitude, 'you look tired, indeed, truly shagged out. Let me give you some good advice, man to man . . .' My father well knew what Robert was up to but couldn't stop himself from cringing. 'One day,' said Robert, 'you'll get married and it will all be lovely, but as time goes by, your eye will start to wander . . .' By now, my father was virtually under the desk with embarrassment, but Robert pressed on mercilessly. '. . . and sooner or later you'll do something about it, you'll have an affair. Now the cardinal rule is, don't get found out, but if you do get found out, always deny it, and if you can't deny it because you get caught with it in, say it was the first time and you didn't like it.' By now my father's face was brick-red and he was incapable of more than an incoherent mumble about Saturday's football match.

My father and Robert Fox formed a wonderful partnership. The Grade Organisation prospered in all corners of showbusiness. If only the two of them had not died so young, Britain might have had a properly funded film industry.

My father was so good-natured that he was an easy target for the pranks of his friends. His natural humility shone through and he was always the first to enjoy the joke. He had sad eyes and in repose could look a little glum, so I suppose it was a challenge to get him to burst out in that mischievous grin of his. His first star act was Billy Cotton, whose *Band Show* was hugely popular, at first in the theatre and then on television and radio. Billy had an impish streak and enjoyed getting my father going. I was with Dad one Saturday morning when the phone rang. Sure enough, it was Billy Cotton, who worked himself up into a synthetic rage, ranting on and on, until eventually he allowed my harassed father to placate him. Years later, when Billy Cotton's son, Bill, the television executive, had become a close friend of mine, we reminisced about our childhood and he told me that his father, sitting at home on Saturday morning at a loose end would sometimes say to him, 'Let's ring up Leslie and drive him mad!'

Dad never stood on ceremony and was incapable of pomposity, but I recall one occasion when he got into a real state about a social occasion. He announced that he'd invited some very important business people home to dinner, which was itself a rare occurrence, his office and telephone being the twin poles of his professional existence. He kept on telling my stepmother Audrey that things just had to be perfect, there was a huge deal in the offing, EMI were keen to buy his business and it was the corporation's chairman, Sir Joseph Lockwood, who would be the chief guest. Since the talk around the dinner table would be very

high-powered, Audrey, my half-sister Anita and I were told to
remain out of sight in the kitchen where, bemused, we sat
watching the staff hired for the night coming and going. Suddenly, at the end of the first course, all the guests, led by my
dad, trooped into the kitchen helpfully carrying their empty
plates; that was the end of my dad's one and only attempt at
presiding over a smart dinner party.

One of Dad's endearing qualities was that he couldn't have
kept a secret if his life depended on it. He bought a gorgeous
flat with magnificent views overlooking Hyde Park and Kensington Palace Gardens, and long afterwards I found myself playing
golf with the man who built the block, Louis Mintz. When he
discovered I was Leslie Grade's son, he explained how he'd put
the flats on the market at a hundred and twenty thousand
pounds each, which was a lot of money in 1966. Not surprisingly,
he found them hard to sell. Dad wanted one but he wouldn't
pay the asking price; he offered eighty thousand pounds and the
inducement that when people heard he'd moved in, there would
be no problem selling the rest. Louis Mintz agreed on condition
that Dad didn't tell a soul how much he'd paid. The problem
was, said Louis, that every time a potential buyer went round to
view a flat, Dad would pop his head out of the front door and
tell them not to pay a penny more than eighty. Louis, of course,
dropped his profit margin as a result but had the grace to smile
about it.

Dad treated the staff at the agency as his family. He could be
a hard taskmaster during working hours, but in his dealings with
them after six o'clock, he was the epitome of the paternalistic
employer – before that expression became a term of abuse. He
bought them houses and cars and sent them on paid holidays.
He involved himself in all their family joys and tragedies. I think
he felt himself one of them, for at heart he was a very simple
man. He loved fish and chips and telly-watching and rooting for
Leyton Orient on a Saturday afternoon. It's true he had all the
accoutrements of wealth, a chauffeur-driven Bentley, a house in
the South of France, a splendid flat in Kensington's Millionaires'

Row, but none of it ever changed him. He never developed the appetites, attitudes or interests of the *nouveau riche*. He'd no desire to mix with the social set or do the fashionable thing.

He may have been personally self-effacing but he knew how to use financial muscle when it suited him. After I took my first job with the *Daily Mirror* I opened my first bank account with Barclays in Marylebone High Street. By Grade standards it was a modest account: there was rarely more than a tenner in it if I was lucky. But one day I got a very snotty letter from the manager informing me that I was two pounds overdrawn. I went to see him and, like the pompous seventeen-year-old I was at the time, huffed and puffed and warned him that dire consequences would follow his discourtesy to a good customer. I might even close my account and take my overdraft elsewhere. He bore my threats with an equanimity bordering on contempt.

Later that day, I called in to see my father and his first words to me were, 'Who do you bank with?' The blood drained from my guilty face as I thought, Oh, my God, the bank manager's rung him! In fact, he said that he'd been having a lot of trouble with Barclays. Apparently, they'd refused his request for a bridging loan to buy a number of cinemas and, on Bernie's advice, he'd decided to move the accounts of the entire Grade Organisation to Lloyds. After due consideration, I agreed that out of loyalty to the family I would also move my account. I then asked for another interview with my Barclays bank manager. I told him that having thought things over, I was moving my account to Lloyds. He didn't look too distraught, but his smile vanished when I added that the entire Grade multi-million-pound organization intended to do the same, and if he didn't believe me, he could pick up a phone and check. I swept out, hoping he was suitably chastened at the thought that the Grades were such a close-knit family they were prepared to move millions in support of a junior member in dispute over a measly two-quid overdraft. Even if I'd told him it was the sheerest coincidence that both my father and I were having our differences with Barclays at the same time, I doubt he would have believed me. The story probably went the rounds of whatever circles bank managers move in and added to the Grade legend. But the incident didn't do much for my humility or, I suspect, for the career of the manager of Barclays Bank, Marylebone High Street branch.

My stepmother Audrey had been a dancer and met my father in 1947 at a charity show he was putting on in aid of the Star and Garter Home in Richmond. She loved and understood him, and provided him with a secure, homely, quiet environment in which he was truly happy and comfortable. She was fiercely loyal, but I suspect her one complaint might have been that she fought a never-ending battle against the flaming telephone for his attention. She once pointedly baked him a phone-shaped birthday cake. During the twelve frustrating years of disablement Dad endured between his first stroke and his death, Audrey cared for him with utter devotion. I'm inclined to think it is a moral universe, after all, because the pain my father undoubtedly felt at my mother's desertion was more than compensated for in the years of joy Audrey gave him. She was the perfect mate.

Dad did his good works the way he lived, very quietly. Professionally he would drive a hard bargain, but away from the business he showed great generosity of spirit towards anyone in need who crossed his path. Bert Knight, his general manager, said that Leslie would fight all day to take ten bob off you or knock you down to the lowest price, but then he'd give you back two pounds as a present and never mention it again. When Dad was hospitalized with a stroke, my uncle Bernie, trying to hold the fort, went through the stuff in his desk and came upon a host of post-dated cheques Leslie had never presented because those who'd written them were hard-up. There were also letters of gratitude for help he'd given to all kinds of people and other evidence of unsung benevolence.

At Dad's memorial service, Bill Cotton told of how, when his father died, he was clearing out his effects and found a faded blue forces air-mail letter dating back to the war tucked down the back of an old bureau. It was from my dad to Billy

Cotton, thanking him for looking after the family while he was stuck out in the Middle East and promising that one day he would repay the debt. When Billy Cotton died, though he'd lived in a very grand style, he left little money and Mabel, his widow, was in trouble. Dad bought her a house and looked after her until the day she died. He never forgot.

In April 1966, my father came back from a crowded round of film and agency meetings in New York and we went that night to see Barbra Streisand in *Funny Girl* at Bernie's Prince of Wales theatre. The following afternoon, he collapsed in his Kensington flat and was rushed to Guy's Hospital, where they diagnosed a cerebral haemorrhage. For three days he was unconscious and we kept vigil by his bedside; it was a close thing but he slowly made a partial recovery because of some marvellous nursing care and the skill of a consultant physician called Charles Joiner, who became a family friend. He was paralysed down his left side and off work for a year and it was clear that he wouldn't resume the pace that had helped to cause his illness. He tired more quickly; he was physically impaired and also developed diabetes, so had to put up with an irksome routine of daily injections of insulin. He was a shadow of his former self, and knew it, which added to his frustration.

Dad was much diminished by his stroke. He spent a short time in the office if he was feeling up to it. In the days of his vigour and health, he could, in a business sense, walk on water, it all came effortlessly to him. But Audrey told me of his frustration and despair when, after his stroke, some minor business deal went wrong. He feared he had lost the instinct for shrewd judgement that made him successful. I never heard him complain, though I do recall an occasion when we were sitting quietly in his splendid Kensington flat. Suddenly he looked round the spacious sitting room and said purposefully to me, 'I'd gladly give all this up to get my health back.' A lesson I have never forgotten.

But there were compensations. The family, especially its younger members, became increasingly precious to Dad. He

adored Lynda's three children, and when my first wife Penny
got pregnant, he told me a hundred times that having children
and bringing them up was really what life was all about.

He died in October 1979 at the age of sixty-three. I was
separated from Penny and living in the Barbican when my
brother-in-law Brook rang me to say that Dad had suffered
another stroke at his home in the South of France and was in
hospital at Fréjus. We caught the next plane. He had lost the
power of speech and could communicate only by using Scrabble
letters to spell out what he wanted to say. He couldn't swallow so
he had to be fed intravenously and had virtually no control over
his limbs. But after a few days, his condition became more stable
so I felt it safe to get back to my job at LWT. As I said goodbye
to him he smiled, but I had a premonition that I would never
see him again. Two days later he was dead and I was flying back
to the South of France to bring him home.

He was buried in Willesden Liberal Jewish Cemetery. His
favourite rabbi, John Rayner, performed the ceremony and gave
an address. His death didn't attract much attention in Britain
because, unlike his brothers Lew and Bernie, he had always kept
out of the public eye, so I was astounded by the size of the
congregation both at his funeral and at the memorial service at
the Liberal Synagogue in St John's Wood. The stars paraded in
force and it turned into a celebration rather than a wake. Robert
Morley gave a witty and perceptive address, Cliff Richard, Frankie Vaughan and Mireille Mathieu sang, and the entire Leyton
Orient football team turned up to salute one of their most
dedicated fans.

It was a most moving demonstration of how deeply he had
touched many people's lives. He certainly touched mine, though
'touched' is too weak a word. For such a mild-seeming man, he
had an immense impact on me. He was a genius at business with
an unerring eye for spotting talent, but that's not why I loved
and admired him. For me, he was a benchmark of essential
decency, goodness and humour. When I'm uncertain about a
course of action, I still find myself asking, 'What would Dad have

done?' I think of him every day, even have a 'conversation' with him. I don't know whether or not I believe in reincarnation and I'm agnostic about an after-life, but I know my father lives on, and not just in my memory.

As a dutiful son should, I said the *kaddish*, the Jewish prayer for the dead, at Dad's graveside. But I was so determined to hold the rest of the family together and be strong for them that, to this very day, I have not fully mourned his passing. It is the unfinished business of my life.

I was much helped by Rabbi Rayner. Discussing grief, he once told me that he'd lost most of his family in the Nazi death camps, but at the time he was unable to grieve. Then, twenty-odd years later, long after he thought the pain of the loss had passed, a tiny domestic incident triggered a burst of uncontrollable crying that lasted for days. In much the same way, I often feel emotionally choked for no obvious reason and know that at any time some internal barrier in my psyche might be breached to allow my pent-up grief to spill out. I suppose until we have mourned our precious dead we can't let them go and reach the stage where we recall them with joy rather than sadness.

Because my mother left us when I was only fifteen months old, I clung ever more closely to my elder sister, Lynda, but then I lost her too. It all started when my father married Audrey. Olga, with the unassailable logic of her generation, decided it was not seemly for children to attend their father's wedding, so Lynda and I were not allowed to go.

We didn't move in with the newlyweds permanently but stayed on with our grandmother. I think Olga was determined to stop the rot at our generation. She persuaded my father to let us remain with her so she could make sure we were brought up as good Jewish children, for his new wife was yet another *shiksa*, though eventually, and with much joy, she converted to the Jewish faith.

Then came the day when my father made an unscheduled visit to the flat. He obviously had something on his mind. He always found it hard to speak about intimate family matters but eventually he announced that Audrey was going to have a baby. Lynda burst into tears and fled the room. I followed her to her bedroom and found myself, at the age of twelve, trying to be grown-up about the whole thing, pleading with Lynda to be fair and recognize that Audrey had every right to have children if she wished. I don't think Lynda was convinced. She never forgave my father and nurtured a growing enmity against him which had terrible repercussions later on.

Ever the Grades' blue-eyed boy, I joined enthusiastically in the family's pleasure at this new arrival. I was quite intrigued by the prospect of a baby half-sister and recall, when I was at prep school, Audrey and my dad coming to visit me with Anita, in a carry-cot, which caused a mild sensation. A year later, there was another child, Anthony, who is now a successful car designer for Renault in Paris. Anita and I became and have remained very close, even though she is twelve years my junior. In a way, she came to replace Lynda in my affections.

In fairness, I think Lynda had a tougher time than I had with our grandmother, who, like many Jewish matriarchs, tended to be strict with the girl but to indulge the boy – especially as he was a bit of a crawler. However, in 1959, Lynda, then nineteen, met Arthur Davidson, a sales rep for the Percy Dalton peanut company. He came from a decent East End Jewish family, who owned a little cream cheese and bagel factory.

Arthur, who was a personable character, seemed to get on quite well at first with my grandmother, but for some reason my aunt Rita took against him and decided that he wasn't good enough to be a member of the Grade family – 'A peanut salesman, I ask you!' – and began a campaign to discredit him with my family, the line being that he was obviously a gold-digger, after the Grade money, for my father was doing well and had become quite wealthy. She went to some lengths to malign poor Arthur. Having discovered that he had been to parties at Cliveden with the Astor set, which would have been a social coup had it not been the era of the Profumo scandal, she put two and two together and made twenty-two.

In those days, of course, the age of majority was twenty-one, so Lynda couldn't marry Arthur without her parents' permission. The combined forces of Grandmother and Aunt Rita were too much for my father, who, probably against his better judgement, was persuaded to consider having Lynda made a ward of court to prevent her eloping. But Lynda was made of stern stuff and went to court herself, seeking permission to marry, which was granted. That took some courage. It certainly showed how much she cared for Arthur and how bitter she felt about my father. Because the Grade brothers were wealthy, famous and constantly in the public eye, the newspapers revelled in our embarrassment. Press scandal apart, Lynda's marriage caused a huge rift within the family.

Throughout all this rumpus, I tried to remain close to Lynda, which wasn't easy because she was angry at the way Arthur was being treated and held my father and grandmother responsible. I was miserable and bewildered that the people to whom I was closest were at such odds. They had provided me with emotional security in my mother's absence, and now the bond of affection that had held us all together was being torn apart. If I took Lynda's part, how could my father forgive me? I couldn't bear to upset him. And the blunt truth is that I chose the unity of the family over my loyalty to Lynda. I still don't see what else I could have done.

Not all the Grades lined up against Lynda: Lew and Kathy were kind to her. Lew gave her away when she and Arthur had a synagogue ceremony some months after the register-office service, and he was host at the reception in his own flat. My father was pretty miserable about the whole episode because he was a soft-hearted, tolerant man, liberal in all his attitudes. And inevitably Lynda and he were reconciled. Dad even loaned money to Arthur so he and Lynda could set up an antiques business.

But when my father was in hospital recovering from his first stroke, Arthur went to see Dad early one morning before any of the rest of the family were around, to confess that he was in financial difficulties and needed another loan. Here was Dad at death's door and Arthur was asking him for money. When we found out, we were outraged. This insensitivity confirmed the worst suspicions of those members of the Grade family who'd taken against Arthur from the outset. However, the last thing anyone wanted was a family row that might impede Dad's recovery, so by common consent the incident wasn't spoken about. But it increased the tension between Lynda and the rest of the family. The climax came when Anita decided to get married and precipitated another family crisis.

Anita had fallen in love with Brook Land, whose father David was an impresario and a long-standing family friend. Everyone was delighted at the prospect of the wedding. Plans were laid and excitement mounted. Dad's stroke may have slowed him down but he had lost none of his organizing ability, so he set about with a will to arrange the details of the wedding. The family seemed united for once. Lynda thoroughly approved of Anita's choice of husband, and was pleased that her daughter Laura had been asked to be a bridesmaid.

One evening a few weeks before the wedding, Dad was checking the list of replies from guests and noticed that Lynda and Arthur's names had not been ticked off. He rang Lynda to ask why she had not formally replied to the invitation. I guess Lynda had gone beyond the point in her strained relations with my father where she was prepared to humour him so a row ensued. In a state of great distress, Dad rang me to say that Lynda had taken offence at his asking for a formal reply to the wedding invitation so that he could complete his table plan. Now she wasn't coming to the wedding. I rang Lynda, spoke to her and then to Arthur, pleading with them to understand that Dad was ill and tired and these little organizational courtesies associated with the wedding meant much to him. I conceded that perhaps it might have been better if he hadn't phoned them, but surely they could see his point of view and excuse him? They couldn't and they wouldn't. Did they realize that they seemed intent on being as hurtful as possible to a man who was so ill?

In the event, Lynda and Arthur didn't come to the wedding, Laura wasn't a bridesmaid and I've never spoken to Lynda since, except to pass the time of day if we bump into one another socially. It was all very sad and unnecessary and, to my mind, gratuitous. Given all the ups and downs the Grade family had been through in their journey from the wilds of the Ukraine to the tough world of British showbiz, it is pathetic that such a trivial incident should have caused such deep and lasting scars. In retrospect, I realize that Lynda must have been suppressing really deep-seated grievances against my father and maybe the Grade family generally, and Leslie's possibly unnecessary phone call was, for her, the last straw. Maybe she never got over the birth of Anita.

From my angle, first I had lost my mother, which drove me ever closer to my sister Lynda, and now I had lost her. It was a 180-degree turn of events, from incredible emotional closeness to frosty distance. I suppose it counts as one more tick on a Hollywood shrink's checklist of my psychological traumas.

In some ways, although I was upset on my father's behalf because of Lynda's behaviour, it was my grandmother I particularly felt for. She cared deeply for Lynda and had given over much of the middle period of her life to bringing us both up. But after the wedding rumpus, Lynda cut off all contact with her. Olga was deeply hurt, for despite the generation gap, she treated Lynda as a cherished daughter. It felt to me like spiteful behaviour, which, if it was so intended, I find hard to forgive.

Life with Olga, the surrogate mother who lavished love and care on Lynda and me, was a constant fascination. She was remote from us both in generation and in attitudes, many of which had their origins in the Jewish subculture of old Russia, yet she devoted years of her life to seeing that we lacked nothing. My relationship with Olga must have seemed strange to outsiders who knew nothing of our family history. I recall the puzzlement of my boarding-school mates when she pitched up on parents' days. To the others she was a most curious figure, a Jewish-Russian *émigré* with a quaint turn of phrase; to me she was the only mother I had and I was proud of her. I suppose this made me different from my contemporaries, and to stand out from the rest in a boarding-school invites all kinds of attention, not always pleasant. The bonus is that, provided you don't go under, your survival capacity and resilience are greatly increased.

Lynda and I were aged four and fifteen months respectively when we moved in with Olga, and it was less of a trauma for us than it would have been for many children because the Grades lived *en famille* anyway, the generations all mixed up as is the style in traditional societies. There was my grandmother, my sister Lynda, my then unmarried aunt Rita, and my father, who was in and out all the time. We children also did the rounds of my uncles' families. Lew and his wife Kathy had a big flat in Cavendish Square; they were childless then so we got plenty of treats. Bernie and Carole had three children so there was no shortage of playmates. And, of course, we spent time with my dad. In some ways it was a nomadic life, though a luxurious one, as we gyrated between my father's homes, my grandmother's flat, our uncles' places and various boarding-schools. But I suppose in the end, our real home was where Grandmother was.

My grandmother was unforgettable. She was short, stocky, heavy-featured, had the physical constitution of an ox and an iron will to go with it. She could be hilariously funny in the Jewish manner, firing off quaint sayings and curses in a mixture of fractured English and Yiddish. She could also be utterly impossible, stubborn to the point of mulishness, imperious, unforgiving and fiercely insistent on what she thought was proper behaviour. Though literate in Russian and fluent in Yiddish, she never learned to read English, so the London telephone exchange names of those days – Regent, Ambassador, Renown *et al* – was a problem to her. She *could* make sense of

English numerals, so she devised for her own use all-figure telephone numbers, long before British Telecom got round to the idea.

She had· made not one but two enormous cultural leaps during her lifetime, from a remote village in Tsarist Russia to luxury in a penthouse suite at the Grosvenor House Hotel in London via a poverty-stricken existence in a couple of rooms over a shop· in the East End. The result was that she still harboured all kinds of peasant superstitions. I remember when I was small, and walking down the street with her hand in hand, if she caught sight of a nun, she would do a 180-degree twirl, muttering something unintelligible. It says much for her influence over me that I didn't at the time think there was anything odd about this. It was only when I noticed that no one else in London streets seemed to behave so strangely at the sight of nuns that I began to feel embarrassed.

Once I was with her when she put her knowledge of the Russian language to good use; it was, of all places, Marks and Spencer on the Edgware Road. A customer slipped and fell over and couldn't make herself understood to the people standing around her. It turned out she was speaking Russian and my grandmother was able to interpret what she was saying. That's the only time I heard Olga speaking her mother-tongue.

She was full of lovable contradictions. Though very strongly Jewish and usually orthodox, she didn't let the kosher regulations stand in the way of Lynda and I getting what she thought was a healthy diet. I was a weedy kid with boundless energy, very thin because I burned off calories easily. Grandmother, having noticed that many *goyim* seemed strong and fit, decided that their diet had something to do with it, and bacon in particular seemed to have special health-giving properties. It suited me; I had no religious preconceptions and enjoyed bacon regularly at school. She would close all the windows of the flat to prevent her Jewish neighbours catching a whiff of the strong aroma of frying bacon then cook it for us in kosher margarine. In summer, the heat in the closed flat was unbearable and the smell pungent, but our health came before the letter of the Torah. Among many other things, the distinctive smell of frying bacon will for ever remind me of her. She never touched it herself.

Grandmother had an older brother, Moishe (Morris), who lived in Stamford Hill. He could have been a character in a standard Jewish novel. He had brought his wife Rosa with him from the old country and they lived happily here until their daughter first got married, then divorced and came back to live with her parents. Moishe went to almost comical lengths to treat his daughter as though she didn't exist, and his daughter returned the compliment with a vengeance. When they had to, they communicated through Rosa. As children we often went round for Sunday tea and found this state of affairs both baffling and fascinating. What was even stranger was that no one ever commented on it. It was just taken for granted as the sort of thing you expected from Moishe.

He was a small-time wheeler-dealer who would buy or sell anything, even within the family. He and my grandmother haggled constantly in a mixture of Yiddish and English but he wouldn't allow her out of the house without trying to get her to buy something. He spoke broken English and had trouble with his aspirants. I vividly recall one exchange. He said, 'Golda, I gotta real bargain for you.'

'Vot is it?'

'A humberella.'

'Vot do I vant vid a humberella?'

'Golda, you're gonna love this humberella. It's no *h*ordinary humberella, it's a parasol.' He produced it.

'*Feh!*' she retorted. 'Vot do I need vid dat?'

'Golda, look at this humberella. It's got a hebony, hivory hendle vot you couldn't buy at Herrods for a hundred pound.'

This knockabout routine she did with Moishe was typical of a certain generation's Jewishness, as was her tendency to fall in and out of love with her daughters-in-law, Lew's wife Kathy and Bernie's Carol and, of course, Audrey. Her mercurial temperament kept everyone in the family slightly on edge, and I think she enjoyed that. First Kathy and then Carol would be at the top of her hit parade until her mood changed. If they upset her, however unwittingly, it was obviously because they were *shiksas*. Could you expect anything better from non-Jewish girls? Yet again, when something they did pleased her, it must be precisely because they were *shiksas*, for no Jewish girl could be such a paragon.

One day when I was very small I was sitting on the beach at Bournemouth with my grandmother. Surrounded by her cronies, she was discoursing on the evils of Jewish boys marrying out of the faith. As any good Jewish mother knew, no *shiksa* could possibly make a satisfactory wife for her son. Eventually one of the old ladies plucked up the courage to interrupt the flow. 'But, Olga,' she said, 'your three sons married four *shiksas*!'

'*Feh!*' she replied. 'That was different, it was *beshect.*' Fate.

There was a deep fatalistic streak in her, as in many of her generation who had been persecuted and dispossessed. The suffering she endured in her early life, then the heartache that family rifts caused her – and she outlived both a son and a son-in-law – made her stoical about matters of life and death. One of her favourite sayings was, 'From worry you don't die.'

She would talk endlessly about the 'children' and wasn't thinking of any of the toddlers in the family but of Lew, Bernie and Leslie who by this time were rising seventy, sixty-five and sixty. She took an almost childlike pride in their success. She often went on holiday to a Jewish hotel and would arrive loaded down with photographs and press clippings about Lew and Bernie, and she would tell an admiring throng of old ladies in the lounge that they had gone from glory to glory, first they were sirs and now they were lords.

She loved her summer seaside holidays, usually at Bournemouth or Torquay. Once when she went to Torquay, I wanted to call her to find out how she was settling in. I was told by the hotel there was no Mrs Grade registered or even expected. I called another half-dozen hotels to be told the same story. 'No Mrs Grade.'

I felt very uneasy but I didn't want to ring my father and worry him. It looked as though Grandma had disappeared. Then the penny dropped. The summer-season shows in Torquay's theatres were presented by Bernard Delfont not Leslie Grade, so somewhere between London and Torquay, Mrs Grade had become Mrs Delfont. I called the original hotel again, asked for Mrs Delfont and was put straight through.

Olga had never been in an aeroplane in her life so she had only the haziest idea what was involved. I'd call in on her and tell her I would be away for a week or so because I was flying to, say, New York on business. '*Oy*,' she'd say. 'Be very careful, and when you're on the aeroplane, don't talk to the driver.' To her, Concorde was just a bigger version of the chauffeur-driven car she went around London in, and everyone knew that if you talked to the driver, he'd take his eyes off the road and hit something.

I lived with her in Wimpole Street until I married for the first time in 1967. By now she was in her eighties and the flat was much too big for her, so the brothers moved her into a magnificent penthouse suite in the Grosvenor House Hotel in Park Lane. She had constant room service but still lived as though the Winogradskis were in two rooms over the shoe-shop in Brick Lane and had to make every halfpenny count. She had only to pick up a phone and anything she wanted was delivered, but she hated to be waited on, especially at Forte's prices.

When she saw the Grosvenor House's room-service menu, she was incredulous. 'How can they charge one pound for half a grapefruit?' I tried to explain to her that it was quite a complicated operation getting that grapefruit on to her breakfast tray: it had to be imported, shopped for, cleared away, then there was a tiny share of the hotel overheads to come out of it, etc., etc. Even though all her three sons moved in the world of high finance, she was unimpressed and wanted nothing to do with this capitalist exploitation. From then on she would only use room service with the greatest reluctance, which meant that I ended up having to do her shopping for her. By this time I was director of programmes at LWT, which was a demanding, often exhausting job, but each week at some point I'd have to dash out of my office to the nearest supermarket, buy what she wanted and carefully remove all the price tags before delivering it to her. Then I had to go through an elaborate charade, assuring her that I'd got everything cheap, wildly inventing prices I thought were low enough to impress her.

When she had to have room service, she'd store any spare bread rolls in a long cupboard in the hall; it was stacked with them. Then we went through another ritual. She never let me leave her suite empty-handed. '*Babula*,' she'd say, 'I got something for you.' I was a married man with a place of my own but I still had to stagger home with an armful of bread rolls.

Penny and I used to collect her from the hotel and bring her over to our house at the weekend. I watched the first moon landing on television with her. She got more and more agitated and finally stood up, went to the window, drew back the curtain and stared at the moon in the night sky. 'Tell me, Michael,' she said, pointing to these space-suited figures bouncing round in the television screen, 'are they on the moon?' I assured her they were.

'That moon?' she said, pointing through the window. I nodded.

She pulled back the curtain and sat down. 'Nah, it's impossible!' And as long as she lived, we could never convince her that man had set foot on the moon.

Weddings, she loved; and since we were a large extended family, there were always assorted cousins and second cousins getting married. She never sent a wedding present but always took it with her, and when we got to the reception she'd feel in her handbag then pull out an envelope containing either five or three guineas. I eventually worked out how she decided which amount was appropriate to the particular wedding: if it was a full sit-down nosh-up, that was worth a five-guinea present, if it was only a finger buffet, out came the three-guinea envelope. Occasionally, she got caught out and paid out five guineas for what turned out to be a three-guinea snack. Then she'd curse like a Yiddish trooper.

She was so grateful for the freedom and comfort she'd enjoyed in Britain after the privations of the Ukraine that she was a fanatical royalist and a Conservative of the 'Land of Hope and Glory' variety. Winston Churchill was her idol. She became a paid-up member of the Tory Party and always kept her membership card in a safe place because she still had dim memories of harassment by the Tsarist regime and feared that the unthinkable might happen in Britain. Her legal status was that of a stateless alien and she thought there might come a time when the police knocked on her door to eject her from this country. She could then produce with a flourish her Conservative Party membership card and everything would be all right – for who could doubt the patriotism of a true Tory?

When my grandmother died, *The Times* obituary of her reported that she was '*approximately* ninety-four'. She either never knew or never let on her age, and there was no documentary evidence to settle the question: all her papers had been lost somewhere between the Ukraine and Tilbury. From time to time she'd decide to celebrate a birthday and chose what she thought was a sensible age, which tended always to be on the low side. The family would then gather solemnly to mark another spurious landmark in her life.

In her late eighties, she started to go blind and the doctors said she had cataracts on both eyes. The family was in two minds as to whether at her advanced age she ought to be exposed to the risk of a general anaesthetic. My aunt Rita's husband, Joe, who was also her GP, had real doubts, but it grieved me so much to see her groping around in semi-darkness that I took the responsibility for insisting that the operation should go ahead. In the event, she sailed through the surgery and had two or three extra years of decent, independent life before she finally succumbed to great old age.

In January 1981, when I was at LWT, I went with John Birt, who then worked for me, to the States to try to persuade Walter

Cronkite, the Richard Dimbleby of American TV, to present a documentary series we were planning. In my hotel room I got a phone call from Kathy, Lew's wife. At this point, I need to acknowledge that Kathy has had a unique role in the Grade family. Although she is a *shiksa*, as Olga would say, and through a long marriage has had to put up with my grandmother's irrational spells of disapproval, she has been a calm and gracious presence in the family, a universal aunt with an instinctive gift of tact – she was perfectly cast as Prince Charming when she played pantomime in the fifties. She's done more than her share to keep the peace and hold the family together. Kathy rang to tell me that Olga had died peacefully in her arms in her bed at the Park Lane apartment that morning. Her last words were in Yiddish: 'Oi, my lovely kinder!' I like to think that I was one of them.

Lynda turned up at Olga's funeral. At the time, I thought that was pretty rich, given the unhappiness she had caused my grandmother, whether she meant to or not. And yet I suppose my reaction to seeing her at the graveside revealed the ambivalence of my relationship with her. By then my alienation from her was all the deeper because we had once been so close; however she had reacted to my grandmother's death would have been wrong in my eyes. I felt it was insensitive of her to attend the funeral, but had she not turned up, I would have been furious at her ingratitude. Families!

Despite these upheavals, I managed to get an education of sorts. At a *Sunday Times* breakfast forum in the 1980s, I sat on the platform with Rupert Murdoch, who was delivering his customary anti-public-broadcasting diatribe, opining that British television is dominated by a bunch of élitists who think they know what's good for viewers, but the introduction of the competitive market into television would free consumers from this cultural tyranny and give them what they wanted, not what the bunch of élitists on the panel thought they ought to have. Then it was my turn. 'Well, Rupert,' I said, 'you are the one who went to Oxford

University, not me. My education was in the front stalls of the London Palladium and on the back page of the *Daily Mirror*, so which of us is the élitist?'

It was certainly the case that the entertainment business and the *Daily Mirror* fulfilled the role that university played in many of my contemporaries' careers. Dad's office at Regent House was directly opposite the London Palladium, and even when I was quite small he took me to opening nights there. We always sat in the same seats in row C of the front stalls. I saw all the big stars in action, but it was Johnnie Ray who made the deepest impression on me. Observing him performing, I was at first mystified and then realized what an indefinable thing star quality is. Here was this gaunt, gangly figure with a hearing-aid and, to my untutored ear, no great voice, yet he had the place in uproar. This was prior to the days of Beatlemania but I recall thousands of screaming girls besieging the stage door of the Palladium for a glimpse of a most unlikely superstar.

Before the show, my father would take me to the Palm Court bar and I'd sit there, listening open-mouthed to all the stage gossip. Mingling with the performers would be the power men of the business: Val Parnell, who ran the Moss Empires, my uncle Bernie and his colleague Billy Marsh, who afterwards taught me the agency game. It was sheer magic and that's when I caught the showbusiness bug. I couldn't wait to get back to whichever school I happened to be attending at the time to tell all my pals that I'd actually talked to Johnnie Ray or the Ink Spots or Buddy Holly. I was a right little name-dropper, but when you're weedy, Jewish and insecure, you'll do almost anything to find popularity.

My first boarding-school was in Bournemouth, but its owner went bust or sold out, so I moved on to a wonderful prep school in Bognor run by a Church of England cleric and his wife. I loved every minute of it and ended up as headboy, my first taste of power. I was promoted from the ranks instead of having to work my way up through the various grades of prefects. Academically I wasn't brilliant but passed Common Entrance without any trouble and got into Stowe. The one subject at which I excelled was music, though I owe my original love of it, as I owe so much else, to my grandmother. She provided the first music in my life. She had a beautiful voice and sang Russian folk-songs around the house or played opera of the more sentimental variety on the gramophone. Then I discovered Sibelius – almost inevitably from television. Associated Rediffusion, now defunct, had a current-affairs programme called *This Week* and its theme-tune came from Sibelius' *Karelia* Suite. Though I knew somehow that this music had been composed by Sibelius, I didn't know where it came from, so I went into HMV and bought umpteen 12-inch vinyl LPs full of Sibelius' music, especially his symphonies, in the search for the elusive TV theme. By the time I reached *Karelia* I was addicted to classical music.

Just before I entered Stowe School in September 1956, I had my *bar mitzvah*. The Grade family's religious situation was complex. Ethnically, we were Russian Jews, no argument about that. Olga, who never knowingly underplayed any aspect of her character, was almost a caricature of the Jewish momma with her thick accent, distinctive dress and constant anguished concern for her children and their families. She enthusiastically kept some Jewish customs and turned a blind eye to others when it suited her. Politically, the three brothers, unlike some Jewish immigrant families who made good in Britain, were never active Zionists. They generously supported Jewish charities but never regarded Israel as their true homeland; they were grateful for the hospitality and opportunities Britain had given them and repaid that debt by being keenly patriotic and royalist.

None of the family were strictly orthodox Jews. Olga had the instincts and some of the attitudes of traditional Jewry but she could never have cut herself off from her sons, who had married non-Jews and would by orthodox believers be regarded as outcasts. The family were not regular synagogue attenders and only gave Jewish festivals a nod of respect much as non-churchgoers keep Christmas. Our on-and-off Jewishness produced some strange results. When I was five or six, I recall Lew's wife, Kathy, who is a Catholic, providing a sumptuous traditional meal for the Passover, the Feast of Unleavened Bread, and mixing bread-crumbs into the chopped liver. We never told Grandma.

Of the three brothers, my father had the strongest personal faith. He was fond of the Liberal Synagogue at St John's Wood and would sometimes slip in for a quiet prayer. And he kept abreast of the Jewish calendar. On his death-bed, unable to speak and almost immobile, he spelt out to my half-sister Anita the words 'Yom Kippur' to signify he was aware that it was the eve of the most sacred of Jewish festivals the Day of Atonement.

Technically, because Winifred was a Gentile, I wasn't Jewish. According to religious law, it is through the mother alone that lineage is transmitted. But Olga was determined that I should pass from boyhood to maturity with all due ceremony and in the time-honoured Jewish manner. Knowing her as I did, I guess she also had some superstitious belief that the rite would keep me on the straight and narrow in later life and safeguard me from bad, which is to say Gentile, ways much as inoculation protects against certain diseases.

Leslie was deputed to set the whole thing in motion. It was a formidable challenge for the great fixer to find a rabbi prepared to coach me in the Torah and a synagogue in which the ceremony could be held. My aunt Rita, who was probably the most traditionally Jewish member of the family, had been mar-ried in the orthodox synagogue at St Petersburgh Place in Bayswater, so that's where he started. The son of a *shiksa* being a *bar mitzvah* boy in an orthodox synagogue! The idea was unthink-able, but Dad pulled it off. He never said how, but there had to have been a deal in it somewhere. Perhaps the synagogue needed a new roof.

I remember little about the ceremony, for which I was coached by Rabbi Reuben Turner of Brixton. I was blessed with a good treble voice and a reasonable memory so I didn't fluff my lines on my first public engagement. The Grade family might have been no great shakes at religious observance but they knew how to throw parties, and the reception afterwards at the Marble Arch flat was, as they say in the trade, a star-studded occasion, with some of Dad's biggest stars, such as Alma Cogan, Arthur Askey and Bill Cotton, congratulating me and pressing cheques and banknotes into my hands as I stood there solemnly in my best suit. Afterwards Dad popped the cheques into his office safe and I never saw them again!

I venerated the headmaster of my prep school and owe him a great deal, but I do hold one thing against him: he chose my next school. Thus I embarked on the most miserable period of my young life. I loathed every day I spent at Stowe, which was a second-division public school taking a nose-dive down the league tables. The regime was repressive, the atmosphere grim and forbidding, I was lonely and I learned nothing much except that anti-Semitism was alive and well among public-school boys. I was subjected to vile racist abuse. We Jews weren't hard to distinguish: on Sundays when the rest of the boys went to chapel for morning service, we were outcasts sent to a form room to do Hebrew. It was my first and only experience of the ghetto.

It was around then that chance, or fate, handed me *The Diary of Anne Frank*. I devoured the book faster than anything I had read before or since, and the memory of my feelings on reading it lives with me today. I was moved as never before in my young life. Her simple, accessible narrative offered a vivid testimony of the unimaginable and I think it was then that I first realized what it means to be Jewish. I could have thought the anti-Semitism I experienced at school was just another species of the thuggery that passes for schoolboy japes, but not after I had read Anne Frank. Then I knew I was different, and different in a way that had cost millions of my people their lives.

One path to popularity in a public school is to excel at sports. Being a devout coward, I hated rugby and any other game which involved robust physical contact. My natural timidity was increased around this time because I began to wear spectacles. I read somewhere that my eyes were damaged while I was at Stowe because of a particularly vicious beating-up at the hands of one of the prefects. I would willingly blame Stowe School for every catastrophe that has struck the human race from the Black

Death onwards if I legitimately could, but the truth is more prosaic: my eyesight deteriorated at the onset of puberty. It does make you blind!

I was a good hockey player and had inherited from my father a great love for soccer, where I played in goal. But pleasant interludes on the sports field were no compensation for the daily wretchedness of my life, and at the end of a couple of terms I could stand Stowe no longer. I rang my father in despair. Dear Dad! He had this simple yet profound belief that people are meant to be happy: he saw no point in my misery at Stowe being prolonged and told me to come home. I learned later from my friend the writer Reg Gadney, a contemporary at Stowe, that the school authorities, to explain my sudden and unscheduled departure, put it about that my father couldn't afford the fees, which was laughable. Stowe has since claimed me as an Old Boy, an accolade that for me has a lack of fascination all its own.

Of course, being a public-school drop-out wasn't a good qualification for getting into another school. Even my father, the great fixer, who could conjure Cup final tickets out of thin air and call in favours from just about anywhere on the globe wasn't able to get me into St Paul's School or Dulwich College. I eventually ended up at St Dunstan's College in Catford, South London. It was a boys' day school with a decent academic record, dating back to the fifteenth century.

It was at St Dunstan's that I discovered and expressed a streak of rebelliousness in my nature. I had obviously been suppressing it up to then because I was expected to behave as the family's blue-eyed boy, the apple of my grandmother's eye, always obedient and co-operative in contrast to my strong-willed sister. Indeed, at St Dunstan's my nickname was the Card, which would have astounded the family. I got up to all kinds of mischief, nothing heavy, just silly pranks, culminating at the end of my fifth-form year in an incident at assembly when I unstitched the name-tag from my school cap, which had a heavy peak, and hurled the cap into the rafters. It whizzed about like a boomerang and eventually dropped on to the piano with a loud thud during the singing of the last hymn. The headmaster demanded to know who was responsible and I had to own up otherwise the whole school would have been gated indefinitely. When taxed by the headmaster, I said it was just an outburst of boyish high spirits, whereupon he sent me down there and then.

I phoned my long-suffering father on the way home and told him I'd been expelled. When I told him why, I think he was vastly relieved it wasn't for some nameless sin that would have brought lasting shame on the family. In the event, the headmaster relented and took me back the following term, by which time my O-level results had come through and I'd performed pretty well, but I was a marked man and they never gave me any responsibility. I suspect I was only taken back at all because my dad did another of his deals.

I left school with a couple of A levels, having had a whale of a time. There's no doubt that after the misery and futility of my spell at Stowe, St Dunstan's restored my faith in education. And that was the end of my boyhood.

On hearing the story of my early life, my second wife said it was a childhood from hell. That's not how I felt at the time but I was in my forties before I was really able to draw a line under it and be at peace with myself about all that had happened to me. I was, after all, a member of the amazing Grade family, three brothers who had built what the *Sunday Times* Insight team called 'probably the most powerful entertainment network in the world'. To be close to the centre of great power is always intoxicating: the glamour of mixing with great stars, the adrenaline flow of seeing big deals done, showbusiness extravaganzas mounted, the Grade juggernaut moving in to conquer one new territory after another – and all this with the bonus of a wealthy and hectic lifestyle. I had neither the time nor the maturity to ask any serious questions about who I really was and what I wanted out of life.

I never had to apply for a job or worry about an unpaid bill or battle for tickets for the best shows or the most important public events. There seemed to be no obstacle that the Grade charm or money or influence couldn't overcome. You cannot grow up watching three of the best operators in the power game negotiating, persuading, and occasionally muscling their way from one deal to the next without learning the tricks of the trade, though I was slow to realize that while such techniques may work in business, they are deadly to personal relationships.

It was all heady stuff – success and money are great motivators – and to outward appearances I was happy and ambitious, apparently without a care in the world. But deep inside, I was immature. I recall a professional boxer once telling me that when you are taking punishment in the ring, you don't feel the pain as much if you keep on the move. That was me, presenting a swiftly moving target to the world; the problem was that I was carrying my adversary around inside me.

Enough of the kiss-and-tell stuff. Back to the spotty youth just leaving school and wondering what to do with his life.

Chapter Two

GRADY OF THE *MIRROR*

THE DAY I FINALLY left school in the summer of 1960, I popped in at 235 Regent Street to see my father. He asked me how school was, and I told him it was over, I'd finished that very day. He blinked. 'I suppose you'll come into the business, then?'

'Not really, not unless I have to.'

'Well,' he said, mentally putting Bill Haley and his Comets on hold while he sorted out my career, 'let me think about it and I'll phone you.' I went back to Olga's flat at Marble Arch. He rang almost immediately. 'You can write, can't you? How about being a comedy scriptwriter?'

'Doesn't do much for me,' I mused, rather churlishly for a seventeen-year-old being offered the chance to be the next Johnny Speight or Roy Clarke.

'OK,' he said, like an agent who knows his client isn't taking the bait, 'I'll call you back.' The phone rang again.

'I've got it,' said Dad. 'You love football. How would you like to be a sports writer?'

'Sounds good to me,' I replied.

'I'll call you back,' he said. That telephone of his! Nothing could happen in the universe except through its agency. Now it was a magic wand that would turn me into a Peter Wilson, J. L. Manning, George Whiting or any other of the great sports writers *circa* 1960. Twenty minutes later he rang again. His manner was crisp, he'd done the business.

'Get a pencil and paper. On Monday, you go to see Hugh Cudlipp, C-u-d-l-i-p-p, he's the boss of the *Daily Mirror*. He'll interview you and give you a job as a sports writer. The office is in New Fetter Lane off Fleet Street. Ten o'clock Monday, Hugh Cudlipp, got it?'

'Yeah, great,' I replied, with genuine excitement. 'I'll be there, don't worry.'

I was trying to absorb this unexpected turn of events when the phone rang again. 'I know you, you'll be late for your appointment. He's a very important man, so wear a suit and look smart. You've got a suit, haven't you? I'll send Arthur for you. Be ready and waiting at nine fifteen on Monday morning.'

Arthur, my father's chauffeur, duly collected me in the blue long-wheel-base Bentley, registration LG1, and off I went to my appointment with destiny. I doubt many seventeen-year-old ex-schoolboys have arrived in such style for a ten-quid-a-week job. I was saluted into the *Mirror* car park by a commissionaire who had obviously assumed a VIP would step out of the gleaming limousine. Instead, he was confronted by a spotty teenager in his best suit who announced he had an appointment with someone called 'Er, Cudlipp.' At the very mention of the name of one of the titans of British journalism, I was ushered up smartly to the executive suite.

'So, young Grade,' the Great Man began, 'you want to be a sports writer? Well, make a note of this name. We're going to meet the sports editor of the *Daily Mirror*, Harold Hutchinson. No, on second thoughts, that should be *Jack* Hutchinson.' That was more or less it. He didn't ask for a sample of my written style; for all he knew I could have been totally illiterate. Yet he treated me with a courtesy, even cordiality, that could only have been a reflection of the regard he had for my father. I doubt he imagined the *Daily Mirror* was about to gain a precocious new journalistic genius. I was in and out of his office in a couple of minutes.

Cudlipp took me down to meet the sports editor on the vast, almost deserted editorial floor. Jack Hutchinson was obviously startled to see the Boss advancing on him at ten o'clock in the morning and probably thought he was about to be fired.

'Harold,' boomed Cudlipp, 'this is young Grade. He starts on Monday at ten pounds a week and I want you to turn him into a sports journalist. So he's all yours. Cheerio.' And out he marched. Once Cudlipp was out of earshot, Hutchinson said, 'My name's Jack, not Harold. What's your name, again?'

'Grade. Michael Grade.'

'Mike,' decreed Hutchinson, thus incurring my father's lasting displeasure; he thought the contraction of my name was undignified. But the name stuck, first at the *Daily Mirror* and then throughout my media career ever since. Hutchinson told me to report to him the following Monday morning, and ushered me out of the building. Arthur was waiting by the Bentley, the commissionaire saluted us out of the car park, and I sank back in the car's rich leather seat, having joined the most powerful newspaper in Britain.

They say genius will out, but I suspect that, were it not for the friendship sparked by common interests between my father and Hugh Cudlipp, the *Daily Mirror* would have staggered on without me. And perhaps the fact that Hugh Cudlipp was a major shareholder in Lew's ATV may also have helped. Otherwise, I got the job on sheer merit.

At this time the *Daily Mirror* had the largest circulation of all the popular daily newspapers and its editor-in-chief Hugh Cudlipp was a genius. Founded in 1903 by Alfred Harmsworth, later Lord Northcliffe, it became thirty years later the first of the tabloids, renowned for its ability to compress complex stories about, say, economic matters or foreign affairs into a few lines, accurately and interestingly expressed in simple but vivid English.

The *Mirror*'s sports coverage was immensely strong, led by columnists such as Peter Wilson, whose byline proudly declared he was 'The Man They Couldn't Gag', the urbane cricket writer

Brian Chapman, and John Bromley, later to be one of the pioneers of television sports coverage.

So I found myself on my first morning in the *Mirror*'s new headquarters in New Fetter Lane. I had three almighty handicaps: I couldn't do shorthand, and these were the days before portable tape-recorders became widely available; I was the son of a millionaire who was a pal of the boss, without the formal qualifications to justify a desk on a local give-away journal, let alone the most powerful newspaper in Britain; and though I loved sport, especially soccer, I was a rank amateur among top professionals. I realized my only chance was to keep my ears open, my mouth shut and my head down. I did as I was told and learned all I could as quickly as possible. A smart Alec wouldn't have survived a week among those corrosive cynics of the sports department.

Jack Hutchinson had been an amateur boxer. He was a sweet, rotund little man, nearing the end of his career. His worst enemy couldn't have accused him of mental sharpness. I remember one day editing the cricket scores and he came over and asked me, 'How's Surrey doing?'

I said, 'They're two hundred for five and Tony Lock's got fifty-four.'

'Oh,' he said brightly. 'Batting or bowling?' This from the sports editor of the nation's biggest-selling newspaper!

He once summoned us to a crisis meeting. As is the usual practice in the world of journalism, we would eagerly scan the first editions of our rival papers to see whether they had picked up any stories we'd missed so we could rectify things by ripping off their scoop. On this occasion we'd missed a big story because the journalist who was supposed to work late and scan the opposition had bunked off home to Sussex. Jack wound himself up into what he thought was righteous indignation about this appalling lapse, assured us he wouldn't tolerate any playing fast and loose with the late rota. 'After all . . .' He paused, lost for a suitably horrendous illustration, then finally settled on '. . . what would happen if Stanley Matthews was assassinated at midnight?'

The room dissolved into hilarity and 'Sir Stanley assassinated at midnight' became a much-quoted news room metaphor for the unthinkable.

To compensate for his limitations Jack had a lovely fatherly way about him: he was a great encourager who wandered around the department chatting to everybody, enquiring about their families and making himself generally agreeable. 'That's right, Mike,' he would say, gazing over my shoulder at the story I was just writing. 'Give the copy a healthy bounce!' I soon learned that his indispensable role on the paper was keeping happy the star columnist Peter Wilson, who was of a mercurial temperament exacerbated by an enormous daily intake of alcohol. If Peter was happy then so was Hugh Cudlipp, and so were we all: hence, Jack earned his feed.

At first, I was terrified of Peter, 'The Man They Couldn't Gag', until I discovered that under the surface he was a real pussy-cat. He was one of the last of the journalistic toffs with a Homburg, silver-topped cane and an urbane charm that could change instantly into irascibility if he was thwarted. One of the great strengths of the *Mirror* at that time was its gaggle of star columnists – the doyenne of agony aunts, Marjorie Proops, Bill Connor who wrote as 'Cassandra', Peter Wilson and Godfrey Wynn. Periodically, there was a certain amount of friction when their egos collided. I recall one day shortly after I joined the *Mirror*, sitting at my desk in the sports department, which was a huge open-plan office at one end of which was Cassandra's office out of which came the sounds of an almighty altercation. The entire sports department fell silent, typewriters stopped clacking, all heads turned. Suddenly Godfrey Wynn flounced out in a state of great distress, turned his head and shouted back at Bill Connor, 'I may be queer but at least I'm sincere!' It was never boring working for an organization dominated by such colourful characters.

One of the real personalities of the sports department was star photographer Monty Fresco. Monty had a whimsical turn of phrase, which sometimes led to misunderstandings. On one occasion he was dispatched to cover Roy Castle's wedding, which was, as they say, a star-studded event. When he got back and handed in the roll of film for developing, he was asked by a distracted picture editor how it had gone. 'Great!' he said. 'They were all standing on their heads to have their photos taken!' Monty went home and the picture editor, whose speciality was obviously photographs rather than metaphors, awaited the promised film. As deadline time approached, the editor came screaming through the news room demanding to know of anyone within earshot how he was to fill a bloody great five-column hole on his front page where the picture of Roy Castle standing on his head should have gone.

Besides being an excellent photographer, Monty was a virtuoso of the expenses game, and he taught me the secret of his success. The system was that we had to set out our expenses in full, then submit them to Jack Hutchinson who would countersign them, pass them on to the accounts department, and we'd go up to collect them. You never wanted to have your expenses queried or you became a marked man. The trick was to claim the maximum expenses that wouldn't cause a complaint. 'What you must remember,' said Monty, 'is that accountants can't help counting things. If they see a row of figures they've just got to add them up, it's an instinct, they won't take your word for it. What you do is to put down all your expenses, but enter a total that's wrong but still within the norm. Then, when the form has been signed and the accounts people get hold of it, they'll find the error and when you go up for the cash, they'll sneer at your incompetence but still pay you out the correct amount.' It worked like a charm.

After a few months, I went up in the world and was given the job of phoning Peter Wilson's copy into the news room, which meant that I went off with him to big fights at Wembley and Earls Court, carrying his typewriter. We would sit on the front row with our chins virtually in the ring watching boxers such as Henry Cooper, Dave Charnley, Terry Downes and Billy Walker in action. Peter would describe the fight, touch-typing, as it happened while I leaned over his shoulder, read his copy and phoned it in to the *Mirror*. My other main task was to keep him supplied with large vodka-and-tonics. Jack Hutchinson had warned me before he first sent me out with Peter that he was not only a great journalist but a world-class toper, so it would be a shortcut to the cemetery to match him drink for drink. I resolved to touch nothing but tonic water or a half glass of beer in the fight hospitality room, and as the evening ended was well pleased with my abstinence.

Then Peter invited me back to his home in Twickenham for supper. His American wife Sally laid on a real feast. I was still resolutely refusing Peter's invitation to join him in a nightcap or two when in came the first course, a delicious soup liberally laced with sherry followed by a steak swimming in brandy sauce, then a luscious rum sorbet, and, as an afterthought, a beautiful Stilton cheese floating in port. They put me to bed utterly pie-eyed even though not a drink had passed my lips all evening.

Passionately keen on sport, I adored my job and was constantly invigorated by the buzz in the sport news room. At first they paid me a tenner a week but I would have paid them for the privilege of working on a world-class newspaper alongside journalists who were the best in the business. I rapidly became one of the boys, soon christened 'Grady', and felt I had finally passed some test or other when I was invited to join them in the White Hart pub across the road from the *Mirror*. It was nicknamed the Stab in the Back because legend had it that some of the most spectacular coups at editorial level had been plotted there. At Grandma's insistence, I took my new friends to meet her at the flat in Wimpole Street where I was still living. She was quite convinced we were all suffering from malnutrition and no one was allowed to leave without being fortified with lashings of her chicken soup. Even if we were on our way out for a meal, it made no odds, she still served up her special soup so we often enjoyed – or endured – two dinners.

Quite apart from my love of football, one of the bonuses of my job was that it offered me another level of contact with my father. For the first twenty years of my life, I didn't see as much of him as I would have liked, and when we did spend time together he was so painfully shy that there were few of the father–son exchanges many of my contemporaries seemed to enjoy. But we were both soccer fanatics; he was a director of Leyton Orient Football Club and I often reported its matches so I spent many a Saturday afternoon in the directors' box with him. Though I shared his passion for the game I didn't share his loyalty to Leyton Orient. When I was seven years old, he once took me with his old friend Billy Cotton, the band leader, to the Valley to watch Charlton Athletic play, and my devotion to the club has never wavered since. I'm now a director and my eldest son Jonathan is also a fan.

At that period, against all the odds, Leyton Orient was enjoying an amazing run of success, winning promotion to the then, top First Division with what was really a scratch team. Determined to spread his enthusiasm around, Dad inveigled brother Bernie to join him on the board, convincing him that he needed a diversion from business affairs, and football would take him out of himself. I suspect the old man also had an eye on Bernie's cheque book. As Bernie told the story, he was sitting in the directors' box at the first match he attended when he was handed a slip of paper on which were set out the figures of attendance and admission money. Whereupon the directors began an animated discussion of them. Bernie shook his head in disbelief. Here he was, supposed to be taking a break from a business where he worried all the time about the number of bums on theatre seats and box-office takings, immersed in more of the same. His foray into football didn't last very long and he went back with relief to his first sporting love, the betting shop.

Leyton Orient's brush with glory in the First Division didn't last very long either. After a few matches against giants such as Manchester United and Liverpool, they began to flag. Alarmed, Dad called an emergency board meeting and summoned their manager, a wonderful veteran called Johnny Carey who had played with Matt Busby for Manchester United. Dad sat at the table with his cheque book open and his pen poised and asked Johnny the critical question: 'Johnny, how much will it cost to keep the team in the First Division?'

After a long pause, Johnny replied, 'Mr Grade, save your money.'

When I heard the story I sighed with relief and commended Johnny Carey to the blessing of whichever gods watched over football managers. It would be bad enough for my inheritance to be squandered on an ailing football team, but even worse on one I didn't support. Had it been Charlton Athletic, that might have been different.

My dad might have managed to drag Bernie into football for a while, but he had no luck with Lew, whose great love was snooker, both as a player and as a spectator. After I left the *Mirror* and became an agent I, too, got hooked on snooker and used to go to a place called the Empire Snooker, Billiards and Table Tennis Club, which was an upholstered sewer under Frith Street. It had a card room and eight snooker tables, and was vastly popular with showbiz personalities, song-pluggers and theatrical agents. The manager's name was George Maggs and if you were involved in a needle match it paid to slip him the odd token of appreciation otherwise you might end up playing at a table with threadbare cushions. Before the war, Lew had been a regular customer and seemed to win the snooker tournament with amazing regularity: the evidence was up there on the board for all to see. I once commented on this to George Maggs, adding, 'I didn't think he was *that* good.'

George said, 'Well, he had a bit of help. First, it was his cup, he'd paid for it, and that had to be good for a bit of favouritism in the handicapping. Then he invariably won any dispute about free balls.'

'How did he manage that?' I asked.

'Well,' said George, 'if the cue ball was touching another ball, the opponent had a free ball, and I was the one who had to decide the issue. Lew would summon me and say, 'Tell me, have I a free ball or not?' He'd take my arm and drag me over to the table, at the same time expertly pressing a pound note into my palm. I'd inspect the lie of the balls from this angle and that and then declare that Lew indeed had a free ball. And he was on the way to another win.'

I think the family love of sport, especially football, in some way compensated for our very conventional and buttoned-up family life. The great thing about soccer is that for ninety minutes enthusiasts can run the whole gamut of human emotions – excitement, tears, boredom, anger, frustration, exhilaration – and express them in a safe, controlled environment. This offered the Grades, especially my father, a form of catharsis. The only time I saw my father out of control, all his inhibitions swept aside, was when he was roaring in support of Leyton Orient.

Because I was a sports reporter, I had to be careful that I didn't breach any confidences and reveal to the *Mirror*'s readers information I'd overheard in the directors' box at Leyton Orient. But I felt showbiz gossip was different. Given my family background, it was inevitable that I should become pally with Don Short, who was the *Mirror*'s entertainment reporter. I was happy to pass on to him the odd snippet of gossip I'd picked up round the family table.

I gave Don one of his biggest scoops when Bruce Forsyth decided to quit *Sunday Night at the London Palladium* and everyone in showbusiness and Fleet Street wanted to know who would take his place. I overheard Lew and my dad discussing who should get the prize slot and duly noted that they had eventually settled on Jimmy Tarbuck. I decided to leak the story to Don, assuring him that he could take it as true without worrying that it might turn out to be unfounded speculation. Don ran the story, which made the *Mirror*'s front page. The next morning Don Short, came past and mumbled that he'd been summoned to see the boss. Apparently, Lew and Dad had been on the phone to Hugh Cudlipp, outraged that the *Mirror* had stolen their thunder and undermined a big press conference they'd called to announce Jimmy Tarbuck's appointment. Don eventually came out of the editor's office and winked at me as he walked past my desk; I was reassured that he hadn't revealed his source.

Anyway, since the story was true, the editor couldn't be too hard on a star reporter for getting his paper a big scoop. It may be my imagination, but I thought my dad looked at me a little strangely for a while afterwards. However, no one in the family accused me of base treachery.

After I'd worked for the *Mirror* for about a year, Jack Hutchinson took me off the subs desk and made me gofer to John Bromley, who wrote a daily column called 'Sportlight', which was filled with snippets of gossip about sports personalities and events. For a fully fledged reporter, the job would have been a demotion, but in my case it was a first step up in my chosen profession and I happily dashed around after John, making the coffee, running errands, answering the phone and chasing up the odd story.

John agreed to Jack's proposal with the ringing endorsement, 'He's not a great intellect but he makes a good cup of coffee.' We became firm friends and he taught me all I knew about sports journalism. Pity he didn't teach me all *he* knew. As part of my apprenticeship I learned how masters of the art of publicity handle the press, feeding us the line they wanted us to take, offering us quotes we couldn't refuse because we had deadlines to meet and rival papers to outsmart. The late boxing promoter Jack Solomons was a brilliant publicist; it was a joy to watch him in action. Bromers and I went to the legendary Cassius Clay versus Henry Cooper heavyweight contest at Wembley, which is, of course, an open-air stadium. We planned to write some preview features, and the critical question was: what would happen if it rained? Bromers put the question to Jack Solomons before the event. Without a flicker of amusement, Solomons replied, 'Anyone arriving at Wembley for the fight carrying a raincoat and umbrella won't be admitted' – a perfect quote, certain to hit the sports-page headlines and reassure any punters nervous about the weather.

If Jack Solomons was a journalist's dream, the late Sir Alf

Ramsey, the manager of the England football team, was a reporter's nightmare – which was bad news because by far the biggest sports event of 1965–6 was the World Cup, which England was hosting, so there was great press interest in the England manager. Alf was a monosyllabic man who hated the press; he gave the impression he'd rather have teeth drawn than speak to us. His background might have had something to do with it. He was a real Cockney born in Dagenham and had played for Tottenham Hotspur. One of his team-mates was another Cockney, Eddie Bailey, with whom I once watched Alf, after he became England manager, giving a press conference on TV. Bailey couldn't believe his ears. Alf's thick Cockney accent had given place to a kind of seaside-landlady posh voice. 'Alf's obviously had elocution lessons,' said Eddie. 'His cockney accent used to be so thick even I couldn't understand it.' The end result was that Alf tended to be over-generous with his Hs and niggardly with the Gs at the end of words. He'd developed a formula for dealing with the hated press. If England had a bad game he'd content himself by saying, 'H'our passin' left something to be desaired', if they'd done well, he'd announce, 'The H'England passin' was pleasin'.' And that was it; end of statement. You couldn't fill many column inches with that.

I remember covering an England warm-up game as a back-up to the *Mirror*'s main football correspondent who wrote about the match while I lurked about the tunnel leading to the players' dressing rooms to pick up any usable quotes after the game. When it ended, we waited and waited for Alf to appear. He probably thought that if he delayed long enough, the reporters would get fed up with hanging about and clear off. When Alf eventually came down the tunnel, his face dropped a mile: he'd have to face the press, after all. The big news of the match was that the England full back Ray Wilson had been carried off injured and this could be very serious as the World Cup began in a few weeks' time. Alf gazed at the assembled press appraisingly as though trying to decide to which species of insect life we belonged and then announced, 'H'our passin' left somethin' to be desired.' We'd already written that down in advance so someone asked him about Ray Wilson's injury. Alf had a curious mannerism, he'd stroke his upper lip with his finger while he pondered what to say next. Eventually he offered, 'Ray Wilson 'as 'ad stitches.'

'How many?' I asked, eagerly.

His finger frantically brushed his upper lip then he said, 'Suffice it to say, that it is h'official, Ray Wilson 'as been stitched.' Those exact words – 'Ray Wilson stitched' – were the *Mirror*'s sports lead the next morning.

Well, we may have made fun of Alf's tortuous diction but the laugh was us. Under his managership, England won the World Cup and Alf collected a knighthood. After I'd left the *Mirror* and was making my living as a theatrical agent, Bernie asked me to help organize the *Royal Variety Performance*. He wanted some kind of dramatic climax to round off the show and I suggested that we could bring on Sir Alf Ramsey and the England team, complete with trophy. I also announced brashly that I knew Alf well. With much trepidation, I rang him up and took him out for a sumptuous tea. He could not have been more charming or co-operative and duly appeared on stage at the Palladium for the *Royal Variety Performance*. I took great pride in the England team's appearance that night because it symbolized a kind of rite of passage for me, from journalism to enter-tainment.

It wasn't all blood, toil, tears and sweat at the *Mirror*. There are many advantages to having been brought up as part of a close-knit family, highly conventional in its moral attitudes, endlessly concerned for my health, welfare and happiness, but it can be frustrating to a high-spirited young man to live with all those eyes watching, however benevolently, his every move. So I made the most of my new-found freedom and there then followed a constant battle of wits between the family and myself in which they tried to fathom out what I was up to and I went to great lengths to cover my tracks.

In due course, I joined the National Union of Journalists, my salary went up fourfold to forty quid a week, and since I lived entirely free with Grandma, I had disposable cash in my pocket. I decided to rent a flat for one of my first girlfriends, Julie, who was a topless dancer and therefore unlikely to be welcomed with open arms into the, um, bosom of the Grade family. I found a one-bedroom flat on the Upper Richmond Road in Putney, signed all the necessary forms and installed Julie in it. She was a real character, vivacious and bubbly, with a colourful turn of phrase, always the life and soul of the party. In my immaturity, I was besotted with her, quite convinced that she was the love of my life. Naturally, when they found out, the family disapproved and began to badger Leslie to put me straight about the whole thing. I was duly summoned to his house in St John's Wood, where he sat me down and squirmed in his chair and gazed earnestly at the ceiling and hummed and hawed and eventually said, 'Now what's all this about a girl?' I told him. He then volunteered the opinion that there was such a thing as sexual obsession, letting drop the dreaded S-word as though it were a red-hot pebble in his mouth. He then mumbled a sentence or two about infatuation, the foolishness of either getting her pregnant or marrying her, and subsided. I said OK, fine, and that was that, the only heart-to-heart talk I ever had with him. It took about ten minutes. He didn't say much but what he said made sense.

Some weeks later I was having lunch with my father when my half-sister Anita, who must then have been about eight or nine, suddenly asked how many Grades there were in Britain. Dad explained there were only us, but Anita wasn't satisfied: she insisted on consulting the telephone directory to check for herself. Sure enough, she went down the list and suddenly read out, 'M. Grade, Upper Richmond Road, Putney'. I blushed brick-red and cursed myself for my naïvety in signing the telephone contract for Julie's flat under my own name. I still had a lot to learn about the subterfuge a man-about-town needed to develop. Neither Dad nor Olga said anything but I felt I'd been rumbled.

I could never fool Grandma: she seemed to have a built-in

crap detector, which cut like radar through all the obfuscation I
cast around the identity of my various girlfriends. On my twenty-
first birthday, Dad and Audrey gave me a splendid party at their
home in St John's Wood. I was determined that Julie shouldn't
be left out but I daren't bring her openly, so I hatched a plot
with some of my pals. The idea was that they would all arrive in
a gang, Julie among them, mingle with the other guests and
sooner or later I'd seek her out as though meeting her for the
first time. The party duly began, the doorbell rang and there
were my mates, including Julie, on the doorstep. They all swept
in, laughing and joking. Suddenly, through the hubbub, my
grandmother's voice rang out: 'That's her!' she screamed, pointing at the cringing Julie. The entire party froze. When normality
resumed, Grandma sat Julie down and, like a Jewish momma
interviewing a potential daughter-in-law, proceeded to eulogize
about her wonderful Michael and warned her against sullying
my innocence. Julie, with superhuman charity, refrained from
telling her the sordid truth about my virginity.

　　Whenever Olga went off to visit her cronies in Bournemouth,
it was party-time home-alone at Wimpole Street. One evening, a
mate and I got decked up in dinner jackets to cover a boxing
match at the National Sporting Club. After the match, we went
to one of our favourite watering holes and picked up a couple
of girls. After a spell of conviviality back at Grandma's Wimpole
Street flat, my mate accepted his girlfriend's invitation to spend
the night at her place. After a night of passion, I got up, put on
a pair of jeans and a T-shirt and set about getting a cab for my
girlfriend, who was still in long ballgown, full-length gloves, the
works. We went downstairs and stood on the pavement to attract
the attention of a cab. As my girlfriend was getting into the cab,
another cab drew up behind it and out got my mate still in his
dinner jacket. The cabby looked from the girl in her evening
dress on the pavement to my mate in his dinner jacket and then
said, 'I hope you don't mind my asking, but are you early or
late?'

　　One mega-thrash I specially remember. It went on all

through one Saturday night and by the time the last guest dragged himself off at eleven next morning, the flat offered a passable imitation of a Second World War Blitz site. I had to go in to the *Mirror* on Sunday afternoon to help get Monday's edition out but I wasn't too bothered about the state of the flat because Olga would be away for a couple more days, I could clean things up when I got back from work. I put in a hard late shift and got back to the flat to find that the front door had been jemmied off its frame and was lying on the sitting-room floor. We'd been burgled. I called the police, who came round quickly. 'Gawd's truth!' said one constable, surveying the wreckage of the weekend party. 'I've seen some terrible acts of vandalism in my time but never anything on this scale.'

My aunt Rita was probably the most conventional of all the Grade family and had a curiosity *not* short of nosiness about my private life. I once had a girlfriend from Norfolk who served in a coffee bar. We became very close and one day she rang and said she had to talk to me urgently. Without preamble, she announced that she was pregnant, then, seeing the look of utter horror on my face, added quickly, 'Don't worry. You're not the father.' She told me the whole story and then said that she just didn't know what to do, whether to have an abortion or go through with it. I advised her to talk to her parents and added that if there was anything I could do to help financially I'd be glad to do it. I didn't hear from her for ages, then one evening I got home and there to meet me was Aunt Rita with a face like thunder. She'd opened a letter from this girl addressed to me. This included the phrase that she'd decided to go through with having the baby but she was grateful for my offer of financial help. Rita and I had strong words about the immorality of opening private correspondence and I tried to convince her that I was not the putative father. To her credit, Rita said nothing to the rest of the family but I am quite convinced that she went to her grave utterly convinced that I was the baby's father.

*

One afternoon in 1964 Bromers came into the office and told me that ABC TV had invited him to set up a sports department and become their network's first sports producer. He asked my opinion. I had no doubt that in the future, television would be where the action was, so I encouraged him to accept the offer, even though it would be a severe personal blow because Bromers was not just my great mentor but also a dear friend. Certainly, much of the fun went out of the department when he left. For me, the sole consolation was that I inherited his column, and at twenty-one had a daily five hundred words headed by my own byline and picture in Britain's biggest selling paper.

But even before Bromers left the *Mirror*, I'd become restless and worried about the future. My salary as a sports journalist couldn't possibly support my rather lavish lifestyle, and thoughts of marriage had begun to preoccupy me. I'd met Penny Levinson, who later became my first wife, and we were talking seriously about our relationship. Out of all this mental ferment emerged a business proposition. A wild Irish promoter called Billy Morton gave us the idea. Both Bromers and I loved track and field events. The attraction was a combination of the calibre of the performers, champions such as Mary Rand, Robbie Brightwell, Adrian Metcalf, Ann Packer and Lynn Davis, and the purest of mental and physical skills uncluttered by any equipment other than a running surface and a stop-watch. At this time, athletics events were organized and run by county officials who were amateurs in the wrong sense of the word. Granted these officials were unpaid, but confronted by a galaxy of talent they had no idea how to go about exploiting it to give the sport a higher profile and more popular appeal.

This is where Billy Morton came in. Every year at the Santry Stadium outside Dublin, Billy ran an athletics meeting, and to everyone's astonishment, managed to persuade world-class athletes to compete in events that regularly broke records. We sports commentators couldn't afford to miss the Santry gathering. Billy ran the whole thing like a three-ring circus; he'd stand on the track with a microphone and, like a showman, announce the competitors with great dramatic emphasis: 'AND NOW, ALL THE WAY FROM AUCKLAND, NEW ZEALAND, THE MAN HIM-SELF, THE ONE AND ONLY PETER SNELL, THE WORLD RECORD HOLDER!' He would whip the crowd into a rare state of excitement. In watering holes around Dublin, we sports journalists would often discuss the secret of Billy's success. After all, the stadium was dilapidated, Billy obviously couldn't afford to pay much, and yet year after year he enticed the world's greatest runners and jumpers to take part in the event. In the end we concluded that Billy employed time-keepers who had the fastest stop-watches in the world. We knew *that* for a fact because, like all professionals, we invariably timed each race, lap by lap, and when Billy crowed, 'HERE TONIGHT, THE WORLD RECORD FOR THE MILE HAS BEEN BROKEN AT THREE MINUTES FIFTY-SIX SECONDS EXACTLY', we'd look at our watches in disbelief, and compare timings. It must have been some kind of unwritten understanding that the athletes who agreed to compete at Santry had a pretty good chance of taking home a world record. The amazing thing is that, though everyone present who could tell the time doubted the accuracy of Billy Morton's watches, no one shopped him; none of the journalists present ever blew the whistle on him. It was such a magical occasion, we couldn't do anything to undermine it.

After the goings on at Santry Stadium, athletics meetings in Britain were an awful anticlimax. Bromers and I went to one at the White City shortly after the Tokyo Olympics, where Lynn Davis and Mary Rand had won gold medals. We listened to this dreary voice announcing flatly that the next competition was the men's long jump and reading out the names with as much dramatic emphasis as the speaking clock. Here we were, a country able to boast world superstar athletes such as Lynn Davis and then introduced him casually as 'Competitor 146, L. Davis, Glamorgan', as though he were a complete unknown.

Bromers and I were outraged: what British athletics needed was robust, unapologetic promotion, Santry-style, and we were eager to provide it. We formed a sports promotion company with Terry O'Connor, then the rugby and athletics correspondent of the *Daily Mail*, and another chap who was a specialist in marketing. We called it Voice of Sport and set about finding sponsoring companies to brighten up track and field events. My dad put up five thousand quid and we bought a small company that had handled golf tournaments, then started the search for sponsors. Things looked promising until my father's stroke, then life for all the Grades changed.

For weeks we thought that Dad would die, so nothing else mattered, business affairs were swept aside. Once it was clear he was going to recover but would remain very frail, the future of his empire had to be settled. Bernie had been holding the fort and one day he took me out to lunch. What he said in effect was, 'Thank God your father's going to be all right, but he'll never be the power he once was, and I'm not getting any younger myself. I think it's time you got serious and took the agency on.' Obviously, Bernie's proposal didn't surprise me. My attitude to the business had changed since Dad had offered me a job when I first left school. To take on a job because it's expected of you, just because you're a Grade, had no attraction for me, but to be offered a job because you are genuinely needed was very flattering. I couldn't remotely see myself filling my father's shoes, he was a legend throughout the entertainment business, but I was determined to do my best and I knew that he would be pleased I was carrying on the Grade tradition.

Bernie promised me I wouldn't be on my own; he would put me in an office with Billy Marsh. Billy had originally worked for him but came over to my dad when Bernie merged the agency part of his empire with the Grade Organisation. I would be taught the trade by the greatest of them all, the man who had discovered Bruce Forsyth, Morecambe and Wise, Harry Worth, Norman Wisdom, Charlie Drake and Frankie Vaughan. He was truly a genius, and I was privileged to be the sorcerer's apprentice.

I went back to the *Mirror* and put in my notice. They had

been happy and productive years. I had learned much about the inner workings of the press and the motivations of journalists. Later, when I joined a BBC that was almost paranoid about the press and paid good money to people whose job seemed to be to keep things out of the newspapers, my attitude was completely at odds with the official line. I had learned not to fear newspapers but to use them constructively. I've seen usually confident people freeze when they know that they have to face the press, and what they may not realize is that the experienced journalist can smell the fear and act accordingly. Having been on the other side, I know the terms of engagement. It's true that the fact I've been a journalist hasn't protected me from getting a terrible press from time to time, but however upset I was, I never felt the reporters were driven by any personal malice – with one exception I'll talk about later. Journalists have a living to make and egos to satisfy, so there is everything to gain by treating them as allies rather than enemies. In spite of all the opprobrium heaped on tabloid reporters as 'reptiles' and 'sleaze merchants', my experience is that most can be trusted if one plays fair with them.

My years at the *Daily Mirror* counted as the university education I never had. I was fortunate to have served my apprenticeship in a Fleet Street which was PM – Pre-Murdoch – and his decision to take on the *Daily Mirror* using the *Sun* as his battering-ram. Ironically, he bought the *Sun* from the Mirror Group, who thought they were selling him a loser. How wrong they proved to be. Murdoch took the tabloid formula the *Mirror* had developed and drove it to the very limits of public tolerance. The *Mirror* boasted page-three girls but they weren't naked; it stood for investigative journalism but it wasn't the kiss-and-tell variety based on bribes and the betrayal of confidences. Until Murdoch's *Sun* blasted through the frontiers of taste, the *News of the World*, with its erring scout-masters and naughty vicars, was as raunchy as the tabloids ever get.

The *Mirror* was fun and frothy but it had a real social conscience and a proper sense of responsibility. It was the finest flower of popular journalism. The anguished debate about privacy, which culminated in the death of Diana, Princess of Wales, really began the day Rupert Murdoch took over the *Sun*. There is no doubt that he is a brilliant entrepreneur and a very shrewd political operator. But I'm glad I served my apprenticeship on a true tabloid and got out of Fleet Street before the worst excesses of cheque-book journalism became apparent. It was Hugh Cudlipp who – perhaps fittingly – had the final word on my career as a journalist. Some time later he told my father, 'If Michael had stayed with the *Mirror* he could have ended up as sports editor.'

Chapter Three

INTO THE TWICE-
BRIGHTLY FUTURE

FOR ME 1966 WASN'T just about England winning the World
Cup. It was a year of personal turmoil. My father's stroke
had changed everything. It ended my brief career in journalism
and disturbed the balance of power within the Grade Organisation, forcing Bernie to turn his attention from his theatrical
empire to take my father's place. Olga's future welfare also
became a matter of anxious discussion within the family. While
Dad's life hung in the balance, she stayed with Lew and Kathy at
their Cavendish Square flat, which in turn meant that I was
homeless. Within a year though, Penny and I were married and
had moved south of the river to Dulwich. I was delighted that
Dad was fit enough to attend the ceremony, and the press got
some rare photographs of all three Grade brothers in morning
dress outside the Liberal Synagogue in St John's Wood. Even
before he was ill, my father, unlike Lew and Bernie, shrank from
publicity, so this photograph became the official portrait of the
Grade showbusiness dynasty, endlessly reproduced in newspapers and books.

In the summer of 1966 I became part of the Octopus, which
was the *Sunday Times*' less than flattering name for the Grade
empire. The paper attempted to disentangle all the complex
filaments of what it claimed was 'probably the most powerful
entertainment network in the world'. The organizational chart
it printed certainly rivalled the famous map of the London

Underground for its interconnecting complexity. The implication of the Octopus image is of a sinister monster of the deep, whereas, though I'm hardly a disinterested judge, I believe that the Grade brothers exercised their great power benignly and as a result the public benefited from high-quality, value-for-money entertainment.

The Grade Organisation was no soulless monolith: the three brothers were great characters, true individualists, who specialized in different areas of popular entertainment. They squabbled frequently and often competed against each other. Lew's company, ATV, used to televise the *Royal Variety Performance* until Bernie decided that every other year the BBC should do it. Lew was appalled but his disappointment changed nothing. Billy Marsh used to tell me that when he shared an office with Bernie, he'd listen bemused as Bernie and Leslie had screaming matches over the phone. He could hear Leslie accusing Bernie of stealing one of his acts. 'It's all over, we'll never do business with you again. I don't care if you are my brother, it's finished,' shouted Leslie.

Bernie would slam down the phone. 'That brother of mine's impossible. That's it! Tell everyone in the office, no more business with the Grade Organisation!' Billy grinned and waited until the phone rang again. Bernie would pick it up, and say, 'Yes, Leslie?' then listen for a while. 'That's a great idea!' he'd enthuse. 'We'll split the commission fifty-fifty.' We Grades were devoted to each other round Olga's table, but when it came to business, family loyalty always took second place to commercial judgements.

Together, the Grade brothers embodied a concentration of knowledge and experience of showbusiness that we will probably never see again, especially since we are now in the age of the great corporations where accountants rather than talent-spotters decide what constitutes public entertainment. By a combination of skill in recognizing talent, an instinct for showbusiness, immensely hard work and some luck, the Grade brothers had come from nowhere to dominate the world of mass entertainment by the 1960s. Bernie was the great impresario, putting on shows in all the important West End theatres and beyond, Lew was running ATV, one of the biggest television stations, and he also owned Moss Empire Theatres, which included the London Palladium, the Coliseum and the Theatre Royal, Drury Lane. And my father was by general agreement the most successful theatrical agent in Europe if not the world, at a time when British talent was flourishing. His Grade Organisation was actually a conglomerate of individual agencies run by brilliant talent-spotters such as Robert Fox, Laurie Evans, Denis van Thal and Billy Marsh.

When I joined the Grade Organisation, some newspaper ran a gossip-column item to the effect that one of the younger generation of the family had become a showbusiness tsar. The truth was laughably different. If I had become part of an octopus, I was its most hapless sucker. The day I walked into the office at 235 Regent Street to join Billy Marsh I knew absolutely nothing about the business. Of course, I had been equally ignorant about sports journalism when I joined the *Daily Mirror*, but the great difference was that the giant shadow of my father wasn't cast across Fleet Street. Wherever I turned in showbusiness, I was told colourful stories about Leslie's legendary coups, his many kindnesses and his business genius; it seemed that everyone I met had a tale to tell me about my dad. He was the undisputed master of the game, and in his absence through illness, the legends and myths about him multiplied. It was one thing for Bernie to assure me that I would grow into the job, quite another to justify that confidence or to vindicate my father's trust in me.

But Bernie did me a huge favour in asking the legendary Billy Marsh to teach me the trade. The *Reader's Digest* used to run a series entitled 'The Most Unforgettable Character I've Ever Met', and if I'd been asked for my choice, Billy Marsh would have been very near the top of the list. His name is one of the most honoured in the history of showbusiness, yet he was the most unassuming and deferential of men. Even at the height of his career, when he could count illustrious stars and

impresarios as personal friends, he would still address the
greenest of stage beginners as 'sir'.

Billy was a small, tubby man with glasses who, during all the
years I knew him, never seemed to age because he started out
looking old. People would often say to me, 'I saw Billy last night.
He's looking really old and ill.' He *always* looked old and ill, but
it would have been a great error to judge by appearances and
underestimate his mental sharpness and business grasp. He was
simply the best, and I felt immensely privileged to be appren-
ticed to him.

He was a farmer's son from Deal in Kent who hated rural life
and fell in love with showbusiness at an early age. He had an
indifferent career as a performer. Taking the stage name of
Peter Dare, he did poor impressions of Edward Everett Horton,
Basil Rathbone and Robertson Hare and eked out a precarious
living until he was picked up by a touring show headed by a big
radio star of the time, Issy Bonn. Billy became his general
factotum. In 1944, this led to a job in the Bernard Delfont
Agency in Jermyn Street. He discovered he loved the graft of an
agent's work, which suited Bernie because it gave him the
freedom to do what he did best, being a impresario.

Billy and I worked in an office almost totally obscured in
wreaths of blue cigarette smoke. He was a chain-smoker with an
untipped Player's cigarette always dangling from his lower lip;
his secretary, Bunty, had to empty his ashtray every hour on the
hour. He had a habit of flicking cigarette ash over his shoulder
and would invariably miss the ashtray so that his jacket looked as
though he'd been caught in a snowstorm. Eric Morecambe, who
was devoted to Billy, used to do a wicked impression of him.
He'd scatter talcum powder across the shoulders of his jacket
and say, 'Guess who?'

In all the years I worked with him, I never saw Billy in a
panic. We were responsible for supplying artists for venues such
as the Talk of the Town, the famous nightclub in London's West
End, and every now and then we'd be told at the last moment
by, say, Shirley Bassey's agent that the star had a sore throat and

wouldn't be able to appear. In our world that was one of the worst disasters that could befall an agent – eight hundred expectant customers and no show. Always calm, Billy would ring me at home, tell me the bad news and give me a list of 'substitute' stars to call while he phoned others. He was totally imperturbable.

He wasn't just a great agent, he was also a great humanitarian. He worried about his stars not just as public performers but as vulnerable human beings. He'd share their anguish and misery; he understood their inner motivations. They might storm into his office making a big fuss because their dressing room was too small when in reality they were fearful their new material didn't work or they felt they were losing their nerve. Billy would sit them down, hear them out, then talk to them, reassuring them that it would be all right on the night. And they *were* reassured because they knew that his understanding of how they ticked was profound and his compassion genuine.

Billy was a master psychologist. One of our favourite clients was the comedian Harry Worth, a chronic worrier. At the beginning of every year, we'd take him out for lunch and go through the list of engagements we'd proposed for him. He would be profuse in his thanks for all our efforts on his behalf and then off he'd go on the train to Berkhamsted, where he lived. When we got back in the office I'd set to with a calculator working out what commission we'd earn on Harry's engagements. Billy would ask me what I was doing and, when I told him, would grin. 'Don't bother. Any minute now the phone will ring and it'll be Harry and he'll say, "Billy, I was sitting on the train thinking . . ." and the whole deal will come unravelled and we'll have to start again.' It was uncanny. Sure enough the phone would ring and it was Harry having second thoughts. Billy used to call it the Train Home Syndrome.

Billy was a tough but fair negotiator. If he had all the cards, he would never drive too hard a bargain. He wouldn't squeeze his victims until all the pips squeaked; he'd stop after one pip and leave them the rest. The important thing was to allow them some dignity and show magnanimity. This was not only good human relations but also sound business sense. We were, after all, not just selling talent as agents but buying it as show producers so we never knew when we might need a favour. He was a man of transparent integrity and he taught me not only about the mechanics of showbusiness but also its ethics.

Billy's supreme skill was as a talent-spotter, and he had an infallible instinct for a good comedy act. Norman Wisdom, Harry Worth, Bruce Forsyth and Morecambe and Wise: Billy either discovered them or raised their careers from the dead. Given the veneration in which Morecambe and Wise are now held, it is hard to believe that there was a time when they were regarded as abject failures. Eric used to carry a newspaper cutting around about their first television performance. The critic wrote, 'Is that a television set I see in the corner? No, it's the box in which they buried Morecambe and Wise last night.' In desperation, they came to Billy and asked him to handle their careers. Billy recognized their talent and advised, guided and pointed them unerringly into the big time. Of all his stable of stars, he felt particularly close to them and always referred to them as the Boys.

When Billy died, his business partner, Jan Kennedy, in a brilliant stroke, persuaded the Palladium management to let us put his ashes under the stage on which many of his protégés enjoyed their moments of triumph. I like to think of him at rest amid music, laughter and applause, the characteristic sounds of the showbusiness he loved.

The first job Billy gave me was to keep up to date what he called the most important document in the building. This was a ledger in which we recorded what were referred to simply as the Figures. Besides running his own stable of stars, Billy was also responsible for booking summer-season shows and pantomimes. This was the last gasp of traditional vaudeville – twice-nightly revues in seaside resorts such as Blackpool, Bournemouth, Torquay and Great Yarmouth. Every morning when I got into the office, awaiting me on my desk would be a pile of telegrams from the managers of the theatres putting on the shows, setting out in code the size of the audience and the takings at each performance. It was a very rudimentary code, no Enigma machine would have been necessary to decipher it, but it was one of Billy's fond illusions that a code such as A equals 1, B equals 2 and so on kept the agency business secret. I had to compare the figures week on week and year by year, and we would hold a post-mortem before Bernie rang us from his office at the Prince of Wales theatre for a report on the previous night's activities. Keeping this ledger made me realize for the first time that showbusiness *is* a business; that it has as much to do with finance as with talent and entertainment. My father had been taking me to shows since I was about six so I'd long been familiar with the stardust but now I had to knuckle down and master its less glamorous elements.

Our string of summer shows brought us into contact with the municipal corporations of seaside towns and their entertainment managers, who often ran the pier-head theatres. They were usually local government officials who found themselves utterly out of their depth in the world of showbusiness. I recall Bournemouth's entertainment manager once lecturing Billy and me about the stars he thought would go down well in the town. He'd decided that for the following season a combination of Burns and Allen and Bert Weedon would bring in the crowds. As always, Billy listened politely to this expert opinion then laughed all the way back to London. The thought of American TV superstars Burns and Allen doing a summer season at Bournemouth was in itself utterly bizarre without the additional twist that they might need the support of Bert Weedon, a guitarist of modest fame. But Billy never threw his professional weight around; he always reacted respectfully to the most asinine opinions.

He was a marvellous teacher with endless patience, and from the beginning he included me in everything that went on in the office. He didn't hog our more important clients, excluding me from meeting them because I was junior and had nothing to contribute. I sat in on every negotiation, keeping quiet and learning as quickly as I could. Often, we'd adjourn to Verry's for a convivial lunch where his guests, especially if they were comedians, would tell funny stories and I constituted an open-mouthed audience.

One of the great skills in putting together variety shows wasn't just booking the right acts but also working out the correct order in which they should perform. I recall Lew once telling me that putting together variety bills as an agent had taught him the art of television scheduling when he took over ATV. And any aptitude I developed in turn for scheduling television programmes originated in Billy Marsh's office, where I gradually learned that there is only one correct running order for variety acts, and that the show will be a flop if this sequence isn't followed. Bill and I used to play a game amid the haze and smoke of our office. He'd say, 'Let's take the Britannia Pier, Great Yarmouth. These are the acts we have booked, now do a running order.' We'd compare notes, and once I'd got the hang of this arcane art, we would invariably come up with an identical arrangement of variety turns. So I slowly learned the tricks of the trade.

Though sitting somewhat self-consciously at my father's old desk in the agency, I had a certain number of dealings with him in his role as an impresario. He was less active after his stroke but continued to produce the shows at the London Palladium; Billy and I found him the star turns, especially for the Christmas pantomime. Every year just before he went away for the summer to the South of France Dad would ask me who we had in mind. I once suggested Engelbert Humperdinck, who had three out of the top five numbers in the hit parade. Dad said, 'Fine, but I'm not paying him too much; I don't believe in all the money going out of the stage door.' Engelbert Humperdinck had a brilliant but awkward manager called Gordon Mills who drove a very hard bargain. We eventually signed Humperdinck to play Robinson Crusoe. We saw the show-stopping possibilities of his coming on stage after the ship had gone down and singing his great hit, 'There Goes My Everything'. The problem was he wanted 10 per cent of the box-office takings. 'Don't be ridiculous,' said my father. 'I've never paid that much in my life, not even to Bob Hope and Jack Benny.' Eventually I decided to go down to the South of France and spend the weekend with him. We never mentioned the subject until I was leaving. Eventually, he said, 'Not a penny more than nine and half per cent.' And that's what we settled for, whereupon Humperdinck packed out the Palladium for sixteen weeks. My dad may have been family, but he was no soft touch when it came to business.

I'd been with the agency for less than a year when Bernie got a huge take-over offer from EMI, which at that time was the premier record company because its top performing artists were the Beatles and Cliff Richard. They wanted the Grade name as well as the family's showbusiness instincts and management skills. My father, though slowly recovering from his stroke, knew he would never again regain his original drive and flair, and Bernie, by nature an impresario, welcomed an even larger platform on which to operate, so the brothers recommended to the shareholders of the Grade Organisation that the offer should be accepted. EMI took over the entire business and we all became employees of a huge conglomerate. No sooner had we come to terms with this turn of events than Bernie persuaded his new employers that they should buy the ABC cinema chain, which also owned a film studio at Elstree. ABC saw things differently and there followed an acrimonious take-over battle, which in the end EMI won. Bernie now found himself in charge of the entertainment side of EMI and proved himself a natural corporate executive. He loved the internal politics and the power-play, and for the first time in his professional life had financial security. Dad, who had slowly returned to work after his stroke, did not find it congenial to be someone else's employee. He was a natural loner who had been a law unto himself since he was sixteen. His discontent boiled over when he was sent an EMI organization chart that showed him linked to top management by a mere dotted line. 'A dotted line!' he snorted in disgust. He became obsessed with this symbol of his subordinate status in the organization and announced his intention to quit EMI. Bernie tried to dissuade him, but it was no use. Dad broke away from the conglomerate and set up his own modest business as Leslie Grade Limited in Wardour Street.

Billy and I were now also employees of EMI, which led to an embarrassing incident when we were trying to do a deal with an Australian hotel owner who was interested in booking some of our stars for his entertainment circuit. We received him in my dad's old office with due ceremony and were busy assuring him that ours was the premier agency in the business when there was a knock on the door and in walked a girl with a tray. It was the wages clerk. In those days we got our salary in an envelope that contained both notes and loose change. The girl was obviously new. She went up to Billy and asked him his name. 'Marsh, Billy Marsh,' he replied humbly, whereupon she dropped an envelope on to his desk with an audible rattle of coins. Then after enquiring my name, she also tossed me a clinking envelope. Our VIP guest was obviously puzzled since we'd just been pointing out how frightfully important we were in the entertainment world. There was an embarrassing silence during which Billy lit another cigarette. To rescue the situation I picked up my envelope and dropped it into Billy's wastepaper basket with the dismissive comment, 'It's not worth bothering about!' And we got back down to business. On the way into the office next morning I suddenly remembered that I'd consigned my wage packet to Billy's bin and, sure enough, during the night, all the litter had been taken away so I never got that week's salary. Billy laughed himself sick, rang up all his showbiz mates to tell them the story, and another Grade legend was born.

EMI's take-over of ABC ran into political trouble. Both the Board of Trade and the Independent Television Authority were unhappy about the possibility that a monopoly was being created, so EMI agreed to give up their agency interests, which meant that all the so-called Robber Barons of the Grade Organisation could acquire their own bits of the company through management buy-outs. Billy Marsh, Denis van Thal and I decided to go into partnership. Billy was keen to include Denis in any arrangement because he felt that with his legitimate theatre clients, such as Franco Zeffirelli and Alec Guinness, Denis would bring a touch of class to our organization. With financial help from my father, we launched London Management, and at the age of twenty-four I found myself owning a third share in a big agency.

Good agents combine a wide range of skills: they need to be tough negotiators, shrewd talent-spotters, passionate lovers of showbusiness in all its aspects, and also opportunists, ready to leap in and push their clients when show producers are in a hole and in no position to bargain. One of Billy's clients was John Hanson, a somewhat ageing matinée idol who used to tour the provinces doing cheap versions of *The Desert Song* and *The Student Prince*. He had a very good voice, bags of charm and a very popular radio show. He desperately wanted to play the West End but Billy doubted he had the indefinable quality that marked out a national star. Then one day Bernie rang to say that Emile Littler, who owned the Palace Theatre, was with him in the office and had a problem. The theatre was about to go dark unless they could come up with another show at very short notice. Billy took a deep breath and said that, as a matter of fact, we had a really exciting possibility. 'Yes?' said Bernie eagerly. 'John Hanson in *The Desert Song*,' suggested Billy diffidently. There was dead silence at the other end of the phone, so Billy gulped and pressed on: 'He could put the show on for about twenty thousand quid all in,' which was peanuts for the Palace Theatre. There was another pregnant silence while Bernie passed on the idea to Emile Littler, who obviously decided to make a virtue out of necessity and promised an immediate contract. Billy put down the phone, took a deep breath and said, 'What *have* we done?'

We went to the rehearsals for John Hanson's show, which Billy was convinced the critics would savage. Luckily the opening scene in the Arab camp was so dark that no one in the audience could see that the scenery was falling apart after being lugged around the country a thousand times or that all the Arabs had their legionnaire costumes showing under their burnouses. Billy decided to open with two shows on a Saturday night because the London critics were unlikely to attend, and we arranged for coach parties of Hanson fans from all round the country to converge on the Palace Theatre to support their hero. We needn't have worried. The show ran and ran, and John Hanson deservedly became a big star.

The good agent must also be an agony aunt or uncle, prepared to nurse temperamental public performers through their personal and professional traumas. With some exceptions, the greater a star's talent, the more wildly his or her moods tend to oscillate between exhilaration and deep depression. One of the stars Billy particularly cared for, even loved, was Tony Hancock, a comic genius who when I came on the scene was a giant in decay, racked by depression, drink and loneliness.

We booked Tony to appear on *The Frost Programme* and Billy asked me to go along and hold his hand. 'Tony's a very lonely man and needs all the support he can get,' he said. I was honoured to be given the job: from my youth on, Tony Hancock had been as a god to me. We got on famously and after the show we went back to his flat in Kensington where he paced the floor restlessly, played records, drank vodka and talked about his great showbiz heroes such as Sid Field. In the early hours of the morning I left him, still pacing the floor, an infinitely sad figure. It was painful to watch him in the throes of such depression that he was utterly incapable of dealing with life, of facing even the most mundane responsibilities and often driven by totally irrational thoughts. He would seek relief in drink, though he wasn't an alcoholic according to any strict definition; he just drank to ease his mental pain. Then, just occasionally, the mist would clear and it was as though a bright light had gone on inside him: he would radiate charm, wit and ebullience. Tragically, those periods of positive high energy became fewer and fewer during the years I knew him.

There are certain rare spirits in showbusiness whom the public take to their hearts; they will forgive them anything. Even at his lowest ebb, Tony never lost the loyalty of his audiences. The old genius had vanished, he had difficulty remembering his lines, he'd quarrelled with Alan Simpson and Ray Galton, the script-writers who had crafted his most memorable sketches, and then got rid of any actors in his sketches whom he thought were competing with him for laughs. Truly, he had a death-wish, and yet the public still flocked to his shows, hoping against hope that the Tony Hancock who once entertained them would rise again. But it never happened.

One day Tony pitched up in our office bubbling with enthusiasm and announced that he'd found a couple of young writers who were absolutely brilliant, they would undoubtedly replace Simpson and Galton and put him back on top. He pleaded with Billy to get him another television series. Billy could never resist Tony's blandishments, so in spite of our worst fears we headed off to see Philip Jones, who was head of Light Entertainment at ABC TV. We assured him that Tony was back to his old form, had these brilliant script-writers and was keen to do another television series. It would be the greatest comeback since Lazarus materialized out of the tomb. Philip was delighted and we did a deal there and then.

Billy and I went along to the recording of the first show. It was an absolute disaster. The script didn't work, Tony kept forgetting his lines and had to have idiot boards dotted round the studio, and he was never in the right spot at the right time for the correct camera angles. There were so many retakes the show overran to the point where the technicians were on the verge of pulling the plugs on it. It was just too awful for words. Years later Mark Stuart, who had had the thankless task of directing it, came to work for me at LWT. Apparently, immediately after Billy and I had done the deal with Philip Jones, he sent for Mark Stuart and told him he'd been chosen to direct and produce Tony Hancock's great television comeback. Mark said words to the effect of 'Over my dead body!' but it was too late, Philip had already signed the contract, so Mark having registered his misgivings had to bite the bullet. At the end of that awful night, when everyone in the studio was slipping sadly away after witnessing the abysmal conclusion to a unique television career, Philip Jones appeared and, according to Mark Stuart, patted him on the shoulder and said, 'Never mind, Mark, you were right to try.'

Eventually we booked Tony for a tour of Australia, and a long way from home in a hotel room he put a permanent end to his inner turmoil. Surveying the ruins of a great career, one looks for redeeming features. However low or incapacitated he was, Tony never let us down. If he agreed to an engagement, he would pitch up as arranged whatever state he was in, and, like a child, seek reassurance, ask plaintively, 'I've never let you down, have I, Billy?' But Tony had his glory days and his legend lives on. The word 'genius' is often loosely applied to anyone of outstanding talent, but Tony at his peak wasn't just better, he was different, and he'll be remembered long after many other performers of the time have been forgotten.

Another showbusiness genius who nearly drove us demented was Judy Garland. Billy and I used to book the Talk of the Town, which Bernie ran for Charles Forte. The evening programme included a meal, a floor-show, then dancing until eleven o'clock when the star turn came on, and that was the slot Billy and I were contracted to fill. Over the years we had booked Diana Ross and the Supremes, Cliff Richard and the Shadows, Sammy Davis Jr and Liza Minnelli. One day out of the blue we got a phone call from Judy Garland's agent. She'd like to come to London and play the Talk of the Town. Though we gratefully acknowledged that she was a living legend, one of the true superstars of our time, we also knew she had a history of heavy drinking, was notorious for reneging on her commitments, having acrimonious rows with all who worked with her and dissolving into bouts of maudlin self-pity. We expressed polite interest and cautiously enquired what shape she was in. We were assured she was fine and rarin' to work in London, so we booked her for four weeks at the Talk of the Town. It was a brave agent, or a very rich one, who would turn down a chance to book Judy Garland.

We gave the job of looking after Judy to probably the greatest road manager in the history of showbusiness, Glyn Jones, who was on first-name terms with stars the world over, so remarkable was his gift for getting along with them. He anticipated their every need, smoothed their path and ensured that they were able to concentrate on their performance without worrying about anything else. Superstars such as Frank Sinatra, Johnnie Ray and Sammy Davis Jr had their quirky side: they could be arrogant, unreasonable and utterly demanding, but nothing they said or did fazed Glyn. He was chameleon-like in his capacity to adapt to their moods and, as a result, they adored him.

Glyn was an interesting character. He was married and lived in a council flat in Clapham with his wife Doris. Though he travelled the world first class with big stars, whenever he was in London he went home to Clapham, his jealously guarded private world to which none of us had access. He even kept us at a physical distance from the block of flats where he lived. If we offered him a lift home he'd say, 'Drop me at the urinal' – there was a public lavatory on Clapham Common – and he'd make his own way from there. Given the job of meeting Judy at Heathrow, Glyn rang International Car Hire from my office and booked the Big One, a Rolls-Royce Phantom. After discussing arrival times with the hire company, he said, 'Have the car pick me up as usual at the urinal.' I've often wondered what the citizens of Clapham made of the bizarre sight of this nondescript figure in a battered fedora standing outside a public lavatory in the small hours of the morning and being ushered into a gleaming Rolls-Royce by a liveried chauffeur.

The Friday Judy arrived was a day of good and bad news. The good news was that she'd actually made it – she was here! The bad news was that she had arrived without a sheet of her music. In some marital dispute, an ex-husband had impounded her property, including her music library, and without her backing music, Judy couldn't perform. We were distraught. Her show opened on Monday night.

The ever-enterprising Glyn came up with a solution. He dashed round to every record store in London and bought a dozen copies of Judy's famous Carnegie Hall performance, which included all her great hits. Then he assembled a team of musical arrangers and copyists and they worked round the clock for forty-eight hours, each assigned a different track, transcribing the music to create a new set of band parts. On Monday morning our office was in chaos with sheet music scattered all over the floor and dispatch riders arriving at regular intervals to add to it.

Judy opened at the Talk of the Town that night, and she was magic. Awestruck, we watched and listened to her. As Billy said, hers had to be a divine gift, for here was someone who, to all appearances, was a shrunken old lady, ill-used by life, but the moment she went on stage and the first spotlight picked her out, her whole personality changed, it expanded until it filled the entire stage and her matchless voice effortlessly dominated the building. It was uncanny, almost like one of those transformations in a fairy-tale where the witch becomes a princess. Judy's body and her voice just didn't match.

Judy stayed at the Ritz Hotel and didn't use the dressing room at the Talk of the Town before the show. She'd change in her bedroom, then go down to the Rolls-Royce waiting at the main entrance and be driven the five hundred yards or so across Leicester Square to the nightclub. As she was leaving the hotel, Glyn would warn us by phone of her imminent arrival so we could cue the orchestra to play her overture, which was a five-minute compilation of her songs. After a quick glance in a backstage mirror, she'd sweep on to the stage and go into her routine. That opening night, the audience were ecstatic, the press universally approving. Billy and I were vastly relieved that everything had gone smoothly.

Unfortunately, on the second night, Judy decided that she wouldn't appear at eleven o'clock. It was a quarter to twelve when she arrived. We had to pacify an audience growing increasingly restless as the time of the last bus, tube or train approached. As the week wore on, she became less and less punctual, and one night caught Glyn phoning to warn us of her departure. For some obscure reason, she decided we were spying on her and punished us by going back to her room. In the end we had to plant someone in a telephone box outside the Ritz to whom Glyn would signal surreptitiously with his hanky when she was about to leave.

We now had a potential disaster on our hands as Judy was turning up as much as an hour and a half late. With trepidation we decided to have it out with her. After the performance, she would hold court in her dressing room. I took a deep breath and said, 'You must be very pleased the place is sold out and the press is good, but we have this problem. You may not know that after midnight in London all public transport stops, so it would be tremendously helpful if the show could begin on time. Then people who've come a long way will get the chance to hear you before they have to leave.' She eyed me narrowly and said, 'Young man, people do not pay to see Judy Garland appear on time. All I have left to sell is drama.' She knew exactly what she was doing, and we knew we couldn't win, so we engaged Lonnie Donegan and his skiffle band to go on before her so that if people had to leave at least they'd seen a show.

One night, or rather early morning, she came off stage and announced that she was hungry, she felt like an Italian meal. I phoned an excellent restaurant nearby and they agreed that for Judy Garland they would keep the chef on until we arrived. She put on her coat and as we were about to leave the place we encountered the night-watchman, who was patrolling the building with an Alsatian. Judy's eye lit upon the dog and she proceeded to make a great fuss of it, then announced that the darling pooch must come with us to dinner. By now, Billy and I were so desperate we would have laid on a man-eating tiger if it would keep Judy sweet, so a bemused night-watchman looked on as we marched out of the building accompanied by his dog. It sat at the table in the Italian restaurant with a napkin round its neck for three hours – night after night, for Judy adopted it and took it out to dinner after every show.

Coping with one drama after another, the imperturbable Glyn steered Judy through an extended run at the Talk of the Town. She did *Sunday Night at the London Palladium* for ATV, and took a liking to the microphone she'd been using. Afterwards she demanded a pair of scissors, cut it off the cable and put it in her handbag. Then her husband, an ex-nightclub bouncer decades younger than she was, precipitated a crisis by making an unauthorized recording of her show at the Talk of the Town to market it in America, whereupon the Musicians' Union ordered a withdrawal of their labour, which left us without an orchestra. It was Glyn as usual to the rescue.

By the time Judy eventually boarded a plane for Sweden, Billy and I had aged years. Tragically, her spell at the Talk of the Town was her last engagement: shortly after she returned to London from Scandinavia, she died. She infuriated, entranced, baffled and exhausted us, but we never doubted that we'd been in the presence of a great star.

Ethel Merman was another superstar we booked for the Talk of the Town. Cole Porter claimed that no one could sing his songs as well as Ethel could. She brought with her the first radio microphone any of us had ever seen and stuck it down her cleavage, which left her hands free so she could move around the stage unencumbered by cable. The radio mike was a rarity at that time and we didn't know it was transmitting on a police frequency. Every night at eleven, police patrol-car radios throughout London would suddenly resound to 'There's No Business Like Show Business' belted out in Ethel Merman's inimitable style. It took the CID ten days to track down the interference, then our engineers had to make some adjustments.

I got to know Ethel well. She was a great lady, but humour was not one of her strong points, neither was generosity; in fact, she was downright mean. When she first arrived, she asked me if I knew any jewellers in London who would give her a discount on a certain make of watch as she wanted to buy a number for her family back home. I rang a friend in the trade and asked him if he could get me a discount on this particular brand of watch. He said 'Are you having me on? Its the cheapest watch you can buy.' I bought a dozen and ceremoniously presented them to her as a gift. I could do no wrong after that.

Before Ethel arrived, she sent over instructions that she wanted a certain musical director with whom she had worked before. The problem was that this chap may have had some talent for music but his undisputed genius was in emptying whisky bottles. He was an Olympic-standard toper who had been unemployed for years. We tried to point her at a number of other distinguished musical directors, but Ethel was stubborn to the point of mulishness. Her chosen musical director was duly brought back from oblivion and united with her in the rehearsal room. She pronounced herself satisfied with his musical backing, then said, 'I have a problem. I haven't got my overture with me. I want a two- or three-minute introduction before I come on stage. Please compose me something that doesn't include any of my own songs because if the audience recognizes them and applauds, they won't applaud as loudly when I sing them.' A real professional was our Ethel. Her musical director hurried off to spend the weekend composing and on Monday we assembled to hear the result. The overture began with a great martial build-up, all blaring trumpets and clashing cymbals, then the main theme gradually emerged. It was 'Ol' Man River'. Ethel exploded with rage. 'How old do you think I am? Ethel Merman doesn't come on to "Ol' Man River".' In vain, her musical director tried to explain the rationale behind his creative effort – Ethel was in London and at the heart of London is the river Thames and . . . His voice tailed off as Ethel's laser eyes transfixed him. She went on that night and for the rest of her tour to the theme from *Sunday Night at the London Palladium*.

We worked closely with the stage producer of the Talk of the Town, Robert Nesbitt, an Old Etonian of great taste and elegance and the best in the business of presenting stars. Bernie always asked him to direct the Royal Variety Performances. We'd booked Dusty Springfield, who could be as temptestuous as she was talented, and I was relying on Bob's legendary charm to get us through. Dusty duly arrived, she was on great form and we began the dress rehearsal. Its main purpose was to test the technical aspects of the show; all we required of Dusty was that she should more or less walk through her songs, but she was on a high and began belting out her numbers at full blast. Bob and I got worried about the effect on her voice, but she dismissed our anxieties and sang her heart out.

That night we had a full house, including a number of stars. The big moment arrived, but Dusty didn't. We hurried up to her dressing room, knocked on the door and, in a hoarse whisper, she asked us to come in. She was sitting in her street clothes, her gown hanging up on a hook. She croaked at us that she'd lost her voice and couldn't go on. By a superhuman effort, we forbore to point out that we'd told her so, and tried to coax her to give it a try. Bob, in his most winsomely wheedling tones, invited her to put on her dress. She looked at him, then snarled, 'You fucking well put it on!' We beat a hasty retreat.

I'd noticed Elton John in the audience, so I explained to him that Dusty had lost her voice and asked if he would be prepared to sing a few numbers in her place. Like the gracious gentleman he is, he agreed. As we mounted the stage so that I could make the announcement, there standing in the wings in her gown, fully made up, was Dusty Springfield. I thanked and apologized to Elton John, and Dusty croaked her way through her numbers. I went home to have a nervous breakdown.

Most great stars play games. I recall Shirley Bassey's agent ringing me and telling me that she had a sore throat and wouldn't be able to appear. I said, 'Don't worry, Petula Clark's in town. I'll ask her to step in.'

The agent said, 'Hang on, I'll ring you back,' and Shirley duly appeared. It was just as well: I hadn't the foggiest notion where Petula Clark was.

We also supplied the artists for the cabaret at the River Room of the Savoy Hotel. The show was managed by Ethel Levy and Freddie Lloyd, who also ran the D'Oyly Carte Opera Company so they weren't really light-entertainment specialists, but they loved the comedian Jimmy Wheeler, one of the last of the classical working-class vaudeville artists. We booked Jimmy for them, and because he didn't go on stage until eleven thirty, he could usually be found in the pub round the corner. One night, totally sozzled, he staggered back to the Savoy. The star didn't need a dressing room: he had the use of a beautiful art deco suite. Somewhat disorientated, Jimmy went into the bathroom to use the toilet, noticed an ornate chain hanging down, assumed it was the flush and pulled it. In fact, it operated an art deco shower, and Jimmy got soaked. Just then the stage manager summoned him. Jimmy picked up his violin and staggered on to the stage dripping wet. He looked at the crowd and said, 'Cor blimey! It's hissing down outside!' The toffs at the Savoy loved him.

The Savoy was anxious to have Petula Clark as top of the bill at the River Room and I persuaded her to appear. I knew she was going to be a big hit because I was besieged by personal friends pleading with me to get them tickets, but the place was booked solid. Yet on the opening night, about half a dozen of the thirty tables were empty. I couldn't believe my eyes. Back in the dressing room, Petula was in tears, convinced her career was over, that she'd lost her star appeal. I confronted Ethel Levy. 'You assured me the place was sold out!' I cried.

'It's nothing to do with me,' replied Ethel. 'I only book the artists, it's the restaurant that controls the tables.' So I stormed off to have a word with Monsieur Antonio, who was voluble in his praise of Petula's performance. 'Sod that,' I said, 'We had empty tables tonight and my artists don't appear to empty tables. If there are any empty tables tomorrow evening then that stage will be empty too.' He shrugged. 'Of course, we could have filled the tables many times over,' he said, in a thick Gallic accent, 'but we couldn't have given that many guests our renowned

Savoy service. We'd need extra waiters.' I shook my head in disbelief. Petula was one of the most sought-after stars in the business and the Savoy was paying her an absolute fortune to appear, yet it balked at a few quid for casual wages. When I regained my sanity, we compromised and took out ten tables. To her credit, Petula saw the joke.

We did a lot of business in Australia with Dennis Wong, who owned the Chequers restaurant in Sydney. I'd never met him but we often spoke on the telephone. He rang one day and asked me if I knew P. J. Proby as he was anxious to book him for Chequers. 'Dennis,' I said, 'I don't advise it. He's a very odd character.' Dennis persisted and I continued to resist because it wasn't only *his* business but *my* reputation that was on the line. I told him to take twenty-four hours to think it over. The next day he rang back, adamant that he wanted P. J. Proby. So I booked him.

The deal included three air-fares – for P. J., his manager and musical director. A few days later, I got a phone call from a distraught Dennis Wong. 'It's been a disaster,' he wailed. I eventually discovered what had happened. Apparently, a tired and emotional P. J. Proby had arrived at Heathrow airport to meet his manager, who flourished the three tickets. 'Who's the third for?' asked P. J. and, when told it was for the musical director, pointed out that they didn't have one. His manager grinned. They could engage a musical director once they got to Australia, but meanwhile they would cash in the ticket and make a few bob. P. J. demurred. 'We've got a spare, we'll take someone with us,' he said, and wandered around the concourse until he found a penurious student looking for a standby ticket. Dazed at his good fortune, the student went off to Australia with P. J. Proby and his manager. It would have been nothing more than a quixotic act of charity had not P. J. insisted that since the student had travelled as a musical director he'd better do the job. He took the stand on the opening night of the show and tried to conduct the orchestra. The result was musical bedlam.

In 1967, the day came when, for the first time, I found myself in negotiation with my formidable uncle Lew. One of our agents had a call from a Werner Schmidt who had a television game-show called *The Golden Shot*, which he was anxious to sell to British television. I phoned ATV, to be told that the big boss himself, Lew, was keen to acquire the show and he would handle the deal personally.

I turned up at Lew's office with Werner Schmidt, and I suppose I made the mistake of being a little too cocky for my own good. Until that day, the head of ATV had always been my uncle Lew, but as I sprawled in one of his sumptuous leather chairs, I said grandly, 'Lew . . . Lew, my client and I are prepared to listen to an offer.' Lew fixed me with his beady eyes, then ignored me completely and made a fuss of Werner, offering him a large cigar and a business card with his private telephone number on it. A deal was struck that put *The Golden Shot* on British television for fourteen years. With great ceremony, Lew ushered Werner through the door, then just as we were leaving he spoke to me for the first and only time. 'Get your hair cut!' he said. Collapse of smart agent.

I did once score a rare victory over Lew. He was renegotiating Morecambe and Wise's contract with his company and they were unhappy both about the money and that colour TV was coming into vogue, as Lew proposed that their next series should still be in black and white. Negotiations got bogged down, Billy Marsh went on holiday and left it to me to offer the act to my friend Bill Cotton Jr, who was at that time head of Light Entertainment at the BBC. Bill couldn't believe his luck and was convinced I was just playing him off against Lew to get the Boys a fatter contract. Once he realized I was serious, he gave them a series on BBC2 in colour and launched them on a dazzling television career.

During my time as an agent, I often pondered the question: what makes a great star? Talent alone is not enough, neither is hard work, though both are necessary. As much as anything it's an instinct for knowing what material will work for you and what won't; which engagements to accept and which to reject. It's partly self-knowledge and partly an acute sensitivity to what your audience expects of you. We used to handle Mike and Bernie Winters, who were an excellent double act but they never had quite the same instinct for the right material that Morecambe and Wise always demonstrated. It was an education to watch Eric and Ernie developing a routine. They once spent a week rehearsing a flamenco sequence in which Ernie played the guitar and Eric danced and sang, if that's the word for the wailing noise he made. Everyone in the studio thought it was wonderful, but one morning Eric walked in and said, 'This isn't working. We're playing the wrong parts. I should be doing the guitar while Ernie does the singing.' And he was right. They changed places and the sketch was transformed. Nine out of ten artists would have been content with the original sketch since it was obviously very funny, but not Morecambe and Wise: it was missing perfection by a whisker, and that wouldn't do.

We once booked them at a theatre in Great Yarmouth and Billy and I went along to watch them rehearse. It was a sketch in which Eric was doing some ventriloquism while Ernie hid behind the curtain to supply the voice. For hours, Eric had been sitting in a chair with the dummy on his knee, but this time he looked at it perched astride his knee, and on an impulse lifted up one of its legs, put them both together, and quipped, 'Sorry about that, son, you must have been in agony.' A new routine was born, and I watched a sketch originally timed at around two minutes expand, quip by quip, until it ran a full fifteen.

Morecambe and Wise were as clever at handling their personal relationship as they were brilliant on stage. They'd seen so many double acts, such as Jewel and Warriss, Laurel and Hardy and Abbott and Costello, end up personally at odds that they made a vow to the effect that if there was a disagreement between them about anything to do with their routine, the one who was against change got his way and they would never discuss it again.

Comedy double acts can be pre-programmed for disaster: the comic who wins all the laughs may object to the straight man getting half the pay and, in turn, the straight man often resents the fact that he bowls the balls the comic smashes over the pavilion to the adulation of the crowd. Psychologically, all the elements are in place for a relationship of mutual loathing. But if Morecambe and Wise ever quarrelled, no one heard them; neither was there even the whisper of a rumour that they had fallen out. They were both happily married and rarely mixed socially, preferring their own separate circles of friends. Billy Marsh adored them. Transfixed, he would watch them in action and murmur, 'This is as good as it gets.' In all the years he was their agent, and in spite of the astronomic sums involved when they were at the peak of their career, no piece of paper ever passed between them. They and Billy did business on the basis of casual conversation and absolute trust.

Eric was totally devoid of jealousy at the success of other comics. He had great generosity of judgement and loved to watch stars such as Ronnie Barker, Harry Worth and Tommy Cooper at work. As a master of the witty *ad lib* himself, Eric particularly admired Tommy's ability to bring the house down while apparently making up the script as he went along. I once went with Eric to Caesar's Palace in Luton where Tommy was performing. During the act, a waiter dropped a tray and glasses crashed to the floor with a deafening clatter. I could see Eric, his eyes alight with anticipation, already rehearsing in his own mind how he would have exploited the situation. There was a long, long pause, then Tommy, his voice rich with irony, said, 'That's nice.' When Eric had stopped laughing, he said, in mock exasperation, 'How *dare* he? How dare he get a laugh with a line like that?'

Morecambe and Wise were Billy's clients, but I was slowly building up my own list. Clive Dunn was the first. He was one of those actors who didn't fit neatly into any category: he was neither a straight comedy nor a dramatic performer. He needed a special niche. The BBC were casting *Dad's Army* and they

offered the part of Corporal Jones to another of our clients, Jack
Haig, who was an excellent character actor. He turned the part
down so I suggested Clive Dunn. Then I added to my list Leslie
Crowther, Mike and Bernie Winters and Freddie Starr. And,
because I spoke fluent French, I looked after the UK careers of
French stars such as Sacha Distel, Gilbert Becaud, Françoise
Hardy and Mireille Mathieu.

I hadn't been in the business long before I realized that TV
was destined to be the entertainment medium of the future, just
as in the immediate post-war period radio had been the great
shop window for stars such as Tommy Handley, Kenneth Horne,
Ted Ray and the Goons. I started handling freelance TV producers and directors such as Stuart Allen, who produced the popular
comedies *On the Buses* and *Love Thy Neighbour*, William G. Stewart
and Jon Scoffield. Through them, I slowly learned the mechanics
of TV and they kept me informed about new programme slots
that were being planned.

I was frantically busy – too busy: I lost control of my life. It
wasn't uncommon for me to leave Dulwich, spend a couple of
hours in the office then drive myself to Blackpool, where I'd
watch the first house at the North Pier, go to the opera house
and see the second house of another show, then drive home to
Dulwich the same night. I insisted on being at all my clients' TV
rehearsals to make sure they weren't being exploited. I just
didn't know when to leave well alone and when to delegate; I
had to be in on everything, no detail was too trivial for my
attention. I recall booking Jack Parnell's band for a *Royal Variety
Performance* and being unimpressed with their suits. I found a
tape measure and solemnly measured each one of them, including their inside legs, then went out and hired new suits. Some
might call it perfectionism but lunacy would be more apt. Of
course, it impressed my clients. Other stars would complain that
their agents didn't come to see them rehearsing, whereupon I'd
slip them what was known in the trade as the Unhappy Pill.
'Really?' I'd say sorrowfully. 'Your agent's an excellent man. I'm
very, very surprised he isn't here.'

It was all good clean fun, but I had a new wife at home who saw nothing of me. Then, in 1970, my daughter Alison was born and I saw little of her either. The stresses of being an agent, always the man in the middle, began to take their toll. It was a nightmare trying to match the wishes of my clients and the prospective producer who invariably wanted my client to do what my client didn't want to do. Then, when each party's expectations had been brought into line, they'd fall out about money and negotiations would have to start all over again. In retrospect, I realize I was becoming too emotionally involved with my clients, zooming up and down on the roller-coaster of their moods, which is tolerable if you are looking after a single client, but I had a dozen of them, all in various stages of emotional turmoil. I lacked the clinical detachment to step back at a certain point and make objective judgements unclouded by personal loyalties, by which I mean I hadn't the temperament of a Billy Marsh. I began to measure my self-esteem by my clients' successes and failures. It wasn't just my commission or even my reputation that was on the line: it was my ego. And looming over my career was the shadow of my father. He went to great lengths to avoid intimidating me by his great knowledge and formidable reputation, but deep in my heart I knew I would never match up to him as an agent.

I took up golf as a relaxation, and for the second time in my life came across anti-Semitism. We were living in Dulwich and within walking distance of our home was a golf club. I wasn't a member, I just paid a green fee and Len Rowe, the club professional, gave me lessons. One of my old mates, J. L. Manning, who was sports editor of the *Daily Mail*, was a member. 'Why don't you join?' he suggested, then added, 'Fat chance! If I put you up, it's odds on they'll blackball you.' I couldn't see why they should, but I filled in the forms and sure enough I was blackballed. J. L. Manning wrote a fierce article on anti-Semitism in British sport, and I then joined Coombe Hill in Kingston, which was virtually a Jewish club.

There was plenty of racism in golf clubs at that time. When I was at LWT, I went with Bill Cotton to Scotland for the Edinburgh

Festival. Bill Brown, the chairman of Scottish Television, offered
to get us a game at Muirfield. The secretariat at the club asked for
the usual information, the name of my home club and my
handicap, and the game was arranged for Thursday morning.
The afternoon before Bill Brown rang to say the club secretary
had been in touch with him, apologizing that they had made a
regrettable error in booking us; apparently there was a junior
tournament that day. Later he told me that as soon as the club
saw 'Coombe Hill' on my application form, that was it. I'm not a
paranoid Jew, I don't assume that all my enemies hate me because
of my race; most of them just find me honestly detestable, and
that's fine. But it is almost impossible not to be alert to fancied
slights. When Marmaduke Hussey was chairman of the BBC he
once described me to a mutual friend as an 'itinerant talent'.
I'm *almost* sure he meant that I was a restless character, not
'Wandering Jew'.

One compensation for this intense involvement in my clients'
careers was that I got a tremendous buzz when I pulled off a
coup. One day, Peter Dulay, a comedy writer who'd written
material for some of my clients, phoned me and said, 'I've seen
this comedian and I was so impressed I've signed him up as
manager, and I'd be grateful if you'd come and have a look at
him.' So off we went to a seedy nightclub where at one in the
morning there was some kind of transvestite show going on. My
heart sank. My dad frowned on artists using any expletive more
shocking than 'damn', so this load of drag artists had more
chance of doing the *Royal Variety Performance* from the moon
than being signed up by the Grade Organisation. Then a comedian came on and did a five-minute turn, which was only mildly
camp. It was Larry Grayson, and I'd been in the business long
enough to recognize a potential star when I saw one. Within
twenty-four hours, I'd signed him up and got him his first
engagement as an early-turn comedian at the Palladium. There
was a kind of innocence about Larry's campness. He was never
overtly blue, let alone suggestive; he dealt in single rather than
double-entendres, but I was afraid he'd get the wrong reputation

early on. I was also nervous about Dad being in the audience; if he took against Larry we were in deep trouble, so I went through Larry's material with a fine-tooth comb. He was a winner, a great career was launched. And I was on top of the world.

Sacha Distel was one of my biggest stars. Because he was about to do a British tour, he invited Penny and me over to the Paris Olympia to see his act. Besides being a vocalist, Sacha was a fine jazz guitarist and at one point in his act a group of musicians ambled on to the stage to join him and play some jazz. One was a silver-haired fiddler and the moment he touched bow to violin I knew he was a genius. I looked more closely. It was Stephane Grappelli. I'd thought he was dead! He'd been a star back in the 1930s when Lew, then still an agent, had handled him. After the show I introduced myself to him and asked him to come to London. He said it was impossible because he played in the restaurant at the Paris Hilton; it was the only regular job he had and the manager wouldn't release him. In the end I rang a friend in Las Vegas, who was part of the senior management of the Hilton chain, and explained the problem. He must have had a word with the Paris office for Grappelli was given four weeks' leave of absence. From the moment the great jazz violinist walked on to the London stage in 1969, his career took off again. Television engagements, concerts at Carnegie Hall, duets with Yehudi Menuhin – it all happened for him as a result of my chance visit to Paris. That was perhaps the most satisfying achievement of my time as an agent.

But all this took its toll on my marriage and my mental health. I now operated from my father's old office. For me it was a kind of shrine: nothing from his day had been touched or changed, including his old glass-topped desk. One afternoon, after a frantic morning on the telephone, clients flowing in and out of the office dumping their gripes and complaints on to me, a desk piled high with contracts to be read and signed, letters to be answered and an evening ahead that might take in a couple of theatre performances and a visit to a television studio, I freaked out. In a sudden burst of rage and frustration, I hurled all the papers into the air then slammed my fists on the desk-top so hard that the glass shattered. It was a momentary nervous breakdown. Billy came dashing into my office and began calming me down and sorting me out in the way he had nursed Tony Hancock and dozens of other stars through their bad times. But it was a warning signal that something was wrong.

Penny had created a wonderful home for us – she was a great mother and a loyal wife – but we had become virtual strangers, and when she went through an appalling crisis with her mother, I just wasn't there for her. I really tried to be, but the endless distractions symbolized by the ringing telephone, my nightly dates at theatres and television studios all round the country and my total preoccupation with a world that was foreign to her did irreparable damage to our relationship. In 1974, shortly after I joined LWT, our daughter Alison was joined by a brother, Jonathan, but though they permanently enriched both our lives, the marriage was in terminal decline.

At about the same time, as my doubts grew about whether I had the temperament to be a good agent, my interest in television blossomed. I got drawn into working more and more with TV producers and directors. I recall being at ATV's Elstree studio looking after the interests of one of my clients and, as usual, getting fully absorbed in the technicalities of programme-making. A producer called Colin Clews took me for a drink after the recording and gently pointed out that TV directors and producers don't take kindly to their artists' agents telling them their job. Then he said, 'Michael, you've a big decision to make. You've either got to be an agent or go into television, but you can't do both.'

He was both articulating my dilemma and quite unconsciously helping me to resolve it. Ironically, the opportunity presented itself through London Weekend Television, a company whose name had been a byword for administrative chaos and poor programming since it went on air in 1968. It started out with a number of hugely talented executives: David Frost had secured the licence, Michael Peacock was managing director, Cyril Bennett was controller of programmes, Frank Muir was head of entertainment and Humphrey Burton was in charge of arts programmes. One by one they had jumped ship.

Then Rupert Murdoch took a financial stake in the company and began to sort it out. Until the Independent Broadcasting Authority (IBA) objected on the grounds of conflict of interest, he was, for a short while, programme controller as well as part-owner. Some of his ideas were certainly original, though they betrayed a startling innocence about the realities of the television industry. One of my clients, Stuart Allen, produced for LWT their one very successful comedy called *On the Buses*, which impressed Rupert so much that he sent for Stuart and proposed he increase its twelve-programme run a year to fifty-two, an idea that to anyone familiar with the problem of getting even a handful of scripts out of top writers was almost risible in its naïvety. Then John Freeman, who had exchanged a successful career as a television interviewer for the post of High Commissioner to India and then British Ambassador in Washington, was invited to become executive chairman, and he in turn reappointed Cyril Bennett as programme controller with the brief of restoring the station's ruined reputation.

Lew thought highly of Cyril Bennett and I knew him slightly. He struck me as tough, unpredictable, charismatic, intelligent and very funny. A sense of humour was one quality he would need for the nightmare task he'd taken on. Since Cyril had what virtually amounted to a blank sheet of paper on which to draw up a programme schedule, he was bound to be in the market for good ideas. Jon Scoffield, one of my producer clients, and I had a brainstorming session, then I went to see Cyril, who bought two of our programme proposals, a situation comedy called *The Upper Crusts*, about a couple of aristocrats down on their luck, and *Who Do You Do?*, a show using impressionists, which turned out to be the launch-pad for Freddie Starr's television career.

A common interest in programmes drew Cyril and me closer together. I was sitting in his office one day in 1972, and when we'd finished our business, Cyril suddenly said, 'You know, you could save yourself the taxi fare over here. I'm looking for a head of Light Entertainment.' I ignored him and went on gossiping. Almost as soon as I got back to my office, Cyril rang and said, 'You didn't respond to my offer, and that means you're interested. Let's talk about it.'

The longer I thought about it, the more interested I became, but there were two big problems: first, it would mean letting down my partners Billy and Denis, who were decades older than I was and looked to me to carry on the business when they retired; then there was my dad, who had put up the money for our management buy-out and gave every indication that he was pleased with my performance as an agent. During this period of indecision, I used to drive most mornings past the LWT building and, though it was a twenty-storey concrete tower of surpassing ugliness, I wished I could be part of what was going on inside it. I was convinced by now that not just my personal future but the future of entertainment lay in television. Lew had seen this years before when he took over ATV, realizing that the variety theatre was living through its last days.

Eventually I confided my problems to Cyril. 'I just can't face my father and tell him I'm leaving the business,' I said. Cyril suggested that the chairman, John Freeman, should fly over to France and talk to him. Dad wouldn't have been human had he not been flattered when Freeman, a former cabinet minister and ambassador to the United States, took the trouble to visit him and ask for his blessing on my move to television. He readily agreed, and Billy and Denis were, as always, understanding and supportive. And that was that.

At the end of 1973, I became deputy controller of programmes (entertainment) at London Weekend Television for a salary of £11,000 a year, a considerable financial sacrifice, but worth it because I felt I was now where the action would be in the future. My life among the carpet-baggers and robber barons of the entertainment business was over, and my career as Corporate Man had begun.

Chapter Four

CYRIL'S BOYS

A T MOST CRITICAL stages in my life I have been blessed with mentors who guided and inspired me. Throughout my childhood, my grandmother was my lodestar; at the *Daily Mirror* John Bromley taught me the trade; Billy Marsh showed me how to be a theatrical agent; and when I joined LWT, Cyril Bennett took me in hand and led me through the strange and exciting world of television. He took a huge gamble when he appointed me, and I can't in all honesty say it paid off. I was not a particularly good head of Light Entertainment and therefore his patience and unwavering support for me was devotion beyond the call of duty.

I had a lovely ninth-floor office overlooking the South Bank, a company car, a pension package and a modest but secure salary. I was completely ignorant about TV comedy. Though I'd been fairly successful as an agent selling programme ideas and stars to television, I knew absolutely nothing about the nuts and bolts of the business, and to make matters more confusing, I found that much of my theatrical-agency experience was worse than useless because the whole value system of television was different. In live variety you kept the best until last, starting the show with the minor artists and building up to a climax featuring the star or stars at the top of the bill. On television, you had to start with a bang: if you didn't grab viewers in the first few moments, they would switch off or turn over to rival channels.

In the theatre, you could try out risky ideas or unproven actors in out-of-the-way places before exposing them to the pitiless spotlight of the West End. On television, and particularly at LWT, a weekend channel, there was nowhere to hide an experimental formula or new talent. By the time we came on air at seven o'clock on Friday evening, most people had finished their week's work and were looking forward to being entertained, so every night on LWT was Saturday night at the London Palladium: there was no televisual equivalent of a wet Monday evening at the Hackney Empire. Nemesis was swift. If a show failed, you knew it first thing the next morning.

The sheer scale of television was daunting. In the theatre we counted our audiences in hundreds or occasionally in thousands, but television measured its viewers in millions, so if you fell flat on your face, it could hardly have been in a more public form. And of all forums of television, comedy is probably the riskiest because it is totally unpredictable. My judgement of television humour was unformed. The comedy I knew most about was seaside end-of-the-pier slapstick rather than the sophisticated narrative comedy that should form the spine of a successful weekend schedule.

I took over a department that hadn't been functioning well for some time. In one sense my timing couldn't have been worse because a whole raft of programmes that had served LWT well in winning high ratings and popular approval had reached the end of their natural lives. Reliable war-horses, such as *Doctor in the House, Please, Sir!* and *On the Buses,* survivors of Frank Muir's creative spell as LWT's head of Comedy, were being put out to grass. There were huge holes in the schedules that had to be filled with dreary sit-coms whose titles I blush to recall. We hadn't much leisure to experiment with new talent, or money to spend on pilot programmes that might end up on the cutting-room floor but from whose failure we would learn how to do it better next time. We were so strapped for resources that almost all the programmes we made, good, bad or indifferent, *had* to be transmitted – the sure sign of a station in deep trouble. As

Cyril Bennett himself said of LWT, 'The trouble is, we're the last shop in town. We know that the talent only comes to us when no one else wants it. We've got to get off the bottom of the league table.'

My fledgling comedy judgement was soon put to the test. Shortly after I arrived at LWT, Cyril Bennett asked me to read a script submitted by the actor Warren Mitchell and Leslie Randle, a writer and comedian. He commented that, having skimmed it, he didn't think it would work in its present form but it might have potential. Apparently Warren and Leslie had met Cyril over a liquid lunch in a Soho nosh bar and they'd caught him in a buying mood. I read the script and to my untrained eye it seemed utterly unfunny. I told Cyril that in my opinion there were no laughs in it. He sadly agreed, but then brightened up and said he'd ask the Old Master himself, Frank Muir, to do a rewrite. I was delighted and also curious to see what an acknowledged expert could do with such unpromising material. I was secretly pleased when even Frank's virtuosity couldn't rescue the scripts from mediocrity, because it confirmed my own judgement.

Cyril decided to give it one more try and called Warren and Leslie to a TV production meeting. From the outset it was clear that we were playing the old nice-cop, nasty-cop routine with me cast as the villain resisting Cyril's inclination to buy the idea. He asked me to spell out my hesitations so I bluffed my way through a strictly amateur diagnosis of the weaknesses of the script. Then Warren Mitchell, with a vulpine grin, said, 'Of course, Michael's right. The script is crap, but miracles happen at rehearsals.' At that point I saw a lightbulb go on in Cyril's head and it was a red one. He murmured his regrets and the meeting ended. After our guests had gone, Cyril thanked me for getting him out of a hole. 'Miracles happen at rehearsals?' He snorted. 'I tell you, Michael, they don't!' That was lesson number one from a television guru. If the original script is a dud, nothing you can do afterwards will revive it.

I learned a fantastic amount from Cyril. He was a fiercely competitive East End Jew from the same kind of background as mine. He prided himself on being working class and he and Ron Miller, the head of Advertising Sales, who was also an East End 'goy', had a kind of running gag in which they tried to outdo each other about the modesty of their origins. Cyril would say, 'Tell me again, Ron, where were you born?' and Ron would reply, 'Eighteen Sebastopol Terrace E8.'

'E8?' enquired Cyril. 'Where's that?'

'Hackney,' said Ron.

'Hackney?' sneered Cyril. 'We used to go there for our holidays!'

Cyril was a neurotic, high-energy enthusiast, a chronic depressive with wild mood swings – even his thumbs trembled when he talked. He used Valium to calm his nerves and the excitement of television to jolt him out of melancholia. He had a deeply unhappy family life and lived alone in a Westminster flat while his wife and children occupied their Surrey home. Perhaps some of his anxiety came from the weight of expectation resting on him. He had been brought back to LWT to rescue it from disaster, a nightmare task although he was having some success. When I'd been with the company for a few weeks I had to go to the BAFTA dinner in the Albert Hall where we learned that LWT under Cyril had won seven awards from *The Stanley Baxter Moving Picture Show* and Humphrey Burton's arts pro-gramme *Aquarius* to Peter Barkworth as Best Actor for *Crown Matrimonial* and Peter Jay for *Weekend World*. The BBC, who had grown used to regarding the Academy Awards as their annual entitlement, were for once outclassed. But Cyril wasn't easily pleased. He shook his head and muttered lugubriously, 'I don't know what we're going to do next year.'

Cyril knew television backwards and was always firing off sharp little comments that showed just how broad his knowledge was. When I was an agent I negotiated with him about the renewal of Reg Varney's contract. Reg had become a huge star as a result of appearing for years in *On the Buses*, but now he was restless and wanted his own TV variety show. I set out my stall for Cyril, spouting statistics about the ratings *On the Buses* had been getting. Cyril looked over his half-glasses at me and said sadly, 'Reg Varney isn't a star.' I expostulated that *On the Buses* had beaten *The Morecambe and Wise Show* the previous year.

'Nah, Michael,' said Cyril. 'Reg isn't the star. Stan Butler, the character he plays in *On the Buses*, he's the star,' which encapsulated the truth that many actors who make a hit in long-running comedies or soap operas are in a rut too deep to climb out of.

As the executive responsible for Light Entertainment, at first I floundered, delivering few shows that could stand up to the fierce competition offered by a BBC in one of its golden periods. But by the application of a certain degree of low cunning I was able to help Cyril in his struggle for ratings. The big battleground was Saturday evenings when the BBC dominated the schedule, rolling out an immensely strong succession of programmes over the months: *Jim'll Fix It* followed by *Dixon of Dock Green* then *The Generation Game*, *The Two Ronnies*, *Starsky and Hutch*, *Match of the Day*, culminating with *Parkinson*. ITV couldn't get a look in. It was dispiriting trying to find a point of leverage where we might squeeze one of our shows into the ratings. Cyril thought we would have a better chance if he knew the precise running order of BBC programmes for the following quarter, and gave me the job of trying to get hold of this highly secret information. After some thought I decided that, administratively, the BBC operated very much like the civil service, bureaucrats talking to one another, having established their respective places in the pecking order by means of lengthy acronyms, so I invented a BBC acronym for myself. I rang the BBC Television Centre and asked to speak to the Transmission Planning department, identifying myself as HTV Ad. and Fin. Bristol. When I was put through to the appropriate planner, I apologized profusely for bothering him but there was some confusion in our region about weeks thirty-six to fifty-two on Saturday evenings and would he be kind enough to run through the schedule for me? He obligingly recited the following quarter's Saturday-evening schedule and I passed it on to Cyril.

Cyril was surprised, grateful and tactfully uninquisitive about my methods. From time to time after that, HTV Ad. and Fin. Bristol checked out the Saturday evening schedules with the Transmission Planning department and, knowing the BBC, I wouldn't be surprised if HTV Ad. and Fin. Bristol still gets a Christmas card every year from the head of Transmission Planning. There was a beguiling innocence, in those days, about the BBC, which seemed to be run more like an Oxbridge Senior Common Room than a hard-nosed business; the very notion of a practice so unsporting as industrial espionage probably never entered their heads. That said, my James Bond-like tactics didn't help us much. Even knowing the BBC schedules in advance was of little value if we didn't have the shows with which to outgun them on Saturday evenings.

The first big programme idea I ever sold to Cyril was built round Tommy Steele, who was packing West End theatres at the time. It was a highly expensive spectacular and did wonders for our ratings. We did two shows, then got Tommy to agree to a third. On the day we started to rehearse it, I was sitting in my office at peace with the world when Cyril rang and asked me what was happening about the Tommy Steele Show. Apparently he hadn't turned up for the rehearsal. In a panic I rang Tommy's agent, who confessed he had no idea where Tommy was, he had assumed he was in the studio as arranged. I reported back to Cyril that Tommy's agent knew no more than we did. Cyril said, 'Well, Tommy's just rung me. He's in New York.'

'What's he doing in New York?' I asked.

'His exact words were "I've got an 'eadache, Guv'nor",' snorted Cyril, in Tommy's Cockney accent. 'I've spent forty thousand quid mounting this show and the star's got a headache!'

My first Christmas in the job fell across a weekend, which meant that LWT would share with the BBC the main burden of entertaining the public. 'We need a mega-event,' Cyril kept muttering in our early planning meetings. After one of them, I was sitting at home watching the Winter Olympic Games in

Innsbruck where John Curry became the first Briton to win a gold medal in the figure-skating event. I was entranced by the grace and athleticism of his performance. It was clear that he was transforming skating from a sport into an art form. Why not an ice spectacular for Christmas, whose climax would be John Curry repeating his gold medal-winning performance?

I recruited Jon Scoffield. We decided to hire the Streatham ice rink for a week, and he had the idea of putting a cyclorama round the rink so that the ice seemed to stretch to infinity and the show didn't look like *Holiday on Ice*. We even positioned the cameras on the ice so that viewers would get an excitingly unfamiliar perspective on the spectacle. Cyril, grateful for any imaginative way of capturing the Christmas ratings, did not demur as the budget escalated. The *pièce de résistance* was to be John Curry repeating his Olympic performance, finishing with a triple salchow or lutz or whatever you call one of those breathtaking spinning aerial leaps.

I had a radio link between the TV scanner outside the rink and my office. On the final day of shooting I turned on my television set to see how things were going, only to catch the boy with the clapperboard announcing, 'Take thirty-six.' Thirty-six? John Curry was on his *thirty-sixth* attempt to do the triple, which was the pivot of the show? Alarmed, I dashed down to Streatham to find that John had had a complete mental blockage: every time he attempted the triple he fell. Without the triple, we had nothing. I watched with growing dismay as takes thirty-seven, thirty-eight and thirty-nine ended in disaster. John Curry, his feet bleeding, was distraught.

Eventually the director, Jon Scoffield, came dashing from the TV scanner, tiptoed across the ice and whispered earnestly in John Curry's ear. Take forty began. The music swelled and John hurtled round the rink, jumping, twisting and dancing. As the moment of truth got nearer everyone watching tensed. John threw himself into the air and executed a perfect triple. We roared our applause and relief. I called in on Jon Scoffield in the scanner: 'What did you say to him?' I asked.

Jon grinned. 'I said, "Listen, son, either you do it this time or you can fucking well go home!"'

At last, after delivering a long series of glowing progress reports to Cyril, I was ready to unveil my masterpiece and hurried along to present the cassette for his approval. Modestly, I thought it represented my emergence as the Cecil B. De Mille of LWT and our company's passport to the next franchise. I accepted a congratulatory scotch from Cyril and sat preening myself as he played the cassette, trying out in my head a few phrases for the press launch such as 'Ground-breaking Television!' and 'Every frame a Rembrandt!' The credits rolled, then the screen faded to black. Cyril went over to the video machine, took out the cassette and pressed it into my hand. 'Michael,' he said quietly, 'you're allowed one of those!' He knew his viewers and what they'd expect in peak viewing time at Christmas. The show was too arty-farty. In the event it was well reviewed and nobody watched it. And I learned that, when dealing with Cyril, it is wise to undersell your products.

I'd been in the job for about two years before I delivered to Cyril a genuine hit show. I was lying in bed with the flu and idly glanced at an unsolicited script, which had been sent in by a writer called Bill MacIlwraith. I started to read it and was instantly gripped. It was brilliant. A few weeks previously, Cyril and I had been to see a Stephen Sondheim show imported from Broadway called *Company*. Like everything Sondheim did it was very clever but rather too cerebral to appeal to British audiences. However, we both agreed that the American star, Elaine Stritch, was stunning. I rang Cyril and told him I had found the perfect vehicle for Elaine.

The basic plot revolved around the endless comical misunderstandings between a wisecracking American widow and crime-writer living in London and her pompous British butler. Our head of Casting came up with the clever notion of Donald Sinden as the butler, and *Two's Company*, a series with wit and style, was launched. It was probably the only eighteen-carat winner I commissioned during my time as LWT's head of Light Entertainment and its success gave me some much-needed self-confidence.

Slowly I became more adventurous. I saw a show in America called *Good Times*, a working-class comedy, produced by Norman Lear and featuring only black actors. At first I thought of buying it in, but Humphrey Barclay, who was LWT's head of Comedy, felt that it wouldn't work in Britain although the basic idea of an all-black comedy was good. We bought the scripts and adapted them for a series called *The Fosters*. It introduced Lenny Henry, then all of seventeen, to his first acting role, made a star of Norman Beaton and exploded the myth that there weren't enough talented black actors in Britain to star in an intelligent sit-com.

I was in a curious position as an ITV programme executive because many of the stars on the opposition channel, BBC 1, had been my clients when I worked as an agent with Billy Marsh. I knew them well, they were my friends, we occasionally had a drink together and they confided in me about their triumphs and troubles, which meant that I knew about the tensions between themselves and the BBC. For instance, I was aware that Bruce Forsyth, who for seven years had been the star of BBC 1's Saturday night anchor show *The Generation Game*, was feeling tired and stale. He wanted a change, ideally in the States but, failing that, in some programme that would exploit his considerable general-entertainment talents as a singer, dancer and comedian rather than the more limited and limiting skill of game-show host. I therefore enticed him over to LWT and we evolved a comprehensive format for him, *Bruce Forsyth's Big Night*, in which Bruce sang, danced, joked and interviewed celebrities. Sadly it never caught on but Bruce went on to do greater things.

Cyril's core team at LWT was made up of myself, my old mate John Bromley, who was head of Sport, Tony Wharmby, head of Drama, and John Birt, whom Cyril had recruited from Granada to run the Current Affairs department. My first impression of John was of a rather dishevelled Oxford-donnish figure, already prematurely white-haired, peering through his moon-shaped glasses at my Light Entertainment staff as though they were an alien species who disturbed the peace of the floor shared with his department. He seemed solemn, which was entirely appropriate, given that he was responsible for the heavyweight *Weekend World* and its heavyweight presenter Peter Jay. In fact, everything about the Current Affairs set-up was heavyweight – except for its ratings, which were feather-light. I guess we in the tits-and-tinsel department would have been solemn too, if we'd been competing with the BBC test card for viewers.

The Current Affairs lot were very serious but not very tidy. We'd get into the office on a Monday morning and the place would be littered with the remnants of Chinese takeaways and mountains of newspaper. Then they'd sidle in and start an inquest on the previous day's show, recriminations often reaching the state of intensity where one of the women producers would flee the office in floods of tears. We watched bemused as they cogitated on the likely repercussions in 10 Downing Street, the Kremlin and Washington to their fearless journalism. *Our* only worries were whether Larry Grayson would forget his lines or Freddie Starr turn up.

As the months passed I began to notice that more and more of LWT's output seemed to be gathered mysteriously under John Birt's wing. First Education then Features disappeared into his capacious maw. Painstakingly, brick by brick, he was building an empire, which didn't worry me in the least. I was a-political and had no interest in corporate power games. Cyril thought highly of John and we all acknowledged his competency so the departments he annexed would come to no harm. He was a thoroughly loyal colleague with whom, work apart, I didn't have all that much in common until Cyril's tragic sudden death threw us together.

Early in 1976 it was announced that Brian Tesler was to leave Thames Television, of which he had been director of programmes since 1968. There was much speculation in the business about his next appointment. Brian is one of the most experienced and highly respected figures in television, but we were astounded and indignant when John Freeman brought him in as managing director over Cyril Bennett. It is true that Cyril was not enjoying a period of great success, but television viewers were creatures of moods, and half a dozen shrewd programme commissions could change everything. To interpose another layer of management between Cyril and John Freeman seemed to us a vote of no confidence in Cyril, and many of the staff were deeply resentful. That the interloper should be from our traditional rival, Thames, made it worse. Quite unfairly, Brian became the Enemy.

A short while after he joined the company, Brian announced that there would be a residential programme conference at the Selsdon Park Hotel near Croydon. Equipped with a first-class honours degree from Oxford, earned the hard way with a state scholarship, Brian had worked his way up through the BBC via ATV to Thames. He knew the entertainment business backwards and had a cool analytical mind so we weren't in for a comfortable time. I suspected, too, that Cyril and I would be on the receiving end of the most stringent criticism, I because I hadn't really delivered much exciting popular entertainment and Cyril because, as controller, he carried the can for everything that appeared on the screen. To make matters worse, Cyril was in the depths of one of his periodic depressions, triggered by events in his domestic life – as I alone knew because he confided in me.

As always, John Birt prepared meticulously for the conference. He arrived bearing a huge wodge of documents, one lot being a defence of his own empire, buttressed by pages of statistics, the other containing carefully marshalled arguments for LWT's poor showing. To some extent, because I was responsible for many of the areas of popular programming, I suppose I was the main target for John's scathing analysis, but curiously I didn't feel as though *I* was being got at. I sensed no undercurrent of personal animosity in his words. John was doing what he does best, bringing a mind of forensic sharpness to bear upon a problem. There was nothing much I could do in my response other than plead guilty but insane. If anything, John Birt and I got much closer during the Selsdon Park conference, partly because of our common anxiety about Cyril, whose gloom deepened by the day. Brian Tesler, well aware of the negative cross-currents swirling around his appointment, chaired the conference brilliantly. In his closing speech, he was clear-eyed about LWT's failures but hopeful enough about its future prospects to send even Cyril away in a reasonably positive frame of mind. I, too, felt much better by the end of the conference and left with everyone else on Saturday afternoon sensing a new camaraderie among the senior staff.

Early on Sunday morning I got a phone call from John Bromley telling me that Cyril was dead. Apparently, he had fallen out of the window of his sixth-floor flat and died instantly on the concrete courtyard below. I wept buckets: I loved the man. The next morning, press speculation was feverish. It was common knowledge that he was a depressive, that he had been passed over for the managing director's job in a company that was having a hard time because of indifferent programming for which he was responsible. The *Daily Mail*, just in case any of its readers were ignorant of the laws of gravity, helpfully printed a front-page picture of the mansion block with a dotted line linking the window of Cyril's flat to the spot on the concrete courtyard where he landed. I have never forgiven the paper for what must rate as one of the most gratuitously cruel newspaper pictures I have ever seen. It made me ashamed to think that I was once proud to call myself a tabloid journalist.

We gathered in the office on the Monday morning, desolate. We were all Cyril's Boys, he'd selected each of us, nursed us through our bad patches and now we had lost our leader and inspiration. John Birt, though clearly distraught at Cyril's death, took charge of things. As I look back on those awful days following Cyril's death it was clear that even then John was a strategic thinker. We realized that now our champion had gone, we were at the mercy of Brian Tesler and might be picked off one by one unless we stuck together. This was monstrously unfair to Brian, but in a sense we were casting around for someone to blame for Cyril's death and Brian was the obvious scapegoat; had he not been brought into the company, things might have been different, though even then we did not share press speculation that Cyril had committed suicide in a fit of deep depression. I believe at the time, and still do, that Cyril's death was accidental. I knew him well. He was incredibly clumsy, often abstracted in thought. The explanation offered at the inquest chimed with what I knew of Cyril's habits – he leaned out over a window-sill cluttered with bric-à-brac to see whether his chauffeur had parked the car round the corner of the flats rather than in the front courtyard. Tragically, he overbalanced and fell to his death.

John Birt became our spokesman, insisting that with things in a state of flux we were entitled to a say in our future. It is quite possible that in the deepest recesses of his mind he was also weighing his chances of becoming Cyril's successor as controller of programmes. If so, it was a perfectly honourable ambition and he had a better claim than the rest of us to the job. He asked for a meeting with Brian, which became a four-hour confrontation. We got very heated, as people whose anger is unfocused tend to do, but Brian demonstrated his quality by hearing us out, quite unruffled by our wilder tirades. We were able to give vent to our pent-up feelings and Brian's calm confidence reassured us that our future was in safe hands.

Brian told us he had decided against making an immediate appointment of Cyril's successor; that he would do the job himself for a time while he sized up the likely contenders. We formed a small committee, which Brian chaired, and so politically naïve was I that it never occurred to me he was auditioning each of us for Cyril's old post, which was to have a different title, director rather than controller of programmes. So unconcerned was I about promotion that, a few months into the interregnum, I asked to see Brian and confessed I was feeling unsettled and wondered about going back to the theatrical agency business. I'd been very much Cyril's protégé and wasn't sure I wanted to work for anyone else. He was quite noncommittal and merely asked me to keep him in touch with the drift of my thinking.

A few weeks later, he sent for me again and told me it was now very important that he knew within twenty-four hours whether I intended to stay or go. I couldn't see any reason for the urgency, but, then, the motivations of top management were a closed book to me. When I got back to my office, there was John Birt, looking gnomic as usual. He told me that I was to be offered the post of director of programmes. I was astounded. Had it been anyone but John I would have laughed them out of my office, but John dealt in the currency of information. He had grasped the basic principle that knowledge is power; he made it his business to know what was going on in the company and he ran a sort of internal market, trading fact for fact. If his own ambitions had been thwarted by his advance knowledge of Brian's intentions, he gave no indication of the fact. Though John was an impeccable source of intelligence, I decided to keep the whole business under wraps until the following morning when Brian sent for me and asked me if I'd made up my mind about leaving the company because, if not, he'd decided to offer me Cyril's job.

I was genuinely humbled and puzzled. I had certainly made no great shakes of the Light Entertainment job and I could not conceive of myself growing in the post until I was worthy of filling Cyril's shoes. Apparently, Brian, against the conventional wisdom, decided that my lack of programme-making experience was an advantage because it meant I had interests right across the board rather than confined to a narrow specialism. Perhaps my experience as an agent worked in my favour. An agent has no option but to be interested in whatever range of skills his clients possess – comedy, drama, live variety, music.

I accepted Brian's offer gratefully. My family were thrilled and Lew capped my delight by assuring me that, had my name not been Grade, he would have made me controller of programmes in his own ATV – which did wonders for my confidence.

Given the press speculation about my strained relations with

John Birt after he joined me at the BBC, it is necessary to record that I could not have had a more loyal colleague or firmer friend at LWT. Whatever happened later, he was a tower of strength to me when I took over the job of director of programmes. We had our professional disagreements but we never exchanged a cross word; nor did I ever feel threatened or undermined by him. I thought the world of him. He was still busy empire-building, but he did that as naturally as a squirrel hoards nuts. I brought in David Bell to my old job as head of Light Entertainment, John Bromley was still head of Sport, Tony Wharmby was responsible for Drama and John was head of Everything Else.

Temperamentally, John and I were poles apart. With staff he could be demanding to a point just short of brutality whereas I was probably too happy-go-lucky. On one occasion he persuaded us to take on some graduate trainees. After working out the scheme with his usual thoroughness, he chaired the interview boards right up until the final round when I came into the picture. I listened goggle-eyed as he interrogated the candidates on the short list. On and on he went at them, grilling them over two or three days. It was like watching someone pick the wings off flies: terrifying. Over a drink, I confided to Brian Tesler, 'I wouldn't have got past the first round and I'm supposed to be running the place.' Brian replied, 'You and John complement each other. You get there by instinct, John works it out step by step in painful detail.'

When I first met him, I thought John was humourless but discovered over time that he had a nice sense of irony. I recall going to see a Royal Shakespeare Company production of Sean O'Casey's *Juno and the Paycock* with him and his wife Jane. It is a bittersweet, harrowing play about the travails of a doomed family. They suffer mayhem, murder and starvation. On the way out I said to John, 'What do you think?' and he replied, 'They were a very unlucky family weren't they?' Mind you, I came to realize that John always brought to his relationships a nice sense of calculation, but I was his boss so he gave me little trouble.

I certainly discovered that he was obsessive in his passions. If something caught his fancy, say, the music of Beethoven, he would buy every book on the subject, compare the available CD versions of his works and generally absorb all that was to be known about the composer. Whether this engineering approach to music would capture the essential spirit of a genius is another matter. He was equally relentless in his pursuit of good cuisine. We once went to New York, and he introduced me to a great restaurant called the Palm, which specialized in lobsters flown in every morning from Maine. They were monsters, seven or eight pounds each in weight. I watched in awe as John tackled his specimen. It was like observing a pathologist in action. It must have taken him two hours to dissect the creature, excavating parts of the lobster that even the lobster didn't know it had. I got through mine in a rough and ready sort of way, leaving about half in an untidy mess on my plate, whereas John pressed on remorselessly until it was just a tiny neat pile of shell. I'm sure there's a moral in there somewhere.

LWT won the Prix Italia three years running, the first time with a brilliant programme from Melvyn Bragg's department called *MacMillan's Mayerling*. It was a narrative ballet; the story of the affair between the Crown Prince Rudolf of Austro-Hungary and seventeen-year-old Mary Vetsera, which culminated in their deaths in the hunting lodge at Mayerling. It was choreographed by Kenneth MacMillan and set to Liszt's music. We filmed the whole ballet, including rehearsals and conversations with the music arranger and orchestrator John Lanchbery. It was a ground-breaking programme, which nearly didn't happen. Kenneth MacMillan decided at the last moment he didn't want the ballet filmed because it would give away the ending and spoil the experience for those who afterwards saw it live in the theatre. What Kenneth really needed was reassurance: beneath all the layers of genius he was a diffident man, uncertain of the quality of his work. I got over his objection by agreeing to use the ballet sequences out of due order, which was no problem since they were only illustrations of the dynamics of ballet. The programme got a million viewers, which for high art was a massive number.

So we won the Prix Italia, and to express my gratitude, I took Melvyn, Nick Elliott, the head of Arts, and John Birt and their wives to the prizegiving in Italy. We stayed on Lake Como, had a splendid dinner at Bellagio and afterwards sat on the terrace. The whole evening was wreathed in a deep brandy-gold glow, when in a lull in the conversation I happened to say, 'One of the great problems with our country is the state of education.'

'Quite right,' replied John, and launched into one of his painstaking analyses of an intractable problem, in the course of which he was challenged by Nick Elliott. There ensued a row of extraordinary bitterness. For the first time we saw the usually self-controlled John Birt almost incoherent with rage. There was obviously some unfinished business between him and Nick that went back to their days at Oxford. Then their wives joined in and Melvyn and I sat back aghast. It all got incredibly personal. I remember Nick asking John, 'How can you send your children to state schools when you even charge your haircuts against tax?'

Melvyn and I cleared off to bed. The next morning, two by two, the antagonists appeared for breakfast and, like naughty schoolchildren, apologized formally for their outrageous behaviour. It was a fascinating insight into an often inscrutable character: deep passions stir beneath John Birt's unruffled exterior.

In 1980, John came to see me and told me he was thinking of applying to become the first chief executive of the newly established Channel 4. I told him frankly that I hoped he wouldn't get it because I couldn't do without him, but I offered to help him with his application. In due time he arrived in my office with a document ten inches thick setting out his masterplan for the channel's future. I read it through carefully and made some comments on it. And off he went for his interview. In the event, the job went to Jeremy Isaacs. It was, I suspect, a great blow to John's pride. He had exposed himself and his ideas to the scrutiny of his peers and had been rebuffed. He and Jane went off on holiday. When he returned, he came to see me and said, 'I've reached a decision, I've decided that my future lies with you. I am really happiest working with you.' I was deeply touched. We were good comrades. At one of our weekly strategy meetings, John said, 'We'll always look back on this time as a golden period in our careers.' On whether this was a golden period for TV, historians of the business will eventually pronounce, but it was certainly the golden time in my relationship with John Birt.

When I first took over as director of programmes, Brian sat alongside me, but then set a deadline and told me I was on my own from that day, though he was there to be consulted if I needed him. With his backing and guidance and a first-class team, we slowly turned the place around, took risks and began to win prizes. We launched *The South Bank Show*, *The Professionals*, *Lillie Langtry* and several Agatha Christies. Taking over Cyril's old job forced me for the first time to come to terms with the higher politics of the television business. London Weekend Television was part of a network that had a total monopoly of air time, companies who wished to advertise their products on television had to deal with one of the ITV stations, which made us very powerful and eventually very rich. There was, however, a price to be paid for that monopoly. ITV was tightly regulated by the Independent Television Authority (ITA), a statutory body that had the power of life and death over us. They had a veto over every aspect of our work from programmes to transmission schedules, from advertising slots to taste and standards.

The ITA, which later became the IBA, was a bureaucracy designed to do several things. It had a parallel function to that of the BBC governors, standing between the companies and Parliament to guarantee our independence from political interference. It had a concern for programme standards, ensuring that the ITV companies did not use their monopoly position to make only cheap and cheerful programmes, thus lining the pockets of the shareholders at the expense of the viewing public. It exerted a constant and generally wholesome pressure on the companies to discharge their public-service broadcasting duty to make and transmit loss-leaders such as operas, serious plays and documentaries that would elevate public taste at the price, very often, of derisory viewing figures. It also approved the schedule and its programmes.

I recall being summoned to the IBA to discuss a proposed programme in our *Weekend World* slot about Northern Ireland to be presented by the distinguished journalist Mary Holland. This was quite an ordeal for me as I hadn't been schooled in serious journalism: Alf Ramsey interviews were about my mark. I went along to Brompton Road with the editor of *Weekend World* and my head of Current Affairs, Barry Cox and David Cox, who were unrelated. Colin Shaw, the IBA's director of television, opened the meeting, talking in the measured cadances of a former barrister and ex-chief secretary of the BBC. Like most bureaucrats, although his very English style was elegant, what he said was opaque. He murmured vaguely about there being some unease around the IBA about our programme idea. Nothing specific, just a slight feeling of unhappiness in certain quarters. I couldn't make head or tail of this circumlocution and asked him to spell out exactly what he was saying. Eventually, he said that the unease centred on the choice of Mary Holland as presenter. I pressed him further. This was my first blooding in the presence of my troops and I couldn't afford to give any ground, especially since all I knew about Mary Holland had impressed me. Somewhat sheepishly Colin confessed that the feeling in some quarters was that Mary Holland's connections might cause some people to believe she was unable to hide her sympathies for the Republican cause.

I flared, 'Are you suggesting that Mary Holland is partisan and unacceptable? If that's the level of the accusation, I've no interest in continuing this conversation.' Whereupon I closed my file, picked up my briefcase and said to the two Coxes, 'Come on, we're going.' They looked at me aghast, quite convinced I was committing professional hara-kiri and probably sinking LWT in the process. In truth, I was way out of my depth when it came to Northern Ireland, but my every instinct told me that if I lost this battle my role as a director of programmes would be untenable. Whether the Northern Ireland Office or MI5 or

Special Branch had been lobbying the IBA I had no idea, but the lack of transparency in the whole business was quite foreign to me, having come up through the world of entertainment where everything is up front.

We'd just reached the door when Colin called us back and withdrew his comments about Mary Holland. We then got down to a civilized, helpful discussion about the content of the programme. When we got back to LWT I was the hero of the hour with the Current Affairs department for daring to lead a walk-out at the IBA, and at a stroke, it established my credibility as a champion of my staff.

But dealing with the IBA was a civilized doddle compared with trying to handle the trade unions in the pre-Thatcherite days. There was virtually no legislation to curb their power so that in labour relations the companies lurched from crisis to crisis. We could do nothing without the approval of the ACCT, run by Alan Sapper, whose hobby was flexing his muscles at the slightest provocation. One reason why the ITV companies were so craven was that our air time was an irreplaceable asset, if we lost any of it through disputes, we forfeited the advertising slots that went with the programmes that had not been transmitted. Unlike the newspapers, we couldn't print extra pages to accommodate any advertising that had been lost in disputes. The IBA would not help us by allowing us to sell alternative advertising time. Their position was simple. They believed that the public interest was best served by keeping the screen alive, so we must accommodate the unions at whatever cost to ourselves. Because a local argument involving one of the companies could black out the entire network, the IBA was singularly unsympathetic to our plight. And, of course, we had a duty to our shareholders to maintain our advertising revenue. The companies were making huge profits out of the monopoly, so kow-towing to the unions was the order of the day.

A kind of collective madness had infected the entire industry and distorted any rational sense of priorities. Not infrequently we ended up with distinguished actors and entertainment stars, fully made up, sitting around our studios twiddling their thumbs while we begged technicians not to walk off the set. Though union agreements assured them of double and even triple time for extra work, they had to be bribed to finish the job. We were totally at the mercy of their moods: should they be out of sorts, they would shrug their shoulders and walk out, and there was nothing we could do about it. One more programme had to be aborted, to the great frustration of talented artists and at huge financial cost to the company.

One of the most flagrant abuses was the misuse of the so-called rostering system. In certain technical departments, if staff worked more than a statutory number of hours they could take time off in lieu or set in motion a gravy train of fantastically escalating wage rates. Since these technicians did their own rostering, they established the quaint old custom of arranging for each of them in turn to do excess hours, so triggering huge payments – LWT had one videotape engineer who earned over £100,000 a year at 1979 prices. The standard joke in the industry ran: What is the difference between an Arab oil sheikh and an LWT video engineer? The answer was that the Arab oil sheikh didn't get London weighting.

The companies were powerless in the face of rampant trade unions. Most technicians were on the staff and almost impossible to fire, however incompetent they were. We had one senior film cameraman who on his best day could just about get his subject into focus, but anything more creative or technically advanced was beyond him. We were anxious to produce some of Dennis Potter's plays on film, using guest directors who liked to choose their cameramen, so we spent weeks begging the house camera-man to go off at our expense on holiday. This was the reality of our life in management. All of us were demeaned by the necessity of adding bribes to high wages to get technicians to work.

Eventually ITV decided that enough was enough and at the 1979 wage round negotiations, we rejected the union bid as exorbitant and offered a lower though still generous figure. The unions didn't argue, they simply pulled the plugs on the entire network in an eleven-week strike. In the end, the companies found themselves in their usual humiliating posture, on their knees begging the workers to return to work, which they condescended to do, having secured a settlement even larger than the one they asked for in the first place.

Programme quality was almost impossible to sustain in a culture poisoned by cowardice, greed and the abuse of power. Many distinguished programmes went under or were never completed. The pioneering anthropology series *The Disappearing World* lived up to its name and vanished, its budgets having escalated into the upper stratosphere because the unions insisted on regarding the rainforests of Brazil or the sands of the Kalahari as extensions of the *On the Buses* studio in London, to be covered by identical work practices.

Whatever may be said of the Thatcher regime in general, there is no doubt that through her trade union legislation she saved more than one industry from medieval servitude. Out went the closed shop and secondary picketing; in came pre-strike ballots. In a short time, the ACCT shrank to a mere shadow of its former self. The long-standing monopolies began to break up. The companies lost their exclusive access to air time as new channels began to transmit on cable and satellite, and the union stranglehold on employment policy was shattered for all time.

The establishment of Channel 4 also had a salutary effect. Since it was a commissioning house, it had the freedom to choose between a growing number of independent production companies who weren't hog-tied by restrictive union agreements. The channel's earliest team of managers had not been drawn from ITV but from the BBC, journalism and entertainment generally, so they had never been habituated to ITV's suffocating union culture. The first managing director of Channel 4, Justin Dukes, was pressed hard by the ITV companies who were financing the channel to extend existing ITV union agreements to its labour relations. Dukes, recognizing that it would be lunacy to embrace voluntarily the work practices that virtually paralysed

ITV, fought the proposal to a standstill and won. Channel 4 was free to establish new, liberal, healthy relationships with the unions and with those of its employees who chose not to be union members.

In 1981, at LWT I commissioned a television version of Trevor Nunn's production of Dickens's *Nicholas Nickleby* at the Aldwych Theatre. Melvyn Bragg and I had been to see the eight-hour show and came away convinced we had to televise it. We began to negotiate the usual minefield laid by the unions and, as we feared, the provisional budget had almost as many noughts in it as the National Debt. Layers of overmanning, Spanish practices, penalty payments for trivial infringements of the union agreement and grossly inflated wages sank the project without trace.

But this became Grade's Last Stand. I was grimly determined that the unions wouldn't beat me this time. I called in a man called Richard Price, who was our distributor of programmes but had production ambitions. I astonished him by proposing that he set up an independent production company to make *Nicholas Nickleby*, furnished by me with a budget and a guaranteed sale at an agreed price when it was finished. As an independent producer he could use freelance crews, and the LWT unions could not black the production. We sold this mammoth TV version of *Nicholas Nickleby* to Channel 4, where it became one of Jeremy Isaacs's first great successes.

Dealing with the unions involved an immense amount of committee work, but so did the rest of the job. The director of programmes of an ITV company was part impresario and part bureaucrat. I once calculated that I was a member of twenty-nine committees, working parties and study groups. One of the most critical was that which dealt with network scheduling. Every Monday morning the programme directors of the five big companies, Granada, Yorkshire, Thames, LWT and ATV, would sit down together with the chairman of the controllers' group and the director of television of the ITA and discuss a draft schedule that had usually been drawn up by the two London companies.

This would be picked about and knocked into shape. Just as the speed of a convoy is determined by that of its slowest ship, it didn't matter how daring and radical an individual controller might be for he would get nowhere unless he could sell his project to the other controllers, some of whom were very conservative. The programme content of the network was inevitably an uneasy compromise, which gave the BBC, if it was fortunate enough to have a talented controller of its main channel (as it did in the days of Bill Cotton), a decided advantage. Within limits, the controller of BBC was a law unto himself, so the programme content could reflect his personal strengths and taste.

Being a weekend contractor, LWT felt the full blast of BBC competition. Bill Cotton, having a showbusiness background, believed that Saturday and Sunday on BBC 1 should be given over to high-ratings entertainment. Serious documentaries and minority plays were shunted over to BBC 2. Bill knew his target audience and their expectations. This is where the weakness of ITV's federal system was revealed. Obviously, we at LWT could not hog the entire weekend with our own programmes; we had to take the output from other companies who did not make programmes specifically designed for weekend consumption. Much of this output was of high quality but needed protected slots, and there was nowhere to hide at the weekend from the fierce blasts of BBC competition.

One area of our dealings with the BBC nagged at me constantly: sports coverage. I thought it ludicrous that the BBC and ITV together deployed something like fifty cameras with an army of expensive technicians to cover the Cup final, following the same twenty-two players around kicking the same ball, getting their pictures from virtually identical vantage-points. Again and again we tried to persuade the BBC to agree to alternation for the great national events that both authorities were expected to cover: by the toss of a coin we would decide who went first and take it in turns to cover the Cup final, the Grand National, Open Golf and so on. The BBC wouldn't play. They took it for granted that they had an inalienable right to be present at all great national sporting events. Eventually my patience snapped and in 1978 I triggered a head-on confrontation with the BBC over the television rights to football matches, pulling off a coup which the tabloid press called 'Snatch of the Day'.

It all began when I was contacted by a friend I'd had since my days as a sports writer. His name was Jack Dunnett and he was the Labour MP for Nottingham Central, as well as being a successful solicitor, property developer and chairman of Notts County Football Club. Jack had become president of the Football League, the controlling body of professional soccer. At that time the only soccer on TV was BBC's *Match of the Day* on Saturday evenings with ITV showing edited highlights of league matches on Sunday afternoons. Jack invited me for a drink at the House of Commons, told me that the TV football contract was due to expire and asked if I would be interested in bidding for a new one. It had been traditional for the BBC and ITV to negotiate jointly as a cartel and tell the Football League what the clubs were going to get in fees – an arrangement that prevented the League from playing off the BBC against the ITV companies to raise the bid. It was a carve-up between the two channels with the BBC, by divine right, getting the main slice. Dunnett thought it was time to change the rules and get the football clubs a better financial deal.

I went back to LWT and talked the idea through with John Bromley. He thought that it would be a sensational coup if we could pull it off but warned me that there was bound to be blood on the walls when the BBC got to hear about it. For years ITV had been locked into this complex arrangement with the BBC and the Corporation would not abandon it without a fight. We worked out all the angles in strict secrecy, and when all the pieces were in place we confided in Brian Tesler. Brian, as always, brought a first-class analytical mind to bear on the deal and its likely consequences and agreed to support us, provided we could get the other ITV companies to back the deal. We would also have to keep the IBA informed: they had the last word and certainly would not allow us to break the concordat with the BBC in any unethical manner.

For the time being we kept the deal secret from the other ITV companies until negotiations had reached crunch-point. Meanwhile, I met Alan Hardaker, the Football League's influential secretary who, like Dunnett, was dissatisfied with the existing arrangements which, he felt, allowed the BBC and ITV to exploit the clubs. He agreed that the deal was worth exploring, though he wondered where the cash for an improved offer from ITV would come from. The companies operating together, I assured him cheerfully, though at that moment the other ITV companies knew nothing about any deal other than the traditional BBC–ITV concordat, which was being laboriously reactivated.

I then called a telephone conference to include the major ITV companies. The key players were Paul Fox for Yorkshire TV, Brian Cowgill for Thames, though he was away from the office sick, and in any case Thames were not affected because they were a mid-week company, Charles Denton for ATV and David Plowright for Granada. Also listening in was Colin Shaw, representing the IBA. I laid out the scheme, and after some discussion it was agreed by everyone present that we should go ahead. In order to ensure the IBA's approval, Brian Tesler had come up with a proposal to deal with a long-standing ITV grievance, the unwillingness of the BBC to agree to alternation in covering major events. We could toss a coin to determine who went first, then split the big events on a turn-and-turn-about basis. Brian's idea was that if we could get the football contract we could use it as a bargaining counter with the BBC to get our ultimate goal: alternation. The IBA took the line that since alternation would obviously be in the interests of viewers, it would support our football bid.

Everyone on the conference call signed up to the deal. There was one problem: the head of Sport at Granada, Gerry Loftus, was our representative on the joint BBC–ITV negotiating committee and he would be placed in a difficult position if he was told about the new proposal. Granada's chairman, David Plow-right, agreed to tell him as much or as little as was prudent about the plan. In the event, Loftus claimed to have been kept in the dark.

I confess to an ulterior motive. *Match of the Day* was the crown of the BBC's Saturday evening schedule, and if ITV could take it from them, then LWT's toughest competition would be removed at a stroke. John Bromley and I went off to negotiate the deal with Jack Dunnett and Alan Hardaker. After hours of hard bargaining, the Football League agreed that ITV should have the exclusive right to televise matches for a sum of five million pounds over three years.

Hardly able to credit the audacity of what we had done, Bromers and I called a press conference at which we announced that we had signed an exclusive contract with the Football League to televise their matches. The BBC's divine right to soccer coverage had finally ended. We had a few drinks, then went home to my flat and stayed up much of the night listening to news bulletins. The following day the press went berserk. Had I not been naturally diffident I might have become big-headed as I read the *Daily Express*, which trumpeted: 'There is a new phrase in the language of television power these days. It says, "Whatever Mike Grade wants, Mike Grade gets." His stunning £5 million ITV soccer coup is seen as merely another example of the ruthless brilliance which has made him a giant in the industry at 35.' A *giant* in the industry? I felt more like the guy in the cartoon who leans against an ugly skyscraper, it topples over and he's hailed as an environmental champion.

The *Express* went on, 'BBC chiefs have nightmares about him. One by one he is knocking down the Beeb's institutions. First Morecambe and Wise, then Bruce Forsyth, now the biggest scalp of all, *Match of the Day*.' It would be fair to say that the BBC were not entranced by LWT's coup. Indeed, all hell broke loose at Broadcasting House when they heard the news. They had been completely outmanoeuvred and knew nothing of the snatch until a magazine reporter told someone at the BBC that

apparently there were wild celebrations going on at LWT and
asked if he had any idea why. In fact, once the documents had
been signed, as a courtesy Alan Hardaker phoned Alan Hart, the
BBC's head of Sport, to tell him about the deal.

Once it grinds into gear, the BBC is a veritable juggernaut of
a war machine. The Corporation attacked ITV on three fronts,
with a civil suit for breach of agreement, an appeal to the Office
of Fair Trading and an action for infraction of the Treaty of
Rome. As we reeled under the furious assault, we wondered why
they hadn't gone the whole hog and taken the matter to the
General Assembly of the United Nations as well. The IBA, most
of whose senior officals were ex-BBC employees who shared the
Corporation's value system, began to wobble as allegations of
ungentlemanly conduct flew around, conveniently forgetting
that they had been in on the original telephone conference and
had agreed to its outcome. Lady Plowden, the chairman of the
IBA, sent for John Freeman, who knew he was treading on
delicate ground since the new franchise round was looming.
The IBA told him that if matters were not resolved satisfactorily,
heads at LWT must roll. When Brian Tesler reported this to me,
I asked, with more than a little self-interest, 'Any idea whose?'
Brian replied that John Freeman had told him that if any head
must roll, it would have to be his own since he had told the IBA
he was responsible for the idea in the first place. Little wonder
the staff venerated their chairman.

John Freeman decided to take legal advice, so he, Brian
Tesler and I went to see Sam Stamler QC, known to the Inns of
Court as the Bionic Brief or the Six-million-dollar Man. Sam was
a top commercial silk, who looked disconcertingly like Ronnie
Barker. We had an all-day conference, at the end of which Sam
poured us each a whisky then proceeded to dictate to his
secretary a twelve-page memorandum off the top of his head
summarizing the whole case and the interrelation between the
three suits. A cascade of immaculate English prose, perfectly
punctuated, flowed from his lips. We were awestruck.

Gerry Loftus, ITV representative on the joint negotiating

committee, bled all over the newspapers claiming that I had stabbed him in the back and precipitated a full-scale war with the BBC. Even as Loftus emoted, Brian Tesler was sitting down with Alasdair Milne, then managing director of BBC Television, to negotiate an alternation agreement. The cartel was restored, the BBC got back *Match of the Day* and ITV secured alternation rights.

It is at such times that you learn who your true friends are. One of the staunchest was Bill Cotton, then controller of BBC 1. Understandably, I was a veritable pariah at the BBC. One evening when the controversy was at its most feverish, I went to a show at the London Palladium and bumped into Bill. I feared he might cold-shoulder me, but he was as friendly as ever and chuckled 'You've caused us a bit of trouble.' The affair put me on the television map and earned new respect for LWT from the BBC. When I was due to leave LWT, John Freeman reported a conversation with Sir Ian Trethowan, the BBC's director general, who had told him that as far as the BBC was concerned, the only competition for quality programmes from within the ITV system came from LWT, which for me was the ultimate accolade.

There was one further irony to the whole affair. The manager at the BBC who benefited most was Alan Hart, head of Sport. From being a competent but relatively unnoticed executive, the *Match of the Day* crisis had pitched him so far into the thick of the negotiations that he had come to the attention of the BBC's governors. When Bill Cotton moved on, Alan Hart was appointed controller of BBC 1 in his place. Later Alan thanked me for inadvertently advancing his career.

I got on well with my ultimate bosses, the board of LWT, for whose executive chairman, John Freeman, I had infinite respect and great affection. Then there was Robert Clark, a rather dour Scottish lawyer, who'd made a fortune in the property business. In one of his ventures he had lost out to the Grade family when we took over ABC but he always behaved with great magnanimity towards me. He was invariably supportive and kind, though when it came to programme budgets he did a passable imitation of the tight Aberdonian, grumbling that things were too expensive and couldn't we cut out the frills – which usually meant half the production. David Montagu, later Lord Swaythling, of the banking family, taught me a great deal about money and human nature. And the newspapers were well represented. Bert Hardy was Rupert Murdoch's man on the board. There was Roger Harrison from the *Observer*, and Lord Hartwell, then the owner of the *Daily Telegraph*, who was deputy chairman. I clashed with Michael Hartwell over a programme series on minorities which John Birt sold to me and I endorsed with enthusiasm. When the idea was reported to the board, Lord Hartwell noted that gays were one of the minorities listed and told John Freeman he felt he should resign because he did not wish to be associated with such programmes. As always John was the supreme diplomat: he defused the issue, persuaded Michael Hartwell to stay but also protected me and my staff. Finally, there was banker Evelyn de Rothschild, representing *The Economist*. 'Diversification' was the in-word of the time and Evelyn intoned it constantly like a mantra. He attended board meetings fizzing with ideas, all imaginative, some bizarre, the odd one brilliant. On one occasion he solemnly proposed that since LWT was a metropolitan company we ought in the interests of diversification to buy Fulham Football Club.

In 1979, we began preparing for the franchise round, which would determine whether we got our licence to broadcast renewed; in fact, for various reasons, the meeting did not take place until 1981. Not surprisingly, given the general quality of our programmes, we won the renewed franchise handsomely and were awarded an extra hour and three-quarters so that we went on air on Friday evenings at five fifteen instead of seven o'clock.

During that meeting with the IBA, I learned a trick from our chairman, John Freeman. Having submitted our written evidence, it was a sort of beauty contest from then on, a face-to-face encounter with the IBA members being the clincher. As part of our strategy for handling the questions the IBA might direct at us individually, John Freeman decreed that initially he would field every question regardless of at whom it was aimed, and then he would bluster, as he put it, for thirty seconds or so before turning it over to one of us, thus giving us a breathing space to collect our thoughts. The tactic worked brilliantly and we gave a good account of ourselves.

A few weeks after we had won the new licence agreement at the end of 1980, Brian Tesler sent for me. Most uncharacteristically, he seemed a little nervous. He said, 'Michael, everything has gone very well, you've made an enormous contribution, we've got the new licence, but I've just discovered that your current contract runs out in a few months.' Then I realized the cause of his anxiety. In a franchise bid, the candidate company's director or controller of programmes is a key figure in selling its future plans, and not simply by his or her advocacy on the day. The IBA weighs the programme ideas and proposed schedules carefully, but the question at the back of their minds is always: Is there someone in this company with the authority and experience to deliver these promises? False modesty aside, I knew that my name and track record had been material factors in winning the application.

Brian was not in a strong negotiating position. I could have cost him a lot of money, but I was perfectly relaxed about the whole thing. I had no desire to be anywhere else in TV; John Freeman and Brian Tesler were a joy to work for and I had an excellent team supporting me. I was well contented, so I told Brian that whatever contract he placed in front of me I would sign without a quibble. Within a week or two a document arrived on which I scribbled my name almost without glancing at it.

Under the surface of my life, however, things were neither so simple nor so satisfactory. My marriage to Penny had ended and, as these things do, the settlement had left a gaping hole in my finances. I had built up no capital and, quite properly, Penny and the children received our house. I found myself with a financial crisis, underscored by a huge overdraft at the bank. I worried and spent sleepless nights trying to square the circle and think of ways of paying off my debts without undermining my lifestyle, which I honestly believed I'd earned by unremitting graft since I had left school.

About nine months after I'd signed the new contract with LWT, I had a phone call out of the blue from my friend Norman Lear in America, from whom I had bought *Good Times*, the show that became *The Fosters*. He told me that his partner, Jerry Perenchio, was coming to London and would like to meet me. I knew Jerry slightly: he'd been an agent for Andy Williams and other big stars, but was now Norman's partner in a successful TV company called at that time Tandem, later Embassy Productions. Jerry invited me to have supper with him at the Connaught. It was the night of the siege at the Iranian Embassy and there was traffic chaos in that part of London. I arrived at the hotel very late to find Jerry glued to his television set, totally absorbed by footage of the SAS storming the embassy, convinced there was a great action movie in it all.

We hit it off well. He said, 'I'll come to the point, Michael. I need someone to run our TV business because Norman's retiring. Would you like to come to Hollywood?'

Hollywood! The idea was mind-blowing! I told him I needed to think about it so we exchanged telephone numbers.

I got home with my head buzzing. I didn't respond immediately and worried at the possibility like a dog with a bone, attacking it first from this angle and then that. President of Tandem Productions was no empty title: it commanded all the financial rewards that went with it. Things began to come together. In London, I was working all the hours that God sent, had no private life worth talking about and my financial problems were crippling me. Things could only get better in Hollywood and about that name there was a certain magic for someone like me who had been bred and nurtured in the world of entertainment. I went into negotiation with Tandem and a friend in Hollywood who was an agent did the deal for me. I was earning thirty-six thousand pounds a year at LWT with a Christmas bonus that might run to a bottle of Scotch, but no share options. Tandem offered me $250,000 a year plus bonuses plus as many first-class air tickets as I needed to visit the kids or bring them out to me. They were my chief concern. Alison was eleven and Jonathan seven. I didn't want them to grow up not knowing their father; neither was I keen to lose the chance of watching them develop and become distinctive personalities. But I consoled myself that they would love Los Angeles and could spend every long holiday with me.

Although LWT was in good shape, partly thanks to my efforts, I knew they couldn't afford to pay me any more, so there was no way out of my predicament in trying to get Brian Tesler to raise my salary. I took a deep breath and went to see him. As always, he put me at my ease and listened sympathetically as I explained my financial difficulties and this fortuitous opportunity to find a way out of them. I told him with absolute sincerity that I felt rotten about letting him and the company down after all they had done for me. There were no recriminations from him, only instinctive understanding. Then, because the future of LWT was his first concern, he became businesslike and asked me about a successor. I never hesitated. 'It has to be John Birt,' I said.

In January 1982, I finished with LWT on a Friday and started as president of Tandem Productions in Hollywood the following Monday. My colleagues gave me a wonderful farewell party, organized brilliantly by John Birt (who else?). He and the others knew my propensity for dashing from place to place in a semi-panic, relying on a benign conspiracy between my PA and Bill, my driver, to get me where I ought to be. One morning I jumped into the car and said to Bill, 'Where are we going?' He said to the City. 'What are we doing there?' I asked.

'You've got a meeting with John Freeman.' Agitated, I asked why I'd been given no papers for the meeting. 'The chairman will explain when you get there,' he said firmly. I buried my head in some papers for an afternoon meeting and didn't look up until Bill turned down this poky little ally in a rundown part of the City. I said 'Bill, there's nothing down here, it's a dead-end. For God's sake, check the address.' Eventually we arrived at a moored barge on a deserted stretch of waterfront. 'This is it,' said Bill. I was by now semi-hysterical. 'Are you mad? Why would the chairman want to hold a meeting on a bloody rotting barge?' Bill insisted it was the address written down in his instructions. I jumped on to the barge, and a deckhand pointed below without saying a word.

In the cabin were John Birt, John Bromley, Tony Wharmby, David Bell and a big bucket of champagne. I'd been well and truly had. As we opened the bottle, a helicopter arrived and whisked us off to Heathrow where a suitcase awaited me, care-fully packed by my PA. No one would tell me what our desti-nation was. In fact it was Paris. We had dinner at a marvellous restaurant, tears and liquor seemed to flow at the same rate, and I was so tired and emotional that I fell asleep in the middle of the meal. We were supposed to go to a nightclub, but I was legless, so they took me back to the Hôtel Bristol, tucked me up in bed then went out on the town. I slept away the celebration in a somewhat anti-climactic end to a great relationship with colleagues who had become my treasured friends. Despite the bitterness of my subsequent dealings with John Birt, it is good to recall this act of warm friendship on his part.

Someone else was involved in my decision. Through my half-sister Anita Land, who was running a theatrical agency, I had met Sarah Lawson, a lawyer, who was interested in a career in the film and television industry. Anita and her husband Brook organized a dinner in Hampstead, and Sarah and I got on famously. She struck me as elegant, intelligent and determined not to be impressed by my reputation, though she did laugh at my jokes, which is the quickest route to a man's heart. I had a lucky break when I asked her to the pictures and chose the première of *Chariots of Fire*. Although I didn't know it, her parents' home, Hall Barn, near Beaconsfield, had been used as the location for part of the film; she didn't know that I didn't know it, so she was much impressed by my thoughtfulness, and one thing led to another.

I'd never bothered much about my appearance and my flat was a mess. One pole of my existence was television, the other, the rather traditional Jewish culture Olga had imposed on the family, in which women, though treasured, knew their place. Sarah gave as good as she got, she was an independent spirit, making her own way in the world and asking no favours on account of her sex. Her father, Lord Burnham, was an aristocratic land owner so through her I became part of a much wider social circle than the one in which I had grown up.

Sarah and I were engaged, there was nothing about me she didn't know, including the size of my overdraft and my frustration that British television could not offer the rewards to match my tastes. Lord Thomson may have declared that commercial television was a licence to print money, but that was an owner's perspective. In the days before the fat-cat culture, those who ran television were modestly paid. Sarah knew that I had a streak of the Grade lust for power in me. Lew, Bernie and Leslie had made their fortunes and reached the top in their chosen area of the entertainment business, and I could never do that while I was a mere manager in a medium-sized television station. Like many generations of European Jews before me, I felt America beckoning with the promise of unlimited opportunity. That's what I believed and that's what I told the press: 'There's a whole new world of television opening up in America ... It's a once-in-a-lifetime opportunity ... A gamble but I want to take it.'

Chapter Five

'HIT HIM WITH THE FISH IN THE FACE.'

As president of Embassy Television I became an independent producer without having the foggiest idea what the job involved. As soon as I arrived in Los Angeles I went to see the financial wizard of the business, Jerry Perenchio, at his house on Malibu in the exclusive Colony enclave. He had only one bit of advice for me. 'Just remember one thing,' he said. 'Shows are like pancakes – you keep throwing them against the wall and eventually one of them will stick and we'll make a lot of money.' And that was it. His partner Norman Lear's advice was different. 'Always remember this, Michael, it's OK if you don't make even one show, but when you do I want it to be a show we can all be proud of.' Jerry and Norman were usually in perfect accord, though once early on in their partnership they had had a costly disagreement. They were offered a picture that was looking for a distributor and previewed it. Jerry said, 'This film will make zillions!' Norman replied, 'I don't care if it makes zillions, I'm not having my name associated with a piece of garbage like that. It's everything I hate. It's exploitative, violent and self-indulgent.' *Rambo* indeed made billions of dollars, but not for Embassy.

The change in my lifestyle was dramatic. I had a palatial office with a private bathroom – the privilege of peeing in isolated splendour was the indispensable symbol of high rank in American big business. I bought myself a pink Cadillac convertible, partly because I wanted to have the benefit of the perpetual sunshine and partly because I was, after all, in California. It was long, powerful and smooth, and marked me out from the other executives who wouldn't be seen dead in an American car: they all drove top-quality Mercedes, BMWs and Jaguars. Everything in Hollywood seemed to be a status symbol. I soon noticed that when I came out of a restaurant or a hotel after a meal and handed over my keys for my car to be brought round, even if whoever was with me had already collected theirs, they would hang around, making conversation, to see what sort of car I was driving. I was the butt of much jocularity about my pink Cadillac but everyone seemed pleased that I was identifying with my new home.

I soon got the hang of the status-dominated culture of Hollywood. All the main restaurants had A, B and C tables and you were seated according to the *maître d*'s estimate of your importance. When I first arrived in Hollywood, I would be taken out to breakfast, lunch or dinner by one of my colleagues and introduced to the *maître d*': 'Now this is Michael Grade. He's come out from England to be president of Embassy. I've told him this is *the* place to eat, so I know you'll look after him and see he gets a good table . . .' The *maître d*', smiling ingratiatingly, would palm the hundred-buck bung he was offered with a dexterity worthy of Paul Daniels. Being English and therefore pompously determined not to succumb to this blatant bribery, I pitted my wits against Bernice, the formidable brassy blonde *maître d*' of the legendary Polo Lounge in the Beverly Hills Hotel to whom I had been introduced a few days after I arrived in Hollywood. I decided to stand the bung system on its head. If she gave me a good table, *then* I would slip her the note. For three years, week in and week out, I would arrive at the Polo Lounge to be greeted by Bernice as though she had never set eyes on me before. 'Your name, sir?' she would ask me, and sweep on to the next customer while I was shown to a table adjacent to the swing-doors of the kitchen. I saved a few hundred bucks and lost endless social face.

The only compensation for all this elaborate social

manoeuvring was the joy of walking into a public place and coming face to face with a Hollywood legend. I once went into Ma Maison, a fashionable eating place, and there was Orson Welles, his huge bulk spilling all over his table like a quivering jelly. I was awed to be sharing the same space as Citizen Kane. In my early days there, my old LWT buddy John Bromley came out to Hollywood on business and I made a great fuss of him. I took him to the best restaurants, gave him a tour of the historic film studios and introduced him to some of the most powerful media moguls, but afterwards he claimed the highlight of his visit was encountering Fred Astaire, loaded down with carrier-bags, coming out of a hypermarket.

I rented a house in Miller Drive, up in the Hollywood Hills. It had the requisite swimming-pool and wonderful views of the ocean all the way to Santa Catalina island, provided the area wasn't shrouded in smog: for most of the year, the sky was the colour of putty and the atmosphere oppressively heavy. On my first night in the house, as I lay in bed, I was startled by a sinister banging noise echoing through the house. I'd heard all the horror stories about crime in Los Angeles so I decided to stay put rather than wander around in the dark trying to investigate. Next morning, I discovered where the noise was coming from: it was the thump of the avocados falling off the tree on to the roof, not a sound I heard too often in London.

In September 1982, Sarah and I decided to get married. Neither of us wanted a register-office wedding, but without Sarah converting to Judaism, we couldn't have the ceremony in a synagogue; in any case, there was a strong C of E tradition in the Burnham family. I was happy enough to get married in church . – after all, I'd been a choirboy at Stowe so I was comfortable with the liturgy. I belong to the Liberal wing of Judaism and believe passionately in the mystical element in religion but regard the institutional restrictions of various religions as little more than control mechanisms to keep the troops in order. A religious label seems to me to have no more significance than a

particular school badge. This may be heresy but I have a strong
faith. However, because I was divorced, the problem was to find
an Anglican priest willing to perform the marriage ceremony.
Sarah's first choice was the local parish church at Beaconsfield,
but it was part of a diocese whose bishop frowned on the
remarriage of the divorced. Then Sarah's father, Lord Burnham,
had a brainwave. He'd served in the Scots Guards and decided
to approach the authorities at the Guards Chapel in Knights-
bridge in the hope that his request would get a more sympathetic
hearing.

The Scots Guards chaplain was a minister of the Church of
Scotland, which has a much more enlightened attitude to
divorce than the Anglican Church so the venue was settled. He
not only agreed to perform the ceremony but promised he'd say
a couple of prayers in Gaelic which, to the uninitiated, sounds
like Hebrew; he felt this would make my side of the family feel
more comfortable in church. Sadly, my father had died but my
uncles Lew and Bernie sat behind me, resplendent in morning
suits. I couldn't help overhearing their whispered conversation
– in fact the entire congregation heard them because neither
was accustomed to moderating his voice. I heard Lew say, 'That's
a nice suit you're wearing, Bernie. Is it yours or Moss Bros?'

'Of course it's mine,' replied Bernie. 'I don't wear it very
often. Matter of fact, I can't remember the last time I wore this
suit. Wait a minute . . . Now I remember. It was for Michael's
wedding.' At this point, the occupants of the half-dozen pews
behind them erupted with laughter.

The reception was held at Sarah's family seat, Hall Barn,
after which we took off in a helicopter for the Savoy. Sarah
organized the whole thing. One of my colleagues at LWT, Tony
Wharmby, was in hospital at St Thomas's and we popped in to
see him. The next morning we travelled by the Orient Express
to Venice and then on to Salzburg.

Sarah made the move to Hollywood and got a job in the
West Coast office of Don Taffner, a producer who successfully
adapted British shows for American television. She made a great

impression at business meetings and on social occasions, not
least because she had this upper-crust English accent but also
because every now and then she would suddenly interject a
Yiddish word or phrase. Yiddish is the *lingua franca* of Hollywood
and, thanks to my grandmother, I spoke it fairly fluently and
had passed some of its colourful vocabulary to Sarah, who used
it to great effect. Much to my surprise, Sarah took to Hollywood
with enthusiasm. I half expected her to hate Los Angeles: its
brashness, pace and ostentation seemed to war against her laid-
back, blue-stocking upbringing in the English shires. But, whatever her initial hesitations, she settled down contentedly and was
soon immersed in a job she loved.

We bought a house in the Mediterranean style in Sierra Alta
Way above Sunset Boulevard on the edge of Beverly Hills. We
also acquired Henry. He was a Münsterlander, a cross between a
springer spaniel and a pointer, bred by Sarah's parents. On one
of my periodic trips to Britain, I inspected their dog Poppy's
litter and chose Henry. I had him crated and he flew back in the
hold of a jumbo jet while in the cabin above I worried myself
sick all the way across in case he was cold, lonely and frightened.
When I collected him with my luggage at LA airport, he was in
much better shape than I was. Henry dominated our lives and
was quite indestructible. He survived the usually fatal parvovirus,
smashed through a glass patio door and several times collided
with cars. When we returned to England, we went every weekend
to the kennels where he was in quarantine; it was like visiting
kids at boarding-school, except that we couldn't take him out
for a cream tea. By then I was at the BBC and, through the good
offices of Biddy Baxter, the producer of *Blue Peter*, we found him
a golden retriever called Lily as a friend.

It was Sarah who insisted that I needed something distinctive
in Hollywood to mark me out from the army of sombre-suited
executives who swarmed around the place. She said, 'You've got
to have a trademark, something they'll remember you by. I don't
know – try wearing red socks, do something crazy.' So I bought
some red socks and wore them constantly, evoking from curious

Yanks the hesitant enquiry, 'Excuse me, but do you always wear red socks?'

'Oh, yeah' I replied. 'Always.' They nodded understandingly, probably assuming that since my wife was the Honourable Sarah Lawson, the red socks had some kind of aristocratic associations. But the ruse worked. I'd ring up an office and ask to speak to someone, and as soon as I stated my name, he or she would say, 'Wow! The red socks!' The red braces came later.

In Hollywood, marketing was everything. First you had to sell yourself, then your product. The contrast with Britain was jarring. The English middle classes are embarrassed by the whole business of selling: it is redolent of a class system where those 'in trade' are pretty low down in the natural order of things. Luckily, as a Grade, I had little of the social reserve of the British, which was just as well, for in Hollywood you had to be an unashamedly high-powered salesman to survive.

In spite of its fancy title and splendid offices, Embassy Television was a sit-com factory. I inherited five shows, which were long in the tooth, and my first task was to see that they stayed on air. The big television networks, unlike their British equivalents such as LWT, made few programmes other than their flagship daily news and documentaries. They bought everything else from companies like ours, and we specialized in comedy. Every year, Nero-like, the big networks would give the thumbs-up or thumbs-down to our existing shows while we tried frantically to develop new ones. Our studio complex on the Universal lot was a mass-production unit, steaming at the seams with activity as shows in every stage of development were scheduled with military precision.

Norman Lear had built up Embassy from nothing. He was a benign gnome of a man whose smiling face radiated goodwill to all humanity. He invariably wore a pork-pie hat with the front brim turned up, vaudeville-style. We used to call him the Alchemist because he conjured up plots like a magician. His favourite method was to get a team of scriptwriters into a room and then get them chatting about *anything* – families, hobbies, money, hopes and fears – then he'd pounce on a casual remark and cry, 'That's it! Let's develop that.' His other key technique was to compile an exhaustive CV of each character in each show: every last detail of their lives was catalogued, not only the particular newspaper they read but the page they turned to first. Though it was tedious to put together all these facts, the fat volume, which was known as the Bible, could be a life-saver. A comedy series on British television rarely ran longer than six episodes at a time while Lear and his team were having to write anything up to twenty-odd episodes, so when inspiration ran dry and they couldn't decide what to do next, they'd trawl the Bible and come up with some detail of a character's life as a hook on which to hang a new twist in the plot. It was damned hard graft. American sit-coms didn't get their reputation for being highly polished by accident: whole teams of scriptwriters burnished the dialogue until it sparkled. In spite of all their work, a sit-com might still die the death in the ratings, but there'd be a high sheen on the corpse.

By the time I arrived in Hollywood, Norman was in his early sixties and exhausted after being responsible for the production of twenty-six episodes each of five or six shows every year. He had had enough and just wanted to relax. He could not have been kinder or more considerate, always on hand if I needed advice but never throwing his weight around. He would read scripts for me and come up with casting ideas, but it never bothered him if I rejected them. As one of the leaders of Hollywood's liberal intelligentsia, he gave much time and money to fighting the so-called Moral Majority, the Reverend Jerry Falwell and other right-wing bigots who used religious programmes on television to raise billions of dollars from the faithful in a crusade against the ungodly, who were reckoned to be Roman Catholics, Jews and secular humanists. The Moral Majority was frank about its political aims: to ensure the election of a right-wing president and bring America back to God. Night after night, the television evangelists poured out tirades of moralistic religiosity, and the very television they were using was one of their major targets. In their opinion, it was infested with left-wing activists and gays; its drama and comedies purveyed sexual filth; its science programmes took evolution for granted; and its investigative journalism challenged the unquestioning patriotism and US world supremacy they believed to be biblically ordained.

Appalled by all the Moral Majority stood for, Norman Lear had founded People for the American Way. He gave himself totally to the battle against bigotry, even producing a big national special for ABC network with Robin Williams, Billy Crystal, Martin Sheen and many other stars. Its theme was the Stars and Stripes and its argument was that the American flag belongs to everybody, not just to the evangelical Right. When Norman retired he first brought in Alan Horn, a brilliant deal-maker who lacked creative flair; he could talk poetically about a balance sheet, but production scripts were in a foreign language. Alan held the fort until Norman decided that I was a kindred spirit. Norman and Jerry greatly admired British television: they had, after all, made a fortune from adapting *Steptoe and Son* and *All In the Family* for an American audience, thus importing a new realism into a comedy market accustomed to the blandness of *The Beverly Hillbillies* and *I Love Lucy* – which was so prissy that when in 1952 the star, Lucille Ball, got pregnant, no reference to her condition was allowed in the script even though it was apparent to tens of millions of viewers – hers was the first immaculate conception in nearly two thousand years. Norman wanted to take comedy in a new direction and drew some of his inspiration from pioneering British TV shows.

I had barely settled behind my palatial desk before the buying season was upon us. In May every year, all the television production-company executives go to New York and sit in a hotel for a week, chewing their fingernails, while the networks play God and decide how to fill their schedules. New York heaves at the seams with perspiring Hollywood producers wheedling, bribing, pleading and cajoling the networks to give their existing shows another run and to buy new ones. On that one week, the jobs, prospects and careers of thousands of some of the most highly talented and neurotic performers and producers in the business depended. As the jargon had it, the battle was to get or keep your shows 'on the board', the 'board' being an enormous wall chart to which were stuck labels bearing the names of the pilot shows the networks might buy. Like Rommel in the desert moving symbols of his Army divisions around a map of Africa and consigning some to oblivion, the bosses of ABC, NBC and CBS would leave some dockets in place and drop others in a pile on the floor. All this took place behind closed doors, but rumours swept through the bars and restaurants where we whiled away endless hours. 'I hear you're off the board,' your rivals would say sadly, shaking their heads in a rueful gesture of shining insincerity.

After a week of this I was a wreck, but the luck of the Grades held. As I was packing to go back to Los Angeles, I had two phone calls. The first was from CBS. The man said, 'I'm delighted to tell you we'll take your new shows *Square Pegs* and *Gloria* and continue three of your existing shows.' Shortly afterwards, an NBC buyer rang to tell me that the pilot of a show called *Silver Spoons* I'd submitted had been accepted. *Square Pegs* was about the trials of high-school life – two freshman girls who are desperate to get into the right social clique but are not quite cool enough to do it – one is skinny and wears glasses, the other has braces on her teeth. The show was to do good business for Embassy.

I thought I'd better let the office in LA know what was happening. The news that we'd had three new shows accepted was received with almost hysterical shrieks of joy. And, to my astonishment, I was greeted at Los Angeles International Airport with flowers and champagne and ushered into a stretched limousine that carried me to the office in triumph like Montgomery after Alamein.

This is when it first dawned on me what a precarious business I was in. A whole industry lived holding its breath from year to year; thousands of livelihoods went into the melting pot annually during the buying season. People like me had to be supersalesmen, engaged in life or death commerce: at stake was food for

Christmas, kids' shoes, the condo, the divorce and the house in Palm Springs. That's what made Hollywood sing – not brilliant programmes but successful deals.

Embassy had eight sit-coms on the air and that first Christmas I got a call from Norman asking if I would pop over to his home in Brentwood. He expressed his delight at the way things were going and told me he wanted to extend my contract. I told him I would have to talk that through with Sarah, which he quite understood. After some convivial chat and a couple of drinks he showed me out and, as he did so, he handed me an envelope: 'A little Christmas bonus,' he murmured. I expressed my thanks and shoved the envelope in my pocket. I opened it when my car was halted at some traffic lights, recalling my Christmas bonus the year before from LWT, a bottle of whisky, some shortbread biscuits and a £5 Marks and Spencer voucher – a thoughtful gesture for which I was grateful. I opened the envelope and found a cheque for $75,000, as much as my yearly pay from LWT. At a stroke, I was able to pay off my overdraft and clear all my debts in London. It was easy to see why people put up with the madness and insecurity of Hollywood: the rewards were truly fabulous and the risks on the same scale, but if life on a roller-coaster suited you, Hollywood was the place to be.

The sit-com was a highly lucrative but limited genre. A couple of veteran gag-writers, Bob Schiller and Bob Weiskopf, who'd cut their teeth writing for Lucille Ball, the queen of sit-coms, explained how they had reduced the art to a formula. One said, 'All comedy is two Jews fighting.' Certainly, there was a strong ethnic strain in US comedy writing – Neil Simon, Norman Lear, Woody Allen and Nat Hiken, who wrote *Bilko*, were not only Jewish themselves but exploited their deep insight into the Jewish psyche and customs to create comedies with depth and poignancy. Another of the two Bobs' sayings was that 'Two things killed Hollywood – Mel Brooks and special effects.'

Thus, some months after I'd settled into the job, Norman Lear, by then supposedly retired, told me about a Hispanic comedian he'd heard in a nightclub. He was so impressed that he was prepared to supervise the writing of a sit-com in which Paul Rodriguez would star, set in a Spanish-American community. I was delighted to welcome Norman back to work. He put together a team of writers who spent time in a Los Angeles *barrio* absorbing the atmosphere. On the strength of Norman's name alone, ABC bought the pilot. He brought me the script. I read it and, with great diffidence, suggested it didn't quite hang together. He agreed and went off to do a rewrite, then another. We still couldn't get it to work, the writers couldn't seem to write their way into Hispanic culture. Then Norman suddenly said, 'There's only one thing to do, we'll have to write it Jewish.' I thought he was being funny, but he eventually produced a brilliant script with all the classical Jewish stereotypes – immigrant family, matriarchal mother, lazy, irascible father, pampered sons and neglected daughters but with Mexican names. It was very funny and ran for a while under the title *A.K.A.Pablo*, but the audience didn't really take to it. Nevertheless, the affair taught me that the immigrant experience is central to all American culture.

Just before I arrived in Hollywood I was interviewed for *Broadcast* magazine and rhapsodized about my future life – 'I like to imagine myself in Los Angeles, taking a bunch of scripts with me on a beautiful sailboat. I'm a lousy sailor but I love the sea. I'm not a businessman, I abhor the deal-making side of the industry. I'm happiest and thrive on being a creative being.' So much for my expectations. Hollywood fosters fantasies: I had much the same illusions about Tinsel Town as the starstruck teenager from the sticks.

The reality was that week after week, I'd sit there reading scripts: eight shows times twenty-two episodes times seven drafts of each script produced by a team of up to a dozen writers. This was comedy by committee with a vengeance, but it was slick stuff. Between them this army of talented writers honed every word. But even the most professionally produced material doesn't always work when it is lifted off the paper and transferred to a studio. Then I'd have to go down to the lot and confront some enormous egos fighting to keep intact every word of a script as though it were Holy Writ. I soon wearied of the standard Hollywood gags. American writers were addicted to jokes about psychiatrists, lawyers and, at that time, *nouvelle cuisine*. Every script seemed to have its statutory restaurant scene with slick word-play about tiny helpings and camp waiters. American television humour was much more verbal than visual, wisecracks peppered the pages of every script, and each show had to have what was known as the Golden Moment near the end:

'Oh, gee, Dad, I love you!'

'I love you too, son.'

There was a writer on the lot called Rick Mitz, who'd worked with Norman Lear. I appointed him my assistant and he became a close friend. He had a great analytical brain for comedy and we'd sit across the desk from each other and read the various parts aloud. I became quite a pocket Olivier. We'd act our way through the whole thing, which was the most effective way of identifying problems with the script. It also brought a little light relief to the grinding business of ploughing my way through a mountain of paper that never seemed to get smaller. In addition to the scripts delivered by staff writers, there was a constant flow of unsolicited material. Occasionally a gem was hidden in the pile of verbal sludge, but there was only one way to find it: the hard way.

It was both immensely flattering and quite intimidating to take Norman Lear's seat. He was the undisputed genius of TV comedy and I used his writing as a kind of counsel of perfection. He was a great risk-taker and taught me that no *subject* is too serious for comedy, though there are *occasions* when comedy would be an insensitive or inappropriate way of dealing with it. Of course, there are some circumstances of life so awful that only the victims have the right to joke about them. One of the funniest stories I ever heard was told by a BBC radio producer, about a blind housewife reading a cheese grater as a page of braille. Had anyone else told it, the cringe factor would have been overpowering. But he himself is blind and told the joke to alert a sighted audience to the dangers of patronizing blind people by overweening prissiness about their condition.

Norman insisted that by its nature comedy is a serious business even though it deals in funny incidents or jokes; indeed, we can only make a joke about serious things; frivolous things already are a joke. There can be no humour where everything is serious or everything is funny. It is this contrast which is the key to much comedy. For example, one episode of Norman's classic sit-com *Maude*, which starred Bea Arthur, who later became famous in *Golden Girls*, is set in a mortuary where a friend is lying dead, and it concerns Maude's efforts to retrieve someone else's brooch, which she'd lent to the dead woman. In another episode, Maude plans a surprise birthday party for her husband Walter, a manic depressive. She arranges for his wartime buddy, whom he hasn't seen for forty years, to be a surprise guest. The friend duly arrives and drops dead on the doorstep, so Maude is left with a suicidal husband and a dead guest to cope with, and the plot has to be resolved in the second half of a thirty-minute programme. Norman specialized in dangerous humour where a wrong word or misplaced emphasis would destroy everything, but he had knife-edge sensitivity and supreme virtuosity in writing dialogue. I never found any other scriptwriter to match him.

A writer who had her own kind of genius was Anne Beatts, who had worked on NBC's satire show *Saturday Night Live*. She wrote a pilot episode of a show called *Square Pegs*. The series was one of my first successes, enthusiastically commissioned by CBS. We cast the teenage Sarah Jessica Parker as one of the Square Pegs and she was to become a big star. The problem was that Anne Beatts was a neurotic perfectionist, at her best writing sketches rather than sit-coms. She spent a whole year writing the pilot programme but couldn't repeat the process over twenty-two episodes. She had what might be kindly called an exotic lifestyle and there were damaging reports in the press of drugs on the set, a charge I was unable to substantiate. But it was the worst possible pre-publicity. Anne was highly intelligent, observant and sensitive, but for some reason she took against me, announcing at the top of her voice that my every critical comment, however well meant, was evidence that I was a male chauvinist pig. Nevertheless, the pilot she wrote was the best Hollywood show I delivered to the network.

Part of my job was to sound out the networks about promising ideas, to avoid putting in an enormous amount of work on a project that was doomed because it was a repetition of one they'd already bought or didn't fit in with their programme philosophy. I would present myself at the local office of NBC, CBS or ABC and announce, 'The story begins this way: there's this Mary Tyler Moore type who's a shop girl in New York—'

'Stop right there,' interrupts the network buyer. 'Shop girls are out this year.'

'Ah!' I'd say desperately. 'You think she's a shop girl. . .' and on I'd go, busking it, looking for a gleam of interest or mercy in the stony eye of the network executive. He would hear me out politely and murmur something about being in touch. Then, like a travelling brush salesman, I'd put my goods back in my briefcase and, after protestations of mutual regard, off I'd go to knock on the next door. It had little to do with creativity, it was all about high-pressure salesmanship. Commerce was everything; the claims of culture came a long way behind. My friend Bill Cotton said that in America they make programmes to make money, whereas traditionally in Britain it used to be the other way round. That was my experience too.

Even when we struck a deal, casting the show could be a nightmare. There was none of the laid-back British system of inviting actors in to read for a part, discussing it amicably afterwards then coming to some agreement about whether they were suitable. In Hollywood, I was shocked to discover that I wasn't allowed to audition actors for a part unless their agent and our Business Affairs department had tied up a five-year deal. A long-term contract had to be in place before the show went on the air, otherwise if its first run was a success, the star's agent would have you by the balls and squeeze you until your eyes popped out. Quite often, actors had to hang around the rehearsal room while their agents and our people haggled. Treating actors as a commodity was completely alien to my way of doing things.

In this hothouse atmosphere, values became so distorted that one had to struggle hard to keep one's grip on reality. Actors in great demand became bargaining counters with real power in the commercial game. The central character of *Silver Spoons*, one of my first successes, was a twelve-year-old boy, the estranged son of an eccentric millionaire who suffered from arrested development; he'd just never grown up. The series covered the changes in their lives – how the boy starts out as father to the man and the man has to learn to be a father to his child. We cast a pre-pubescent boy actor called Ricky Schroder whose stock-in-trade was that he could cry to order – on the director's cue, he would drench the set in floods of tears.

The show was a huge hit and twelve-year-old Ricky became a mega-star who went everywhere in a stretch limousine with an entourage consisting of his mother, father and sister, business manager, lawyer and agent. One day his agent rang me and asked for a meeting. Was I going to play hard to get when young Ricky was single-handedly servicing Embassy's overdraft? I pitched up, eager to please, only to be told that Ricky was unhappy. His entourage nodded mournfully while Ricky stared at me, tearful. If Ricky was unhappy, then Embassy was thoroughly miserable. I feared I was facing a hold-out, a venerable Hollywood tradition where the star of a hit show stayed at home pleading depression until we were forced to renegotiate the contract, upon which the black cloud that hovered over him or her would miraculously lift.

It wasn't a hold-out: the boy genius had a list of demands as long as my arm. First, he wanted me to fire his co-star, a boy called Jason Bateman who was getting too many laughs for his liking. Then he demanded a part for his sister, who'd decided that at fourteen it was time she won an Oscar, and to cap it all, in the upcoming series he insisted on directing at least six

episodes, with the appropriate credit in large letters and a fee
to match. Ricky 'Spielberg' Schroder was still wearing short
trousers.

I promised to consult the network and expected their jeering
laughter as I told them of the Boy Wonder's demands. I waited
for them to say, 'Tell him to **** off.' Instead, there was a pause
on the line and then the executive drawled, 'I guess we can live
with that.' They didn't want any pain: we were talking serious
money. After long and tortuous negotiations, I managed to
persuade Ricky's agent that the co-star Jason Bateman was critical
to the show's success. He was the black velvet against which our
little star Ricky shone so brightly, I suggested oleaginously.
Ricky's sister made an occasional appearance, but I forgot to
give Ricky any directing. For me, it was truly astonishing that a
giant network would cave in without protest to the crazy
demands of a twelve-year-old.

By far the hardest part of my job was firing people, and it
was a daily routine in Hollywood. When I took over from Alan
Horn as president of Embassy he warned me on my first day that
one particular executive would have to go. I said to Alan, 'I'll
invite him in and explain the problem in detail, then I'll ease
him out of the company.' I went on to sketch out a complex
scenario I hoped would make the victim feel a little better. It
was the classic, oblique English way of doing things.

Alan just looked at me and said, 'What are you talking
about?'

'I thought I'd handle it delicately.'

'Michael, you're so English,' he said. 'Just hit him with the
fish in the face. We don't have the time to play around. Fire
him. People are used to it in this town. You're part of the "pink
slip" culture now. Hit him with the fish.'

And that's what I learned to do, and it certainly toughened
me up, but I hated it.

Years later, when I was working at the BBC, I remember
discussing the problem of firing people with Sir John Harvey-
Jones, the management guru, at a conference in Paris. He told

me that when he was chairman of ICI, one of his senior executives had had to sack an employee who was simply not performing well enough in a strategic job. Harvey-Jones discovered when the deed was about to be done and arranged to be hanging around the corridor at the critical time. Sure enough, the employee came out of the office but he wasn't ashen-faced and shaking: he was all smiles. Harvey-Jones asked him how he was getting along. 'Oh, fine,' he said. 'I had a great chat with the boss. We cleared the air and agreed some objectives for the future. I'm really focused now on the job in hand.' And away he went, whistling merrily.

Sir John called in to see the man who was supposed to have done the firing. 'How did it go?' he asked.

'Oh,' said the executive. 'These things are never easy, but I did what I had to do.' The manager was quite convinced he'd fired the man, the employee felt they'd had an inspiring chat. That story illustrated my weakness as a boss in Hollywood. I had a kind of English circuitousness in giving employees bad news that often turned out to be more cruel than whamming them across the face with the fish.

Even then, as my grandmother Olga used to say, there's a time and place for everything. We had a very successful show on the air called *One Day at a Time*. The star, Bonnie Franklin, was an excellent actress but very demanding. She decided that if the show was going to remain fresh in the following year, it needed a change of director. CBS, who were not about to get into an argument with her, agreed, and it fell to me to give the director, Alan Rafkin, the bad news. I arranged to have breakfast with him at the Westwood Marquis Hotel. When the menu arrived Alan, who had a typical American appetite, ordered about half a dozen courses. I was fairly hungry so I did the same.

'So,' says Alan, 'you want to talk about next year?'

I launched into a prepared spiel. 'Yes. As you know the show is in its eighth year and we're struggling to keep it on the board . . .'

'Well,' he said, 'I've got some very good ideas for next season.'

'Before you spell them out, Alan, let me tell you, I've been talking to Kim LeMasters at the network and Bonnie Franklin and we're kind of beginning to think about the personnel for the next run . . .'

'You're going to fire me,' he said flatly.

I took a deep breath and mumbled something inaudible.

He never said another word. He picked up his napkin, threw it down on the table and walked out. At that moment, a procession of waiters arrived, laden with plate after plate of food, which they arranged on the table. I was sitting alone looking at fifty bucks' worth of grapefruit, whole wheat oats with pitchers of fat-free milk, a mountain of bacon and eggs sunny side up, hominy grits, succulent sausages and crispy toast. I asked for the bill and left.

I'd learned my lesson: never fire anybody at the beginning of a meal. Even the Mafia have their rules about such things. When the mob killed Carmine Galante in Joe and Mary's Italian restaurant in Brooklyn in 1979, they waited until he was enjoying his post-prandial cigar before they dispatched him with a sawn-off shotgun. It was simple good manners.

In addition to their television operation, Jerry Perenchio and Norman Lear had bought a feature-film business, which started to haemorrhage red ink. There was the inevitable drive with people being fired or made redundant. Jerry addressed the troops, a couple of hundred of them, at a theatre in Century City. He ended up saying, 'We're going to sharpen up our act and, to do that we're going to have a dress code in the company. I want to see everyone in smart, dark suits, looking tidy. If you look the business, you'll do the business.' The slogan obviously appealed to him because he repeated it a couple of times. All the while Norman Lear was sitting on the platform like a benign gnome in his invariable outfit – pullover, blue slacks and a white pork-pie hat with upturned brim. He never wore anything else, but such was the affection in which he was held that no one imagined a dress code could possibly apply to him. But it could be a big problem to me. I had seventy writers under contract and I'd swear there wasn't a decent suit between the lot of them; they felt overdressed in sneakers and jeans. 'I agree with the new policy one hundred per cent,' I told Jerry, 'but I think it should be discretionary in the studio.' He liked the sound of that and incorporated the phrase into his memo.

At the Edinburgh Festival in 1983 I described my job in Hollywood as 'selling crap to assholes'. I wish now I hadn't said it. It was a cheap, disloyal crack made when I was demob happy and running off at the mouth, a poor way to reward my Holly-wood bosses, who were very kind and stood by me while I learned my trade. But, as time wore on, I found it strangely dispiriting to spend my days as part of a company grimly dedicated to the business of making people laugh. I began to understand the psychology of the sorrowful clown. I was missing the broad sweep of programme production I had become used to in LWT, the documentaries and news, music and sport, light entertainment and serious drama. In my down moments I felt I was little more than a door-to-door salesman selling joke books. I also realized I lacked the ruthlessness of the successful Holly-wood producer. I thought I was tough and, by British standards I was, but in Los Angeles I was out of my league as a hatchet man. The procession of colleagues leaving the lot clutching their pink slips because I'd failed to sell the shows they'd been working on depressed me unutterably.

I confided my frustration to Sarah, who wasn't in the least surprised. For months she'd been expressing her concern that I seemed to have lost my zest for life generally and my enthusiasm for television in particular. We had everything going for us in Hollywood – a beautiful house, plenty of sunshine, loads of money and lots of good friends. We were right at the very heart of the film and showbiz world, which was the Grade family's spiritual home, yet I wasn't happy. At her urging I went to see Norman and confessed that I was utterly played out. If I didn't ever see another sit-com script it would be too soon. I was tired of Golden Moments and happy endings, slick word-play and uproariously funny predicaments. I was weary of talking average shows up and pulping brilliant pilots because they didn't meet the networks' relentlessly commercial imperatives.

As always, Norman understood perfectly. He nodded mournfully when I protested that there are only so many times you can read, 'Hi, honey, I'm home!' without the brain rotting. He knew exactly how I felt and assured me that the company didn't want to lose me. He proposed that I could set up an independent production company, which would be financed by him and become a division of Embassy. I could make whatever programmes I liked and offer them to the networks. I was delighted; my head was buzzing with ideas and I couldn't wait to get back to my old trade. Predictably, the British press claimed that Embassy had fired me, but Norman Lear made a public statement saying that, far from being sacked, I would be heading up a new arm of Embassy and he was most anxious to secure my long-term future in the company.

The Grade Company's first project was Jeffrey Archer's *Kane and Abel*. I'd known Jeffrey since his running days when I was a sports writer on the *Daily Mirror*. Though his books were well known in the United States none of his work had yet made it to film or television so I persuaded him to let me have the rights to the book for a modest sum. CBS put up the development money. That was the first stage, than we had to produce what is known in the trade as a 'Bible', an extended treatment, and if the network bosses liked that, then we would get to write the first two hours, and so on and on, one hurdle after another to surmount.

I brought in Jud Kinberg, with whom I'd worked on dramatic development at Embassy. He was a fine writer as well as producer and he got to work on the show. Eventually, all seven hours of scripts were ready and we arrived at the crunch meeting with CBS, after which *Kane and Abel* would either run on network television or end up in the wastepaper basket. Jud and I sat up until the small hours for several nights rehearsing our final pitch. We tried to put together convincing responses to any possible quibbles from CBS's buyer, whose name was Bob Markell. He had the power of life and death over us at this meeting. We agreed that I should go first and then Jud would come in at the end to deliver the *coup de grâce*. I was in full flow about the drama and excitement of the story when suddenly my honeyed words were punctuated by a curious snoring sound from the sofa alongside me. Jud was fast asleep. Luckily, Bob Markell had a keen sense of humour and *Kane and Abel* went into production, starring Sam Neill and Peter Strauss.

Another project dear to my heart was a history of China from the Boxer rebellion to the flight of Chiang Kai-shek to Taiwan in 1948. With Jud, who was now fully awake, I spent a year doing research on the background. This was programme-making on a grand scale and we needed someone wo could weave a panorama of historical events into a coherent narrative, so I invited Alex Haley, who wrote the slave saga *Roots*, to take a look at the idea. He fell in love with it.

This was 1983, before the Tiananmen Square massacre; China was still a very reclusive society. Alex and I went there to scout for locations and try to persuade the Chinese government to lay on all the facilities we'd need. We had some good contacts and spent a few nights in the State guest-house in Beijing where President Reagan had stayed during his official visit to the People's Republic. As a building it had a certain spare grandeur, though there was no capitalist luxury about the interior furnishings. We were shown around the Forbidden City by Pu Jie, the last emperor's brother. He was tiny and looked like an aged jockey. Some of his comments were gems even when passed through an interpreter. One sticks in my memory. Pointing to a secluded garden, he said, 'This is where my brother and I used to play with the eunuchs.'

News of the project, provisionally titled *The Last Emperor*, got around in Hollywood and I had a call from the great Italian director Bernardo Bertolucci, who told me he also had a China project under way and proposed that we should co-operate. We certainly seemed to be getting under each other's feet: wherever Alex and I went in China, Bernardo had either been there before us or was expected within the next few weeks. The Chinese, of course, were past masters at the art of devious diplomacy and played us off against each other. I was very flattered to be approached by Bertolucci but felt we would be operating on two completely different time-scales. He was renowned for the painstaking thoroughness with which he made his films, but we intended to be in and out of China in a matter of months. His lawyer kept on pestering me and I continued to decline his overtures. I confidently expected we would have made our series, banked the profits and moved on to the next project before Bertolucci had a foot of film in the can. What a shmuck I turned out to be.

We went off to ABC with our fabulous treatment: it had all Alex Haley's flair for spell-binding narrative and some breathtaking visual effects. Conscious of the political sensitivities of the time, we'd peppered it with American heroes and Communist villains. It throbbed with love, lust, action, drama, magnificent scenery and splendid architecture. I could feel a catch in my throat as I reached the climax of my presentation. 'One question,' said the laconic boss of ABC, Brandon Stoddart. 'If we're going to do history, why Chinese, why not American?'

What could I say? I packed up my storyboards and stole silently away.

Two years later, in 1987, Bernardo Bertolucci won nine Academy awards for his film *The Last Emperor*, which told the story of Pu Yi, who began life as the last emperor of China and ended it as a jobbing gardener in post-revolutionary Beijing. He got Oscars for the Best Picture and Best Director. All I got out of it were some very expensive lessons in Chinese history.

In Hollywood, Sarah completed her career move from the law to television production. She found the atmosphere bracing. The point about this place, she told me enthusiastically, is that in the

UK, if you go to a meeting to try to sell an idea or sell yourself, the first thing people ask you is what you've done, what kind of a track record you've got. In Hollywood nobody's remotely interested in what you've done. They just want to know what you intend to do, and if they like what they hear they'll give you a chance. That had been her own experience and as a result she'd become a very successful production development executive. Her boss, Don Taffner, had begun his career as an agent and made a fortune when he bought the rights to the successful British TV comedy *Man About the House* and adapted it for US television. Sarah spent her time looking for other British programmes the American networks might be interested in transmitting.

Like everyone else in Hollywood she was selling, and loved it, but her real ambition as she confided in me during one of our heart-to-heart talks about my future was for us to go into partnership as a husband-and-wife production team. I couldn't see that working: she had been a literary agent and had little experience as a producer, so I suppose I felt she would be a virtual passenger in any joint venture. In the light of what she was later to accomplish when she started her own company, I seriously underestimated her.

Those who knew me best had predicted that I was bound to love Hollywood and Sarah would hate it; in fact, it was the other way round. I was chronically unsettled. I guess I didn't want to revert from being a buyer into being a seller – that, after all, was why I gave up being a theatrical agent. Perhaps it was a subtle form of laziness. I'd been used to sellers making their pitch while I sat back, weighed the odds, then said yes, no, or maybe. A seller has to make all the running, driven by a combination of optimism and desperation, and maybe I just wasn't hungry enough and could only take just so much rejection. Sarah's and my income gave us financial security, which took the edge off my drive. Even my own independent production company couldn't turn me back into a buyer. I was still knocking on doors, smiling in the face of rejection and trying again.

Perhaps the most striking evidence that Sarah had gone native in Hollywood occurred at my fortieth birthday party when one of the guests gave me as a present a voucher for a visit to Hollywood's most fashionable psychiatrist. Sarah didn't find anything odd about it! Everybody had not only their shrink but an army of so-called experts to sort out every aspect of their lives. Sarah and I once went to look at a house for sale up in the Hollywood Hills. It was in the middle of August and Hollywood was sweltering in an airless 98 degrees with smog blanketing everything. We were ushered into the vendor's living room and were struck immediately by this roaring log fire in the grate. He brought out a bottle of Château Margaux from his cooled cellar while this fire was turning the room into an oven. Eventually I had to say something. 'Gosh, that fire works a treat.'

'Yeah,' he said, 'I thought you'd really appreciate it. I took advice from my ambience man.' Ambience man! He had a consultant who advised him on the appropriate atmosphere to be created for any particular occasion, and since his visitors were English, a log fire was mandatory.

Hollywood is all about having the best personal consultants in the business. It was fatal to confess at a party that you had, say, back trouble. You were overwhelmed with personal testimonials. I was once invited to a tribute dinner for Frank Sinatra where the great stars were announced one at a time. 'And now the one and only Miss Elizabeth Taylor!'

The woman on one side of me said, 'Doesn't she look great?'

The man on the other responded, 'Yeah, I did most of her.'

I was intrigued to have Hollywood's most fashionable cosmetic surgeon as a table companion.

Sarah had a kind of wide-eyed innocence about such things: she was avid for new experience. Hers had been a fairly closeted life. Her upbringing was that of the county classes, she'd trained as a lawyer and had never known anything like the exotic milieu that was Hollywood. At one party, the guests started discussing their personal psychics, a pseudo-scientific term for what would be called fortune-tellers in an English seaside resort. Sarah was so impressed by what she heard that she decided to make an appointment to consult one, Ron Portante, up on Mulholland Drive above Hollywood. She arrived back, eyes alight, clutching a recording tape. I had to concede that some of the revelations about her past were amazingly accurate. She pestered and pestered me until I agreed to go and consult her great guru.

Off I went to see Brother Portante, who was a big fat queen enveloped in an enormous kaftan. His cell, as he called it, was lit only by candles and reeked of incense. He had a dark brown voice and soulful eyes. He asked to hold some object associated with me so I gave him my wedding ring. He started by saying that someone who was once very important in my life had a name beginning with the letter P. Penny – my first wife and the mother of my children! Perhaps there was something in this psychic business, after all. He went on to tell me that I had big decisions to make. But, then, who hasn't? Apparently, I was also about to make big money – as though anyone was in Hollywood for any other reason!

Sarah was completely sold on Brother Portante until she went one evening to a party and heard several guests singing the praises of a Mrs Someone or other in the Valley. Sarah just had to consult her and came back in a quandary. Ron, she felt, was excellent, but so was Madame du Bois, and the problem was that they were giving her conflicting advice about a career move she was contemplating. 'I wonder whether I could get them together on a conference call and then they could argue it out,' she mused.

'Whoa, stop right there,' I said. 'Just listen to what you're saying. Here you are, Sarah Lawson, laid back Home Counties girl and ace lawyer, proposing to call a conference of fortune-tellers, highly paid mountebanks, to sort out your future. Enough is enough!' After a while she saw the funny side of it, but there is no doubt that Sarah had swallowed Hollywood, hook, line and sinker.

My fundamental doubts about my great American adventure never really left me and they became most pressing at a time when there was an unexpected flutter of interest from the BBC. I had been careful to show my face from time to time in Britain during my Hollywood era. Every year I would fly over for the Edinburgh Television Festival, remind them that I still existed, crack a few jokes, then head back to Los Angeles. In 1983, I attended the Royal Television Society's biennial conference in Cambridge. In the bar after one evening session, I fell to drinking with Brian Wenham, by then director of programmes for BBC Television. Apparently several of my friends had confided in him that I seemed out of sorts in Hollywood and Brian, after a lucid and biting analysis of the state of the BBC, seemed in his usual convoluted prose to hint that there might be something for me at the BBC, should I consider coming home. It was nothing so definite as a firm job offer, but positive enough to tantalize me.

A month later I wrote to him frankly spelling out my state of mind:

> I left LWT for the fool's gold of Hollywood for several reasons. I felt I had done British TV (foolish boy); I faced a bleak financial future supporting an ex-wife and two children (whom I miss very much), a national debt-sized overdraft at Lloyds, and I wanted to remarry ... My two years here have proved a bit of a roller-coaster ride, at times thrilling, at times sickening, but all the same a heck of an experience. My situation within Embassy is very comfortable and secure, but I find I do miss the excitement of running a broadcasting schedule ... Controller of BBC 1 is the position that I know would reach parts of me that are currently untouched here or by other UK opportunities ... one of which is the offer to become Chief Executive of my Uncle Bernie's Leisure Conglomerate which is on the brink of being floated on the Stock Exchange.

From Brian's response to my letter it was clear that the job that he and Bill Cotton had in mind for me was not that of controller of BBC 1, a post they intended to abolish: they were planning a radical change in the management structure of BBC Television, replacing the controllers of BBC 1 and BBC 2 with a whole group of controllers of output – for drama, light entertainment, sport and so on. They had pencilled me in as controller of Drama and Film; in Brian's phrase I would be 'Lord Fiction'. It would be a huge empire, though Brian admitted frankly, 'The terms are, of course, miserable. We could plug you in at £37,500, which with a following wind becomes £40,000 or so next April. You get a nice motor car and all the food you can eat.' On the other hand, Brian promised, 'You will be extremely well placed to inherit the joint in due time. Alasdair [Milne, the director-general] will register with the governors your long-term potential.'

After that, we exchanged notes and postcards, just keeping alive the mutual interest. Brian came out to Los Angeles on a film-buying expedition and had a meal with Sarah and me. The discussion was all about the parlous state of the BBC, but he was even vaguer than last time about the possibility of my working at Television Centre so I decided he and Bill Cotton must have cooled on the idea.

Then in March 1984 Bill Cotton himself came out to California. He was still keen to restructure the television service and get me to run the fiction side. I had lost none of my enthusiasm for working with Brian and him: it was the draft scheme itself that bothered me. I wasn't convinced that this salami slicing of the power and resources of the TV service was a good idea. If I was to make a drastic financial sacrifice – and the promised £37,500 a year wouldn't have interested a Hoover salesman in Hollywood – then I wanted real power in exchange. I wrote to Bill in March 1984:

> What I am unable to come to terms with is the status of the job in a wider context. In an outside world used to channel controllers, it would be perceived as a step backwards for me. To join the BBC, I would have to feel the job offered to me the full range of opportunities to pick up where I left off two

and a half years ago. Therefore with great regret, after weeks (and long nights) of weighing and balancing, I've concluded the job is just not enough for me to give up everything here.

Reluctant to slam the door shut completely, I proposed to Bill as an alternative that I should run both channels, which was cheeky, since it would effectively make Brian Wenham, as director of programmes, redundant. But, as they say in Hollywood, I was desperately keen to close the deal so I hinted that if the restructuring didn't materialize, I would be open to discuss the possibility of my becoming controller of BBC 1 on the old model.

Much to my relief, Bill's restructuring came to nothing and we reverted to the possibility of my becoming controller of BBC 1. There was one almighty problem: the job was already taken. Alan Hart was sitting in that chair, so his future would depend on my decision, though, alas, he didn't know it. There were vague press rumours: 'We hear,' said a diary item in the *Sunday Times* in April 1984, 'that Michael Grade has been having "muffled talks" with BBC chiefs . . . but what job would Grade consider taking at the BBC? An obvious one would be controller of BBC 1, a role currently held by Alan Hart.' Alan had apparently not heard these rumours for the news of his removal hit him like a bolt from the blue while he and his family were on holiday in Greece. These BBC executives might look and sound like a bunch of bumbling Oxford dons but when it came to wielding the scalpel Hollywood hit-men could teach them nothing. And it was done with such panache: they could cut out your heart without spilling a drop of your blood.

For weeks I was in a state of total mental disarray. For someone who prided himself on acting by instinct I was all over the place, one day utterly sure my future lay with the BBC, the next racked with guilt about casting Sarah's career into the melting-pot. But a deadline was approaching. Bill needed a firm decision by midnight Hollywood time on Wednesday 23 May because the governors would be meeting the following morning.

I had two problems. As always, one was money: the Grade Company was paying me half a million dollars a year as a basic salary with the possibility of huge bonuses. The other was much more important than any financial question: Sarah had no desire to return to Britain. After much agonizing, I decided I had no right to sacrifice Sarah's prospects to my own happiness. After all, I had dragged her to Hollywood in the first place, and by sheer ability and persistence she had carved out a real niche for herself and a wonderful home for both of us. No, I would stay in Hollywood and press on with being an independent producer. But Sarah, who knew me very well and had a capacity, which I lacked, for putting her partner first, insisted on keeping the debate going. We paced up and down Sierra Alta Way in the balmy night air arguing hotly. Our dog Henry had never had such extended exercise. Eventually I looked at my watch, it was five minutes to midnight. I took refuge in cliché: if in doubt, don't. We went into the house to call Bill, with me still muttering about rejecting the BBC offer. Sarah dialled Bill and when he answered the phone she said, 'Bill, this is Sarah, he's definitely coming.'

In retrospect, it seems pathetic that I was relieved to have the decision taken out of my hands by a partner who was perceptive enough to know me better than I knew myself. Sarah was making the real sacrifice. For me there was the prospect of an exciting new job at the top of the greatest broadcasting organization in the world; for her, it would mean transatlantic commuting with all the strains that must put on our relationship. Though she enthused with me, had I paused for a moment amid all the frenetic preparations for the move back to Britain I might have noticed the sadness behind her eyes. Perhaps, deep down, she realized that in going along with my wishes she was sowing the seeds of the destruction of our relationship.

I felt that my career was back on track after a diversion which had added to the sum total of my television experience but didn't really fulfil me. When I left Hollywood, the rumour factory was awash with stories that I had been a failure in the

States. Interesting, then, that on my departure, Embassy TV was sold for $500 million to Coca-Cola. Bill Cotton said afterwards that I joined the BBC because he made me an offer I couldn't refuse. But I almost did refuse: it had been Sarah who clinched it.

Chapter Six

THE OLD INSTINCTS

To exchange Tinsel Town for Auntie was to undergo the ultimate culture shock. It was a voyage into a different thought-world. The BBC I joined was a community of highly creative programme-makers who, according to the Annan Commission, formed the most important cultural institution in the country. At least, it *was* a community until my erstwhile friend John Birt, like the engineer he was, took a spanner to it, then reassembled the resulting pieces to make a factory, all system and no soul. But that was later. Of all the possible problems and challenges I rehearsed in my mind on the flight across the Atlantic, a bruising conflict with John Birt was one I never remotely foresaw.

After the frenetic pace and brutal efficiency of Hollywood, everything about the BBC oozed well-bred restraint, from its temple-like headquarters with a Latin tag across the entrance hall to its senior executives, who talked and behaved like dons on sabbatical from an Oxbridge senior common room. It appeared to be one of those British institutions like the monarchy or the Church of England about whose inner workings it would be vulgar to enquire. Brilliant programmes seemed to get made almost as a by-product of the perpetual war of ideas that raged all over the place – and this was one of the secrets of its strength, for I had learned the hard way that ideas rather than money, resources or technical skills are the scarcest commodity in broadcasting.

On the flight over, I dipped into one of the popular histories of the BBC. Given the never ending debate about sex and violence on television, I was intrigued to read that as recently as 1961, the then chairman of the BBC governors, Sir Arthur fforde, was asked at a public meeting, 'Where does the BBC stand on bare bosoms?' He referred his questioner to Milton's *Areopagitica*, adding that perhaps a passage in Dante's *Divine Comedy* would also be helpful. He then recited the stanza in the original Italian. Since my grasp of Italian stretched to the average trattoria menu, the notion that as controller of BBC 1 I might be required to judge the saucier passages in *'Allo, 'Allo* and *Only Fools and Horses* by the standards of fourteenth-century Florentine literature taxed my imagination to the limit. But that was the tradition I was inheriting.

Being the ultimate outsider, I was apprehensive as well as excited about the prospect of joining the BBC. Unlike many of my former ITV colleagues, such as Paul Fox, Brian Tesler, Jeremy Isaacs, Brian Cowgill and Melvyn Bragg, I had never served an apprenticeship in the BBC: its language, customs and working practices were totally alien to me. I was also a Grade, which to some of the more supercilious BBC mandarins was a name synonymous with entertainment at its shrillest – high-kicking chorus girls and red-nosed comedians. These élitists, who apparently included a number of governors, regarded high-ratings popular shows as a regrettable necessity to fill the gaps between 'real' programmes, which had cultural and intellectual significance. Bill Cotton had been in the BBC for thirty years and was still viewed with deep suspicion in some quarters because he, too, came from showbiz. He fought a constant battle to get the BBC governors and his fellow managers to recognize that entertainment *was* the BBC's main business. Though the BBC Charter set out a trinity of aims, to educate, to inform and to entertain its licence-fee payers, Bill insisted that entertainment came first, not least because programmes that weren't entertaining wouldn't remain on the viewer's screen long enough to inform or educate anyone.

I was looking forward to weighing in on this debate without conceding anything to the culture-vultures about the importance of upmarket programmes. The BBC's founder, John Reith, had talked about giving the public the best of everything, not one sort of programming rather than another but each the best of its own kind. It would be a relief to be dealing again with a range of programmes across the board instead of concentrating on wall-to-wall sit-coms as I had to in Hollywood. Though my name was Grade, I was a classical Reithian, however hard my new colleagues might find that to believe.

A more sensitive matter was my relationship with Alan Hart, the outgoing controller of BBC 1. Back in 1981, when Bill Cotton, the then controller of BBC 1, had been promoted, the board of management was very keen that John Gau, the highly respected head of News and Current Affairs should get his job. John had everything it took to be a good controller: sound programme judgement, strength of character and the respect of the staff. Unfortunately, some months before, he had become embroiled in a major internal row when one of the *Panorama* crew for which he was ultimately responsible filmed an IRA road-block in the Northern Ireland village of Carrickmore, an incident that proved to have been staged for the cameras. The programme was never shown but news of it leaked out and incurred the wrath of the Prime Minister, Margaret Thatcher, who charged the BBC with giving terrorists 'the oxygen of publicity'. An internal investigation revealed that there had been a technical breach of the strict procedures for referring to senior management any proposed programmes on Northern Ireland. John was given an official reprimand, which was duly noted in his file, and life went on as usual, except that Mrs Thatcher now had even more tinder to fuel her vendetta against the BBC. Then John Gau's file with the dreaded leprosy spot on it was unearthed when he was interviewed for the controller's job. Neither Sir Ian Trethowan, the director general, nor Alasdair Milne as managing director of Television could persuade the governors to ignore this solitary and merely technical blemish.

He was turned down in favour of Alan Hart, who was head of Sport. Ironically, it had been my Snatch of the Day that had brought Alan to the governors' attention. He was not senior enough to make routine appearances at their meetings, but he was hauled in to report on the goings on with *Match of the Day*, and had impressed them.

Sadly, Alan's spell as controller of BBC 1 coincided with a period when the BBC's total ratings for both channels fell to 40 per cent and below – a figure felt to be lethal for the prospects of the future of the licence fee. It was therefore decided that Alan had to go. Having got used to the 'pink slip' culture of Hollywood, I was well aware that modern management is a rough old game, so I felt no undue sentimentality about replacing him. From all I knew of him, I had no reason to doubt that our dealings with each other would be highly civilized. But he was deservedly popular in the television service, so I wasn't quite sure how I would be received by his many friends and colleagues.

I was still amazed by the speed at which old Auntie could move when she really shook her bones. Bill Cotton had said he wanted me in London immediately, which left me with the problem of a million-dollar house in Sierra Alta Way to sell. The chairman of the governors, Stuart Young, solved that one by authorizing the BBC to buy the house from me to sell it on, which they did very quickly. I had been impressed by Stuart when he visited us in California during the 1984 Olympic Games. He was a self-made man, an accountant who had built up a vastly successful financial consultancy before being appointed a governor of the BBC by Mrs Thatcher. She assumed that, like his brother David Young whom she made a cabinet minister with a seat in the House of Lords, Stuart fell into the category of 'one of us' who would help bring the BBC to heel and subdue a management and staff totally out of control. To everyone's astonishment, including his own, Stuart went native and became a champion of the BBC's independence. When the contract of George Howard, landowner and larger-than-life eccentric, expired and he relinquished the chairmanship, Stuart was appointed. After a succession of resplendent establishment figures, Stuart was the first chairman in the Corporation's history to have his roots in the world of high-powered business, at home in those fraught areas where finance and politics meet.

The BBC's autumn season was looming and I was out of practice at scheduling television programmes, so before I left Hollywood, Bill Cotton had arranged for the late Roger MacKay, BBC 1's transmission planner, to fly out and show me what was on offer. In civil service terms, Roger was the permanent secretary with the controller as minister. Like all his kind, he had sound programme judgement and was totally discreet yet abreast of all the gossip floating around the production corridors about programmes being made – which were behind schedule or running over budget or experiencing staffing problems, the sort of intelligence vital to a controller trying to fill gaps. He and I sat by the swimming-pool in Sierra Alta Way and rewrote the autumn schedule. On my part it was a matter of trying to get my intuition functioning again, for I had never heard of most of the programmes he talked about. *Only Fools and Horses, Tenko, Just Good Friends* – what were they? Roger talked me through the skeleton schedule, programme by programme, summarizing their content and the rationale behind the time and day each was transmitted.

Tenko, a gripping drama about women from a variety of backgrounds interned in a Japanese prisoner-of-war camp in Singapore in 1942, had been transmitted on Thursday evenings, but to me it had the 'feel' of Sunday viewing. Acting solely on impulse and exhilarated to be getting back to my old trade, I hammocked it between *Only Fools and Horses* and *Just Good Friends*, which would make a solid spine to Sunday evening – a strong, satisfying, varied run of programmes for the culmination of the weekend. I had developed an instinct for television scheduling. A programme in the wrong place not only sticks out like a sore thumb but becomes a wasted resource. Months of hard production work can come to nothing if the slot in which the programme is placed isn't suitable. I had learned much from my uncle Lew, who had scheduled ATV in the pioneering days. I had cut my teeth in the commercial sector where scheduling as an art was most developed because the companies had to sell space at fixed times to advertisers; they needed to match programmes to available audiences with some precision. My spell at LWT taught me that while focus groups and market research can be very helpful, they are no substitute for old-fashioned gut-feel.

I headed for the BBC, hoping to be happy and certain to be poorer. One newspaper reported my appointment with the headline, 'The biggest pay cut in history – half a million dollars to £34,000 – I might just have to give up eating,' was my quoted comment. I knew nothing about the arcane workings of the BBC but I did understand the press, having served my apprenticeship on the *Daily Mirror*. It was clear that I had two options: I could either sink into the Trappist silence traditionally enjoined on BBC executives, or recognize that the press have a job to do and use publicity intelligently to keep the Corporation's achievements in the public eye. And if that meant some of the stories were personalized around me, then so be it.

Shortly after I joined the BBC I came across a headline in the *Sun* saying 'If you've got it, flaunt it!' On impulse I cut it out and pinned it to my office door. No doubt there were some clucks of disapproval from the BBC old guard at the sacrilege of a press clipping from the *Sun* (of all papers!) disfiguring a door on the semicircular management floor of Television Centre, whose heavy panelling and strategically placed plants reminded me of the reception area of a crematorium. But that was my style and it seemed to me that the BBC needed an injection of brazen self-confidence at a time of low morale and serious self-questioning.

In going out of my way from the beginning to court the press, or at least in taking no steps to avoid publicity, I was breaching a long-standing BBC tradition. On the whole, press officers in the BBC were employed to keep stories out of the newspapers. They blenched if the names of any of their bosses appeared in the public prints unless, of course, they were mentioned in the Court Circular or the list of those present at a memorial service. Here was an organization that had high-quality products to sell yet thought it vulgar to sell itself, except in a manner so genteel and restrained that hardly anyone noticed. It struck me when I was at LWT that the BBC just had no marketing strategy: it seemed to rely on serendipity – if listeners or viewers chanced upon a good programme, then it was by happy accident. The Corporation's attitude to selling its wares was still frozen in the era when it had a monopoly of broadcasting with a captive audience, who gratefully accepted whatever was handed out to them.

The creation of ITV against the BBC's bitter opposition changed everything, but it seemed that many at the Beeb hadn't noticed. Some of the governors in particular behaved as though the BBC was still good old Station 2LO transmitting from Savoy Hill and trying to ignore its embarrassingly large, noisy and very expensive accretion at the Television Centre. In 1977, in his report on the future of British broadcasting, Lord Annan had described the BBC as reacting to criticism like a 'hedgehog at bay'; it adopted much the same posture when confronted with publicity it hadn't generated itself. And before I had even set foot in the Television Centre, the *Observer* and the *Daily Mail* ran extensive interviews with me, and even my red socks and braces were matters for comment in the gossip columns. I gathered from Bill Cotton that there were those in the hierarchy who were not keen on all the publicity I was attracting. That was tough. I felt the BBC had the goods and we ought to flaunt them.

The Corporation was under intense pressure politically from the Tory government led by a Prime Minister who had never forgiven the BBC for the way it reported the Falklands War. What the BBC regarded as the principles of impartiality and objectivity, which had governed its news coverage through every national crisis since the 1926 General Strike, Mrs Thatcher interpreted as a lack of patriotism. At a notorious board of management dinner shortly before I arrived at the BBC, Mrs Thatcher, who was guest of honour, berated the BBC for its failure to give enthusiastic support to the British forces during the South Atlantic conflict. She was stopped dead in her tracks by Bill Cotton, who asked bluntly, 'Prime Minister, are you accusing the BBC of treachery?' And he still got the CBE!

Then in another assault, the Home Secretary, Douglas Hurd, complained publicly about the quality of BBC programmes, singling out a popular American mini-series called *The Thorn Birds*, starring Richard Chamberlain. Was this the sort of thing the licence fee should be spent on? he asked rhetorically, comparing it unfavourably with critically acclaimed dramas such as *The Jewel in the Crown* and *Brideshead Revisited*, which ITV had recently transmitted. Here was irony indeed, he opined, that an institution funded by the licence-fee payer was peddling imported pap while the commercial channel, paid for by those unapologetic capitalists the advertisers, was offering an uplifting home-grown cultural experience. And the BBC's offence was compounded by its decision to drop its flagship current-affairs programme *Panorama* for the duration of the mini-series run. This was the last straw for traditionalists for whom *Panorama* was more than a programme. It was an icon, which occupied sacred space and time – as I was to discover when I proposed moving it. Even before I set foot in the BBC I knew exactly where I stood on *The Thorn Birds* issue. Had I been controller at the time, I would unhesitatingly have bought and defended it vigorously. Fourteen million licence-fee payers watched and presumably enjoyed it. No television channel was able to churn out dramatic gems such as *Brideshead* routinely: they could afford neither the immense amount of production effort nor the financial cost. Unless the BBC was provided with a bottomless purse – and the government at the time was resisting any increase in the licence fee – hours and hours of air time had to be filled with comparatively cheap programmes to release the resources to make expensive dramas.

The Thorn Birds was popular entertainment, neither more

nor less. It was one of those 'What happens next?' stories people have been telling since the dawn of time. To 'entertain' means to occupy the mind agreeably, and the series certainly did that. Douglas Hurd implied that in buying and transmitting *The Thorn Birds*, the BBC merely hoped to attract mass audiences. What's dishonourable about that? The former home secretary has now blossomed as a fiction writer: would he regard low sales as a fair indicator of quality? I have never seen the need to be defensive about television programmes with popular appeal. After all, the lives of most people are driven not by high-falutin' cultural experiences but by simple ideas, broad emotional experiences and homespun convictions. Quality and popularity are not mutually exclusive.

The critics said that mini-series such as *The Thorn Birds* were eminently forgettable whereas the experience of watching great drama lingers in the mind long after the programme has ended. It is true that most television programmes are fated for extinction, to be forgotten soon after the final credits roll, and it's just as well. The human mind could not contain the torrent of fact, experience and action beamed at it from the television screen for twenty-four hours every day. Far from regarding the ephemerality of television as a bad thing, I have always been grateful that highly talented television producers are prepared to spend months lavishing skill and care on programmes that will interest viewers then be forgotten moments after the transmission is ended. It's a little like the virtuosity of a great chef, who puts immense effort into preparing a dish that will vanish in minutes.

That was and is my philosophy of popular programming, and there were those in the BBC who thought my appointment would herald a tidal wave of vulgarian programming compared to which *The Thorn Birds* was high culture. In some quarters, my name was associated with wall-to-wall game-shows rather than *The South Bank Show*, Alan Bennett plays and a whole raft of minority programmes for which I was responsible at LWT. I tried to counter the impression in every press interview I gave, insisting that I was not a populist at any price, and holding to the Reithian high ground; I hoped to offer the best of everything, not excluding imported mini-series if they were well made.

There is no doubt that Douglas Hurd's attack on the BBC intensified the feeding frenzy among right-wing papers who had been its traditional enemies. The Corporation was described as 'a juggernaut out of control'; BBC stood for 'British Bonking Corporation' or 'Biased, Bankrupt and Corrupt'. Max Hastings in the *Evening Standard* contemptuously dismissed the leadership of the BBC as 'pitifully inadequate, bankrupt of ideas and lost for a course', and the ineffable Paul Johnson characterized the BBC's Drama department as a Communist-style production Politburo churning out sleazy pornography with a political message. Something like panic swept through the BBC's corridors of power and there was an anguished search to locate the cause of the crisis. The chairman, Stuart Young, concluded that two appointments made by his predecessor had been disastrously mistaken. One was that of Alan Hart as controller of BBC 1; the other was the governors' choice of Aubrey Singer to head up the television service. When Alasdair Milne became director general in 1982, it had been widely assumed that Bill Cotton, who had been one of the most successful programme executives in the history of the BBC, would replace him as managing director of the television service. The governors had other ideas and got things spectacularly wrong. They chose Aubrey Singer, at that time managing director of BBC Radio. Though heading up the radio service, Aubrey had spent almost all his BBC career in television as head of Science Features and controller of BBC 2 and, more to the point, he was a vastly experienced programme-maker with detailed knowledge of the technical side of broadcasting. He would therefore have been the ideal person to launch the BBC's new venture in satellite broadcasting. Instead Bill Cotton, who cheerfully confessed his total ignorance of anything to do with the nuts and bolts of broadcasting, was moved sideways into that job and Aubrey took over at Television Centre.

In January 1984, Stuart Young and Alasdair Milne decided that Aubrey must go. He was dispatched with a combination of ruthlessness and conviviality after being invited to a day's shooting in Berkshire with no inkling that he and not the pheasants was the main target. In the car on the way back, after some desultory conversation, Alasdair suggested that Aubrey should take early retirement, very early, in fact, as soon as the paperwork could be done. Then Bill Cotton was duly appointed managing director of television and he and Alasdair set about correcting what they believed to be the other seriously mistaken appointment of the George Howard era, that of Alan Hart as controller of BBC 1 – which is where I came into the picture.

I inherited a somewhat drab office on the sixth floor of the Television Centre. In stark contrast to Hollywood's opulence, it had nothing much in the way of elaborate furnishings, but there was all I needed: four TV monitors and a couple of telephones. Settling in, I reflected on the convulsions within BBC management that had propelled me there and concluded the BBC's power structure was crazy. You had one group of people, the board of management, who had all the expertise in the world but no ultimate power, and a dozen governors who combined invincible power with total ignorance. Within the organization, the governors' power was virtually limitless. As a succession of chairmen had proudly or threateningly said, the board of governors *is* the BBC. The BBC Charter makes no mention of the director general or of the thousands of employees; the greatest broadcasting organization in the world consists of twelve amateurs appointed by the Government. In theory, they were intended to represent a cross-section of the public, but in reality, apart from the odd trade union official, the horny handed sons and daughters of toil didn't get a look-in. They were classic quango-fodder – landowners, academics, business leaders, assorted do-gooders, former ministers and civil servants. Not only were most of them ignorant of the way broadcasting works, some regarded it as a matter of pride that they rarely watched any programmes – as Sir Michael Checkland, usually the mildest of men, put it in an extraordinary outburst: 'When you talk to the governors about FM, you want to be talking about frequency modulation and not fuzzy monsters.' They were, he concluded, elderly people with no understanding of the realities of broadcasting.

Though historically the Home Office had attempted to maintain a rough kind of political balance in the composition of the board, Mrs Thatcher changed all that and filled vacancies with her kind of people, some of whom manifestly shared her dislike of the BBC. Shortly after he was appointed chairman, Marmaduke Hussey, attending a BBC function and in conversation with some of the staff, began a sentence, 'The trouble with *you* BBC types is . . .' evidently forgetting that, according to the Charter, *he* was supposed to be the BBC and they were just hangers-on.

This group of unrepresentative, undistinguished and uninspiring legatees of government patronage had the power to hire and fire dozens of the BBC's top executives, take any programme off the air and dispose of a billion pounds of licence-fee payers' money – and do it all in one day a fortnight since the job was intended to be a part-time hobby. In reality, the whole thing could only work if the governors refrained from using their great power and avoided interfering in the day-to-day running of the place, and that, in turn, depended on there being absolute trust between the governors and the board of management. By the time I reached the BBC, the two boards were in a state of virtual civil war with the director general Alasdair Milne and the then Sir William Rees-Mogg, vice-chairman of the board, leading the opposing forces. Tragically the chairman, Stuart Young, was now too ill to sort things out. However, my job was to get good programmes on the air, so I resolved to give the governors a wide berth and steer well clear of BBC internal politics. Fat chance!

I had to get used to the BBC's strange customs. The late and much lamented Frank Muir was assistant head of the Light Entertainment department of the BBC for three years in the 1960s. He made much sport of the acronyms by which the various grades of management were known and claimed to have discovered a senior executive in the information branch of the engineering group who was known as EIEIO. When – as well as being controller of BBC 1 – I became director of programmes, television, I was known as DPTel, and a memo addressed to me by the head of Sport, typed by a temporary secretary, went adrift and was eventually unearthed in a dead-letters pigeon-hole having been sent to D. Patel.

This system of nomenclature was a gift from the civil servants who helped Reith to set up the BBC along the lines of the public corporations that ran the water and electricity industries. These acronyms symbolized the formal structure of the BBC as a bureaucracy, and they weren't just for memo purposes: people were addressed by them: 'H Ops has been talking to C N Eye about D Eng's memo of the 3rd, and MDWS is not amused.' For a newcomer like me, ten minutes in a meeting where half a dozen apparatchiks were jabbering away in this sort of patois was like eavesdropping on a gathering of the Esperanto Society. At least in Hollywood the top mogul put his hand on your shoulder and addressed you as 'Chuck' or 'Hank' even if your name was Mike. Of course, he may well have been carrying a dagger in his other hand, but it was all done with hearty informality. In the BBC, the moment you received a memo you knew the degree of notice you'd better take of it because rank was signified by the first initial of the title: an H for Head was junior to a C for Controller, who deferred to a D for Director, who was outranked by an MD for Managing Director, and at the pyramid's point was the DG or Director General.

I found the de-personalizing effect of all this irksome. I was Mike Grade, the guy with boundless enthusiasm for everyone and everything to do with television. For good or ill, my name and personality were part of my stock-in-trade. I was used to picking up a phone or doing the business face to face. I kept my office door open and anyone was welcome to pop in and chat if I wasn't busy. No doubt management consultants would say this wasn't a systematic or economic use of my time, but I was able to talk with some interesting characters, get frank feed-back on programmes and catch up on the gossip around the place. In a bureaucracy as highly organized as the BBC, gossip was an essential means of discovering what was really going on. It added human interest and colourful detail to the sparse information seeping down through official channels.

I'm allergic to paper, but the BBC machine seemed to run on it as a car engine runs on petrol. I reluctantly concede that a percentage of those memos was necessary, but the rest just served to solve the problem of perpetual motion; committees and groups keeping themselves alive by devouring each other's minutes. There was also a pass-the-parcel element to the process: the poor devil who was last in the chain carried the can if anything went wrong because he or she was expected to do something about the memo that had been whizzing around the place before it landed on their desk. The snowstorm of paper that descended on me every morning was an incredibly time-wasting distraction, which I never got used to.

This endless red tape frustrated me because I knew the BBC's bureaucracy was not intended to be an end in itself: it existed to organize and sustain a community of programme-makers. As someone has said, the BBC is a monster, in the strict sense of the word, like the Greek centaur, half man, half horse, a creature made up of two divergent species. It is an industry for the mass production of works of art. The television studio complex is a factory as down-to-earth as those making plastic cups or soap powder and it is governed by financial laws and management principles just as stringent. It would be silly for even the most reluctant bureaucrat not to recognize this. What happens in studios and on location may be the reason for the organization's existence, but behind the scenes there needs to be teeming activity of the most humdrum kind to do with balancing books, equating supply and demand, conserving scarce resources, dealing with the unions and keeping the VAT man at bay. Even in the dream factory, the Television Centre, stardust has to be accounted for, speck by speck.

Yet the BBC is a mass industry only in the sense that an identical product, the programme, is transmitted into millions of homes simultaneously. Unlike a plastic cup, the product is individually crafted and intended to be a major or minor work of art. If the idea of an assembly line for manufacture of *Mona Lisa*s seems far-fetched, then even more bizarre would be an arrangement whereby Leonardo da Vinci had to win the approval of at least 50 per cent of the citizens of Florence for his work to keep the ducats flowing in. Substitute 'licence-fee payers' for 'citizens of Florence', and that was how those who set up the BBC decided its bills should be paid.

But the point is that each of the BBC's thousands of programmes on radio and television is an act of sustained creativity which in the last resort is to be judged not by the laws of industrial production but according to the principles of art. That sounds pompous, given the disparaging names television is known by – chewing-gum for the eyes, the square-eyed idiot, the box, the dream factory, electronic baby-sitter. Television, an art form? How could Goya's great painting *The Third of May 1808*, which depicts a Spanish civilian being shot by French invaders, occupy the same cultural universe as the mock execution of the café-owner Rene in BBC's *'Allo, 'Allo*? Shakespeare's *A Midsummer Night's Dream*, Donizetti's *Lucia di Lammermoor* and Cilla Black's *Blind Date* are all about match-making but Cilla is unlikely to qualify for a grant from the Arts Council – not that she'd need one. Yet what is art but the application of the human imagination, intellect and skill to some medium – words, canvas, musical notes, paint, marble or film stock – to add to the sum of our worthwhile experience? And that is what television does at its best.

And by 'at its best', I do not mean 'at its most culturally highbrow'. I have fought all my life against élitism in every form of entertainment and have nothing but contempt for the classical intellectual view that television is a medium of mindless entertainment, a great trash-generating engine that works against serious thought, critical standards and profound values.

In the early days of television it was considered a mark of virtue
never to watch the small screen, then later on, one might keep
a television set but only in the nursery to occupy the children.
It is fashionable, these days, for intellectuals to declare an
irrational weakness for the odd cult programme such as *Monty
Python's Flying Circus* or *Blackadder*. 'I like my entertainment
moronic,' confessed a Nobel Prize winner recently on radio,
pleading guilty to getting hooked on *EastEnders*. He spoke in the
regretful tones of someone owning up to a weakness for wife-
beating.

   Those who show cultural disdain for TV not only devalue the
creative efforts of others but also seriously underestimate the
impact of television on our society. Even popular entertainment,
which is assumed to have no serious purpose, is influential
because social values are most powerfully conveyed when they
pass unnoticed. A radical playwright who preaches left-wing
sermons through his characters may have less social impact than
a game-show host who cracks racist jokes. What a panel of
football experts do to our mother tongue on *Match of the Day*
('He done good, Jimmy!') influences the way the young speak
more than the precise use of academic English on *The Late Show*.
It is when people watch programmes with their feet up that their
guard is likely to be down. I have never underestimated the
social impact of television entertainment, which is why I believe
it must be treated as an art and judged by exacting standards.

   As soon as I joined the television industry, I discovered that
there is an in-built tension between managers and programme-
makers that cannot be completely resolved. Many talented programme-makers find talk about budgets, resources and staff costs
positively Philistine; they feel that they should be able to spend
on a programme whatever it costs to do it properly without
having to worry about budgets; after all, there is no record of
Michelangelo's work being costed by accountants. On the other
hand, as a manager I soon learned that whereas a solitary artist
in a garret is free to choose between his next meal and an extra
pot of paint, once hundreds of artists have to be supported the

rules change. When there is only so much canvas and paint to go round and an army of mini-Leonardos dipping into it, somebody has to ensure that everyone gets a fair daub or, more controversially, assign priority to A's work over B's. This somebody is the manager and he wins few Oscars for telling a programme genius he or she has to suspend work on the television equivalent of the Sistine Chapel ceiling because the scaffolding is needed elsewhere.

However impatient I was of BBC bureaucracy, I determined to be an efficient manager, but my philosophy was simple: the BBC existed to make programmes, everything else was housekeeping. This was by no means a universally accepted doctrine in the upper reaches of the BBC. The whole hierarchical system operated on the unspoken assumption that policy made programmes: boards of governors and of management, editorial bodies and advisory committees laid down the law about the overall shape of the output and the staff took it from there. In fact, in all but the most global sense – to do with the disposition of huge resources and whole programme strands – things worked the other way round: policy did not make programmes, programmes made policy. The range and quality of a television channel's output owed much more to free-for-all competitiveness among producers than to the decisions of policy-makers.

As I was to learn, good programme ideas rarely originated from the executive suites of Broadcasting House or the Television Centre. The process began when a producer sold an idea to a controller who decided to take a risk on it, putting up the money and resources. Sometimes the gamble failed and the programme never saw the light of day or else it didn't appeal to viewers and took a nose-dive in the ratings. But if the programme worked and became popular, or even if it didn't do too well in the ratings but was highly appreciated by those who did see it, it became part of the schedule. Eventually, the board of governors might endorse it with a lordly murmur of approval, but never in my time at the BBC can I recall an occasion when they proposed programme ideas or urged producers to take more risks.

In spite of saying all the right things in the BBC's annual reports, the governors acted more to curb creative risk-taking than to encourage it.

EastEnders was a case in point. Throughout the entire production process, the governors hummed and hawed, doubted whether the goings-on in a London square would interest viewers, tut-tutted at some of the plot lines and grumbled at the cost. Some even felt that soap operas like *Coronation Street* were all very well on the commercial channel because it was funded by glossy advertising, but they would lower the tone of the BBC. However, once *EastEnders* hit the top ten, the governors could not have been more proprietorial and self-congratulatory had they dreamed it all up themselves in the boardroom. When Mrs Mary Whitehouse launched a public attack on the loose morals of the inhabitants of Albert Square, one or two governors had second thoughts, notably the redoubtable trade union leader and salvationist the late Sir John Boyd. He wound himself up into a fearful rage and distanced himself from the whole enterprise so vehemently that one would have thought *EastEnders* had been slipped through the board's agenda one afternoon when he was dozing after an ample lunch. But this is what comes from allowing arrogant amateurs to second-guess the professionals.

I have always believed that programmes should make policy and not the other way round. Three years later, this conviction was to put me fundamentally at odds with the great ideologue, John Birt, and lead to my abrupt departure from the BBC.

When I first joined the Corporation, though, John was still my dear friend from LWT days. When I got back to London we had a jolly reunion and looked forward to being in keen but friendly competition with each other.

I was fortunate in my immediate colleagues at the Television Centre. Bill Cotton, Brian Wenham and Graeme McDonald were three of the best and most experienced professionals in the business. Bill Cotton had established a unique authority in the BBC's power structure. Though a BBC man through and through, he had none of the standard characteristics of the breed, public-school accent and suave manner. He was noisy, ebullient and convivial, reminding everyone who first met him of his famous band-leader father – prematurely bald with a moon face and horn-rimmed glasses. He also had his father's ability to get on with anybody. He was shrewd, with the kind of street wisdom you are unlikely to acquire at Oxbridge. One of his favourite sayings was, 'The best thing about being mediocre is you're always at your best.' This self-disparagement came partly from genuine astonishment that he had managed to rise to the top in the BBC over the heads of any number of intellectually brilliant, highly professional middle managers, but it was also a tactic he deployed very cleverly. Confronted with a thorny problem, he'd scratch his head, shuffle papers about and mumble that the whole thing was beyond him, and everybody would fall about trying to help him out while Bill listened carefully and decided who was talking the most sense. Theories were not his strong point, but he knew how to size up people; he may not have known the answer but he'd be on first-name terms with someone who did.

One of Bill's great strengths was that he had no unfulfilled ambitions. He knew he would never become director general so he could be brutally outspoken in a board of management most of whose members were auditioning for the top job. Bill venerated the BBC and was quite prepared to take on Mrs Thatcher and other members of her government when they abused the Corporation's hospitality and delivered anti-Beeb diatribes. He was the director general's confidant and spent hours sitting in Alasdair's kitchen chewing the fat over a dram or two of whisky. Stuart Young also came to trust him and talked to him in confidence. It's a great pity that, at crucial points during my time in the BBC, Bill's advice was sought, listened to respectfully, then ignored.

Bill knew the BBC system backwards and he taught me much about BBC psychology. I recall that when Michael Checkland was in charge of all the resources of the television service, he changed the accounting rules – the way in which programme monies were to be spent and resources allocated. As the eager new boy, I went to great trouble to get the new system into my head and then called a meeting of all television heads of department where I explained it to them at length. I thought my exposition a *tour de force*, and even Bill, who had sat in on the meeting, was duly impressed.

'Well,' I said, preening myself, 'just to make sure everyone's got it clear, I'll drift back to my office and spell it out in a memo.'

'For Christ's sake, don't do that,' said Bill. 'You'll set off hundreds of the best brains in the business trying to work out ingenious ways round the thing. As long as it's just verbal, it's your word against theirs and you have the stripes.'

Because there were two generations of friendship between the Cottons and the Grades and we had both cut our teeth in show business, we were on the same wavelength from the outset, but I came to appreciate enormously his generosity of spirit. He had been one of the most successful controllers of BBC 1 in the Corporation's history. In 1996, when he was the subject of Michael Aspel's *This Is Your Life*, an endless stream of celebrities poured on stage to pay tribute to his influence on their careers – Terry Wogan, Russ Conway, Bruce Forsyth, Esther Rantzen, Sue Lawley, Vera Lynn, Ernie Wise, Jimmy Tarbuck, Sandy Shaw, Cilla Black, Mike Yarwood, David Jacobs, Pete Murray and the two Ronnies. Bill probably did more than any other individual in post-war times to shape popular entertainment on television through spotting and nurturing showbiz talent, launching new programme formats and winning large audiences by shrewd scheduling. Human nature being what it is, I would not have been surprised had he felt possessive about his beloved BBC 1, but he rejoiced at my successes, supported me enthusiastically even when I made changes to the structure he had established and, above all, he protected me from all the internal politicking at Broadcasting House.

Brian Wenham was director of programmes at the Television Centre when I arrived. His was the sharpest brain on the board of management and he was generally thought to be one of the most able figures in British broadcasting. He had been controller of BBC 2 and transformed its fortunes at a stroke by introducing snooker to the small screen in the 1970s. Here was irony that this great lover of opera and theatre, a leading figure at the Institute of Contemporary Arts, turned to that working-class sport, snooker, as an audience builder. He made the Crucible Theatre, Sheffield, where the snooker tournaments took place, as familiar a location to millions of viewers as Lords or the Centre Court at Wimbledon. On the other side of the Thames, at LWT, we often spoke of him as a future director general of the BBC.

Brian had been editor of *Panorama* and head of News and Current Affairs so he was a highly political animal. I found his comments on the passing scene in Mrs Thatcher's Westminster perceptive and funny; in fact, whenever something of significance happened in the big world outside the BBC, a coterie of Wenham disciples would gather spontaneously in his office for an animated debate. Since the BBC was going through yet another period of turmoil, there was deep suspicion down the M40 at Broadcasting House that Brian and his little group were plotting some kind of management coup. Nothing could have been further from the truth. Wenham's confidants were much too independent-minded, irreverent and quirky to make effective conspirators. Though I had the office next door, I never became part of the Wenham salon, not because I wouldn't have been welcome but through a rather priggish determination to give time to nothing other than getting BBC 1's schedules right.

Before I arrived at the BBC, I had decided that Brian might be trouble because of his Machiavellian reputation within the Corporation as a schemer and plotter – a game I had neither the expertise nor interest to pursue. A shrewd and experienced former BBC producer called Terry Hughes with whom I had worked in Hollywood said that the only thing BBC managers worried about was their next job. I always felt that about Brian: his eye was on the play two moves ahead, the DG's chair. And

why not? He was up to the job. I remember, when I was still at
LWT, that Brian Tesler, who had some responsibility for appointing the first chief executive of the soon-to-be-launched Channel
4, expressed his disappointment that Brian Wenham had not
applied for the post. He asked me to sound Brian out so we had
tea at the Grosvenor House Hotel. Brian spoke with complete
candour: for him Channel 4 would be a sidetrack. He spelt out
a possible set of permutations and combinations of pieces on
the managerial chessboard that, if he was lucky, would propel
him right to the top in the BBC. The luck ran against him, but I
was fascinated once I joined the BBC to see how close to
fulfilment his battle plan had come.

I always felt that, bright though he was, Brian was not as
shrewd an operator in the internal power game as Bill Cotton.
There are times when it is necessary to brush aside complexities
and thrust to the heart of the matter. Bill was good at that,
whereas Brian's thought processes were so subtle that it was
not always clear to simple minds like mine just what he was
saying. Twice during the time I was in Hollywood I had conversations with Brian about the possibility of my joining the BBC.
When I recalled them afterwards, they were full of hints and
speculations; one supposition piled on top of another until they
made up an elaborate structure of ifs and buts, but nothing
concrete enough to count as a definite offer. His harsher critics
called him elusive and cited his genius for being somewhere
else when a major crisis broke in the BBC. Brian made a joke
of it. He once sent Bill and me a holiday postcard from the
Aegean. A fishing smack bobbed on an azure sea and lying in
the bottom of the boat was a fisherman asleep with a straw hat
over his face. Brian inscribed it, 'This is me, keeping my head
down.'

I don't think Brian was a very decisive man. Beneath the
layers of sophistication there was a kind of tentativeness, perhaps
because he had a family history of cardiac trouble. His father
died young of heart failure and Brian had already had his first

attack when I knew him; I always sensed that behind his formidable exterior there was fragility, detachment, a sense that he was living on borrowed time. He was very much Alasdair Milne's protégé, so his fate was closely tied to that of the director general. In 1982, two years before I joined the BBC, Alasdair had asked Brian to become his assistant director general with responsibility for all the Corporation's journalism. He turned the job down and was instead appointed director of programmes at the Television Centre, which gave him for the first time a seat on the BBC's board of management.

Because of his powerful mind and elegant written style, in 1985 Brian was asked to co-ordinate the Corporation's response to the Peacock Committee on Financing the BBC, which Margaret Thatcher had set up with the expectation that it would tell the Corporation to take advertising. In the event the BBC got a clean bill of health, largely thanks to Brian and his team who wrote the BBC's submission and organized a skilful press campaign making the case for continuing to finance the Corporation through the licence fee.

After this triumph, Brian should have been on course for the top job, but his career was so linked to Alasdair's that when Milne was fired in 1987, Brian was doomed. It must be said that he could be too sardonic for his own good and had a biting, wounding wit, which made him enemies, especially among the governors. In particular, the vice-chairman, William Rees-Mogg, seemed to detest him as a world-weary cynic who was too clever by half and had no convictions.

The post of director of programmes in the television service was a curious one. Brian himself described it as the television equivalent of the managing editor of a newspaper, who is often charged with checking expenses and running the administration. He is also meant to be a super-editor of journalistic content, a sort of clearing house, so that suddenly there weren't four documentaries on fly-fishing being made at the same time. Truth to tell, it was a job with more political than managerial significance – a sort of parking place for executives on the way to the very top where they waited for dead man's shoes or the next reshuffle. In a way, the director of programmes was a nut between nut-crackers. Above him was the overall boss, the managing director, who had ultimate power, and below him were the controllers of BBC 1 and BBC 2 who made all the crucial decisions about money and programmes.

In 1986 when I replaced Brian as director of programmes I also kept my original job as controller of BBC 1 – otherwise I wouldn't have had enough to do. I think that was Brian's problem: he was bored. He was an immensely talented man whose skills were not being fully used, which is why he spent hours running a private debating society. But I liked him enormously. He had all kinds of endearing habits. The first thing he would do on arriving at the office in the morning was take off his shoes and for the rest of the day he'd pad around the corridors in his stockinged feet as though he were still at home, which in a sense he was because television was his life. He shared my aversion to memos: whenever he got one, he'd send it back with totally illegible comments scrawled over it in green ink. And he could summarize hours of discussion in the board of governors with one devastating witty sentence, delivered deadpan. A lovely man.

I became devoted to my fellow controller, Graeme McDonald, who was responsible for BBC 2. In many ways, BBC 2 languishes in the shadow of big brother BBC 1, which gets the lion's share of resources, the high-ratings programmes, the constant attention of the governors and most of the press publicity. Graeme and I devised a way of working together as a team, scheduling in such a way that if I was committed to showing a programme which, for whatever reason, was unlikely to be a ratings success, I would warn Graeme so that he could put out one of his stronger programmes against it. We used this complementary scheduling with great effect against the opposition, for though ITV and Channel 4 were joined at the hip financially, they hadn't at that time found a way of walking in step when it came to joint programme planning.

Graeme was quiet and undemonstrative, with a delightfully mischievous sense of humour. He had been a distinguished drama producer, starting his career at Granada then joining the BBC to produce *Thirty Minute Theatre* and *Play for Today*, before becoming head of Drama, Series and Serials. He had excellent programme judgement and taught me a lot about the finer points of drama production. He was entirely without ego and never showed the slightest sign of jealousy about the enormous amount of publicity generated by my appointment and early days as controller of BBC 1. We shared the same sense of humour and programme philosophy and I was fortunate to have him as a friend.

The colleague I found most enigmatic was the director general, Alasdair Milne. I had the impression he wasn't ecstatic about my appointment, though he must have approved it, probably because he had great confidence in the judgement of Bill Cotton and Brian Wenham, and it didn't hurt my case that the chairman was very supportive. Alasdair was always perfectly amiable, except for a curious habit of addressing me, and most of his other colleagues, as 'Boy'. His father had been a medical missionary in India and I assumed this designation was a hangover from the days of the Raj until Bill Cotton put me right. 'What you've got to understand,' said Bill, 'is that Alasdair was head of school at Winchester.' Another theory was that he had picked up the habit from the charismatic Welshman Donald Baverstock, who had been his boss during the early years of his BBC career. Whichever. It made for a curious relationship with senior executives, most of whom were older than he was. To be fair, his wariness about me was understandable: he had been managing director of BBC Television at the time of my 'Snatch of the Day' coup and went on air in a fury to denounce my ITV colleagues and myself as 'mafia with cheque-books'.

On paper, Alasdair was a classic BBC mandarin – Winchester

and Oxford, a spell as a national-service officer in a good regiment, then straight into the BBC, where he rose effortlessly through the ranks. He was one of the first generation of BBC executives who had spent almost all their careers in the television service. He knew the business backwards. He certainly did not behave like one of the management species referred to disparagingly by the troops as 'suits'. There was nothing of the urbane diplomat about him. He dressed more like a country gentleman than a city slicker and there was often an abstracted look in his eye as though he longed to be up to his thighs in a salmon river fly-fishing rather than dealing with mountains of paper in Reith's old third-floor office at Broadcasting House. He was very bright, quick to get the point of a discussion or document, equally quickly bored by it all and impatient to move on. He could be by turns charming and considerate or irascible and tactless. Those who knew him best claimed that, though he could look and sound fierce, underneath he was a pussycat, which is reassuring unless you happen to be a mouse.

Temperamentally, Alasdair and I were at opposite ends of the spectrum of human types. He had his mates, who gathered in his office in the late afternoon for a convivial dram, and I wasn't one of them. Although the job of controller of BBC 1 was at that time regarded as the most strategically significant in the Corporation, I was only invited to his office twice in three years, and one of those occasions was to be interviewed for his job. By nature, I operated by persuasion and consensus and, frankly, enjoyed popularity so long as it wasn't earned at the expense of my principles. I saw no point in antagonizing people for the hell of it. My experience as an agent had taught me that people are more likely to buy a product, whether it is a programme, a star or an idea, from a friend rather than an enemy. Alasdair was so supremely self-confident in his own judgement that there was sometimes a take-it or leave-it note to his voice, as though he were implying, 'If you don't see things the way I do, you're a fool.' This could be counter-productive when he needed to win people over. It was precisely because he had been unable to persuade the governors to accept his nominee for the job of controller of BBC 1 in 1981 that I was eventually brought in three years later.

But Alasdair was a good man, brought down partly by bad luck and partly by errors of judgement that multiplied until his position became untenable. And one could forgive him almost anything because he had a deep love of the BBC, unlike those who deposed him. They gave the impression that they detested the place and were determined to stamp out every vestige of the old traditions and remake the BBC in their own image. But we haven't got that far yet.

My first and most urgent task was to restore the morale of the producers who had gone on doggedly making programmes while the storms of controversy raged over their heads. They seemed to be working in a vacuum because those responsible for monitoring their output were distracted by the alarms and excursions on the management floors. Programme-makers had no idea whether their work was good, bad or indifferent because no one offered them feed-back. They got their ideas commissioned, fought for budgets and a slice of air time, made the programmes, took their salaries and that was that. They heard no more.

Hence, I spent weeks with a staff telephone directory beside me, sitting and watching the output, programme by programme. When a programme was over, I would phone the producer and, if I decently could, offer words of congratulation and encouragement. I would also discuss with him or her the scheduling process, getting their views about such matters as the length of the programme and the time of its transmission. It seemed to me vital in those first few weeks that I should be very visible so that those in the engine room would know that the bridge was manned and they were valued members of the crew. I deliberately sought high visibility, which besides allowing me to shout loudly about the BBC's achievements, distracted the attention of the press from the internal squabbles that had for months produced countless column inches of damaging stories.

One of my pet hates had long been the Miss World contest. I thought it vulgar in the wrong sense, demeaning to women in its motivation and utterly fatuous in its format. Leaving aside questions of taste, it just wasn't good television, so I was glad ITV had taken it over. But I discovered that BBC 1 still transmitted the Miss Great Britain competition from the Spa Esplanade, Morecambe. As soon as the programme contract would allow, I dropped it. There were bellows of outrage from borough councils on the North Lancashire coast, but I was not to be moved: parading girls in swimming costumes and asking them asinine questions to prove that they had brains as well as boobs was an anachronism, and I didn't want it on my channel. I was accused, of course, of élitism, no doubt by the same critics who were convinced that I had been imported to drive the BBC downmarket.

In those first few days, a jocular off-the-cuff remark I made about the appearance of BBC weathermen created uproar. For three years in the United States I'd become accustomed to weather forecasters who had the dress and manner of encyclopedia salesmen, smooth and slick, then I returned to Britain and was struck by Met Office weathermen dressed for the most part as what they were, boffins, all sports coats with leather patches at the elbow and mad-scientist hairdos. When I was asked at a press conference what I would like to change at the BBC, I realized it was too early for portentous policy statements, and casting around for something to keep the reporters off sensitive BBC management matters, I said that while I'd been away in Hollywood our weathermen didn't seem to have washed their hair. Oh dear! There were cries of outrage from Bill Giles, Michael Fish and Ian McCaskill, one of whom gave me a detailed rundown of his daily coiffure, including the make of baby shampoo he used. The following week, my suggestion to Robin Day that he should not sign off *Question Time* with his usual admonition for viewers to sleep well – for the obvious reason that it wasn't fair to the programmes that followed his – provoked a *Sun* editorial. Stories like this kept the popular press busy and the

BBC in the headlines about something that interested the general public more than the Byzantine power struggles within the organization.

But this was part of the froth and bubble of the business, which helped to create a general buzz of interest and excitement that raised the drooping spirits of BBC staff. The more serious task was to get some good programmes on the air. Though the image is hackneyed, a television schedule is like a supertanker, it's a long, slow business changing its course. The programmes available to me had been commissioned by my predecessor possibly eighteen months or even two years before. I was bursting with ideas, but it would be a long time before most of them could be translated into programmes. Scheduling programmes already commissioned by someone else was alien to my way of doing things. Traditionally, some stars and programme formats had been around the BBC for so long that one series followed another as a matter of course. The result was that the controller ended up taking whatever programmes the production departments gave him, then found slots for them. Ideally, I preferred to work as much the other way round, first deciding the composition of the audience at a particular day and time and what category of programme would fit, then telling a production department to develop some ideas and make it.

But this method will only work if one knows as much as possible about audiences and their tastes. Scheduling is an instinct, which must be backed by research. The BBC had a broadcasting-research department that measured audiences and found out what viewers thought of the programmes they had seen. I found the department very laid-back and unsystematic compared to ITV's equivalent where the profitability or even survival of television companies depended on being able to tell advertisers just how many viewers, and of what class, age and sex, were watching a given programme, quarter-hour by quarter-hour. The BBC's head of Broadcasting Research, Peter Menneer, was a rather lofty academic who gave the impression that his department existed to serve some higher scientific purpose than the practical business of helping to increase BBC audiences. However, the member of his department he had assigned to the television service, Pamela Reiss, a statistician, had flair and enthusiasm which had hitherto remained untapped. I recruited her as a colleague, ignoring the BBC's hierarchical system, which expected me to deal with her through her boss.

Pamela confirmed or challenged my instincts with hard facts. Systematically we went through the schedule, testing each element against the results of a specially commissioned audience survey. It revealed that many of the assumptions which had shaped the structure of BBC Television over the years were fallacious. It all seems very obvious, but we discovered that viewers think naturally in terms of hours and half-hours while BBC programmes had traditionally begun at all kinds of strange times, such as twenty to or ten minutes past the hour; viewers who turned to the channel without consulting the *Radio Times* or television listings in newspapers found that the programme they wanted had already started. We also found that many viewers watched a stream of programming without registering what was on or when, so that they often couldn't tell the researchers which programmes they had seen the night before. This strengthened my conviction that television schedules must have fixed time points that are almost like alarm clocks in viewers' minds, subconscious reminders that six o'clock is news time, seven thirty marks the start of *EastEnders*, and so on.

Slowly the skeleton of a rational and effective schedule began to emerge. After months of casting around for patterns and trends, I began to feel I knew what I was doing. There is, however, little point in matching programmes to slots unless they are vigorously promoted so that viewers know where to find them. We had to sell our programmes much more aggressively. I was astounded to discover that the senior members of the Promotions department had not had regular meetings with the controller for years. I carved a slice out of my diary and conducted a weekly post-mortem on what I had seen on the screen, asking what logic lay behind the choice of clips they used to trail programmes. I also saw to it that more time was made available between programmes to advertise forthcoming attractions and put up more money so that in their own way trailers were as polished as the programmes to which they drew attention.

In general, I was frustrated by the lack of any flair, any showmanship, around the place. At least, if it existed, it had gone rusty with disuse. Showmanship might be a distasteful concept to the purists in BBC management but television was becoming a cut-throat, highly competitive business. The advent of Channel 4 had changed everything. The BBC no longer had the luxury of deploying two channels, offloading minority programmes on to BBC 2 while BBC 1 put out popular programmes against an ITV that had only a single channel. It had to find room both for high-ratings shows and minority programmes to fulfil its public service obligations. Now ITV and Channel 4 were beginning to work more closely together, and scheduling against them was a more complicated business. My first Christmas as controller was a good one, though much of the credit was due to my predecessor, Alan Hart. The festive season is the great battleground between the BBC and ITV when the public, replete with food and drink, settles down to be entertained. For years, the backbone of the schedules on both channels had been feature films suitable for family viewing, but the film studios couldn't produce blockbusters in sufficient numbers to keep television channels supplied. Hence Alan Hart had commissioned a number of full-length editions of popular TV series such as *All Creatures Great and Small* and *Last of the Summer Wine*. The viewers loved them.

Modesty aside, I believe that the pattern of my scheduling also contributed significantly to the BBC's good showing and went some way to justify the hype that accompanied my appointment. But I was in for a long haul and needed to refresh the schedule radically, which meant, among other things, doing an audit of BBC Television's available talent.

Enter Jonathan Powell, the BBC's head of Drama. He appeared in my office one day, blinking through his granny

glasses, with a quiet voice and diffidence of manner that belied
his brilliant record. He had produced John le Carré's espionage
epics *Smiley's People* and *Tinker Tailor Soldier Spy* and the evocative
Barchester Chronicles. The subject under discussion was a soap
opera to compete against ITV's highly successful *Coronation Street.*

The BBC's programme scrapyard was littered with failed soap
operas. There was *Compact* about a women's magazine; *United!*
which recorded the goings on at second-division club Brentwich;
The Newcomers about a number of London families relocated in
a Suffolk town – but none really caught the public imagination.
As I got to know the BBC, I suspected that these attempts had
not failed because of any lack of skill and experience in the
drama department, the deadening pressures of the internal
culture of the Corporation must have had their effect. It was as
though there were an invisible vulgarity threshold over which
the BBC was reluctant to step. Whether it was the ghost of John
Reith snorting from on high or the gravitational pull of
long tradition, there always seemed to be a pall of embarrassment hanging over the Television Centre when the BBC tried
to let it all hang out and produce the kind of popular programmes ITV did so well. There was also a certain intellectual
snobbery at work in the upper reaches of the BBC, which showed
itself in a greater willingness to take the risks involved in, say,
political controversy than those inherent in down-to-earth entertainment. Some governors and BBC bosses would enthuse about
the merits of *The Archers* and other 'wireless' classics but shudder
at the thought of defending *Blankety Blank* or *The Generation
Game.*

Soap operas have always been the targets of cultural disdain.
In fact, they are the offspring of two highly respectable parents,
one of which is talking-heads television. At their heart is always
one or more families, whose members spend much time gossiping about life and relationships, health and money and crime. It
is no accident that pubs figure so largely in the soap opera – the
Rovers Return and the Queen Vic are places where people
congregate and talk. We eavesdrop on the inconsequential chat

of life but salted with serious issues – for the other ancestor of soap opera is the medieval morality play. Though soap operas have come under fire at one time or another from moralists for setting a bad example to young people because drug trafficking, murder, adultery, homosexuality and blackmail may feature in their plots, much screen time is also taken up with the themes of family solidarity, racial tolerance, care for the elderly, battles to save a stormy marriage, coping with depression and a whole gamut of other virtues, earthed in a totally believable community with its share of human fallibility and wickedness.

EastEnders, for example, also dealt with a whole series of social and medical problems and was praised by the government for the responsible way it handled such issues as Aids, abortion, cancer and suicide. Mrs Mary Whitehouse attacked an episode of *EastEnders* in which one of the characters had to become a stripper to stave off poverty. The president of the National Viewers' and Listeners' Association claimed I would stop at nothing short of murder to increase ratings and that the realism of *EastEnders* was a cynical violation of family viewing time. In the event, she won little public support because the situation *EastEnders* dramatized was all too common in a society where unemployment among young people was so high. There was nothing gratuitous about the way one character's decision to take off her clothes for money was handled: it had the ring of true life about it. It would be silly to claim for soap operas the status of deathless works of art, but they have an important role in maintaining the overall balance of television entertainment. They bring stability and continuity to the schedules. If conventional drama is about crisis and resolution then soap operas are anti-drama in the sense that crises are never finally resolved, one just follows another *ad infinitum*. There is no final curtain, only a fade to black. Time looms ahead, open-ended, so viewers can miss any number of episodes and yet hook back without any sense they've ever been away. Individual episodes, though they may be beautifully made and acted, have much the same significance as separate squares in an endless strip cartoon.

This tradition of telling stories in episodes goes back a very long way. Until the end of the nineteenth century it was the custom for prominent authors to recite their works aloud in public. Dickens travelled the world giving readings from the latest instalment of the serials, which later became great novels, often bringing a recital to a dramatic conclusion without having the foggiest idea what happened next. And his fans queued up in the streets to buy that day's newspaper hot off the press because it contained the latest instalment of his current novel. It is this tradition that the television soap opera continues, and I have never felt the need to apologize for the genre. What was good enough for Dickens is good enough for me. When I was at LWT, I once commissioned a series based on adaptations of R. F. Dangerfield's books. Sadly, the project didn't work out, but I did come up with a good title, 'People Like Us'. That's what the soap opera is all about.

Bill Cotton and Brian Wenham had both recognized the urgent need for a successful soap opera to provide the spine of early-evening viewing on BBC 1, and Alan Hart had encouraged research and development. I in turn inherited the challenge and I was anxiously awaiting a progress report from Jonathan Powell. He told me that when he had become BBC head of drama, a trial script had already been written: the location was a caravan site for retired people in the north-east. My heart sank, then lifted again as he went on, 'The first thing I did was to scrap that idea, which meant my casting around for something to replace it.' He then described how he had gone to visit some friends in the East End of London, which was rapidly becoming gentrified, though Cockney life went on in the old way in one or two marvellous old squares around Stepney and Mile End. An East End square: he had decided that was where the projected soap opera would be set. He had brought in the producer of a gritty twice-weekly drama serial about nurses, called *Angels,* Julia Smith, who in turn recruited the writer Tony Holland, who had worked with her on *Z Cars.* They were busy sketching out the characters and story-lines.

I said words of congratulation and encouragement, and Jonathan asked if I would like to see the final scripts as they were produced. I demurred. What was the point in having talented producers like Jonathan Powell and Julia Smith unless one trusted them? But I would be delighted and relieved to see the first episode. We talked money and production schedules and I was a much happier man when he left the office than I had been when he came in. Everything he said and the confidence with which he said it gave me the feeling that this soap opera would work. If it proved to be an audience winner, half my problems were over . . . If it didn't . . . well, Uncle Bernie might give me a job as manager of one of his piers.

I had been at the BBC fifteen months when Jonathan Powell duly delivered the first episode of *EastEnders.* Sarah and I were spending the weekend with her parents at Hall Barn, a whole universe away from Albert Square. We settled down to watch it. Up came the opening shot where Den Watts bashes down the door of Reg Cox's flat to find inside a dead body lying on the floor. Half an hour later I took the cassette out of the video recorder and didn't wait for anyone to express an opinion. I could tell from the pregnant silence that everyone in the room was hooked. We were in business.

I had then to decide where to place it in my schedule. In those days *Coronation Street* went out at seven thirty on Mondays and Wednesdays and regularly got fifteen million viewers; it would be madness to tackle it head on. I pencilled *EastEnders* to go out at seven o'clock on Tuesdays and Thursdays where it would be up against the much less formidable *Emmerdale Farm,* an ageing bucolic saga that took a break every summer, offering me a free run of several months against minimal opposition. Sensing the beginning of a titanic Battle of the Soaps, the newspapers took a considerable interest in *EastEnders* with the result that we won nine million viewers for the first episode. It then settled down at around seven million viewers each week; decent but nothing like enough to recoup our investment either in resources or prestige. *Coronation Street* was still up there at the head of the top ten programmes, apparently unassailable.

One day I was idly scanning the viewer figures and noticed that, according to latest figures in the Broadcasters' Audience Research Board report, the Channel 4 soap *Brookside* achieved an average audience of three million yet it appeared in the top ten with double that figure. 'How can that be?' I asked Pamela Reiss, who knew everything there was to be known about audience ratings. She explained that because *Brookside* had a narrative repeat on Sunday afternoons, its viewing figures could be added together, thus putting it in the top ten. That was it! I quickly arranged to have the two mid-week episodes of *EastEnders* consolidated into an omnibus edition on Sunday afternoons, which sent the show soaring into the top ten.

This worked a treat in keeping the more sceptical governors off my back and prevented the press from trumpeting that *EastEnders* had crashed out of the charts. Privately I still had my anxieties because it just hadn't caught fire, though I assured the producer, Julia Smith, who was a chronic worrier, that we had to give it time. The Queen Vic's landlord, Dirty Den, who had got his daughter's friend Michelle pregnant, was played by actor Leslie Grantham. He had been imprisoned for murder before he became an actor and suddenly his screen persona as a bad lot and his real-life prison record merged in the tabloids, providing pages of blanket coverage and sending *EastEnders* up the ratings until it overhauled *Coronation Street* at the head of the top ten. And there it has stayed ever since. I could relax, the BBC's huge investment would pay off. Perhaps the most instinctive decision in my career as a television scheduler was made when Julia Smith and I discussed the 1986 Christmas edition. She proposed a special one-hour episode. I was less than enthusiastic and responded with a rather more risky alternative.

'Let's do an hour on Christmas night as you suggest,' I said, 'but break it up into two halves, a cliff-hanger at six thirty and its denouement at ten o'clock, but make the action happen in real time.'

Julia grinned from ear to ear. 'I've got just the story-line,' she said. 'I swore I wouldn't breathe a word to anyone but I've decided that Den and his wife Angie are going to split up. They can do it on Christmas night.'

That Christmas, twenty-nine million viewers watched *East-Enders*. It was a sweet moment for me and a just reward for a team who had dedicated years of their life to realizing the original idea and battling their way through all kinds of discouragement and cynicism, some of it coming from within the upper reaches of the BBC itself. Julia Smith had no other existence, the soap opera devoured her life. The regulars at the Queen Vic became her family and she seemed to feel personally their miseries and joy. I recall visiting the set at Elstree while the Christmas episode was being shot. Julia said something about having to sort out some Christmas cards.

'Come on, Julia,' I said, 'you've got enough on your plate. Send your secretary for the cards.'

'Don't be silly,' she replied, 'these are not *my* Christmas cards. I've got to work out just what kind of cards Angie and Dot and Michelle and the rest would send to one another.' Here was a producer who carried the responsibility for the whole show and had a million other things to do, yet she was worrying about a tiny detail. The Christmas cards would barely be glimpsed in shot, they were just part of the background, but Julia insisted they had to reflect accurately the taste of the character who sent them. It was this degree of obsessiveness with the characters which was the key to *EastEnders*' power to capture and hold vast audiences.

While *EastEnders* was planned to anchor the early-evening schedules on Tuesdays and Thursdays, I had to turn my attention to the other three evenings. Bill Cotton was keen to use Terry Wogan to do a kind of *Parkinson* chat-show three nights a week at the end of the evening. I just didn't see how I could carve out the necessary space because I was constrained by the position of the nine o'clock news, which was immovable. The programme that followed it was the main entertainment of the late evening and might be a drama, a film, a comedy or an American show. All these programmes were of different lengths, so I couldn't offer a fixed starting time for *Wogan* at the end of the evening. And it is fatal for the prospects of a programme if it roams around the schedules infuriating viewers who wish to make a regular date to watch it. I was also worried that many of Terry's natural viewers would be in bed by the time we screened it late at night: one of his strengths is that he is popular across the generations. I therefore decided to put out *Wogan* at seven o'clock on Mondays, Wednesdays and Fridays.

When I arrived at the BBC, Bill Cotton had been in confidential negotiation with Terry Wogan's agent about his contract. A few weeks later, *Private Eye* published all the details of the negotiation including the exact amount Terry would be earning. Bill apologized to Terry but was puzzled about the source of the leak. He was even more baffled a couple of weeks later when *Private Eye* gave a verbatim account of Bill's colourful language down to the last sizzling syllable and coruscating consonant as he read the story in the previous edition.

'Did you say all that?' I asked him, astounded at the range of his invective.

'Yes,' replied Bill. 'That's word for word what I said. The frightening thing is I was all alone in here when I said it!'

Wogan did not quite match up to my expectations for it. Though undoubtedly a success, it never achieved importance as one of those rare programmes you must catch or your day will not be complete. It should have been the show everyone rushed home to watch, but it never created that kind of buzz. Terry is a natural broadcaster with a ready wit, great articularity and high intelligence, which he doesn't use to intimidate his guests. But I never found a producer who really understood the possibility of exploiting *Wogan* as a regular platform from which to deal with topical issues. I knew we were in trouble the first time I called into the production office. On the wall was a huge blackboard with all the shows for the following two months listed, and beneath each date a full complement of guests was set out, each one booked in advance. The show was set in concrete. If the End of the World had supervened, we'd have been unable to find a slot on *Wogan* for Jesus. Though that fully filled black-board spoke to me of efficiency and a well-filled contacts diary, it also hinted at an unwillingness to take risks – to take a chance and leave blanks in the expectation that something was likely to happen at the last moment that would dictate who the most appropriate guest should be.

I never got the producer to realize just what the problem was with the show. Big names were not enough: it also needed guests who were there because they were associated with topical issues sufficiently controversial and intellectually challenging to spark Terry off. He had shown on his morning radio show that he could handle serious topics with a light touch. An endless procession of Hollywood stars plugging their latest movie wouldn't extend him or bring out that provocative side to his nature. Terry was nothing if not versatile. He was equally at home grilling a top politician or chatting to an old lady who had tackled a mugger and floored him. But he could do little without the support of producers of a special kind who occupied the middle ground between hard-nosed investigative journalism and light entertainment. The BBC didn't seem to have them – or at least, I never found one to run *Wogan.*

On the other hand, one television personality who did sit comfortably in that middle ground between journalism and light entertainment, both as a talented producer and a popular presenter, was Esther Rantzen. She came to see me one day with an idea for an anti-drugs show and suggested a one-hour special late at night on BBC 1. To her astonishment I countered with a proposal that we should clear the schedules one Sunday evening for a couple of hours and make a programme aimed not just at teenagers but the whole family.

The result was *Drugwatch.* The word must have got around the corridors of the BBC that we were going to tackle the drugs

issue, for Jimmy Savile popped his head round my door. When I
confirmed that we intended to do the programme, he said,
'Would you like the young lady to come on the show?'

Jimmy always talks in riddles, and I was so used to playing
word games with him that instead of asking who he was talking
about, I merely asked, 'Would she do it?'

He replied, 'I'll ask her,' and disappeared.

He phoned a few days later to tell me that the date was in
her diary. I'd read the gossip columns and knew all about
Jimmy's friends in high places so I began to wonder whether he
meant the Princess of Wales; very unlikely, but I thought I
should warn Esther. Sure enough, when the programme went
out, on to the set walked Diana and headed the list of celebrities
signing the 'Just Say No' board on the studio wall. *Drugwatch*
with the added lustre of Diana was a notable success, but
badinage with Jimmy was never quite the same again – I never
knew how seriously to take what he said. Now I would believe
him if he told me he'd arranged with NASA to present *Top of the
Pops* from the moon.

An even more dramatic demonstration of the power of television as a socially constructive force began after I'd been at the
BBC for a few months. My secretary buzzed and asked if I'd take
a telephone call from Bob Geldof. I knew he was a pop star but
for a couple of years I'd been thousands of miles removed from
the British popular music scene so I didn't know quite where to
place him in the firmament. However, I took the call and asked
what I could do for him. He told me he was making a record to
raise money for Ethiopian famine relief and reeled off a list of
stars and pop groups he'd recruited to the cause. He recognized
that the video couldn't be featured on *Top of the Pops* until it was
actually in the charts but he'd be very grateful if I could give it an
airing somewhere in the schedules. I'd become a hardened seller
in Hollywood and I could smell hype a thousand miles away but
Geldof was the antithesis of the high-powered salesman. He spoke
quietly and without emotion, but there was a kind of purposeful-
ness in his voice, which was quite compelling. I found myself

telling him that I would look at the video. It was on my desk within the hour. Then I phoned him back and said that if, as he promised, he could deliver David Bowie to set it in context, I would put back the start of *Top of the Pops* for a few minutes and insert it as a 'filler' just ahead of the chart show, thus ensuring that pop fans could easily find it. This was to disrupt an invariable pattern of scheduling but I didn't see any point in being a controller if I couldn't respond to a great challenge.

I decided not to attend the actual Live Aid event at Wembley stadium but watched the twenty-four-hour continuous transmission at home, at times with tears in my eyes. There was one heart-stopping moment around three o'clock in the afternoon when a weary Bob Geldof appeared on screen, suppressed panic in his eyes. Apparently the phone links taking cash pledges from viewers had gone quiet. Pressing his nose against the camera lens, he snarled, 'Send us your fucking money!' This was the only time the expletive had been used in family viewing time, but no one complained, not Mrs Whitehouse, not the BBC governors. Presumably even they recognized that this four-letter word had been wrung out of a man tormented by the enormity of human need. There's nothing like the sight of pot-bellied, starving children to put the term 'obscenity' in its true perspective. The money poured in.

It was a majestic demonstration of human solidarity, marrying the power of popular music with the global reach of the airwaves to unite people of many nations to help those in distress. I became a trustee of Live Aid/Band Aid and learned a great deal about the challenge of trucking and distributing food to the desert areas of Africa. I was proud to have been one link in an endless chain of compassion.

Those first months were not all unalloyed triumph. *Bread* was a comedy series that crept up on viewers, an acquired taste, but my first attempt at scheduling it wasn't a success. Carla Lane is a brilliant writer who has delivered lots of excellent comedies to the BBC over the years, and *Bread* was as good as anything she had done, an affectionate satire on Scouse scallywags exploiting the welfare system. We transmitted six episodes and they made absolutely no impact; they just came and went and no one noticed. Watching the programme on air at the same time as the viewers is a quite different experience from previewing a cassette in the privacy of my office, and I began to get the uncomfortable feeling that I had scheduled it on the wrong night and hadn't commissioned enough episodes to establish the format and characters.

I sent for Carla, who, understandably, was depressed. She had got used to drawing audiences of around sixteen or seventeen million viewers and *Bread* had barely managed six million. I assured her that I had absolute faith in the series, it was a sure-fire hit but needed a much longer run to bed itself down. I asked her to go away and write thirteen new episodes, a run that should be extensive enough to catch the viewers' attention. To make sure, I preceded them by rerunning the original six. Before the first series was over, the show had taken off and became one of the biggest hits of the period.

It wasn't just instinct that made me invest in a long run of *Bread*. I had studied the figures of the original half-dozen programmes. *Bread*'s ratings provided a rough head-count and they weren't high, but there was a complementary measure called the Appreciation Index which went along with the ratings. Researchers would question viewers and invite them to rate a programme for quality on a scale from one to ten. Then the ratings and AIs were compared. A programme that got a high rating but a low AI was being watched for lack of anything more interesting on another channel. Conversely, if a programme was getting poor ratings but a growing AI week on week, various assumptions were possible. It might be in the wrong slot so few people had found it, or else it was not being promoted energetically enough. *Bread* was a classic case of a series that at the outset had high AIs but low ratings. Obviously those viewers who did watch it loved it, but there just weren't enough of them, which is why I piled on the episodes. The AI research confirmed my instinct about the quality and potential of the series.

The first series of *Blackadder* presented different problems. I inherited the first series in which I watched the antics of Rowan Atkinson as the evil, clownish son of Richard IV. Frankly I was unimpressed. It struck me as expensive, unfunny and self-indulgent. At the annual Offers meeting where heads of department lay out their wares for the coming year, Gareth Gwenlan, head of Comedy went down the check-list of programmes he was offering, then added almost as an afterthought, 'And, of course, we'll have another series of *Blackadder* . . .'

'No, we won't,' I retorted.

He was stunned. 'But this is cutting edge. It's John Lloyd, Rowan Atkinson, Stephen Fry!'

'Tough,' I said. 'It just isn't funny. I'm not doing another series.'

'You must be joking,' pleaded Gareth.

I assured him I wasn't and then told him what I was prepared to do. I wanted a re-jig of the whole concept. The series had been filmed on location at enormous cost – the hire of Alnwick Castle, dozens of extras and a number of horses put the budget way out of line with the average comedy series. I would not have minded had it worked, but using film slowed down the action and created longueurs where the jokes dropped into a kind of void. Actors like Rowan Atkinson and Tony Robinson were quick-witted comedians used to thinking on their feet, they needed an audience to get their adrenaline flowing. I gave Gareth a choice: either cancel the series or convert the show into a studio production in front of an audience. The upshot was Ben Elton was brought in as one of the scriptwriters. He sharpened up the humour with his inimitable one-liners and funny metaphors while Rowan, free from the distraction of worrying about the words he had composed, turned in a virtuoso performance as the wicked and ridiculous Edmund Blackadder.

Rowan Atkinson, ever the consummate performer, had recognized the problem with the first series and told the tabloids he wasn't surprised that I had threatened to pull out after the first series. He agreed that it just didn't deliver enough laughs to the pound. In fact, he and Richard Curtis had already privately decided that they would like the second series to be shot in front of a studio audience, but no one had bothered to tell me. But it all turned out well in the end. The final series, set in the trenches during the First World War, *Blackadder Goes Forth*, was, besides being very funny, one of the strongest anti-war statements I had ever seen on television, yet it wasn't preachy or propagandist; almost incidentally, it showed the supreme idiocy of the whole ghastly business. It was transmitted after I had left the BBC but I was proud to have been associated with it.

Being controller was all about commissioning the right programmes for the appropriate slots, but occasionally it involved getting rid of shows I didn't like. In certain quarters I shall have an assured place in demonology because I cancelled *Dr Who*. Why beat about the bush? I hated it. I thought it had lost its way, was losing its audience and deserved to lose its slot. Its scientific paraphernalia – 1950s telephone boxes and Daleks welded like lavatory cisterns – was totally outmoded in an age when children were watching the sophisticated special effects wizardry of *E.T.* and *Star Wars*. And curiously, for such an old-fashioned show, it could be gratuitously violent. In one story, a creature with the ability to materialize in plastic, turned a shop window full of tailors' dummies into monsters who smashed through the glass and calmly walked down the street killing everyone in sight. Then there was a horrific drowning sequence, which achieved the unique feat of putting Mrs Mary Whitehouse and myself on the same side in condemning it.

Dr Who was a television icon. It had started way back in 1963 as a black and white science fantasy and made cult figures of the actors who played its eponymous hero, including William Hartnell, Patrick Troughton, Jon Pertwee, Tom Baker and Peter Davison. It was a big export earner for the BBC, and had a fanatical following among the anorak-clad train-spotting brigade. In February 1985, I decided to give it a long rest and pulled it off the air. The contrast between the volume of my hate mail and the number of people who actually watched the programme suggested that every viewer of *Dr Who* must have written at least half a dozen letters of protest to me. I was given the Horse's Ass Award from the Dr Who Society of America, which occupies a place of honour in my loo. The *Daily Mail* sent a heavily pregnant reporter up a French mountain where I was on a skiing holiday to challenge me about my act of barbarism. Unfortunately the high altitude brought on premature labour pains and the interview had to be terminated abruptly – a bizarre outcome that was a perfect parable of the whole weird business. I had merely rested a programme that was way past its sell-by date; I hadn't committed mass murder.

Predictably, the BBC governors panicked. What little contact I'd had with them suggested they had no steady opinions of their own, no independent programme judgement. They seemed to be driven by disapproving noises at Westminster or unfavourable newspaper headlines. Here were these august personages who controlled the destiny of the greatest broadcasting organization in the world getting into a lather about a boring children's programme. They huffed and puffed and expressed grave concern and demanded a full inquiry. The storm passed. As soon as the newspapers turned their attention to something else, the governors in turn forgot all about *Dr Who*, a programme I would wager most of them had never even seen. I felt their knee-jerk reaction augured badly if I found myself involved in a really serious controversy. I realized I couldn't bank on their support if public opinion took against me. I sensed, too, that Alasdair Milne felt I was headstrong in provoking the governors' intervention, further agitating an already fraught relationship between the two boards. But this very peace-at-any-price policy towards possibly controversial programme decisions had helped to create the torpor that had led to the slide in the BBC's ratings. I was now feeling confident enough to tackle the major roadblock in my advance towards the schedules of my dreams: *Panorama*.

Panorama is a sort of Albert Memorial of broadcasting, a

proud landmark, loaded down with history, sacrosanct and immovable. People can be a bit miserable on a Monday night, having gone back to work after the weekend, but if they switched on BBC 1 for a little light relief, there at eight ten was *Panorama* sternly drawing their attention to the goings-on in foreign parts or offering them a searing indictment of government policies, local government incompetence, big business greed and soaring crime rates. I yielded to no one in my admiration for the BBC's current-affairs output and *Panorama* in particular. I was keen to give it the prominence it deserved on BBC 1, to open a window on the world and attack the parochialism and complacency of too much of our national life, but a few minutes after eight o'clock was the worst time to do it. Having just finished an evening meal, viewers needed something more relaxing to aid the digestive processes. I also believed we would attract much bigger audiences to an outstanding current-affairs programme later in the evening. From my spell at LWT, I knew exactly why *Panorama* sat across the jugular of BBC 1 choking the life out of early-evening viewing. Way back in the mists of time, when there were but two channels, there had been a gentleman's agreement between the BBC and ITV that they would schedule *Panorama* and ITV's version, *World in Action*, at the same time. They felt it was a Good Thing for the peasantry to have a weekly dose of geopolitics to lift their eyes beyond game-shows to the far horizon. In the absence of such a truce, whichever of the two programmes had raised its head above the parapet would have had it shot off by a fusillade of popular programming from the other side.

As soon as I took over at the BBC, I realized there were two things wrong with this arrangement. The first was that *Panorama* and *World in Action* did not exactly coincide. Both began roughly around eight o'clock but *World in Action* finished at half past eight whereas *Panorama* ran right up to the *Nine o'Clock News*, so for thirty minutes, the second half of *Panorama* was exposed to ITV comedies which, thanks to lack of competition, regularly won seventeen or eighteen million viewers. These comedies were often of poor quality, but it didn't matter: the conventional wisdom in ITV was that if you had what Clive James called a 'howling bummer' of a programme, you could still find a big audience for it against *Panorama*. The other problem was that this agreement was born of the days when there were only two channels, BBC and ITV. Now BBC 2 and Channel 4 were also in the game of winning viewers and they eyed the hour between eight and nine on Mondays with a predatory gleam.

Something had to be done. *Panorama* was dying on its feet with less than three million viewers, and my Monday evenings were expiring with it. I suspected ITV had no intention of moving *World in Action*, which was the sort of Brownie points television that enabled them to claim they were still a public-service broadcaster. So I would have to shift *Panorama*. It would suit my plans if it were on the other side of the *Nine o'Clock News* and reduced in length from fifty to forty minutes. Sounds simple enough. I thought I'd better try it on the managing director of Television first. Bill Cotton told me bluntly that I'd never get away with it: 'You'll be taking on not only the governors but all the journalists at Lime Grove. You'll never do it, but if you're determined to try, start with the Lime Grove lot. If you can get them on side, then we can tackle the governors. And God bless you.'

Over the years, BBC Current Affairs had expanded from the huge, ugly warehouse that was the Lime Grove studio to the row of terraced Edwardian houses adjoining it, a chaotic labyrinth of offices running from one house to the next through holes cut in the walls. Never have such polished programmes issued from such Dickensian premises. Yet those who worked there seemed to rejoice in their squalor. I suppose if you are a BBC correspondent spending much of your life in war zones, famine areas and the scenes of natural disaster, a home base like Lime Grove isn't so glaring a contrast as a gleaming glass and chrome office block. The physical separation of Current Affairs from the Television Centre was a historical accident, but it symbolized the fiercely independent spirit, not to say mulishness, of some of the greatest journalists in the world.

We met in an upstairs office in Lime Grove. The place was crowded and I knew I had to keep my cool because I would be confronting the best inquisitors in the business who were used to subjecting presidents and prime ministers to the third degree. Among those present were reporters like Tom Mangold, Tom Bower, Michael Cockerill, Fred Emery and David Lomax, who had accused Idi Amin of genocide and General Zia of Pakistan of murdering President Bhutto. The BBC rumour mill had been working in overdrive, they were already steamed up. The atmosphere was fraught; I met a wall of suspicion. I knew what they were thinking. Here's a song-and-dance man, what can he know about the complexities of world affairs? I suppose my experience as a theatrical agent came in useful. I had spent years sitting quietly being hectored and lectured by prima donnas indignant about real or fancied complaints. And some of this Lime Grove lot *were* prima donnas, on-screen stars with formidable intellects.

Patiently, I took them through the viewing figures, demonstrating what they already knew, that *Panorama*'s ratings were slipping slowly but inexorably into oblivion, and this not only spelt death for my attempts to improve ratings on Monday evenings, but it was also bad news for them. What was the point of making brilliant programmes if virtually no one watched them? I asked if any of those present could explain to me why *Panorama* went out at eight ten on Monday evenings rather than, say, seven fifteen on Tuesdays? No one knew. This was a prize example of BBC inertia – using that word in the literal sense, the tendency of a body to continue on the same course unless deflected by a great force. Every venerable institution develops it. Things go on getting done in a certain way because they always have been.

I spelled out my plans. I wanted a forty-minute programme. This evoked howls of pain. Didn't I know that it wasn't possible to tackle a major current-affairs story adequately in forty minutes? I sighed: here was Grade's Law in action again. This runs: in the opinion of any programme's producer, it is never quite long enough to tackle its subject thoroughly. An endless procession of programme-makers used to appear in my office begging to extend their programme's length by another ten or fifteen minutes so they could do justice to all the priceless material that would otherwise end up on the cutting-room floor. Occasionally, I agreed with them but usually urged more vigorous use of the razor-blade and scissors. I told the journalists the forty minutes wasn't negotiable and explained that I intended to begin the evening with good light entertainment up to nine o'clock, then put out *Panorama* at nine thirty when it would benefit from the inheritance of all the natural news watchers. Then I would follow it with a big movie.

The journalists weren't entirely convinced and it took a further couple of meetings before they agreed to give my proposal a chance. Crucial to this decision was the positive response of the editor of *Panorama*, Peter Ibbotson, on whom I would depend to keep the programme's quality up to scratch until the viewing public got used to its new placing. Once they were sure there would be no red flag of revolt flying from the roof of Lime Grove, the governors agreed to the change, though one or two expressed misgivings along the lines of that hallowed principle, 'Let nothing be done for the first time.' *Panorama* went out at nine thirty on Monday evenings and in a short time doubled its ratings. I had my Monday evenings back. At last, BBC 1 was eating away at ITV's ratings. That year, the ITV companies had a conference in Monte Carlo with their paymasters, the advertisers, and were badly mauled for allowing the two BBC channels to overtake them. I was a happy man. I knew why I had come back from Hollywood.

I relished the keen but usually friendly competition against my old colleagues at ITV, but I had a bruising encounter with one that was much more unpleasant. Brian 'Ginger' Cowgill had been one of my predecessors as controller of BBC 1, where he had established a reputation as a brilliant and aggressive scheduler. A prickly individual, he left the BBC because he was passed over for promotion and joined Thames Television as managing director. Within limits, the controller of BBC 1 can make decisions unilaterally whilst the ITV system is a federal network where the heads of the various companies must work by consensus and agree about the programmes that will be shown on the network. Brian was never a team player; he found consultation uncongenial – once he had made a decision he went ahead and implemented it. When I was head of programmes at LWT, I was too often on the receiving end of this high-handed attitude because Ginger would make commitments on behalf of the entire network and not bother to tell anyone. You'd only discover once it was a *fait accompli* that he'd signed a contract, say, for ITV to cover the world ice-skating championships for the next five years.

Brian was autocratic, secretive and, over the *Dallas* saga, somewhat economical with the truth, but at the time I joined the BBC, his star was very much in the ascendant in ITV because he had taken on the hugely powerful television unions, provoked a strike and won. He was walking around with a personal letter of congratulation from Mrs Thatcher in his pocket and the confident expectation he would soon be appointed chairman of Thames when Hugh Dundas retired.

It was *Dallas*, the hottest show on television, that put us on collision course in January 1985, after I had been controller for only a few months. There was a convention in the industry at that time about the buying in of programmes from America. Since there were only the two British buyers, the BBC and ITV, to avoid the sellers playing off one of us against the other and pushing up the price, a gentleman's agreement had been in force for years forbidding poaching. There was a Film Purchase Committee, chaired by Paul Fox of Yorkshire Television, which bought for ITV, and on our side, Alan Howden, head of Purchase Programmes, and I did the bidding. Competition was keen, but the rule was that once a side won, the programme in question belonged to them for the rest of its natural life. Every year, the bargain was renewed as a matter of course and only if the original buyer decided to drop the programme was it offered to the other side.

One Sunday evening, Alan Howden rang me at home to tell me we had a problem about *Dallas*. He had received a strange communication from WorldVision, the *Dallas* distributor. They had sent him an ultimatum, full of preposterous conditions, and warning that if he did not respond within the hour, WorldVision would be free to negotiate elsewhere. I knew immediately it was a stitch-up. They must have another customer, but who? I needed time to find out what was going on so I asked Alan to send them a holding statement while I talked to Paul Fox, who assured me that the no-poaching agreement was still in force and ITV wasn't counter-bidding for *Dallas*. We briefly considered Rupert Murdoch's European Sky Channel and then I wondered aloud whether it might not be Ginger Cowgill on one of his raiding expeditions. Just to eliminate the possibility, I asked Paul if he would call Brian.

'Better not,' he replied. 'It might put the idea into his head.'

The following morning an embarrassed Paul rang to say that it was indeed Brian who was trying to do a deal with WorldVision for *Dallas*. Bill Cotton and I decided to get the BBC's retaliation in first. We called a press conference at which I announced that unless Cowgill backed down I would cancel the upcoming run of *Dallas*. This would mean that if he did succeed in his bid for the next series, viewers who watched it on ITV would not have caught up with the plot running through the series we were holding. The press called me 'petulant', 'childish' and 'high-handed', and reminded the public of the occasion when the boot was on the other foot and I had snatched *Match of the Day* from the BBC. The irony of the situation was not lost on me, but there was a big difference between the two incidents. Before I made any bid for *Match of the Day*, I had gone to great trouble to ensure that I had the formal support of every relevant ITV company chief executive and of the IBA. Brian had told none of his colleagues about his secret bid for *Dallas* and thereby caused them acute embarrassment: they were at pains to distance themselves from what he had done. I was unapologetic about my threat to cancel *Dallas*. If Ginger was allowed to get away with his act of piracy, he would be after some of the BBC's other crown jewels such as Wimbledon or the Open Golf.

A self-righteous Cowgill protested to the chairman of the IBA that it was WorldVision who had called to tell him that negotiations with the BBC had broken down and therefore presented him with a golden opportunity he had to take. As a story, it didn't hold water. We *knew* (who better?) that the BBC's negotiations with WorldVision for the next series of *Dallas* had not broken down: they had hardly begun. But arguments were overtaken by events. By his unilateral action, Brian had put such strain on the ITV system and generated the kind of tension within Thames that he had to leave within a few months. We got *Dallas* back, with £300,000 compensation from Thames because we were stuck with a much more expensive contract. *Dallas* returned to the BBC's screen and Bill Cotton and I had smiles on our faces.

'I don't know how you did it,' said Stuart Young.

'We know our man,' replied Bill.

One of the nicer problems I faced in my days as controller of BBC 1 was deciding what to do with Selina Scott, who was one of the most famous faces in Britain. Having been a presenter of *News at Ten*, she had moved on to fronting the BBC's *Breakfast Time* with Frank Bough. The press loved her and followed avidly her every move, speculated endlessly about her life, loves, thoughts and fears. And they were privy to her unhappiness about the breakfast-time slot. She wanted out, and we had to agree; it was unthinkable that the nation's sweetheart should appear before her public first thing every morning looking miserable. She was still under contract to the BBC but now had nothing to do. Every time I met the press in the weeks that followed I was asked what I intended to do with Selina Scott and ritually replied that we were working on a big show for her whose precise format was a closely guarded secret. And it was more or less true; I never lie to the press. I've had to deflect, distract and evade their questions but I have never told them bare-faced lies. We *were* working on finding something for her, but hadn't come up with anything suitable. Then a reporter asked me if she was still under contract to the BBC. This was August and Selina's contract ran until the end of the year. I had to confirm that she was still being paid, and even as I spoke, I could see the following morning's headline under a saucy picture of Selina: 'Paid A Thousand Pounds A Week of Your Money for Doing Nothing'. Sure enough, the next morning, the *Daily Mail* ran just that headline.

Ideally I would have preferred Selina to go on fronting *Breakfast Time* but I recognized that having to get up most mornings at an ungodly hour could ruin any star's life, turning her into a social hermit. An additional problem was that Selina had no firm ideas about the next step in her career, but now the press had the story we had to act quickly. I phoned Selina's agent, who told me she was on a walking holiday in Provence. I asked him to get hold of her at all costs. There was only one thing to do: we had to find a show for her in the next twenty-four hours. The head of Transmission Planning, Roger MacKay, and I began to trawl through the programme offers of the past couple of years to see if we could come up with a format that was remotely possible. Eventually Roger said, 'There was that terrible idea from BBC Birmingham for a fashion show.' Within minutes I was on the phone to the producer at Pebble Mill. I asked him whether he would still like to do the show if I found the money, adding, 'There's one snag. I choose the presenter, and it will be Selina Scott.' He wanted to think about that. Producers are very proprietorial about their programmes and have their own ideas about on-screen presenters, but he was up against *force majeure*: no Selina, no fashion show.

Then Selina came on the phone from a call-box in some village in Provence, reversed charges. 'You have to trust me,' I said, 'I'm going to announce that you will be starring in a new series called *The Clothes Show*.' As she protested, I explained about the likely headlines in the following day's papers. She got the point.

Day dawned and the tabloids exploited the story under absolutely predictable headlines – 'Selina Scott Scandal' and 'How Dare They Squander Your Money On This Idle Woman?' At noon, we put out a press release: 'BBC Television controller Michael Grade announced this morning that Selina Scott is to star in a new series. This will be a thirteen-part programme which looks at the great world of British fashion . . . Said Selina, "I'm delighted to have this opportunity of analysing the world of fashion."' The press were not best pleased and there was a suspicion in Fleet Street that I had deliberately encouraged them to write their Beeb-bashing stories in order to generate more interest in our own press release. Perish the thought! *The Clothes Show* is still running, though without Selina.

The media journalist Michael Leapman summed up my first year at the BBC thus:

> After a year as controller of BBC 1 Michael Grade has succeeded in reversing the decline in its ratings. By the autumn of 1985, the two BBC channels combined were attracting 47.5 per cent of viewers, where the figure had been less than 40 per cent when he arrived. In exceptional weeks, the Corporation's share would advance to just over 50 per cent . . . the entire BBC schedule had a more convincing, thought-out look to it. Thanks to Grade, the argument was no longer heard that the Corporation's claim on the licence fee was illogical because it served only a minority.

I'll settle for that.

A rare sighting of the three brothers together, left to right:
Lew, Bernie (Delfont) and Leslie.

Top left: With my sister Lynda in 1945. I was two years old.

Top right: My first professional photo-opportunity – aged five, a portrait taken by Baron, the society photographer.

Left: Two proud mothers. My grandmother with the Queen at a Royal Variety Performance with Lew looking on.

Spot the Grade – the first XI, 1956.

Dad recuperating from his stroke in the south of France.

Spot the alien – my press pass when I worked on the *Mirror*.

Summer hols 1966. Left to right: Adrian Metcalf, my half-sister Anita,
my stepmother Audrey, Mrs Monty Tresco, me.

Right: In the agent's chair – would you buy a variety act from this man?

Below: Penny and me at our wedding – with full supporting cast. Left to right: Arthur Askey, Eric Morecambe, Jimmy Tarbuck, Ted Rodgers, Albert Finney.

'Snatch of the Day' as interpreted by Giles.

Celebrating LWT's success at the Prix Italia. Left to right: John Birt, Melvyn Bragg, Tanya Bruce-Lockhart, Nick Elliott, me.

'I made him an offer he couldn't refuse.' Laurence Olivier's appearance on the *South Bank Show* was the only major interview he ever gave.

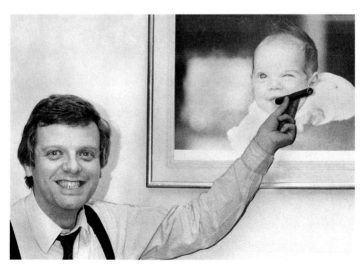

I can never resist a photo-opportunity – even at the expense of my six-week-old daughter's dignity.

Above: Bidding farewell
to LWT with my second
wife, Sarah, and my long-
time friend and colleague,
John Bromley.

Left: Handing the LWT
baton to my successor
John Birt. We would
meet again . . .

Doing the can-can in Albert Square with members of the original *EastEnders* cast.

With Alasdair Milne and the Queen Mother at a Royal Variety Performance.

With Brian Cowgill and Bill Cotton before the *Dallas* Wars.

The *Telly Addicts Christmas Show*. Left to right: Barry Took, me, Noel Edmonds, Larry Grayson, Nina Myskow.

With Magnus Magnusson, presenting the *Mastermind* trophy
to the 1986 winner, Jennifer Keaveney.

The BBC – an equal opportunity employer. Director-General Mike Checkland's
BBC Board of Management.

Dickie Attenborough gave me the original of Cummings'
wonderful cartoon when I arrived at Channel 4.

'Stop me and buy one' – a 7th birthday treat for Channel 4 staff.

Receiving the BAFTA Fellowship in 1994.

Not as nice as he looks! Taking over from Captain Bob as the President of the Television and Radio Industries Club.

Jak's brilliant comment on Channel 4's decision to break the broadcasting ban.

Above: Spot the tinsel – crossing the Atlantic, Christmas Day 1993.

Right: Framed by the mizzen boom of *Laphraoig*, Francesca and me about to step ashore in Mustique for our wedding.

My daughter Alison.

My son Jonathan.

With Francesca and Samuel – pure joy.

Chapter Seven

TWO FRIENDS AND A STRANGER

WHEN I CAME BACK to London in November 1984 to join the BBC, Sarah's father, Lord Burnham, let us have a house on his estate near Beaconsfield. The family home, Hall Barn, a magnificent Queen Anne mansion, had been one of the locations borrowed for the film *Chariots of Fire*, so in contrast to Hollywood our surroundings were classically English and countrified. Sarah and I had spent barely a day apart since 1982; we had been babes in Hollywood together, clinging all the more closely to each other because we were outsiders in a strange, exciting and rather intimidating environment. Now we spent months apart because Sarah's job took her back to Los Angeles, first as the London representative of a big American production corporation, then as the chief executive of her own film and television company.

I guess I was schizoid about Sarah's job. Intellectually I fully supported her in her determination to pursue her own career: she was bright, articulate and hard-driving, and would have withered as a BBC company wife, a decorative appendage to a husband in the limelight. But when we discussed our future in the days before I joined the BBC, I hadn't really taken on board just how great a disruption to the life we'd established would be caused by Sarah continuing a career that involved her spending much of her time in the United States. Some relationships can survive and even thrive on the alternation between physical closeness and distance, but at that time I hadn't the emotional maturity to adapt to a radical change in the conventional pattern of marriage my Jewish upbringing had led me to expect. But I was so intoxicated by the prospect of the new job that I would have agreed to virtually any arrangement between us that gave me the freedom to do what I had set my heart on. I never faced honestly the question: am I capable of sustaining a relationship subjected to the strain of frequent separation?

Sarah was a much more liberated spirit. When she was interviewed by Robert Kilroy Silk about the problems of being a transatlantic commuting wife, she replied with typical candour when asked which came first, her job or me, 'Job!' and then went on to say that she enjoyed her freedom. 'I very much like being on my own. I actually like being in a room all alone. I can sit in my bed in Los Angeles at two in the morning and decide to eat lemons without having to explain myself to anyone . . . I think I'm an independent modern woman.' Well, in contrast, I was amazed to discover the extent to which I was a traditional Jewish boy accustomed to the constant attentions of a loving wife.

For long periods we were apart, and even when Sarah was with me, I would get home in the evening bursting to tell her all about my day, but because of the time difference between Britain and the United States, she was already glued to the phone speaking to Los Angeles. By the time she put down the phone eager to discuss her work with me, I was ready for bed. The telephone bound us together when we were apart but separated us when we were in the same place. I now wryly recall the exasperation of my stepmother, Audrey, because the moment Dad arrived home in the evening he would pick up the phone and make a whole series of calls while the supper wilted in the oven. In my youth I thought it one of his endearing traits but now that I was on the receiving end of someone else's telephonic preoccupation my tolerance soon wore thin.

Truth to tell, for all my protestations about equality between the sexes, I began to build up considerable resentment that, for much of the time, Sarah wasn't around to look after me and share my public appearances. I was a Grade, one of a dynasty of male personalities sustained by loving wives. Lew's Kathy, Bernie's Carole and my father's Audrey had dedicated their lives to their husbands and played no small part in their success by providing them with happy homes and constant support: working partners were not part of the tradition. Because my mother had deserted us when we were small, I grew up with an unquenchable craving for love, I couldn't get enough of it. I needed constant attention; I felt vulnerable and threatened when Sarah wasn't there. It all brought back memories of childhood dereliction. I matured with a skewed idea of love; maternal love you were entitled to, but if that was missing then you had to earn the love of others by being eager to please, which in turn meant avoiding confrontation even when tough problems had to be faced.

I was totally unable to talk about my deepest feelings and fears. Sarah, who was much more emotionally mature than I was, sometimes tried to initiate a frank reappraisal of our relationship, but my response to any painful encounter was to run from it, so I shrugged off her anxieties and assured her that everything was fine. I would talk about anything, her job, my job, anything but *us*. There was a total lack of communication between us. I now realize that to get our marriage back on track would have demanded really hard work on my part and I just hadn't got the commitment. I was too self-absorbed to take full account of Sarah's needs. We were both fairly accomplished actors so we presented a united front to the world, but those who knew us best were obviously worried, particularly Sarah's parents, to whom we were both devoted.

The BBC itself was a cause of tension between us. Though Sarah had been the one who at the eleventh hour insisted I should take up Bill Cotton's offer, she soon became deeply suspicious of the effect corporate culture was having on me. She felt I was becoming a bit of a stuffed shirt and losing my creative drive as a free spirit. In fact, it wasn't true: far from absorbing the Establishment ethos, I had been on collision course with BBC bureaucracy almost from the beginning, I found the governors uncongenial and some of my fellow managers enigmatic, but the BBC was the only game in town and I had to make a success of the job, so Sarah's cynical attitude was dispiriting. We put on a great show of togetherness. The pace of our life was dizzying, but deep beneath the surface of all the socializing and transatlantic commuting, the core of our relationship was being eroded by loneliness and frustration.

I immersed myself totally in my work, and the BBC is the sort of all-embracing community that can take over your life unless you make strenuous efforts to preserve some kind of private existence. Like the Windmill Theatre, it never closes: day and night, there are bright, interesting people around and constant activity – as the evening programme producers leave, the breakfast-time staff are arriving. There's a buzz about the place. If you want somewhere to hide from your problems, the Television Centre is ideal; you need never be alone with your thoughts, you can be swept up in all the razzmatazz of the business and give the impression you are enjoying yourself hugely. I was good at that.

The abiding political reality of my time at the BBC was Mrs Thatcher's detestation of the Corporation, so it was open season as Tory MPs launched one attack after another on us. When they tired of accusing us of left-wing political bias, they got on their moral high horse and condemned us for submerging the nation under a tidal wave of sex and violence. This tendency to classify sex and violence together as though – like Marks and Spencer – they were two halves of an indivisible whole always marked out those critics who were looking to give television a ritual whipping rather than engage in a rational debate about serious issues. Sex and violence have their roots in diverse emotions, evoke different reactions from viewers and do not march together in the schedules – bonking and bashing incidents do not increase or decrease at the same rate. Lumping together in a single phrase all television's spicier causes of offence – sex, violence, language and taste – casts a kind of generalized moral fog over an area that needs much more research and less heated rhetoric.

Having been director of programmes at LWT and at the sharp end of Mrs Mary Whitehouse's wagging finger on a number of occasions, this was an issue I knew something about. In Hollywood I'd had to run the gauntlet of the successor to the Hay's Office, the censorship authority which decreed that male and female actors in bed together must keep at least one foot on the floor. I certainly understood where most politicians were coming from. Many of the problems they faced were intractable and had little pay-off in public-relations terms, so an issue like sex and violence on TV was a godsend: it interested the public, had a high profile and was good for tabloid headlines. MPs hadn't the foggiest notion what to do about rising crime rates, prisons heaving at the sides, the disintegration of the family, the collapse of public morality – and who can blame them? But, to add to their discomfiture, *there* was television, confronting them with a vivid picture of the society they had done much to shape. And they didn't like what they saw so, like exasperated parents, they turned on the broadcasters crying, 'Whatever you're doing, stop it!'

It is, of course, a venerable tradition to blame communications technology for social problems. A clear historical line joins the beheading of the bearers of bad news in ancient Greece and the Conservative government's 1989 ban on the appearance of Sinn Fein politicians on television. A famous *Times* leader ran, 'Before the children's greedy eyes, with heartless indiscrimination, are presented every night terrific massacres, horrible catastrophes. All who care for the moral well-being and education of children will set their faces like flint against this form of excitement.' 'This form of excitement' was not the video nasty or even *Grange Hill* but the invention of cinematography. The leader was dated 1913. And according to Marshall McLuhan, the arrival of the first comic books on the American scene was blamed for rising crime statistics. As he put it, 'The dimmest-witted convict learned to plead from the dock, "It wuz comic books wot made me do it, m'lud!" '

The Tories decided that a great cultural institution like the BBC, which had decades of experience in drawing the boundaries of taste and practising public accountability, whose policies had been shaped by some of the most creative minds of our time, could not be trusted to show social responsibility: it needed the smack of firm regulation. And in 1985, shortly after I joined the BBC, Winston Churchill MP decided to cleanse the Augean stables by introducing a Private Member's Bill to bring broadcasting within the scope of the 1959 Obscene Publications Act.

Besides making broadcasting organizations subject to the Act, Churchill wanted to replace its famous test of what is obscene – the 'tendency to deprave and corrupt' – with a list of practices whose portrayal on screen would be punishable offences. He was enthusiastically backed by the Prime Minister. The Tory press gleefully reported that on the second reading of the Bill she went into the 'Yes' lobby.

I agreed with Winston Churchill about one thing, though for diametrically opposed reasons. The test of obscenity, 'tending to deprave and corrupt', was vague, confused and difficult to apply. In the famous case involving D. H. Lawrence's *Lady Chatterley's Lover* in 1960, the judge tried to help the jury by consulting a dictionary and came up with 'to make morally bad, pervert, and debase' for 'deprave', and 'render rotten, destroy moral purity, and defile' for 'corrupt'. The Court of Appeal rapped him over the knuckles for trying to go further than what they described as the plain English of the original Act. 'Deprave and corrupt' may be plain English, but in a succession of cases, juries found it impossible to put the test into practice when confronted with specific instances. The phrase, concluded Lord Wilberforce, 'provides a formula which cannot in practice be applied'. A Committee on Obscenity and Film Censorship, set up by the Home Secretary in 1977 and chaired by the philosopher Bernard Williams, came to the conclusion that terms such as 'obscene', 'deprave and corrupt' and 'indecent' had outlived their usefulness and should be scrapped, together with the ragbag of laws based on them, so that the legislators could start again from scratch.

Hence, I was all for getting rid of an Act whose common law origins went back to the eighteenth century, but Winston Churchill wanted to replace it with much more draconian legislation setting out a dirty laundry list of specific words and practices that would be punishable offences. At least the virtue of the old 'corrupt and deprave' test had been that, because of its very vagueness, juries had had to fall back on their common sense and most prosecutions were thrown out. But once specific practices were nailed down they would become offences, regardless of the artistic context or circumstances of their use.

Some years later, when I took over Channel 4, the columnist Paul Johnson was to award me the title of Britain's Pornographer in Chief. I was more offended by his loose use of language than the implied insult. I have never knowingly commissioned, financed or approved a programme I regarded as pornographic. Erotic, yes, but pornographic, never. Pornography is, in D. H. Lawrence's phrase, 'doing the dirt on sex'. Its content is explicit, its immediate intention is to arouse sexual excitement and its ultimate aim is to make money for its producers. Whether or not pornography corrupts many people is a fiercely contested issue, but it certainly cheapens something that civilized people regard as precious. Pornography isolates the sex act from its context within human relationships and makes it serve no greater end than the gratification of appetite. Violence, too, is a key element in most pornography. Lust is magnified and distorted by hostility; it is redolent of the hatred and the humiliation of women. I will have nothing to do with it.

On the other hand, the erotic is a wholesome celebration of sexuality as a significant aspect of human life. It differs from the obscene in emphasizing the attractive and joyous side of sexuality in distinction from its corrupting and disgusting possibilities. There is no moral question mark against it, no suggestion that its representation could be harmful – though as a scheduler, I was always careful to avoid subjecting children to images for which their learning and life experience had not yet prepared them.

I freely confess that I have wilfully transmitted material that could be strictly described as obscene. The word itself, its derivation, has nothing specifically to do with sex, though I never managed to convince Winston Churchill MP of that. It is a term meaning 'ill-omened' and refers to any image or expression that would disgust and offend a normal human being, whether or not sex is involved. A napalm-burned child in Vietnam, a grossly mutilated corpse, a scene of gluttony in a context of starvation might all be defined as obscene. Yet the transmission of such pictures can occasionally be justified to introduce viewers to new thinking or increase their awareness of the raw nature of the world, though the onus is always on the broadcaster to prove that no other image will do.

These were and are my convictions about the portrayal of sex on television. They were first formed as I sat round the Grade family table and listened to my father and uncles discussing the Lord Chamberlain's likely reaction to shows they intended to put on – which naughty words would he ban, how far dare a bedroom farce go in the direction of nudity? In the end, the Lord Chamberlain's role as official theatre censor was abolished because he had become a figure of fun, but not before he had mutilated some great works of theatrical art over the years. Having seen him confined to his ceremonial role, walking backwards carrying what looks like a billiard cue in front of the Queen at the State Opening of Parliament, I had no intention of sitting by and allowing Winston Churchill to give the old buffer a new lease of life on radio and television.

I called a crisis meeting at the British Academy of Film and Television Arts (BAFTA) in Piccadilly. There were representatives of the National Theatre, the Royal Shakespeare Company, the National Gallery, film and television companies, publishers and journalists. David Attenborough made one of the wittiest speeches. It was brief and simply pointed out that every one of the forbidden practices set out in the draft Bill formed part of a normal day's routine for a praying mantis, so if Churchill got his way, it would mean the end of natural history programmes.

I found myself debating the issue with Winston Churchill on radio, television and in the public press, and his Bill eventually died the death, but my high profile had been noticed and disapproved of at Broadcasting House. Alasdair Milne, the director general, summoned me to point out that in opposing the Bill I was not speaking for the BBC. 'The BBC doesn't have a position on this,' he said. I couldn't believe it. Surely the governors will be stating a view on Churchill's Bill? I pleaded. He shook his head. Apparently, the guardians of public-service broadcasting did not have the matter on their agenda. I found Alasdair's passive attitude to the issue baffling. He was too big a man to be jealous of the press coverage I was getting, and in his time had been a doughty champion of the BBC's right to manage its own affairs free from government interference. I could only conclude that over the previous months he had suffered so many bruising encounters with a hostile board of governors that the spirit had been knocked out of him. It was as though he no longer seemed capable of taking a fight to the governors, he could barely cope with the belligerence they aimed at him. He reminded me of one of those referees who is always twenty yards behind the play. He seemed a sad, lonely man.

Probably the most exciting and potentially troublesome part of my job as controller was commissioning drama. The BBC has been well blessed throughout its history with very talented drama producers and a list of the heads of Drama would include the most eminent names in the business. And if proof were needed that television is a serious art form, it is surely supplied by the brilliance of the writers who have chosen it as their chief forum – Dennis Potter, Alan Bennett, Alan Bleasdale, Mike Leigh, Andrew Davies and comedy writers like John Sullivan, Roy

Clarke, Dick Clement and Ian La Frenais, and Eric Chappell. They may write for other media as well, but it is on television that their special skills have come to full flower.

I recall a meeting with the BBC's head of Plays, Peter Goodchild, in 1985. Peter had an unusual background. A chemist by training, he had been a senior producer in Television Science Features and pioneered the use of drama documentaries about scientific issues and personalities. A series he produced about Professor Robert Oppenheimer and the development of the atomic bomb established his reputation as a drama producer and led to his being appointed head of Plays. He had the scientist's precise mind, which sometimes degenerated into pedantry. He was highly strung, voluble and easily offended. My routine meetings with him sometimes ended in tantrums. This meeting was different because he walked out of my office with the promise of an extra £2 million on his annual budget on the strength of a comment he made that he was encouraging Alan Bleasdale to write a drama for the BBC. Bleasdale's stunning serial *Boys From the Black Stuff*, about a gang of Liverpool Tarmac layers, was transmitted while I was in America, but I'd seen the tapes and been vastly impressed by its dramatic power.

Apparently, some Bleasdale scripts had been shuffled from one desk to another in the BBC for a couple of years. The original proposal had been for his drama serial to be a co-production between the BBC and an independent company, but it had been impossible to agree terms. I read the scripts eagerly. They were based on a book by John Fairley and William Allison called *The Monocled Mutineer* – an account of the last mutiny in the British Army, which took place in France at Étaples in 1917. The central character was Private Percy Toplis, half villain, half hero, a deeply flawed romantic who rebelled against the inhumane treatment meted out by officers to their men. I was entranced by Bleasdale's writing, and when Peter, delighted by my enthusiasm, proposed that he should intensify the search for co-production money I told him to forget it, I would pay for the four-part serial.

One way and another, I found the cash, and *The Monocled Mutineer* went ahead. I trumpeted its imminent screening to the press; this was Alan Bleasdale's return to the BBC, the centrepiece of our drama season. But I made a stupid mistake. I approved the advertising copy which, among other information about the series, mentioned that 'it was based on a true life story'. When the advertisement was published, the military establishment went ballistic. It was offical policy to deny that there had ever been a mutiny at Étaples in 1917 and any suggestion to the contrary was a slur on the brave British Tommies and their splendid officers. The right-wing press went berserk. The *Daily Mail* described the series as a 'tissue of lies' and demanded that the BBC governors and the Broadcasting Complaints Commission should hold an immediate inquiry. Here were the lefties of the BBC, glorying in military indiscipline and sneering at patriotism. Inadvertently I had provided yet more ammunition for the barbarians at the gate to hurl at the besieged Corporation. As always, Bill Cotton was a tower of strength. In a public statement, he declared, '*The Monocled Mutineer* is brilliantly directed and acted, and I stand by its integrity. It is based on the events surrounding the life and death of Percy Toplis and reflects the greater truth about the First World War. Every historical drama is open to a charge of bias.'

The serial was a brilliant success, established several actors as stars and achieved very high ratings. When the row broke out, I had written to Alan Bleasdale apologizing for my carelessness in dragging him into a row that seemed to put his dramatic credibility on the line. He was magnanimous and shrugged off the attacks. 'The truth will out,' he said. How right he was. As each programme was transmitted, letters began to reach me from old soldiers who had been at Étaples and confirmed that the mutiny had indeed happened. This was evidence that military historians could not discount. These were not academic theorists or offical spokesmen but men who had lived through the hell of the trenches and were determined before they died to see that the whole truth was told. *The Monocled Mutineer*, they insisted, portrayed an awful reality.

Other sources became public. James Davis, the real-life officer who was portrayed in the *The Monocled Mutineer* as the captain who tried to persuade the mutineers to give themselves up, described the scene in which he featured as 'chillingly accurate'. William Allison, one of the authors of the original book, joined the fray. He pointed out that as long ago as 1929, a secret-service agent, afterwards a member of Scotland's Special Branch, had described in a volume of memoirs how he had captured Toplis, and the Brigadier who commanded the garrison at Étaples gave an account of what happened in 1917, though he carefully avoided the word 'mutiny' and used 'disorder' instead. And in 1978, the government officially acknowledged that there had been a mutiny at Étaples in 1917 but claimed the papers relating to the board of inquiry had been lost.

The anti-BBC clamour in the tabloids died away for a while, but there was always another stormcloud on the horizon. Another play, another drama, this time not on the screen but in my office. I walked into a crisis not of my own making, which culminated in my rejecting a script about the Falklands War by the distinguished playright Ian Curteis. I had been far away in Hollywood four years before in 1982 when Alasdair Milne addressed the Writers' Luncheon Club. In his speech he spoke highly of Ian Curteis's three-hour drama *Suez 1956*, which the BBC had transmitted. This was an account of the Suez disaster seen through the eyes of Anthony Eden, the British Prime Minister at the time. Curteis specialized in twentieth-century historical dramas; his *Churchill and the Generals* was specially admired. After the lunch, Curteis wrote to Alasdair Milne thanking him for his kind words and mentioning casually that he would like sometime to write a play about the Falklands War from the perspective of Mrs Thatcher. He had been dismayed by what he perceived as a vendetta against Mrs Thatcher in the left-wing press and would love the opportunity to put the other side of the picture. To his astonishment, he got a reply from the director general commissioning him to do just that and telling him that the head of Plays would be in touch about the details of the project. No one should have been under any illusion from the start about Ian Curteis's political stance, he was an unapologetic admirer of Mrs Thatcher so the result was bound to be hagiography rather than searing criticism – a position a dramatist is perfectly entitled to adopt.

The final draft reached the director general in April 1986. Alasdair was delighted with it and decided that it should be transmitted on BBC 1 for the fifth anniversary of the Argentinian invasion of the Falklands. I had heard about it in general terms as a project which the director general had sponsored personally and wished to see made and transmitted. One of the DG's traditional titles, which goes back to Reith himself, is that of editor-in-chief; besides being the BBC's chief executive, he also has the final say in what goes out on air. If he wished to assume temporarily the role of head of Plays, it was his constitutional right.

I had enough to do, so I got on with another project which, quite coincidentally, also dealt with the Falklands War. Charles Wood had written a script entitled *Tumbledown* based on the real-life experience of Lieutenant Robert Lawrence MC. He had been hit in the head by a high-velocity bullet and suffered terrible wounds in the battle to recapture Tumbledown, the high ground above Port Stanley. What made Lawrence's story so poignant was his anger that once the victory had been won, the military and political establishment were desperate to protect the British public from the true human cost of the campaign. He was one of the wounded heroes of the Falklands War, but once peace returned he felt that no one wanted to know about survivors like him. What particularly rankled with him was the great difficulty he had in getting a ticket for the service of thanksgiving for the end of hostilities at St Paul's Cathedral. He was still severely incapacitated and needed crutches to get round, and at the service he found himself stuck in an obscure corner of the nave behind a pillar. He felt this was a deliberate tactic so that the public wouldn't be disturbed to see concrete evidence of what the war had cost. He was a very angry young man.

Charles Wood's script was outstanding and Richard Eyre, who later went on to run the National Theatre and become a governor of the BBC, was keen to direct *Tumbledown*. Then Ian Curteis's script arrived on my desk. Why it had taken so long to reach me was puzzling, not least because, according to the system, I ought to have agreed the money and assigned the production effort some while before. The script came via Bill Cotton but he refused to make any comment until I had read it. I was very disappointed by the script. I had no problem with Ian Curteis's political stance but the quality of the writing was uneven and in places downright bad, which I found surprising since he had been nominated four times for a BAFTA award as dramatist of the year. I recall one scene in the script where General Galtieri in his study at Casa Rosada is poring over a file on Mrs Thatcher. His adviser, Costa-Mendez, launches into a eulogy of the British Prime Minister which even the Conservative Central Office would have thought was gilding the lily. The war is going to be hard to win, he declares, because they are up against a leader who knows what the British people think and feel, and by instinct gives it a voice. 'It is a woman's thing and comes out of here,' he says, thumping his chest. And so on and on. No doubt the Iron Lady's fervent disciples would have echoed that sentiment but as drama it was toe-curling.

I was relieved to discover that Bill Cotton felt even more strongly than I did about the script. We were about to commit £1.5 million of the licence-fee payer's money to what in Hollywood they would call a turkey. But we couldn't follow our professional instincts and cancel production outright at that point, otherwise a whole raft of baseless conclusions would be drawn from our decision – to do with Mrs Thatcher, patriotism, the glory or futility of the Falklands War and the right of a playwright to express his political views. Apart from anything else, the director general himself had commissioned the damn thing and out of loyalty to him we had to try to make it work.

I sent off Peter Goodchild to see Ian Curteis at his home and tell him that some rewriting would be necessary. I suspect this was the first inkling Curteis had that everything was not going according to plan with the play. He was much too experienced a professional not to realize that when the head of BBC Drama visits him in person to discuss details instead of leaving them to the play's producer or director, something is seriously wrong. The upshot was that Ian Curteis rang me and we discussed my anxieties about the play.

I told him I was worried about the ambiguity of the play's point of view about the sinking of the Argentinian battleship, the *Belgrano*, by a British nuclear submarine. The simplest explanation was that if the warship had got amongst British supply ships, there would have been heavy casualties so she had to be eliminated. However, some commentators claimed that the Argentinian battleship had been sunk deliberately to scupper a Peruvian peace initiative so that Mrs Thatcher could ride at the head of her legions to a glorious victory. It wasn't for me to editorialize. I really wasn't bothered which of all the possible reasons Curteis incorporated into his script, but he couldn't leave the issue hanging in the air. I also felt I should warn him that the production of the play was no longer a foregone conclusion: everything would depend on revisions to the script. Peter Goodchild followed up this telephone conversation with a formal letter.

I told Alasdair Milne of my reservations about the play and wondered whether it would not be fairer to Ian Curteis to come clean and tell him frankly that neither Bill nor I liked the play and would prefer to pay him off before matters went any further. We were very conscious of Curteis's outstanding track record and that we ought not to play him along if, in the end, we had no intention of going ahead with the production. Alasdair felt he himself ought to write to Curteis since he had started the whole thing. This he did but, according to Ian Curteis's own account, the reason Alasdair gave for halting its production was the imminent possibility of a general election, which would mean that a drama strongly supporting the Prime Minister would be *parti pris* so the BBC would be unable to transmit it for many months.

By now, Ian Curteis had received so many confusing signals about his play that it was understandable he thought the left-wing cabal that ran the BBC had taken against his pro-Thatcher, pro-war stance and wanted to abandon the drama. In fact, given the sensitivity of relations between the BBC and Mrs Thatcher's government, it would have been madness on my part to make such a crass attempt at censorship, but the true explanation – that the play was just not good enough – was too banal to satisfy the right-wing press, who fastened eagerly on the controversy. We had another confrontation on our hands. What confirmed the deepest suspicions of the anti-BBC faction in the Tory Party was that while I was expressing grave doubts about Ian Curteis's script, I was also enthusiastically promoting *Tumbledown*, which was anti-war and implicitly anti-Thatcher.

Naturally, the BBC governors, reacting like Pavlov's dogs to warning signals in the *Daily Mail* and *Daily Telegraph*, got in on the act. In October 1986, Daphne Park raised the matter at a board meeting. A Margaret Rutherford lookalike with a back-ground in the diplomatic service, she was rumoured to have worked for MI6 so it was a safe bet that she would not be cheering on Bill and me. *Tumbledown* had been commissioned but hadn't yet gone into production, so these heroic guardians of the public interest proposed that the BBC should placate the Government by dropping *Tumbledown* as well as the Curteis play. I assured them that, in my professional judgement and that of the BBC's head of Plays, *Tumbledown* was a wonderful script the BBC absolutely had to produce. I tried to convince them that the problem with the Curteis play was not its political stance, I enjoyed television polemics, but the script was so bad that to transmit it would lay the BBC open to a charge not of political controversy but professional incompetence.

Three times the governors discussed the issue. In effect they gave me an ultimatum: either drop both plays or transmit both.

I had privately made up my mind I would resign rather than give way to them. If they stopped me from making *Tumbledown* or tried to force me to press on with the Curteis play, I was off. I sensed that this was a crunch-point: if the governors' political timidity was allowed to override the informed judgement of the BBC's professionals in deciding programme policy, the Corporation was doomed. Alasdair said nothing at these meetings. Perhaps he felt his credibility with the governors was at such a low ebb that his support for *Tumbledown* would be lethal, or he may have been musing on the problematic consequences of his one foray into the commissioning of drama.

I went to my third meeting of the governors armed with some family background on the hero of *Tumbledown*. His was a military family, his mother had been decorated during the war, his father had served in the Grenadier Guards and when he retired from the Army became assistant secretary of the Marylebone Cricket Club (MCC). Hardly a rabid bunch of Trots. With carefully concealed irony I told the governors that they were 'people like us', who were angry and ashamed at the shabby way their son had been treated. *Tumbledown* went out to universal acclaim; Ian Curteis eventually published the script of his Falklands play and most of the critics saw our point. I didn't regard it as any kind of victory over him; it just wasn't one of his better efforts and I regretted that he read political bias into our judgement.

Dennis Potter was another playwright who got me into much trouble with the BBC governors, but it was an honour because he was the supreme television dramatist. He claims he chose television rather than the theatre or the novel as the vehicle for his ideas because it short-circuited an educational system that, in his view, was hierarchical and dependent on class. As he put it, he wanted 'all sorts and conditions of human being to share the same experiences'. He told the audience at his MacTaggart Memorial Lecture in 1993, 'I first discovered television in my late teens. It made my heart pound. Here was a medium of great power, of potential wondrous delights, that could slice through all the tedious hierarchies of the printed word and help to emancipate us from many of the stifling tyrannies of class and status and gutter-press ignorance. We are privileged who can work in this, the most entrancing of all the many palaces of varieties. Switch on, tune in and *grow*.'

How could one do anything other than warm to someone who was, through and through, a television animal? He understood the medium, its possibilities and its limitations, and could always find the exact words to match the images in his mind. Shortly before I joined the BBC in 1984, Jonathan Powell had commissioned Potter to write a six-part serial provisionally called *Smoke Rings* about a private investigator looking for a missing girl in London at the end of the Second World War. That's how *The Singing Detective* project began, and by the time the first episode was made in 1986, I had become director of programmes. I sat in my office one afternoon and watched a cassette of the opening scenes, more profoundly moved by it than by anything I had ever encountered on television before. To start with, the plot was so intricate that I wasn't entirely clear what exactly was going on, yet I was totally gripped by it. We had a masterpiece on our hands; it was as simple as that. In all the years I was associated with Dennis, I never once asked to read a script in advance. 'Just do it, Jonathan,' I'd say. When you have a team of all the talents like Dennis Potter, Kenith Trodd and Jon Amiel backed by Jonathan Powell, it's a privilege to be able to offer a shop window for their work; you just trust them. Even so, one afternoon during the shooting of the third episode of *The Singing Detective*, Jonathan appeared in my office, with Ken Trodd and Jon Amiel. 'I've got to show you something,' he said.

They played for me what became known as 'the bonking scene' where the young boy playing in the trees catches sight of his mother having sex in the grass with a stranger. In terms of the depiction of the sex act, it was more explicit than anything hitherto seen on BBC. I quizzed them about the scene's context in the piece, then examined it frame by frame – I wanted to be sure we could defend all the angles at which it had been shot and that we weren't lingering for gratuitous effect. That morning's *Today* newspaper carried a story about 'senior BBC officials' expressing alarm about the episode, though who these might be was a mystery, for until Jonathan Powell had shown me the cassette no one outside the production team knew what the bonking scene contained. Ken Trodd afterwards claimed that Dennis himself had given the story to the press to increase the viewing figures. But whoever was responsible for the leak, it was obviously the opening salvo in yet another round of guerrilla warfare with the right-wing press. I could almost hear the creaks and groans from the third floor of Broadcasting House as the governors remounted their high horse.

I asked Jonathan to step outside so that we could talk privately. I had absolute faith in his judgement, and when he assured me that in his opinion the scene was essential, I told him to go ahead, provided the episode carried an advance warning about explicit imagery. I sensed Jonathan had been worried that I might refer the episode upwards to the director general. It had been Alasdair, as managing director of BBC television, who in 1976 banned one of Dennis's earlier plays, *Brimstone and Treacle*, a mere two weeks before it was due to go out.

Of course, all hell broke loose and, of course Mrs Whitehouse announced that she was writing to the Prime Minister, demanding that broadcasting be brought within the scope of the Obscene Publications Act, adding, 'If Michael Grade thinks this episode with its gross sexual violence did not offend against good taste and decency, which it is his job to uphold, then he is not fit for the position he occupies.' The Tory MP Norman Tebbit, who ran the Tory Party's television-monitoring unit, warned that he would investigate the sex scenes with a view to taking action. I was hauled in front of the board of governors whose chairman, Stuart Young, was by then a very sick man. He and Alwyn Roberts, the Welsh governor, were the only friendly faces round the table; the hostility of the rest was almost palpable. Stuart was still sharp enough to propose that my old scourge Sir John Boyd should open the dicussion. Sir John duly produced a notebook and intoned a litany of four-letter words, suggestive gestures and shocking images the episode had contained. He then uttered what became one of the most-quoted malapropisms in the BBC's history: 'I never believed that I should live to see the day when the British Broadcasting Corporation would transmit into the nation's living rooms the depiction of an organism,' he declaimed.

Shoulders began to heave, hands covered mouths and everyone in the room struggled to keep a straight face. That was the high point of the debate, the rest of the discussion was of the 'yes and no with reservations on both sides' kind of equivocation. They decided the bonking scene was a borderline case involving a difficult decision, but by and large the transmission was justified.

The following year, 1987, I fulfilled a long-standing ambition and finally transmitted Potter's *Brimstone and Treacle*. This was only possible because Alasdair Milne, the director general who had banned it, had been replaced by Michael Checkland. I decided to act quickly before Michael, who was not a programme man, settled in and became the focus of all the conflicting pressures that went with the job. I summoned the head of Religious Broadcasting because the play's theme was the incarnation of the devil as a personable young man who foists himself on to a gullible couple and rapes their brain-damaged teenaged daughter. He didn't like it much because it seemed to connive at the humiliation of women but he could see no theological reason why it should not be transmitted. The new director general was persuaded, so I scheduled a Dennis Potter retrospective with *Brimstone and Treacle* as its climax.

I felt honour was satisfied and I'd repaid a long-standing debt to Dennis Potter. Years before, when I was director of programmes at LWT, I had commissioned six location-based dramas from Dennis Potter's production company, PfH, but pulled the plug on the deal when they incurred a huge overspend. I think my decision was inevitable but I always regretted it. Now at last I'd been able to do justice to Dennis's towering ability.

Like my immediate predecessors, I found Northern Ireland a perpetual broadcasters' nightmare. Many of the controversies that had rocked the BBC over the previous three decades had originated across the Irish Sea. Northern Ireland tested to the limit the BBC's doctrine of impartial reporting. What did it mean to be objective in a society where there was no agreement on the legitimacy, form or even boundaries of the state, where at least three cultures told a different story about the past and pursued irreconcilable goals for the future? How, for instance, could you have common news values in a bitterly divided society where an event or a word or an expression regarded as innocent in one community was inflammatory and provocative to the other? There wasn't even any agreement about the words one used to describe people and places – talk to four people on the streets of Belfast; one might say, 'I'm an Ulsterman,' another, 'I'm Irish,' a third, 'I'm British,' and a fourth, 'I belong to Northern Ireland.' If they mentioned that city in the north-west of the province at the head of Lough Foyle, Protestants would call it Londonderry and Catholics Derry. And so on and on.

Successive governments seemed to make two conflicting demands of the BBC. In one breath they'd warn us that there was a war to the death going on against terrorism and we had a patriotic duty to support the struggle to sustain democracy; in the next breath, they would berate us for not portraying the normality of peace-time life in Northern Ireland. Didn't we realize that the images of violence that appeared on our screens were frightening away tourists and possible investors?

We tried to give a fair hearing to all the contending points of view, but this wasn't like a debate in the Oxford Union, where the votes are counted and then everyone goes home. Some ideas came charged with a bitter history, and in the flesh and blood communities beyond the broadcast transmitters they were not just debating points but killing matters. The strain, particularly on our staff in BBC Northern Ireland, was immense. They weren't just soulless extensions of a microphone, television camera or reporter's notebook: their job was emotionally and spiritually draining; the struggle to maintain impartiality in a deeply polarized society exacted a heavy price.

Then there was terrorism. At first sight, it seemed a clean-cut issue. When challenged at a public meeting in Belfast in 1985 the chairman of the governors said, 'Of course, the BBC is against terrorism,' in tones that suggested that only a half-wit could think anything else. But it was clear that by 'terrorism' he was thinking about the IRA, INLA, the UDA or the UVF. Yet there were whole areas of Northern Ireland where highly respected members of the community who loathed the IRA would insist that if the BBC was to declare itself against terrorism it must not discriminate; it ought also to include that form of terrorism to which, they believed, rightly or wrongly, the state turned a blind eye: so-called shoot-to-kill policies by the RUC, Take No Prisoners operations by the SAS, and the like. It required a strong stomach to report such incidents. The outcry was deafening when Thames Television transmitted *Death on the Rock*, a documentary about the killing of three unarmed IRA members by the SAS.

Leaving aside all the thorny issues of government policy and security, the unpalatable truth from a broadcaster's angle is that viewers in other parts of the British Isles react to news about Northern Ireland with either horror or boredom. Until the Good Friday Accord in 1998, it was one of those stories that just kept going round in circles but never got any nearer resolution. There was nothing in it for us: no glory, no viewers, no thanks – only government hassle and viewer resistance. And yet . . . it has been the most important domestic story running for the past quarter-century and no public-service broadcasting organization worthy of the name could ignore it . . .

. . . which brings me to *Real Lives*, the beginning of the end of Alasdair Milne's career in the BBC, and the first stone in an avalanche that was to sweep me away too. The executives responsible for news, current affairs and documentaries had to make most of the knife-edge decisions about Northern Ireland, but I was drawn in if a proposed programme was going out on the channel for which I was responsible. I was part of a referral process that could stop with me or go all the way up to the director general.

In July 1985, Will Wyatt, then head of Documentary Features, called in to see me with the cassette of a programme in his *Real Lives* series called *At the Edge of the Union*. It featured a day in the life of two politicians, both of whom lived in Londonderry but saw things very differently: Martin McGuinness, then deputy leader of Sinn Fein, and Gregory Campbell, of Ian Paisley's Democratic Unionist Party. At the time there was a general ban on the filming of those who had links with the IRA, which only the director general himself could vary, but the advice from BBC Northern Ireland was that because Martin McGuinness was an elected politician, the usual rules didn't apply. The BBC had a statutory duty to give a platform to publicly elected representatives of the people.

I watched the episode, which showed both men making political speeches in public, and as family men, taking their children to school, going to church and engaging in all the routine business of real life. There was no interviewer: the style of *Real Lives* was to allow the subjects to speak for themselves, so no one challenged their ideas, but since half the time was given to McGuinness and half to Campbell the programme, by definition, was balanced. I realized that there were those in Northern Ireland who would find the portrayal of an alleged IRA terrorist as a normal human being intolerable but assumed that the British government would have a more sophisticated understanding of the realities of Northern Ireland politics. I was wrong.

I was happy with the programme and told Will to go ahead. As a courtesy, I rang Bill Cotton, told him what the episode was about and assured him that I could foresee no problems. Meanwhile the other part of the procedural process was being gone through and the BBC controller in Northern Ireland, apart from suggesting one minor alteration, offered his verdict that it was a difficult subject well handled. The programme was scheduled to go out at the beginning of August, preceded by a three-page feature in the *Radio Times*. Then a *Sunday Times* reporter scanning the *Radio Times* noticed that the BBC intended to put out a documentary featuring Martin McGuinness, a man with known links to the IRA. He got an official comment from Douglas Hurd, who was secretary of state for Northern Ireland. He said he was alarmed at the idea of giving terrorists a platform on the BBC. The Prime Minister was in Washington and a reporter was primed to ask a general question about how she would react if she knew a British TV company was going to interview the IRA's chief-of-staff. She said she would condemn them utterly and then went on to detail the number of people who had been killed by the IRA over the past decades.

It was one thing for the Prime Minister to utter a general condemnation in answer to a hypothetical question about television and terrorism, but the screw was tightened when Leon Brittan, who as home secretary had parliamentary responsibility for the BBC, wrote to the chairman of the governors formally requesting him not to allow the programme to go out. Brittan, after much liberal-sounding rhubarb about the governors' exclusive right to decide what should or should not be transmitted, then smoothly reminded them that he was also responsible for law and order and suggested that the fight against terrorism would be subverted if the programme went out – the BBC, he implied, would be conniving at the murder of its own viewers.

We were appalled. Everything would now depend upon a board of governors made up of eleven members, ten of whom had been appointed by Mrs Thatcher. Stuart Young called an emergency meeting of the board. Before that could happen, Bill took the precaution of showing the *Real Lives* programme to the board of management, who unanimously endorsed our decision to clear it for transmission. There was, however, one member of the board of management who had not seen it. By sheer bad luck, a few days before the row blew up, Alasdair had gone off with his wife Sheila for a cruising holiday in Scandinavia and was out of reach somewhere up a Norwegian fjord. Michael Checkland, the newly appointed deputy director general was acting in his place.

The board of governors had two decisions to make at their meeting: first, whether they should break with tradition and see the programme before it was transmitted; then were they of a mind to agree to the home secretary's request that the programme should not be shown? It was a hallowed principle of the BBC that the governors did not preview programmes as this would be second-guessing the professional broadcasters; they reserved their comments until the programmes had been transmitted. *Yesterday's Men*, about Harold Wilson's former cabinet members, was the last programme the governors had insisted on previewing, and that had been fifteen years before. However, Stuart Young felt that unless the governors had seen the programme, they could hardly give the home secretary an informed response to his request. And Leon Brittan's reference to his responsibility for law and order could hardly be ignored.

The broadcasters' case was weakened because Michael Checkland had to concede that there had been a technical breach of the referral procedure in that the director general had not been informed about a proposed documentary featuring the alleged former chief-of-staff of the IRA. Bill Cotton pleaded that the governors should not break with precedent and see the programme as this would fatally undermine the editorial process and subvert the morale of producers. If Stuart was inclined to listen to Bill Cotton, the vice-chairman, William Rees-Mogg, was determined that the governors must see the programme. And so they did, punctuating the viewing, so Bill Cotton reported afterwards, with audible intakes of breath and murmurs of disapproval every time Martin McGuinness was on screen. It was like Saturday morning at the flicks, he said, with the kids hissing every time the villain made an appearance.

The result was inevitable. The vice-chairman felt that the

programme was totally unacceptable since it portrayed the IRA sympathetically. Daphne Park strongly supported the vice-chairman, saying that she was particularly offended by what she called 'the domestication' of the IRA, showing them as 'lovable people with babies'; Jocelyn Barrow thought the programme 'sinister'; Lord Harewood's opinion was that the programme was 'smooth, odious and hateful'. The only dissenting voice was that of Alwyn Roberts, the sole survivor of the pre-Thatcher era, who believed it would be a grievous error not to show the programme.

As staff, we felt betrayed by the people who had been appointed to protect our independence: they had buckled in the face of a blatant attempt by the Thatcher government to censor the BBC. I confess that as Will Wyatt and I waited in my office at the Television Centre for news of the meeting, we hoped against hope that the immense experience of Bill and Brian Wenham would carry the day against a bunch of amateurs who didn't really know what to think until the *Daily Telegraph* told them. At the very least, I thought, if they weren't prepared to back the programme, they could put the onus on the home secretary to use his reserve powers to ban it, a step that even Winston Churchill shrank from during the Second World War. When we heard the result of the governors' meeting, we knew we had suffered a major defeat. They had sold out the BBC's hard-won independence for the sake of a programme which, but for the mischief-making of the *Sunday Times*, would probably have attracted little interest because it was soft-edged and politically balanced to the point of paralysis.

Next day, most of the newspapers carried the news of the governors' action as their main story. It was the usual ideological split: the right-wing press supported the government and therefore applauded the board's action, while those concerned with civil liberties and freedom of expression were alarmed at the consequences for the independence of the BBC. The *Guardian* dismissed the governors in one contemptuous phrase: 'They copped out; they caved in.' Outraged, BBC journalists called a one-day strike, supported by some of the staff of ITN, the commercial channel's news service.

Alasdair got back from his holiday, saw the cassette, agreed with the board of management that there was no reason why the programme should have been banned and met the governors. Obviously, in the intervening few days, they had been shocked by the amount of criticism from many directions, so they agreed that the programme, with one or two changes, could be shown in the autumn. Sir William Rees-Mogg dissented: he was in favour of continuing the ban indefinitely. Alasdair won a victory of sorts, but any credibility he had with the board was gone. It was a malign fate that he should have been away when the *Real Lives* crisis reached its climax, but things might have been dramatically different if when Michael Checkland had managed to reach him by telephone to tell him about the impending governors' meeting, he had stood on his authority as editor-in-chief of the Corporation and insisted that the discussion in the board should be delayed until he could get back. But he hadn't and eventually paid the price for his uncertain grasp on the power of his office.

On the sixth floor of the Television Centre we held a post-mortem on the whole sorry business. We had only compassion for Stuart Young, the chairman, who was seriously ill and just hadn't the energy to get the result he would obviously have preferred. He was certainly unable to impose his will on the vice-chairman, Rees-Mogg, who had emerged as the strong man of the governors. That was bad news for all of us and for Alasdair in particular. Rees-Mogg, with his supercilious manner, never bothered to hide his dislike of the BBC and his determination to reorganize the entire place, beginning with the firing of the director general, whom he thought both arrogant and incompetent. We could understand why a governor like Lady Faulkner, the widow of a former Northern Ireland prime minister, might find the sight of Martin McGuinness distasteful, but Rees-Mogg had been editor of *The Times*, for God's sake, that great organ of liberty and truth, and here he was, on the same side as the government in the crudest form of censorship.

Some months before, Sir William Rees-Mogg and I had taken an instant dislike to each other when we were having one of our periodic discussions with the board of governors about violence on television. The head of Religious Broadcasting had written a paper outlining the issues and Rees-Mogg was asked to open the debate. I had noticed that Stuart tended to defer to his vice-chairman – perhaps he thought that, as a mere accountant, he was outgunned by the patrician intellectual with the snooty voice and lordly manner. (Rees-Mogg was made a life peer shortly after he retired from the board so he was obviously rehearsing for his future role.) In fact, Stuart had a gift rarer than clever-ness: he was a wise man even when he was racked by pain and heavily drugged.

'I have formed the view . . .' began Sir William. He was always forming views. This circumlocution was longhand for 'This is the word of the Lord.' John Birt was fond of another: 'I have trouble with that argument', which meant 'Shut up. I've made up my mind.' Rees-Mogg once wrote a book called *An Humbler Heaven*; it was surprising that there was *anything* humble in his universe. 'I have formed the view,' he said, 'that in the days before television when there was the wireless, the world was a more peaceful place and traditional values were much more import-ant.' On and on he went: Merrie England, cold tea and warm sandwiches on the vicarage lawn, spinsters cycling to church, the whole nostalgia bit about which John Major was later to wax poetical during the 1997 general election campaign. It was a con. Rees-Mogg may have been an antiquarian bookseller but he was also an up-to-the-minute monetarist, loaded down with direc-torships of banks and companies, including a non-executive directorship of GEC, a firm that was actually suing the BBC for breach of contract over a satellite venture. As he would say, I had formed the view that there was a conflict of interest here somewhere. It must have been a delicate ethical balancing act to sit on both boards, privy to confidential information from each side. Perhaps not: maybe he hated the BBC so much that a clash of loyalties just didn't arise.

As I listened to him pontificating from on high, I wondered what kind of a world he inhabited. Stuart could see I was bursting to say something, and gave me the floor. 'All I know is that, as a kid, I loved the radio, and I was brought up on a diet of mindless pap like *Ignorance Is Bliss*, *Ray's A Laugh* and *Up the Pole*, together with a nightly quarter of an hour of coshes, guns and general mayhem called *Dick Barton, Special Agent*, so where Sir William has got the idea from that the world was a more peaceful place before television, I really don't understand. And I seem to remember that in the tranquil days before television, there were two world wars.'

He said no more to me, but I knew I had made an enemy for life. He was later to describe me as a 'bounder in the Wodehousean sense', which I rather liked. To me, Rees-Mogg was the epitome of the people who ended up on the bodies controlling broadcasting during the Thatcher years. They didn't like television, they sneered at the people who made it and they thought they knew what was best for the people who watched it. This combination of cultural snobbery and political conservatism paralysed the BBC. Every programme innovation we tried to make that involved any degree of risk-taking had to be fought through against a bitching, carping board. We couldn't win: if we put out programmes popular enough to send the ratings soaring, we were accused of offering 'moving wall-paper, no more informative than the penny dreadfuls', as *The Times* put it. If ratings fell, the same newspaper attacked us for taking licence-fee money under false pretences.

Still, there was more to my job than worrying about the political fall-out from the *Real Lives* programme. I got on with the business of strengthening the BBC 1 schedules. Bill Cotton, on a scouting expedition to Australia, recommended an intriguing soap called *Neighbours*. I looked at it and bought it. I decided to schedule it twice a day, putting out an episode at lunchtime, then repeating it in the late afternoon after

children's programmes and before the *Six o'Clock News*. My hope
was that both programmes would benefit – the news through
inheritance and children's programmes by early switchers-on.
The tactic worked a treat.

The pulling power of *Neighbours* proved enormous and was
neatly demonstrated in Northern Ireland. For years there had
been a strand of regional cultural programmes in the early
evening, complete with Irish fiddlers and even a presenter
dressed as a leprechaun. When we scheduled *Neighbours* in the
early evening, Northern Ireland decided to abandon its own
programme and take the soap. There was uproar in the NI
Broadcasting Council and in the Ulster press generally at the
cultural vandalism of replacing Irish high culture with Australian
schlock. The Northern Ireland governor raised the issue in
London, though the Ulster Unionists were pleased about the
change because they had suspected all along that Irish cultural
programmes were crypto-IRA propaganda. BBC Northern Ireland stuck to its guns, and a couple of months later a mere
newspaper rumour that *Neighbours* was likely to be discontinued
in favour of a return to pukka regional broadcasting complete
with leprechauns and Irish harpists almost led to rioting in the
streets of Belfast.

This tension in BBC Northern Ireland between the claims
of a network soap like *Neighbours* and locally originated programmes illustrated what I found to be *the* most difficult aspect
of my job: working out some way of accommodating programmes that originated in the BBC's regions without diluting
the overall quality of BBC 1. The three national regions, Scotland, Wales and Northern Ireland, each had a governor specifically appointed to see that it got a fair crack of the whip, its
share of resources and network air time – and a thorn in my
flesh some of these governors became. It took only my PA to
announce the arrival of a regional controller with his national
governor in tow, usually frothing at the mouth with righteous
indignation because a Welsh *eisteddfod* or Scottish bagpiping

competition hadn't been transmitted on BBC 1 and a black cloud descended on my spirits that took days to lift.

The key issue was: ought the BBC to make programmes *from* as well as *for* the entire British land area in order to legitimize its claim to a licence fee? I knew this was a political minefield because my correspondence tray was packed with letters from MPs who had constituencies in the regions and needed its outlets to address their constituents, so they kept a close eye on the balance between programmes originating from London and from the rest of the country.

There were two aspects to the problem: one was that the regions had recognized times when they could opt out of BBC 1 and show programmes made in the particular region for the viewers of that region, which played havoc with BBC 1's ratings when we were in a life-and-death struggle with ITV; the other was that the regions expected some of their programmes to be shown on the network, for the quite legitimate reason that the rest of the United Kingdom ought to be exposed to the distinctive culture of one part of it. Regrettably, too often a region was only represented on the network in such a way as to give a distorted view or even parody of its culture. There is more to Wales than male-voice choirs, to Scotland than the Edinburgh Tattoo and, God knows, there's more to Northern Ireland than the images of war that packed the news bulletins and current-affairs programmes during my time as controller.

Through no fault of their own, the BBC regions were up against what has been called the critical-mass theory of television. A television programme may well begin as a solitary inspiration thrown up by a writer or producer who evolves, nurtures and fights for it, eventually persuading some controller to back it. Yet once conceived, good programmes are usually the product of teams of people of allied disciplines who rub shoulders together, argue, refine or demolish treatments, exchange experiences and achieve levels of creativity together that none could reach individually. It takes outstanding self-generating creative impulses on the part of individual and isolated producers to compensate for the range of talent a larger team can offer. And the relevance of the size of the creative unit to regional broadcasting is obvious. As a general rule, production teams dedicated to regional programmes tend to be small and modestly resourced, and although it is not true that there is a positive link between quality and cost – any number of brilliant programmes give the lie to the notion that throwing money at the screen is enough to produce a masterpiece – I do think the opposite is true, that there is a certain financial base-line below which it is just not possible to deliver high-quality network programmes. And even with BBC Television's huge budget, it was just not possible to finance regional programming to the same level as network television.

This was the problem that dare not speak its name in the BBC during my time, especially with national governors on the rampage. I became something of a hate figure in the BBC regions because I insisted that I would not transmit sub-standard programmes on my network, no matter how many Brownie points the BBC might get as a result. Now I freely confess that, for as long as the BBC has existed, regional broadcasters have had to battle against the arrogance and parochialism of metropolitan BBC executives who tended to talk about the regions as though beyond the ambit of the M25 there was only, as the ancient maps used to say, *terra incognita*, whose inhabitants had yet to get the hang of the crystal set let alone the subtleties of the on-off button.

In fact, I didn't underestimate the importance of regional broadcasting, having spent six years in Hollywood, where much television output has no sense of place but is rooted firmly in mid-air, originating in a ghostly trans-national realm of unfixed boundaries and deliberately blurred accents so that it will appeal to the widest possible audience. Regional broadcasting is that part of the industry which insists that the reality of people's lives is earthed firmly in a particular place where they are surrounded by family, friends, neighbours, workmates, enemies, where they live and love and die; whose lives are a fully sensuous experience of distinctive sounds and smells and sights and tastes; of a history whose key events are commemorated all round them.

But the centralizing tendency of television is irresistible. Scholars seem to be divided as to whether it is even possible to talk any longer about something called 'British culture' as a coherent system of common beliefs, values and assumptions that bind us together. To the extent that Brixton and Bournemouth, Gateshead and Glasgow, Penzance and Port Talbot can be said to share a common culture, network television has become its chief adhesive force. By its very nature, public-service broadcasting must mark and celebrate as many aspects as possible of our national life, the sporting, political and ceremonial events that transcend local and sectional interests. It provides public symbols around which fragmented groups and individuals can cohere – as, for example, those ritual fixed points at which much of the nation gathers, such as the news, Wimbledon, the Cenotaph, the Cup final and so on.

This understanding of the role of television inevitably elevates the network at the expense of local and regional broadcasting – and where the understanding goes, the money usually follows. I offered a weekly opt-out slot after the *Nine o'Clock News*, and tried to encourage the production of regional programmes of such a quality and interest that the network would be glad to be able to transmit them. Much depended on there being in place talented producers in the various regions. Thus, when BBC Scotland appointed the distinguished theatrical producer Bill Bryden as its head of Drama, *Tutti Frutti* with Robbie Coltrane and Emma Thompson soon followed. But during my time as controller of BBC 1, I never really resolved the regional broadcasting/network tension, and I don't know of anyone else in the business who did. ITV claimed to have avoided this problem because the system is by definition a federation of regional production companies. In reality, many of the producers whose names appear on the credits of ITV dramas from Yorkshire or Granada are actually based in London and spend much of their time on trains between London and Manchester or Leeds.

In June 1986, I replaced Brian Wenham as director of programmes in the television service, then two months later came both good news and bad news: the good news was that William Rees-Mogg's spell as vice-chairman of the board of governors came to an end and off he went to lord it over the Arts Council. He was replaced by Lord (Joel) Barnett, who, at least on paper, seemed to redress the political balance a little because he had been a Labour cabinet minister. The awful news was that Stuart Young died.

Mixed with our sorrow at the loss of a good man, who genuinely cared for the BBC and its staff, there was apprehension about his likely replacement. A shudder of horror ran through the Television Centre when someone in news and current affairs heard a leak in Whitehall that the job had been offered to Rees-Mogg. Apparently, he *was* sounded out by Downing Street for the post but decided to stick with the Arts Council, though he did warmly recommend his friend and neighbour in Somerset. Marmaduke Hussey had two claims to fame: his wife was a lady-in-waiting to the Queen, and as managing director of Times Newspapers he had presided over a long and very damaging strike in 1978. In such a nudge-and-wink way was one of the most important jobs in British public life determined; this was how the Thatcherite establishment operated. Someone knew someone who knew someone within the magic circle of 'people like us'. Lady Susan's brother was the Conservative cabinet minister William Waldegrave, so royal, aristocratic and political cogs neatly intermeshed. Dukey's illustrious connections certainly did not count against him: his career in the media had been so undistinguished that his old employer Rupert Murdoch was dumbstruck when he heard the news of his appointment. 'You'll never guess who they've appointed to run the BBC. Old Dukey!' he crowed. Rupert Murdoch had spread his tentacles over satellite television and had become one of the BBC's competitors, so his glee did not suggest that he was worried by any competition offered by an organization headed by Dukey.

Hussey's insouciance about his new appointment was revealed in a press story that reported he was so ignorant about broadcasting he had to ask his wife where the BBC was. Ah, the drollery of the landed classes! Lady Susan obligingly looked up 'British Broadcasting Corporation' in the telephone directory, and Dukey had to make his first decision: should he show up at Broadcasting House in Portland Place or the Television Centre in Shepherds Bush? The press were asking us to believe that the former managing director of *The Times* had never come across the BBC!

That story didn't reassure us much; nor did the manner in which we were told of Dukey's appointment. It eloquently illustrated the contempt the government had for the BBC. Five minutes before the appointment was due to be announced to the press, Alasdair was called out of a conference to take a phone call from the Home Office to be told that someone he had never heard of was to become chairman of the BBC. We consoled ourselves with the knowledge that at least it wasn't Rees-Mogg, and by then we were equally relieved that the vice-chairman, Joel Barnett, hadn't been promoted either, for in the interregnum he had made himself fairly obnoxious.

Barnett was a boring little man with the stature and aggression of a Jack Russell terrier. He had briefly emerged from political obscurity when Harold Wilson appointed him chief secretary to the Treasury, and didn't he let us know it! Every now and then we had to remind ourselves he had been a *Labour* MP. I recall a governors' meeting at which he presided where it was reported that John Timpson, the veteran presenter of the *Today* programme on Radio 4, was retiring. The Tory press had already consigned his colleague Brian Redhead well to the

revolutionary side of Lenin, so the question was, would John
Humphrys, his replacement, redress the political balance of the
programme or swing it even further to the left? It is one of the
hallowed traditions of the BBC that programme presenters keep
their party allegiance to themselves and give all politicians a
hard time, yet I heard Barnett say, 'I hope he's not another of
those left-wingers.' This was the governor brought in to provide
a political counterweight to the Tory chairman, and he was
actually monitoring the politics of the staff! None of the board
of management present protested at this remark. We just sat
silently. I should have said something, but I was the most junior
member of the board, it wasn't my place to upstage the director
general. That's what I told myself but I knew in my heart that we
were all colluding by our silence in the breaking of the BBC's
independent spirit.

Bill Cotton, who had a keen nose for internal politics, said
that the government had brought in Duke Hussey to complete
Rees-Mogg's unfinished agenda and get rid of Alasdair Milne.
The journalist Hugo Young agrees that this was the plan. In his
study of Mrs Thatcher, *One of Us*, he wrote:

A new chairman [of the BBC] had been appointed and within
months he had sacked the Director General. Early in 1987,
the most important television strategist in the Thatcher circle
gave me his assessment of the different news organizations
which the election managers were prepared to do business
with. ITN, he reckoned, was entirely 'sound'. The right people
were in the key positions and were known to be sympathetic to
the government's problems. Channel 4 News was entirely
unsound, but since it was watched by a minority audience this
deficiency did not matter. The BBC was the problem. Nobody
could be sure who exactly was in charge there: to whom
complaints should be made and pressure applied.

Quite soon, however, this problem was solved with a reor-
ganization of BBC personnel. The steady drip of the Conservative attack had worked its effect on the self-confidence of the
broadcasters. The new priority, unspoken and often unacknow-
ledged, even privately, was the avoidance of rows of the kind

that Tebbit in particular had shown himself cynically adept at orchestrating. By the time the campaign looked all but certain to culminate in a June election, and not to be delayed any further, most of the important television coverage could be accounted 'sound.'

On Wednesday 28 January 1987, there was a farewell dinner for the Welsh governor, Alwyn Roberts. All the governors and about fifty of the senior staff were present in the Council Chamber. The atmosphere was charged: Alwyn had been very much a hero to BBC staff for his lone stand against the banning of *Real Lives* and his consistent support for the board of management, so we were determined to give him a rousing send-off. In retrospect, I recall that the other governors seemed somewhat subdued, but I assumed this was because they felt the staff were comparing them unfavourably to him: too true. There was only one curious incident. Sir John Boyd, who was not a drinking man and quickly became tired and emotional when the port was passed round, got into an argument about *Real Lives* with one of the senior staff sitting opposite him and startled everyone in the vicinity by shouting, 'You lot think you can do what the hell you like. Well, just you wait, you'll see!' No one read any particular significance into his words – until lunchtime the next day. The following morning there was a routine board of governors meeting and I had already asked the chairman to allow me to leave during the coffee-break because Sarah and I were off on a skiing holiday to Méribel. When the meeting broke up I excused myself and Duke Hussey walked with me to the lift. He was a big man, both in stature and presence, who stumped around the corridors of Broadcasting House, booming like an old buffer in a London club. He had gained our admiration for one thing: the way he coped with the pain and discomfort of an artificial limb, the result of losing a leg at the Anzio beach-head. One of my colleagues who had served in the Army explained Duke's psychology to me. Dukey reminded him of generals he'd encountered who treated private soldiers with great respect but were absolutely beastly to their immediate subordinates. I suppose I was too low down the hierarchy to bother him, so he was always hearty, even effusive in his dealings with me. He put his arm on my shoulder. 'Have a great holiday, Michael, enjoy yourself. Come back refreshed, and thanks for your contribution this morning. Cheerio.'

Off I went, picked up Sarah and we drove down to Dover to catch the ferry. I was bowling down the A2 when my car phone rang. It was Graeme McDonald, the controller of BBC 2. He was passing on a message from Bill Cotton. The governors had just fired Alasdair Milne. We were already in the ferry terminal when Bill himself came on the phone. Apparently, when the governors broke for lunch, Dukey had sent for Alasdair and he and Barnett presented him with an ultimatum. It was the unanimous wish of the board that he should leave immediately. The chairman held out an already prepared letter of resignation. Unable to believe what was happening to him, and taciturn to the last, Alasdair said nothing, signed the letter, then swiftly and silently left the Television Centre.

The ferry docked in Calais, we drove off and as we were passing through the customs area, my phone rang again. It was Dukey, very apologetic that he couldn't have told me earlier about the governors' decision and full of 'Steady the Buffs!' rhetoric that had probably worked a treat with the Other Ranks in the Guards. He was relying on Bill Cotton and me to keep things on an even keel. Michael Checkland, the deputy director general, would act until a new appointment was made. We continued with our holiday, though thoughts of the BBC constantly intruded, and Sarah and I debated the matter on and off. I could not put my hand on my heart and swear that Alasdair had been an outstandingly successful director general, but he had given his life to the BBC and it seemed to me the way Dukey and Barnett had dealt with the matter was unforgivable. Perhaps it was right that he should go, but the thing could have been accomplished without robbing him of his dignity as well as his career.

By the time I got back to the Television Centre, the rumour mill was working overtime. The job had been advertised and the names of just about everyone except the commissionaire on the main gate were being bandied about. Bill and I both knew who we wanted. Paul Fox had been an outstanding controller of BBC 1 and had then left the BBC in 1973 to become managing director of Yorkshire Television. I had worked with him when I was at LWT and had great respect for him; he was the outstanding elder statesman of the industry, so he would be no pushover for the governors. He was also a close friend of Bill Cotton and whoever became director general would need Bill's support.

We decided to try out the idea on Dukey and waited on him by arrangement at his Chelsea flat. Lady Susan was off to the Palace and put me in charge of the kitchen. Over supper, Dukey listened intently to our arguments but wouldn't commit himself. Bill thought we had made some progress, though when Barnett heard of the proposal he insisted that Paul, at sixty-one, was too old for the job. But that was our whole point: the BBC needed someone of Paul's stature and experience to calm the place down after a period of turmoil, rally the staff and hold the fort until the next generation of leaders emerged. In fact, Dukey already had his preferred candidate. A few days later, newspaper leaks claimed he was backing David Dimbleby, a proposition we thought eccentric to the point of absurdity. David was a splendid current-affairs presenter but knew nothing about management other than what he had learned from owning a small newspaper company in Richmond. He was also a heavyweight journalist, very much in the mould of his distinguished father, Richard: Bill and I feared that under him, the entertainment side of the BBC, which to us was central, would be neglected. Our opposition hardened when the usual channels let it be known that 10 Downing Street would welcome his appointment.

Bill was close to retirement anyway, but I had a fair slice of my career ahead of me and I was damned if I would spend it in the BBC working under David Dimbleby, so I told Bill I intended to write to Hussey to tell him in a spirit of frankness that, should the governors decide to appoint David, I was off. Bill looked at me quizzically over his glasses and said that if I were going to send a letter like that I was morally obliged to put my own hat in the ring. It is true that, in the newspaper stakes, my name had been mentioned among the also-rans and excluded from the list of favourites for all sorts of reasons ranging from my age (too young), through my song-and-dance background (too frivolous) to my red braces (too vulgar). I had just treated the newspaper odds as a joke.

I have been called cocky and might plead guilty but insane to that verdict, but I've never had an inflated opinion of my own significance, and I knew I hadn't an outside chance of getting the job. Never one to flatter, Bill agreed, but insisted that wasn't the point. An extended interview with the governors in which I set out my programme philosophy would stand me in good stead when he retired from his post as managing director of the television service. 'They'll probably give you my job without an interview,' he said. I would also get the chance to put an alternative view about the BBC to that which David Dimbleby had already been canvassing in one or two well-publicized speeches.

This was the first time in my entire career I had ever applied for a job and been subjected to an interview. I assembled a panel of inquisitors who tore to shreds my answers to the kind of questions I was likely to be asked by the governors. It consisted of Sarah, whose built-in crap detector was second to none, Peter Ibbotson, my deputy at the Television Centre, and, irony of ironies, my old friend from LWT, John Birt. He was repaying me for the time I had helped him audition for the Channel 4 chief executive's job. John hadn't been educated at a Jesuit school for nothing: he made a natural Torquemada, merciless in his logic and persistence. My manifesto included the merger of News and Current Affairs, a reduction of the layers of control that had helped to create chaos in the *Real Lives* débâcle and much greater decentralization of resources as well as power so that many more BBC programmes would be made *in* as well as *for* every part of the British Isles.

There were five other candidates, Jeremy Isaacs of Channel 4, David Dimbleby, Anthony Smith, former editor of *Panorama*, a respected television academic, and my colleagues Michael Checkland and Brian Wenham. Paul Fox had refused to submit himself for interview but let it be known that he would take the job if it were offered to him. I was the last in and presented myself at the director general's office on the third floor at Broadcasting House flaunting my red braces and socks. The interview was to be held in the boardroom next door. As I sat in Reith's chair and waited to be called, in walked a pert, bright lady who introduced herself as Ros Sloboda, Alasdair Milne's former PA, now awaiting reassignment. It was a reflection on the remoteness of the centre of power at Broadcasting House from the Television Centre that in three years I had never even met her. She was refreshing in her forthrightness: there was none of the traditional BBC solemn respect accorded to senior managers by the lower orders. 'You know you won't get the job,' she said, with a grin. She made such an impact on me that when I left for Channel 4, I took her with me as my PA. I tend to act on instinct, and that was one of my better impulses.

I had a very relaxed interview. It was the end of a long day for the governors and I sensed as soon as I went in that I wasn't a serious candidate. They were friendly, even jokey, and laughed heartily at all my quips. They nodded approvingly at my proposals, knowing full well they would never have to live with them. With Bill's help, I'd prepared a final out-cue. When, as is the custom, I was asked by the chairman if there was anything I wanted to say to the Board, I said that Reith had been twenty-seven when he was appointed director general of the BBC and since I was all of forty-three, I hoped they wouldn't hold my great age against me. I left to murmurs of appreciation and Dukey's effusive protestations of immense gratitude that I had offered myself for interview. He could afford to be magnanimous: it wasn't going to cost him anything.

After the interview, I repaired to my office, where a whole gang had assembled to gossip, drink and wait for the white smoke to emerge from Broadcasting House. There were Peter Ibbotson, Ron Neil, editor of television news, Sue Lawley and several others. People drifted in and out to ask about my interview and pass on the rumours and counter-rumours flying around the place – Sir John Boyd had given Jeremy Isaacs a bad time, suggesting he was arrogant and undisciplined; Paul Fox had been spotted entering Broadcasting House by the back door; Anthony Smith had delivered a lecture on his programme philosophy so dense that several governors nodded off. Coffee and sandwiches gave way to drinks as the hours passed and there was no word from the governors. We had assumed the dead-line would be the *Nine o'Clock News* for if the decision hadn't been made by then the biggest news to come out of the BBC for a long time would be a gift for ITN's *News at Ten*.

Finally, at around ten o'clock, the phone rang. Everyone in the room froze. I carefully kept my face expressionless, put the phone down and reached for my drink. They all bellowed at me, 'Well?'

'We fucked Dimbleby!' I shouted triumphantly. The chosen candidate was Michael Checkland. I could live with that, though I would have preferred Wenham. The BBC being what it is, my exultant outburst went round the place like wildfire and afterwards I had to grovel abjectly to David Dimbleby – I didn't want him as director general but I needed him as a presenter.

Radical change was inevitable. One moral of the Milne years was that most of his problems had originated in the Current Affairs department, ranging from Norman Tebbit's attack on Kate Adie for having the audacity to mourn the death of Libyan citizens killed in a Western bombing raid to Michael Cockerill's *Panorama* accusing Maggie of having her own militant tendency. Then there were *Carrickmore* and *Real Lives*, time-bombs from Northern Ireland that exploded in the BBC's face. The new director general was an accountant by training who had spent all his BBC career finding the resources to enable producers to make programmes. From the sidelines, Michael Checkland had watched Alasdair's slide into disaster and he knew that Dimbleby, whose strength was current affairs, had been the chairman's choice for the job. When Dukey realized that the board would only settle for Checkland, he had tried in vain to make Michael's appointment conditional on his accepting Dimbleby as his deputy. Mike refused and Dukey capitulated, but the new director general knew that news and current affairs would have to be sorted out smartly otherwise he would confirm the chairman's judgement that he had been wrong to refuse to work with Dimbleby.

Alan Protheroe, the assistant director general, an experienced journalist, had been responsible for all the Corporation's news and current affairs. A wry Welshman with a sardonic wit and a bolshie streak, Alan had incurred the governors' wrath when after the *Real Lives* affair, he wrote a scintillating article for the *Listener* in which he said that when the home secretary thanked the BBC governors for banning *Real Lives*, it was like the White Star Line congratulating the iceberg for sinking the *Titanic*. It would be fair to say that for the governors the article had a lack of fascination all its own; Rees-Mogg wanted him fired. He barely survived that time but was later held responsible when BBC *Breakfast Time* taped off-air an extract from an exclusive TV-am interview with Princess Michael of Kent. The governors were livid and Alan was shuffled sideways, taking early retirement shortly afterwards. So there was a vacancy.

One of Mike's first acts as director general was to set up a high-powered group to wrestle with the journalism problem, and he accepted its recommendation that there should be created a News and Current Affairs directorate as powerful as the other two, Television and Radio. I was in sympathy with this idea – indeed, I had suggested something of the sort at my interview with the governors. The question was: who would run it? It was clear there was no one suitable within the BBC itself: the strongest candidates had either already gone or were in the eyes of the governors tainted by association with a string of disasters.

The job involved merging News and Current Affairs, two departments who had been at loggerheads for years and had quite different philosophies of journalism. A new structure was needed to implement a new ideology. Now, who did I know who was a wizard at Meccano-like structure-building and had an ideology in his pocket for every eventuality? I had long thought the BBC needed John Birt but I had been unable to persuade Alasdair of this. Now I tried again. Bill and I discussed the possibility of importing John Birt, only to discover that his name had also been proposed to Mike Checkland by Paul Fox.

I was delighted when Mike Checkland told me that Dukey had agreed to the appointment of John Birt. I phoned John immediately, enthusing about my vision of the BBC run by a triumvirate: Checkland looking after the money and keeping the governors happy, John sorting out the journalism, and me worrying about the ratings and the quality of television. John was cautious: there were, he said, matters still to be decided. I presumed he was arguing about money. I just assured him of a warm welcome and rang off. A few days later, John rang me. He asked me if I would mind if his title was deputy director general? Even though this would make him technically my senior, I could see no problem if it merely meant that John stood in for Mike when he was away. I had enough on my plate without worrying about the ceremonial minutiae of the Corporation.

It was so long since I had worked with John that I'd forgotten he always thinks several moves ahead in the chess game of life; nor had I registered the significance of Mike Checkland's role as deputy director general in the *Real Lives* affair. Afterwards, there had been animated discussion in management circles about the phone call Mike made to Alasdair in the Norwegian fjords telling him that the governors were due to meet the next day to discuss banning the programme. There were those who claimed that Mike did not want Milne to return for the governors' meeting because he was anxious to prove that he could handle a tricky situation and so make his mark for the future. I never believed that for a moment, but in there somewhere was an object lesson about the considerable powers of the deputy director general. It was those bloody titles again. I never got the hang of them, and this time it mattered. If one of the director general's titles is editor-in-chief, which meant he had the final word on all programmes right across the Corporation, it followed that John's role could also be construed as having the same breadth of responsibility.

I should have known that John wouldn't press for that title simply to sit in Reith's old office for a couple of weeks every now and then when Mike went off on holiday. But Mike assured me that John's remit was strictly News and Current Affairs, and I believed him. He must obviously have agreed different terms with John, who, I now realize, would never have taken the job unless his editorial brief covered the whole Corporation, including, of course, the television service, for which I was responsible. Since I wouldn't stand for that, Mike had a problem.

I first realized that something was wrong shortly after John's arrival when I started getting handwritten notes from him about television output, asking for clarification of this or an explanation about that. At first I took this as a typical Birtian attention to detail, but I got really narked when I televised a Frank Bruno fight that turned out to be hopelessly one-sided because Frank had been matched with a 'horizontal heavyweight', though I wasn't to know that beforehand. I got a pained note from John sniffily enquiring whether we ought to be televising such travesties? By this time I was managing director designate, about to move into Bill Cotton's office on his retirement date. I went to see Michael, seeking clarification.

Mike seemed to take my point. The notes duly stopped and it looked as though things were settling down nicely. In fact, John and I were on an inevitable collision course because of our diametrically opposed understanding of our reponsibilities; a fatal clash was inevitable sooner or later, and it came when we had to set up a board to appoint new channel controllers for both BBC 1 and BBC 2. I was about to vacate the BBC 1 job on becoming managing director of television, and Graeme

McDonald, controller of BBC 2, was retiring. These were two of the most important jobs in the entire Corporation, arguably more critical to the BBC's health and success than the director general or chairman because most licence-fee payers paid up to watch television; they accepted radio as a bonus. If the ratings and quality of the two television channels fell off, the licence fee was under threat, and that meant the entire funding of the Corporation was in jeopardy. So we had to make the right appointments.

I got a call from Bill Cotton to tell me that the board had been constituted with John Birt a member and himself excluded. This was outrageous. Bill was the most experienced programme man in the place; he'd seen the careers of all the likely candidates blossom. His knowledge was irreplaceable. On the other hand, I had been assured by Mike Checkland that John Birt had nothing to do with the television service. I wrote a note to Michael Checkland, telling him I was deeply unhappy at Bill's exclusion and Birt's inclusion. What had it all to do with the deputy director general, anyway? I pointed out that in neither the internal nor the public announcement about John's appointment was there any hint that his responsibilities would include an editorial role in all the programmes across the directorates: 'If the full extent of the DDG's remit had been explained to me I would have fought strongly against it. To give any DDG a formal position in the programme policy of the television service can only lead to divided responsibility and ultimately confusion in the programme departments where decisions are made. This must in turn weaken the authority of the managing director and divide the team – a miserable prospect.'

It would send out all the wrong signals to the staff in the television service if Birt, who nominally outranked me, had a hand in choosing my two closest colleagues. It meant I was not master in my own house. Mike's deliberate ambiguity about my relationship to John Birt had run its course. Now he had to decide something. Bill Cotton also had a frank exchange with Mike and told him he wasn't going to have the ex-controller of programmes of a three-day-a-week channel like LWT telling him who to choose to run the BBC's two television channels. Mike assured him he would sort it out.

But when Bill and I were summoned to a meeting in Checkland's office at which John was present, Mike began by stating that he still wanted John Birt to be a member of the board. He was acutely uncomfortable, and when pressed for reasons, said that the deputy director general had the right to be there, and the chairman would like it that way. Fateful words. I knew this was a battle I couldn't win, but I decided to appeal to Mike's sense of fair play, pointing out that this was not the agreement about territorial boundaries he had sold me when John was appointed. I also asked him to understand that my authority in the television service would be damaged if I was not able to make key appointments without John Birt's approval. To this point, John Birt had sat silently. Now called on to say something, he was stern and unrelenting. His contract said that he was deputy director general and that's what he intended to be. Checkland made no attempt to defend the gloss he'd put on the whole thing to get me to agree to John's appointment, but mumbled something to the effect that this was the way 'we' wanted it to be. Dukey, Mike and John. That was the game. Once Bill had retired and I was tamed, the old BBC was history. A great new order was about to be born.

That was the moment when I knew my BBC career was over. I am not a bare-knuckle fighter, I recoil from confrontation with my friends, so I pleaded with John, 'I beg you not to push this, not to put me in an impossible position with my own staff. I'm begging you to back off.' But I was looking into the eyes of a stranger; it was as though all the years as colleagues and friends had never been. I'd heard stories about John's cold ruthlessness but had discounted them as the sort of misreading of his character easily made by those who did not understand him. I ought to have realized that John's Grand Plan made no provision for the claims of friendship. It had to be in his interest to have me out of the way because he intended to be the next director general and I was the only possible candidate who could stand in his way. Checkland was a pawn in John's game; Dukey he had sized up and would play on his snobbery and vanity to get his way.

'I'm sorry,' said a tight-lipped John. 'This is the way the director general and the chairman want it and this is the way it will be.'

Checkland proposed what he called a compromise. John would be on the board but I had the chairman's word that the candidates appointed would be the ones I favoured (Jonathan Powell and Alan Yentob as it transpired). I agreed to go along with that. I owed it to the BBC to see that the right people became controllers, though I was embarrassed at the duplicity of it all: here we were rigging in advance the results of a board after inviting a number of candidates to attend whom we had no intention of appointing. And there the meeting ended. Another piece of John Birt's Grand Plan had been slotted into place.

That night I told Sarah about my encounter with Mike Checkland and John Birt. It was the classical Western saloon plot – a poker game in which two guys in cahoots take on a stranger who doesn't realize that they know each other and have fixed the deck. They just carve him up and leave him penniless: two friends and a stranger.

'I'll be gone by Christmas,' I said.

Chapter Eight

THE GREAT ESCAPE

SHORTLY AFTER I left the BBC, I had a handwritten note from John Birt:

Dear Michael,

I still hear of what upset you; indeed I still hear of things which upset me. Could we not talk about it? There's been a lot of hurt but we need to come to terms with it all sometime. May I come and see you?

Yours,

John

I replied a few days later:

Dear John,

I got your note. It's sad to come to this after all these years, but that was your choice. No point in meeting up really, you made your feelings pretty clear by your actions; more lack of feelings, I should have said. Of course we'll bump into one another socially and you can rely on me to maintain the public mask. Let's remember the good times. One of those things I shall always be grateful to you for is that you were the key player in me moving to Channel 4 where I am blissfully happy.

Yours

Michael

John, obviously stung, came back with his side of the story:

> We see things differently. The key moment for me was early
> on in the saga when you insisted I should not be on the
> [appointments] board. That was a real shock. It was an overt
> attack on the job I'd been invited to the BBC to do. By the
> time we met in Mike's office, I felt markedly threatened. Your
> 'plea' to me was months too late. I was keen to meet and try
> to understand why you felt able to treat an old and loyal
> friend in this way. I needed help and a welcome and not
> what I got.

I have since thought a lot about my curious relationship with John Birt, which effectively came to an end that afternoon in Mike Checkland's office. Leaving aside temperamental differences, he and I had diametrically opposed convictions about the relationship between programmes and policy. For as long as I have known him, John Birt has been an ideologue, a fervent believer that out of firmly imposed management strategy good programmes will flow. I always felt that his mindset was fixed when he played with his Meccano set in the nursery. Ever since, with meticulous attention to detail, John has bolted together his theories piece by piece, and after testing them for logical soundness, put them into practice single-mindedly.

I valued John as a colleague at LWT because he thought things through with great care before he made any move: he counterbalanced my seat-of-the-pants approach to the job. His programmes were carefully researched, fully costed and made with infinite care. They tended to be worthy rather than exciting, though let justice be done, he did later champion the format of *Blind Date*, the perfect vehicle for his fellow Liverpudlian Cilla Black. If he wasn't so abstemious I would have said he was drunk at the time because risk-taking has always been anathema to him and popular entertainment is a much more unpredictable area of television than carefully controlled current affairs. Only in one area did he show any spontaneity: his enthusiastic support for Liverpool Football Club. But, then, he had no option, because not even the methodical John Birt could pre-plan the outcome of soccer matches.

At LWT we used to joke about John's Grand Plan, his career strategy, never stated openly but hinted at in all the tactical moves he made. Usually, there was one more item on his agenda than he would admit to. The rest of us sat around gossiping, letting it all hang out, speaking frankly about our hopes and fears, being indiscreet about our bosses, trusting our mates not to shop us. John never said anything even in private that might damage his career if it got out. He was attentive to his superiors but could be dismissive of others who were not his intellectual equals. Melvyn Bragg said of him that he would walk into a crowded room and find the power like a heat-seeking missile. I realized he was nice to me at LWT because I was his boss, not because he had formed a flattering estimate of my IQ.

It was in 1975 before I was promoted to director of programmes at LWT that John unveiled a new phase of his Grand Plan when he wrote three articles for *The Times*, two of them with the paper's economics editor, Peter Jay. They were a classic statement of the Policy makes Programmes philosophy he was later to put into practice at the BBC. Not unduly inhibited by loyalty to his own current affairs staff, he described a scene of chaos and anarchy in the television industry as individual journalists dashed around the place, turning in stories without any context, driven by the movie mentality to get good pictures at any price. In his view, the aim of too many reporters was to grab attention rather than to inform the public, to establish themselves as personalities by bullying the people they interviewed; covering issues so superficially they only reinforced the prejudices of the viewer. All this amounted to 'a bias against understanding' – as the only memorable phrase from the articles put it.

Having stated the problem, John then offered his comprehensive solution, which, not surprisingly, was based on the organizational trinity at whose altar he worshipped: centralization, planning and control. News and Current Affairs should be amalgamated in one department with teams of journalists responsible for different areas such as politics, economics, foreign affairs and so on. The rogue newshound who, by a combination of instinct, experience and contacts, ferrets out stories would become a museum relic. Organization was everything – journalists imbued with the Birtian spirit, and therefore concerned with 'the continuing themes of our time', would work out precisely what the story was, research it thoroughly and even produce a draft script before the cameras began to roll. The final green light must be given by a senior manager, thus eliminating the possibility of inaccurate stories that might lead to expensive libel suits. Fair enough – but at what price? This system would also stamp out the individual authorship, flair and opportunism that have always been the marks of great journalism. This was policy controlling programmes with a vengeance.

John's articles got a lot of attention from the newspapers and in academic circles. He and Jay had chosen their time well. Television and radio channels were proliferating with more news outlets than there was hard news to fill them, so all sorts of dubious material ended up being transmitted under the loose label of current affairs. John turned his attention to this messy scene and, as always, happened to have a theory in his pocket about the way order could be brought out of chaos. The intelligentsia hailed him as a prophet; traditional journalists wrote him off as a control freak. But 'biased against understanding' became the standard charge aimed by politicians and newspaper leaderwriters against television journalism. John was the media guru of the moment.

At LWT we observed the emergence of this latter-day Isaiah with some bemusement. John became rather self-important as he dashed off to seminars, meetings and conferences at which his theories were received with great respect. He certainly practised what he preached. The way he trained an erstwhile MP Brian Walden to be the inquisitor for *Weekend World* typified his approach. Having decided on the subject of the interview for the following Sunday, they thoroughly researched his or her life and speeches, then prepared a list of questions and noted every possible answer to each. Having analysed these answers in turn to throw up a further set of questions, they went on and on in the same way. The result was a series of interviews that had shape and depth, everything, in fact, except the element of surprise. In a sense, Walden and Birt were soul-mates with rigorous intellects and the same air of gravitas – one couldn't imagine them having a giggle together, and I doubt that in all the years Walden presented *Weekend World* he ever tore up the script and allowed his instincts to take over. Even if he had, the viewer would never have noticed, so strictly disciplined was his speech style. Still, *Weekend World* deservedly won many prizes and was a demonstration of the strengths of Birt's methodology.

But John was changing. He'd always taken in good part any leg-pulling about his fanatical attention to detail, especially from John Bromley, who wove wild fantasies about John working himself into a lather as he balanced time against cost in sending a video cassette from one place to another by car, train, bicycle, horse, on foot, or Sellotaped to the back of a tortoise. Now he seemed a more solitary, withdrawn figure, as though he had some secret destiny to pursue. In retrospect, it's clear that LWT was too small a platform from which to deploy his ambitious theories. He had his eye on a larger forum.

In one of his *Times* articles, John had drawn attention to the BBC as an ideal test-bed for his theories. It had a huge news and current affairs output across radio and television and a centralized management, which could make radical changes at speed if it were so minded. Indeed, the BBC governors were so impressed with John's ideas that he and Peter Jay were invited to discuss them with the then BBC chairman, Sir Michael Swann. Sir Michael was an eminent biologist, obviously accustomed to studying the systems and hierarchies of the natural order and therefore he warmed to John's model of a centrally controlled, fully integrated news service. However, the director general, Sir Charles Curran, and Brian Wenham, at that time editor of *Panorama*, poured scorn on Birt's ideas, so the discussions came to nothing.

The journalists in the BBC applauded the rejection of what

they thought of as the cock-eyed theories of the great ideologue, but the laugh was on them. Ten years later, John Birt as newly appointed deputy director general assembled BBC journalists for a five-day conference at the Woodlands Park Hotel near Leatherhead, and after steam-rolling their objections proceeded to reorganize the BBC's News and Current Affairs departments precisely along the lines of his *Times* articles. And the laugh was also on me. I helped to give him the power to do it. After all, I had enthusiastically endorsed the idea of bringing John into the BBC as news supremo. However much his philosophy of pro-gramme-making was at odds with mine, I admired his organiza-tional skills and knew he would relish the challenge of sorting out a vast current-affairs empire in disarray.

I had forgotten all about John's Grand Plan. I ought to have known he would never be content until he had the top job, and though I was keen for him to join the BBC to sort out its journalism, I would never have seen him as director general. He had the ability but not the personality – the DG embodies the spirit of a community, which needs, first and foremost, not to be managed but to be corralled and led; he is the ultimate source of its inspiration. But John confounded me, and many others, by bringing his Grand Plan to fruition. Had he stayed on in ITV, his share options would have been worth a fortune, but to someone of his command-and-control nature I suppose power is more important than money. At the time, I just did not foresee the possibility that the Birtian ideology would spread beyond news and current affairs and end up blanketing the BBC's entire output. But then I was just a showman, not a visionary. Jeremy Isaacs, the founding chief executive of Channel 4, was more perceptive than I. In his autobiography *Storm Over 4* he reports having lunch with John Birt and quizzing him about his precise role as deputy director general of the BBC. John confirmed that he was now my senior and intended to assert himself in deter-mining the overall tone of BBC programmes.

During the few months our time at the BBC overlapped, I observed John bringing to bear both those strengths and weaknesses of personality his colleagues at LWT had long recognized. There was the utter single-mindedness, the sense of certainty that enabled him to press on with his reforms in the teeth of unprecedented hostility from within the BBC and from the press. Those of us who supported his appointment to sort out BBC News and Current Affairs knew he was in for a tough time but we could not have foreseen the degree of vilification to which he would be subjected. He kept his nerve and never deviated from his declared objectives, impervious to insult, scorn and a degree of unpopularity unknown in the BBC's history.

Much of the vilification was sheer blind prejudice against an outsider but some of it could have been avoided if John had gone about things with greater sensitivity. One can't turn upside down one of the most powerful areas of the BBC without sparking off a huge debate and generating opposition, some of it well founded. It was important that John should take the time to argue his case with patience and good humour before laying down the law, but he was so sure he was right that anyone who challenged his ideas became not just a sceptic but an enemy. The place for enemies was outer darkness, into which some of the most talented and experienced BBC staff were cast. I was about to join them.

So long as I had known him, John's convoluted way of expressing himself in public had been a bias against understanding – to borrow one of his favourite phrases. Having spent my early life in showbusiness, I've had plenty of time to study public performers of all kinds, and I find it ironic that the leader of the greatest communications system in the world seems to have difficulty in getting his ideas across in anything other than the ugly multi-syllabic jargon which has become immortalized as Birt-speak. Not all directors general have been orators, nor need they be, but in my experience each of them has been able to make himself understood with clarity: Sir Ian Trethowan was an experienced TV presenter with bags of self-confidence, Alasdair Milne, though laconic by nature, was precise in his use of language, and Michael Checkland had a relaxed, easy fluency.

This skill is important in an organization with its roots in a literary culture where the love of words is prized. The director general, after all, addresses some of the best communicators in the business. He is not just the chief executive, he is also editor-in-chief, and that title implies some facility with language. John has none.

In private, John can be warm and humorous, yet his personality seems to shrink in public, and he becomes stiff, awkward and uninspiring. Dennis Potter's characterization of him as a 'croak-voiced Dalek' was cruel, but both personality and articulacy desert him when he gets up to speak, and this has had serious consequences. Many of John's problems in overcoming opposition and motivating staff were caused not by his policies as such – some of the things he did needed doing – but by his difficulty in establishing rapport with those whose enthusiastic support would have made his task easier. He projected so little personal warmth when he tried to communicate with his staff that they had no way of knowing whether or not he appreciated them or was proud to be part of the BBC. I've heard more charm in the train announcer's voice at Victoria Station. There are still many idealists among the BBC's staff who regard the Corporation not as a meal ticket but a public service it is a privilege to serve. They need and deserve encouragement and inspiration; it's just not in John's nature to provide it.

John is bright enough to sense this communications barrier so he withdraws to a more congenial private setting where he can rule by management fiat and surround himself with Birtites who talk the same awful jargon and assure him that he is infallible. Significantly, many of those closest to him have no loyalty to the BBC as such, they are consultants and advisers brought in to do a particular job. They are professionals whose dedication is offered to whichever organization or company can afford their fees. For the first time in the BBC's history, it is impossible to name a single senior executive noted for his or her rugged independence of spirit. Historically, the Corporation has always tolerated individualists in senior management who challenged official policy but were valued because their loyalty to the BBC and concern for its welfare were beyond question. I recall from my schooldays the Latin saying that no grass would grow where the Emperor Caligula's horse had stood. It's almost as though independent, feisty spirits wither in John's shadow. A larger loyalty to the BBC is now no defence if it leads to a questioning of the director general's policies.

Let it be roundly stated, in an ever harsher economic climate, that the BBC could not have survived without shedding all kinds of wasteful and self-indulgent practices that had grown up over decades, and John Birt had the courage and organizational skill to do it. In fact, the necessary reforms had been started by Michael Checkland but John carried them through ruthlessly to their logical conclusion. In the process, aided and abetted by Duke Hussey, he broke the organization's spirit. His successor, Greg Dyke, will have the daunting task of trying to mend it.

There is one other thing that strikes me about John's dogmatic approach to running the BBC: there are political dangers in it. Though the BBC has long been viewed with some suspicion as a hot-bed of fanatical lefties, in fact it has thousands of highly articulate employees with strong convictions of every political hue, among whom, no doubt, there are some Marxists and the odd closet fascist. What they are prepared to do is put on one side their own personal opinions and try to achieve impartiality and fairness in the programmes they produce. Historically, this has been achieved not by official pronouncements, management directives or production guidelines but by each generation of programme-makers absorbing the large wisdom of the Corporation then passing it on to the next generation, with such liberal qualities as good manners, self-discipline, the refusal to exploit the vulnerable or betray a trust, generosity of judgement and fair play – the classic BBC programme values.

But if you impose an ideology based on the infallibility of one man's convictions upon the whole organization, centralize its control systems and remove the people and mechanisms by which dissenting opinions might be expressed, you have set in place the apparatus of a powerful propaganda machine. Little wonder that the reaction of one senior BBC current-affairs producer to John Birt's exposition of his philosophy at the Woodlands Park Hotel conference in 1987 was afterwards much quoted: 'I don't mind being told what to do, but I'm buggered if I'm going to be told what to think.' The political impartiality of the BBC no longer rested on an elaborate set of checks and balances but on the opinions of its director general.

The general election in 1997 decisively changed the political climate in which the BBC had to operate. All the evidence suggests that John finds both the personalities and philosophy of New Labour highly congenial: his ideology and theirs have clicked. According to Michael Vestey, a respected media journalist, writing in *The Spectator* in December 1998, programme editors were told when the present government was elected that they must not quarrel with the purpose of Labour policy but merely question its implementation; an interviewer who dared to interrupt Tony Blair with a perfectly reasonable question about the future of the monarchy was hauled over the coals by the programme's editor for 'impertinence'. And the bizarre events following the 'outing' of a cabinet minister on *Newsnight* in October 1998 – personal apologies hand-delivered, gagging directives, strong hints of the director general's displeasure – demonstrate how swiftly a centralized machine can move to bring independently minded members of staff into line.

I'm not concerned with the party politics of it all, it would be equally unhealthy were the Birtian ideology to favour the Tories. But a supine group of governors did allow their director general the licence to indulge his strong even fanatical convictions, with the result that his subordinates spend their time trying to read his mind. Even his friendships must be closely monitored for clues about the drift of his thinking. This is not so much management as psychoanalysis. Further down the line, programme-makers faced with critical editorial decisions have grown used to asking, 'How will John Birt react?' rather than 'Does this programme meet the BBC's traditional standards?'

Fear, suspicion and paranoia now stalk the corridors of what was once the most civilized, creative and cheerful of institutions. On the rare occasions I go back to the BBC I don't hear much laughter echoing through the offices. Whatever John put into the organization, he sure as hell took the fun out of working there.

As I left Michael Checkland's office after the confrontation with John Birt I couldn't wait to get out of the BBC. I had no desire to work a moment longer with a compliant director general down whose neck an ambitious and aggressive John Birt was breathing. I would not be one of the claque applauding as Birt put in place the last piece of his Grand Plan and was carried in triumph into Reith's office on a pallet borne by a squad of accountants, consultants and assorted lackeys. I guessed the BBC was going to be a much more rigorously controlled place in the future.

It was entirely in keeping with the spirit of the new BBC that when John was eventually appointed director general, it was done in a way more reminiscent of Tammany Hall than Broadcasting House. Michael Checkland had, after all, beaten a number of other candidates, including me, fair and square at a properly constituted appointments board for the job of director general. When Dukey decided the time had come for Mike to leave, the whole matter was settled at a private dinner over the port and cigars, no board, no manifestos, no other candidates.

Michael Checkland, the chief victim, was not allowed to finish the job he was brought in to do. In a sense, John Birt was a victim too. Had he emerged as the victor at a competitive board, all the tension and resentments that had built up around him would have been dispelled. Instead, he had to live down the imputation that he was the chairman's placeman, not a role to endear him to the staff. The whole business smelt of a cynical fix, and nothing would ever be the same again in the new BBC.

Later, I finally got the whole business out of my system and delivered my summing-up of the state of the BBC under Hussey and Birt when I gave the 1992 keynote MacTaggart Lecture at the Edinburgh Television Festival. Since I had left, the BBC had changed from being notorious as a leaking boat with its internal disputes placarded across the national press to an airtight fortress from which no stray opinion, personal conviction or judgement about public service broadcasting unauthorized by John Birt was allowed to escape. Some might applaud the lash of firm government, but there comes a point where iron discipline is virtually indistinguishable from brain death. The BBC had always been an exuberantly opinionated place where, within reason, individual staff members had the freedom to contribute to the general debate about broadcasting. Once the Birtian regime tightened its grip, the silence became ominous. I knew that some of the cleverest and most imaginative television producers I had ever known were alive and thinking in the BBC – I knew it because I met them socially and listened to their horror stories of regimentation and thought control. It was clear that the Birtian BBC was not prepared to initiate a public debate about its future, even though David Mellor's Department of National Heritage was in the process of unveiling a green paper setting out the government's thoughts about the future of broadcasting. The BBC talked about 'keeping its powder dry' but it was clear that the Corporation was sinking out of sight weighted down by the accumulated paperwork produced by sixteen task forces all talking in jaw-breaking jargon.

The absurdity of this Trappist silence from within the Corporation was well illustrated when the bosses repaired to the Lucknam Park Hotel for a strategy weekend. When the press tried to find out what was being discussed, they were rebuffed by no less than six BBC press officers all assembled to chant the mantra, 'No comment!' thus ensuring a public-relations disaster. The journalists had to do something to justify their travelling expenses so they focused their reports on the expense of the luxury hotel, its sylvan surroundings, the grandeur of its bedrooms and its five-star cuisine. One BBC press officer pointed out stiffly that none of this luxury had anything to do with the choice of Lucknam Park. It had been selected for a classically Birtian reason: it had the right number of power points.

The whole debate about the future of British broadcasting was paralysed so long as there was an ominous zone of silence where the BBC should be, for the Corporation was the biggest player in the game; as I always used to say, it kept the rest of us honest, setting standards for public-service broadcasting we all had to respect. So if no one from within the BBC was prepared to get the argument going at the Edinburgh Television Festival, the annual forum for the airing of broadcasting policy, I put myself forward. I discovered from the controller of Factual Programmes at Channel 4, John Willis, who was on the appropriate committee, that no keynote speaker for 1992 had yet been chosen to deliver the James MacTaggart Lecture. I hinted modestly that if none of the preliminary soundings they had made came to anything, I was willing to serve.

I have no academic background nor am I by nature or training an analytical thinker but I cleared my diary and spent hours and hours in preparation, struggling to make sense of what was happening to the BBC and reliving my experiences there. I tried to avoid being influenced by the tidal wave of scorn and vilification John Birt and to a lesser extent Duke Hussey were suffering in the press; I had no intention of using the name of a great broadcasting pioneer, James MacTaggart, to take cheap shots at John Birt or anyone else. Having completed the lecture I rehearsed the delivery of it again and again. I knew that, as time went by, any authority I had to speak about the BBC must diminish, so this was my one and only chance to say what had to be said, and I didn't want to blow it by sloppy delivery.

Channel 4's press officer, the late Chris Griffin-Beale, took copies of the final manuscript up to Edinburgh on the morning of the lecture and gave them to all media representatives except the BBC. My instructions had been that no one from the BBC should get a copy until fifteen minutes before the lecture began, a mischievous ploy calculated to drive the BBC press brigade frantic since they could sense by the buzz around the place that a big story was brewing and they weren't in on it. I was determined that this was one attack on the Birt regime that his spin doctors wouldn't have time to neutralize by a pre-emptive strike.

The lecture was given in the parish church of St Cuthbert at the western end of Princes Street. The place was packed with broadcasters, television executives and programme-makers. I made it clear from the outset that I was speaking as a friend of the BBC and a keen supporter of the public-service ethos. Nothing less than the standards and quality of all British broadcasting hung on the BBC's success in the negotiations for the renewal of its Charter and licence.

I argued that two events have subtly and fundamentally changed the BBC; indeed, signalled its brutalization. The first was the firing of Alasdair Milne. I wasn't concerned about the rights or wrongs of that decision, nor was I in any way disputing the governors' right to take it: that was one of the duties they were appointed to fulfil. But the barbaric and humiliating manner in which it had been accomplished by the chairman and vice-chairman not only demonstrated personal vindictiveness against Alasdair Milne but also indicated that Duke Hussey, backed by the governors, intended not just to preside over the Corporation but to run it. And, given that the governors had been appointed by Mrs Thatcher, this must mean a decisive shift of emphasis from programme-making to commercial priorities. As the BBC governors involved themselves more and more deeply in the day-to-day management of the Corporation, they forfeited the objectivity required of arm's-length regulators of the service; they indulged in amateurish meddling while the real experts, the board of management, were sidelined. And the manner of firing Alasdair Milne was meant to signal to staff that there would be no more messing around. Duke had run his standard up the mast. The long tradition that the BBC governors demonstrated their supreme power by refraining from exercising it except with subtlety and as a last resort had ended.

And my conviction was reinforced by the second event, the opening speech made by Michael Checkland when he was appointed to succeed Alasdair Milne. He said, 'The BBC is a billion-pound business.' At the time I thought it a worrying proposition and subsequent events were to confirm my fears. I have never believed that the BBC was meant to be a business. What form of business has an assured source of income and, in commercial terms, the one responsibility to spend it? The BBC, I contended, was set up to be a centre of excellence in broadcasting and had earned its place in the hearts and minds of the British public, and the admiration of the world by being a great cultural institution, a patron and purveyor of information, education and entertainment – in short, a spending organization dedicated to public service.

What followed from those two events, I argued, was the elevation of commerce above culture, the strongest evidence of which was the endless flow of management jargon that poured out of John Birt's office – ten-point plans, efficiency initiatives, task forces, 'positioning in the market place' and, supremely, 'downsizing', 'de-layering' and 'out-sourcing' – which are euphemisms for closure, redundancies and dark studios. Programmes had become commodities. This seemed to me a denial of all the BBC stood for. 'In its headlong rush for the myth of demonstrable and measurable efficiency, the governors have forgotten that dramatic weight-loss induces giddiness. The staff are drunk with change. Riding a roller-coaster may be an exhilarating experience for a short time at the fun-fair, but it is not a condition conducive to sound judgement, clear-sightedness and responsible risk-taking. And that's what good programme-making needs. Apprehension and insecurity do not create an atmosphere in which the imagination can flower. And if that elusive flower withers, the BBC will become just one more publisher of other people's ideas. What solid claim would they then have to the licence fee?'

I went on to point out that the worst consequence of all this was on the morale of the staff. I found my handful of visits to the Television Centre distressing. The atmosphere was poisoned by suspicion and fear. Staff were speaking disparagingly of their managers, but behind their backs. Middle managers despaired, in private, of their senior managers, many of whom despaired of the governors. But no one dared say anything openly. In this atmosphere, too many good programme-makers were giving up the ghost and looking elsewhere for jobs. The BBC was haemorrhaging talent.

Low morale breeds timidity. BBC staff used to say that ITV might be rich but the BBC was bold. In recent years, that boldness had been replaced by an enervating caution, which started at the top and quickly became the culture of the whole organization. One of the most damning phrases I had heard used about the governors was that whenever there was any danger of a controversial programme evoking the government's displeasure they adopted 'a pre-emptive cringe'.

'Can anyone in this hall see the BBC in its current mood making, let alone transmitting *Death on the Rock*? Would the governors of the BBC support and allow the transmission of a programme like Channel 4's recent *Dispatches* film on Northern Ireland knowing the legal risks? Would they then carry that support right through contempt proceedings in the High Court? The BBC would have "referred" these programmes out of existence.'

I acknowledged that, given the terrible battering the BBC had taken from the Government over the previous decade, some caution was understandable. But as I reminded the audience, Mrs Thatcher had gone, replaced by a prime minister who had shown that when a good case had been made he was prepared to dump the ideological baggage of the past. And the minister responsible for broadcasting was David Mellor, who had bravely defied the break-up-the-BBC lobby and been booed at the Tory Party conference for his pains.

I ended by stating my conviction that the BBC had an irresistible case for a renewal of its Charter and some long-term licence-fee formula that would obviate the necessity of those periodic grovelling visits to Downing Street for a hand-out.

'If only the BBC could shake off its obsession with secrecy. There is an army of supporters ready to speak out on its behalf. All they need is a sign, not from heaven but from Broadcasting House. The constituency the BBC commands includes the whole creative community and most of the inhabitants of the 20 million homes for whom the BBC is an integral part of their lives. The Government needs to feel the full weight of the argument for a strong, independent BBC so it can continue as the cornerstone of our broadcasting, for an impoverished or marginalized BBC would lower the standard of all UK broadcasting. We must ensure that the BBC doesn't just survive as a shadow of its former self but moves confidently into the next century still able to do what it does best – give the whole of the British public the best radio and television service in the world.'

For what seemed an eternity after I'd finished there was dead silence and I thought, My God, I've blown it! Then the hall erupted in tumultuous applause: there were deafening cheers, which must have bemused the senior BBC executives present since many of their staff were on their feet applauding me. August is a dead month for news so the lecture hit the headlines the next day. It got the main lead in Saturday's *Daily Telegraph* and its repercussions were plastered across the front page of its stable-mate, the *Sunday Telegraph* the following day.

GRADE ATTACKS BBC MANAGEMENT STYLE
GRADE ATTACK ON BBC 'APPEASERS'
BBC LIVING IN WONDERLAND, SAYS GRADE

The first BBC response came from Howell James, the director of Public Affairs. He found my lecture 'spirited and stimulating but wrong. Nowhere in his speech does Michael recognize the considerable changes that have occurred in broadcasting since the current BBC Charter was issued in 1981.' He thought my whole thesis was little more than an appeal that the BBC should face the challenge of change by remaining the same. John Birt was on holiday in the States and contented himself by telling an interviewer that I just didn't understand what was happening. My description of the BBC was 'grossly inaccurate'. My long-time admirer Lord Tebbit opined, 'All I can say is thank God Michael Grade isn't director general of the BBC or we'd face a demand for doubled licence fees and have twice as much dirt, smut and other rubbish on its channels.'

It was Duke Hussey who mounted the main attack. Having refused to make any comment to the BBC's own reporters or speak to the generality of the press about my lecture, he gave an exclusive interview to a paper belonging to the BBC's arch-enemy, his old boss Rupert Murdoch. I found it fascinating that the Murdoch press after kicking the BBC to death for years had suddenly become champions of the *status quo*, offering Dukey a platform from which to defend the Corporation. Some more cynical than I am might suspect that this Damascus Road con-version – from 'Break up the Corporation!' to 'What a splendid job it's doing' – had something to do with the deal the BBC and Sky TV had struck over Premier League football. Dukey described me to the *Sunday Times* as 'A Bourbon in red braces' – I rather liked that: it had a nice Rees-Moggian ring to it. Dukey charged that I had made wild allegations that didn't stand up and the BBC could neither afford my policies nor my salary (flatteringly put by the article at £485,000). 'Michael Grade hasn't learned anything. He is making an emotional and nostalgic pitch for the BBC in the 1980s and has failed to take realistic account of the Government's desire to see the BBC achieve much greater efficiencies.' Failing to take realistic account of the Government's desires was not a mistake Dukey was likely to make, since it was common knowledge that Mrs Thatcher had put him there to sort out the Corporation – and, after all, he presided over a board that had turned the 'pre-emptive cringe' into an art form.

The chairman then turned his attention to a speech made the previous week by Sir David Attenborough to the British Association for the Advancement of Science in which he claimed that the BBC was being 'gravely eroded, the morale of its staff seriously damaged, and the very things that gave it its unique stature and strength destroyed'. It was one thing to savage me, my criticisms could be written off as the rantings of a failed candidate for the BBC's top job, but to attack David Attenborough was like spitting at the Queen Mother. 'It's a bit rich,' said Mr Hussey, 'to be accused by David Attenborough at the beginning of the week of cutting down on the upmarket quality programmes and by Michael Grade at the end of the week of abandoning popular entertainment. Neither is true.' He then went on to give both of us a much-needed lecture on the nature of public-service broadcasting, pointing out, 'I go to great lengths to discover what people "in the lower ranks" think. I have lunch in the canteen and ask them.' For BBC staff who'd served in the forces, this conjured up a wonderful image of Major Hussey, officer of the day, sweeping through the mess hall preceded by a sergeant bellowing, 'Any complaints?'

I had my defenders. Bill Cotton, loyal as ever, contended, 'It wasn't just Michael grabbing the headlines. He was sending out a clear message to the people who make policy at the BBC. They should consider what he said very carefully.' George Russell, chairman of the Independent Television Commission, was very complimentary, pointing out that the speech had been received warmly and thus endorsed by perhaps the most knowledgeable audience, in broadcasting terms, in the world. He emphasized that though ITV was the BBC's main competitor, the commercial companies recognized that the BBC was the cornerstone of quality television in Britain and therefore had to be defended against government attacks.

In an editorial the *Independent* described Duke Hussey's comments 'ill-considered' and contrasted them with the remarks of another BBC governor, Lord Nicholas Gordon Lennox, who rushed up to Edinburgh after the lecture and 'showed greater sensitivity than Mr Hussey when he conceded one crucial part of Mr Grade's case. The governors themselves are apparently unhappy with the way in which their role has evolved and with the BBC's secrecy and lack of accountability. They intend in future to act more as regulators and less as managers, interfering in the day-to-day running of the Corporation.'

When I chose to make the future of the BBC the subject of the MacTaggart Lecture, I knew I would be vulnerable to the charge that I was venting my bitterness at being passed over for the director general's job or pursuing a private vendetta against John Birt, and that line of attack was widely used. But I achieved my main objective and sparked an intense debate about the future of British broadcasting generally and the state of the BBC in particular. The politicians joined in. George Walden MP expressed his concern that the BBC was being tempted to go downmarket. If this happened he could see no point in trying to defend it against the tide of commercialism. The chairman of the Conservative backbench committee, Roger Gale MP, had doubts about the value of my comments. 'I think Michael Grade has a clear duty to run Channel 4 and not act as director general *manqué* of the BBC. He thought Edinburgh had failed to concentrate on the real argument, the BBC in the future.' Labour's broadcasting spokesman, Robin Corbett said, 'After Edinburgh, I hope the BBC chiefs are going to be much more forthright about how they see its future rather than sitting back and letting the Government set the agenda. There is no earthly reason why they have to wait for the Government's green paper and I think there is every good reason why they should wake up and take the lead.'

Philippa Giles, a BBC drama producer who made the award-winning *Oranges Are Not the Only Fruit*, was present at Edinburgh and dared to tackle Dukey Hussey from the audience at a session on the future of the BBC. She said that she was unhappy at his response to my lecture: 'It was just mud-slinging. I am embarrassed and ashamed.' Apparently Dukey was reduced to spluttering silence while Philippa told the press philosophically, 'I expect I will be joining the ranks of the independent producers after what I said.'

Over a hundred BBC staff members wrote to me, 99 per cent of them requesting anonymity – which was eloquent testimony to the point I was making about the fear and paranoia suffusing the Corporation. A senior BBC Radio 3 music producer wrote: 'Thank you for voicing the concerns of so many BBC employees who are too worried about their own futures to dare to voice them in public.' A BBC Scotland cameraman asked me to keep his identity secret and went on, 'I sincerely hope you will continue to state your views for everything you have said is true.' A producer in the Natural History Unit at Bristol commented, 'I have never known a time when the management has been so grey ... those on the shop floor have been treated appallingly.' One of the BBC's best-known TV presenters was biting: 'I know scarcely anyone in the BBC who doesn't share your views. But how to organize the resistance when the leaders are all Quislings?' A Radio 4 current affairs reporter felt that my lecture had 'caused great angst amongst the bureaucracy because in their hearts they know that so much of what you say is absolutely true'. And one of Britain's most distinguished playwrights, David Hare, had grave doubts whether the powers-that-be in the BBC would take much notice of what I said but 'if you cannot reach the powerful at least you impressed the powerless profoundly'.

A few writers, besides expressing gratitude, also conveyed a sense of frustration and disappointment that I had quit the BBC. Since, as my lecture had demonstrated, I could see so clearly the damage being done to the BBC by the Birt regime why hadn't I stayed to fight him instead of abandoning ship? There was no point in trying to justify myself. The plain truth was that as a politician and organizational in-fighter I was no match for John Birt. He was a master-intriguer. He marshalled his forces, demanding a degree of loyalty from his supporters that was downright unhealthy and then systematically set about demolishing any opposition to his plans. I was much too open, spontaneous and trusting a character to be a successful schemer. All I wanted to do was sponsor and schedule good programmes. I wasn't exactly a coward but I wouldn't have made a good *kamikaze* pilot either. I like to be liked and I like to like the people I work with. I just hadn't the energy or the inclination to spend years locked into endless knock-down-and-drag-out fights with a rule-book-waving John Birt.

There was no way I could have out-manoeuvred John, let alone won a power struggle against a combination of him and Duke Hussey with the director general sitting on his hands. And I didn't want to be around when Mike Checkland woke up to the fact that he had made a Faustian pact with Dukey in backing Birt for which he duly paid by being unceremoniously invited to leave the BBC with his work half done. I didn't for a second imagine that anything I said in the MacTaggart Lecture would deter John or cause him to modify his policies – opposition and resistance only stiffen his sense of certitude that he is right. I suspect the Jesuits who educated him gave him a martyrdom complex: unless you are being burned at the stake, you aren't a true believer. But the governors were shaken, BBC staff encouraged and the politicians alerted to the need to let some light in on an increasingly isolated and regimented Corporation.

A bizarre postscript needs to be added to these admittedly partial reflections on my experience of the Hussey–Birt years at the BBC. Ten years after I had left, in a debate in the House of Lords, the by now ennobled Lord Hussey of North Bradley attacked the BBC for spending too much money on bureaucracy and not enough on good programmes. He condemned 'over-bloated policy units and management expansion' and concluded, with a flourish, 'The future of public-service broadcasting in the UK will flourish so long as the BBC remembers that people and programmes are more important than policies.' The only adequate word for that is *chutzpah* – the definition of which takes the form of a joke about the man who murdered his father and mother, then pleaded for leniency in court on the grounds that he was an orphan. Could this be the same Dukey who bulldozed the traditional BBC with its concern for people and programmes to erect the very bureaucratic structure, teeming with managers and consultants, he now felt would spell the end of public-service broadcasting? What misery and heartache, what draining of talent and loss of staff morale could have been avoided if Dukey had undergone his Damascus Road conversion years earlier?

Back to that fateful afternoon in Mike Checkland's office. Having decided I could no longer work at the BBC, the question was, what next? From time to time I'd been sounded out about joining with some of my friends to compete for an ITV franchise, but I saw nothing on the horizon that would interest or challenge me. No one other than Sarah knew of my intention to quit the BBC. I didn't even tell my closest confidant and friend Bill Cotton, probably because I knew how much it would disappoint him after all the effort he'd made to get me to the BBC in the first place. I probably underestimated his grasp of *realpolitik*. He had been as shattered as I was by the incident in Mike Checkland's office and must have realized that the BBC couldn't contain both John and myself indefinitely.

In the weeks that followed, I just got on with the business of seeing in the two newly appointed channel controllers, Jonathan Powell and Alan Yentob, and began mentally withdrawing from the BBC. It was a phone call from Lord Attenborough that set in motion an extraordinary turn of events that had many of the characteristics of a Whitehall farce. Dickie Attenborough is, of course, one of Britain's leading film directors and he had just made a film about South Africa called *Cry Freedom*, whose subject was the death in custody of the black activist Steve Biko and the attempts of a white newspaper editor, Donald Woods, to bring to justice the policemen who had killed him. Apparently, a couple of producers for whom he had great respect had made a television documentary about the background to *Cry Freedom* and he would like me to look at it with a view to the BBC buying it.

I liked what I saw very much and agreed to buy the documentary, provided there were some fairly drastic cuts, chiefly of the extended pieces to camera by Dickie preaching about the evils of apartheid, which in the fraught days before the release of Nelson Mandela could be construed as blatant propaganda. Wearing a different hat, Dickie as chairman of Channel 4 was also in the process of appointing a new chief executive to replace Jeremy Isaacs. Sitting at home one evening, I told Sarah that I was about to ring Dickie to let him know the transmission date of the documentary. I wondered whether they had found a replacement for Jeremy and if I should tell Dickie I was on the brink of leaving the BBC. 'Do it,' said Sarah decisively. I rang Dickie and told him we'd found a slot for the documentary, which fitted in well with the release of *Cry Freedom*. He was delighted.

'By the way,' I added artlessly, 'How's the search for Jeremy's successor going?'

'Well, you know, darling, it's not easy but we're getting there slowly.'

'I don't know whether this is of interest to you or not but I'll say it twice so that there's no misunderstanding. If you were to offer me the job, I would take it.'

There was silence at the other end of the phone, then: 'Oh, darling!'

'Yes, if you were to offer me the job, I'd jump at it.'

'Oh, really, darling? I say, I'll call you back.' He rang back and said, 'Are you serious?'

'Dickie, absolutely. I don't even want to know about the conditions. Whatever they are is fine by me. If the job's going, I'll take it.'

Dickie explained that Channel 4 had formed a sub-committee of the main board to make the appointment – John Gau, former head of BBC News and Current Affairs, Carmen Callil, the co-founder of the Virago Press, George Russell, who had been deputy chairman of the IBA, my old friend Paul Fox and Dickie himself. They would have to interview me as soon as it could be arranged.

To avoid any possibility of a press leak we agreed that I would meet the committee at Dickie's home in Richmond at ten o'clock the following Saturday morning. That was the earliest moment at which the board could be mustered, but it presented me with a problem. It was the day I was due to fly to Hollywood for the buying season with my senior BBC colleague, Peter Ibbotson. Sarah had flown out to Los Angeles ahead of me, and a housekeeper was taking care of things at Beaconsfield. I was in a quandary. Even if the Channel 4 board could be postponed, it would be quite unethical to engage in a buying trip for the BBC knowing that if all went well I would be scheduling for Channel 4 in competition against the very programmes I had bought. On the other hand, if I cried off the Hollywood trip for any reason, it would set alarm bells ringing around the BBC. I decided to follow the example of John Stonehouse, the Labour MP who organized his own disappearance from a Miami beach. I arranged to stay for a few days with my sister Anita in Hampstead while I sorted things out. I didn't want to put my housekeeper in the position of having to pass on lies, so as I left the house, I specifically didn't say I was off to the airport.

Come departure time, and my trusty lieutenant Peter Ibbotson was drumming his heels at Heathrow. When I didn't show up, he phoned my housekeeper, who speculated that I must be on my way to the airport. Then she added, 'Would you tell Mr Grade, when he gets to the airport, that a Mr Paul Fox called?' Ibbo hadn't been in the BBC political game for years without having a keen nose for intrigue. He knew that Paul Fox was not just a friend of mine but also a member of the appointments board of Channel 4, which was actively seeking a new chief executive. He also knew that I was bitterly unhappy at the BBC under the Checkland–Birt regime. Ibbo didn't know what to do. Should he track me down to find out exactly what was going on, or board the aircraft and carry on with the trip? BA and LA won.

As soon as he reached the Bel Air Hotel in Los Angeles, Ibbo phoned Sarah's home. No reply. He knew that she should be there. So he tried an old trick and redialled, let the phone ring three times and hung up, then he immediately dialled again. Assuming it was me, Sarah picked up the phone and said, 'Hello, Michael.' At first, Sarah wouldn't say a word about my where-

abouts but Ibbo managed to persuade her to come round to the
Bel Air Hotel, where after a few drinks, she told him about the
Channel 4 offer.

   In fact, as yet there was no offer. While Ibbo was tucking into
his in-flight lunch, the members of the Channel 4 appointments
board were making their way in great secrecy to Dickie's splendid home on Richmond Green. I drove myself straight round
into Dickie's garage; the door closed behind the car and I
moved swiftly through a connecting passage into the house. Paul
Fox, despite parking his car in a remote street, walked right into
one of the BBC's senior executives outside Dickie's home;
luckily, the BBC mandarin didn't think there was anything odd
about a Channel 4 director popping in to see his chairman.

   I knew most of the members of the appointments board
pretty well, well enough for them to cut through the usual
preliminaries and get to the heart of their main reservation
about me joining Channel 4. Some months before at the Royal
Television Society in Cambridge when the debate about the
future of Channel 4 was at its most intense, I had suggested that,
instead of being funded by the ITV companies, Channel 4
should be privatized. I was not delivering a formal speech but
making some off-the-cuff comments as one member of a panel.
It was really a mischievous suggestion to deflect the discussion
from the BBC, which was the invariable target at those sort of
conferences. And, after all, I was wearing my BBC hat. If Channel
4 were to become a direct competitor to ITV for advertising,
that could be to the BBC's advantage.

   As a diversionary tactic, my privatization of Channel 4 ploy
worked a treat, though Paul Fox, who was present at the conference, came up to me afterwards and, speaking with the brutal
candour of a very close friend, told me to mind the BBC's
business and keep my nose out of Channel 4's affairs. Now some
months later, boomerang-like, my casual remarks had come back
to haunt me, and here was Paul Fox on behalf of the appointments board probing me about what I had said at Cambridge. I
held my hands up. I'd been stirring it at the Cambridge confer-

ence. I was prepared to sign in blood that I would do everything in my power to resist the privatization of Channel 4 and, anyway, I added earnestly, even in a few short months the whole landscape of broadcasting had changed with the arrival of Channel 5! This was not a group to be easily fooled, there was a wealth of broadcasting expertise in that room, and I could only grin disarmingly at their sceptical snorts. But I insisted that, apart from a single comment, my record showed I had consistently championed public-service broadcasting all my career, and no one in the room disputed it.

After about an hour, I was smuggled out of Dickie's house as surreptitiously as I'd arrived and went back to Anita's home. Dickie had spelled out the timetable of events. Assuming the group was in favour of my appointment, he would tell Jeremy Isaacs, the founding chief executive of Channel 4 at lunchtime on Monday. Then there would be a tea meeting with the members of the IBA at the Hyde Park Hotel at 4 o'clock, after which the appointment would be ratified by the full Channel 4 board on Monday evening. Meanwhile Paul Fox rang round his fellow ITV managing directors to make sure they would support my appointment – an assurance the IBA would undoubtedly seek before endorsing me. He then phoned Beaconsfield to tell me they were all on side, but I wasn't there, and it was Paul's call my housekeeper asked Peter Ibbotson to pass on to me, thus raising his suspicions.

Sunday was a dead day; I lounged around at Anita's place. On Monday morning I wrote out my resignation from the BBC and addressed it to Mike Checkland. I pointedly said that I would remember my time in the Television Service under Bill Cotton with affection and much appreciation – the not too subtle implication being that I wouldn't miss the rest of them. I couldn't in honesty thank Mike for his support and leadership because I didn't think he had demonstrated either. I gave the letter to Trish, my PA, and told her to deliver it by hand to Mike Checkland's office: 'Trish, get Bill, my driver, to take you to Broadcasting House and on the dot of five, not a minute before or after, drop it off in the DG's office.' I had been assured by Dickie that the meeting with the IBA was a mere formality so I reckoned an hour at the outside would give me plenty of time to meet them, have a quick cup of tea, indulge in a round of pleasantries and then it was off out of the BBC and into a bright future.

As soon as I arrived at the Hyde Park Hotel at four o'clock I sensed that something was wrong. Though hiding it brilliantly as a great actor should, Dickie seemed ill at ease and the director general of the IBA, John Whitney, who was not a brilliant actor, was very agitated indeed. They asked me to wait and engaged in a lengthy conversation at the other end of the room, Dickie doing his thespian thing, plucking at his beard, rolling his eyes and wagging an admonitory finger. Eventually they came over and asked me to join them in an adjacent room. I glanced at my watch. It was twenty to five. Trish would be well on her way to Broadcasting House to deliver my resignation letter. In a panic, I realized that I could be about to quit one job and still not get the other.

'Darling,' said Dickie, 'there's been a hitch.'

'Jeremy,' I said. I had not expected Jeremy Isaacs to be ecstatic at the prospect of my replacing him as chief executive. Jeremy felt proprietorial about Channel 4 because he had largely shaped it. He was also something of a culture vulture and would undoubtedly feel that the channel could only go one way under the direction of a song-and-dance man – downmarket. Apparently, after announcing his intention to move on to the Royal Opera, he had discussed no possible successor with Dickie. Perhaps subconsciously he couldn't bear the idea of *anyone* replacing him.

I was saddened by Jeremy's reaction to the prospect that I might succeed him. I admired him greatly. He was the perfect choice as Channel 4's founding chief executive and I could never have achieved what he did. Dickie told me he had antici- pated a certain amount of scepticism from Jeremy but was not

prepared for what turned out to be an almost hysterical performance – rage, tears and accusations of treachery.

'Jeremy was very upset when I told him about your appointment,' said Dickie. 'He thinks it's the end of Channel 4 and he's
not going to stand for it. He's behaving very badly.'

'Well,' I said, 'just let me make a quick phone call and then
we can talk about it.'

Thank God for car phones! I reached Trish sitting in my car
outside Broadcasting House waiting for the hour of five to strike.

'Trish, you've got the letter? Well, do not, repeat, do not
take it in. Just hang on there until you hear from me. I'll phone
you again.' Then I went in with Dickie to meet the IBA. I was
absolutely gutted. Things had been going splendidly. Dickie and
the appointments board could not have been more enthusiastic
or welcoming. I really didn't want any more grief. I hadn't
ducked out of a guerrilla war with John Birt at the BBC to find
myself engaged in one with Jeremy and his supporters at Channel 4 so I asked Lord Thompson, the IBA chairman, if I might
make a statement before any discussion began.

'I want to clear the air,' I said. 'I've no desire to be the cause
of any problems at Channel 4. I'm quite prepared to withdraw
now and disappear into the night and you'll never hear from me
again. Rather than create a schism at Channel 4, I'd rather
forget the whole thing.'

George Thompson wouldn't hear of it and made it clear that
he and the other members of the IBA had no intention of
allowing Jeremy to tell them what they could and could not do.
They were unanimous in supporting my appointment at the full
board meeting of Channel 4. Dickie went on to his board
meeting, no longer gung-ho about my appointment and fearing
a full-scale row since he had no idea whether Jeremy had been
at work persuading board members to blackball my appointment. At any rate he promised to ring me as soon as the board
meeting ended.

I felt Bill Cotton was entitled to know what was going on so I phoned him and arranged to have a meal with him at a Chinese restaurant in Kensington. I told him I intended to leave the BBC whether or not I got the Channel 4 job. He was pretty upset because he had gone to immense trouble to smooth my path into the BBC, but as I explained my reasons he made no attempt to dissuade me, realizing that there was no way I could work with Birt.

'I know when you made up your mind,' Bill said. 'That day in Checkland's office when you looked John Birt in the eye and begged him twice. That was the moment, wasn't it?'

'Yes,' I replied. 'That was when my heart left the BBC.'

Bill felt much as I did about the baleful regime at the BBC but his imminent retirement made it unnecessary for him to take any drastic action. We mulled over events for a while and then I was called to the phone. It was Dickie to tell me that the Channel 4 board had endorsed my appointment with one dissenting vote, that of Jeremy Isaacs. We had a celebratory drink and wallowed in a certain amount of 'What might have been!' reminiscence. Had John Birt moderated his ambition and Michael Checkland been straight with me, the three of us could have created a huge success for the BBC. But the single quality necessary to make it all work was trust, and I could no longer trust Michael. Curiously, I didn't feel that John had betrayed my trust, whatever else he'd done. He'd always had his eye on the main chance so he was just acting true to type.

I had arranged for my much-travelled letter of resignation to be on Michael's desk when he arrived in the office on Tuesday morning, but somehow the *Daily Mail* had got wind of the story and when Michael picked up his morning paper he was confronted with the main lead: ANGRY GRADE MOVES TO CHANNEL 4. I regretted the apparent discourtesy, though the leak had nothing to do with me. I had gone to extraordinary lengths to keep the manoeuvrings of the weekend secret, if only for the selfish reason that had the Channel 4 board not backed Dickie I needed to be able to carry on at the BBC until something else turned up.

Dickie chaired a press conference later in the day. The various media correspondents gave me a hard time over my dramatic change of heart about the privatization of Channel 4. It was a fair cop. I could only come clean that my Cambridge intervention had been a spoiling tactic to take the heat off the BBC and put it on ITV. I couldn't think of a single one-liner to get me out of that tight corner. My hesitancy was duly noted by a press corps who knew me well. I did assure them that I had agreed to accept board policy on the structure of Channel 4 for at least five years. Short of government legislation changing everything, the *status quo* would remain.

Only one interpretation of my short-lived proposal about privatizing Channel 4 baffled me: it was alleged that I had had a political, even Thatcherite motive in making it. The theory was that my speech, given at a time when Channel 4 was looking for a new chief executive to replace the non-Thatcherite Jeremy Isaacs, signalled to 10 Downing Street that I was one of Them. The PM need expect no trouble from Channel 4 with me at the helm and so might exert subtle pressure to get me appointed. I was astonished at this Machiavellian interpretation of what had been a spur-of-the-moment remark. I wouldn't be capable of such serpentine thinking. I had just been making mischief, not sending secret messages to Downing Street.

As I left the press conference I ran right into a very emotional Jeremy Isaacs, who had been clearing out his office. He wished me well, then added he was handing on to me a sacred trust and that if I screwed it up he would throttle me. I was startled at the vehemence with which he spat out the words, and he amplified them in a press statement, which ended, 'I will bloody well hold him to his undertakings.' I was shaken but not outraged. I didn't feel that Jeremy's reaction was driven by personal malice but out of love and concern for Channel 4. And he became a tower of strength to me in some of the long battles with the Government that lay ahead.

The BBC issued a press statement. While Michael Checkland declared himself to be 'very sad. It is a tremendous blow and a shock', Dukey ascribed my move to itchy feet – I was, he said, an 'itinerant talent'. William Hickey in the *Daily Express* wrote:

> A roar of feigned surprise and a flood of crocodile tears from the BBC has greeted the announcement that Michael Grade is deserting them for Channel 4. In the time-honoured way, the bad-mouthing operation has clicked into operation. When he was employed by the Beeb he was credited with commissioning *EastEnders* and bringing *Wogan* to our screens. Now he is leaving, they are saying – predictably – that Grade had nothing to do with these top-rating shows and that the coffer of ideas is empty, plundered mercilessly by the man they say couldn't make the Grade.

I was given until 2 p.m. to clear my desk but all my stuff arrived at Channel 4 much sooner than that – the BBC acted with the speed of medieval sanitation bods getting rid of a plague victim's bedding. At the end of the press conference, I had remarked that in spite of the apparent unheaval I had caused it would only be a matter of weeks before the BBC forgot I existed. I said, 'There's an old Corporation proverb that the hole heals as soon as you leave the BBC car park.' That same afternoon a friend called the Television Centre to wish me well. He was told by the switchboard, 'We don't have a Michael Grade working here.'

In the following days, my appointment was mulled over in the press. Brian Wenham, by then retired from the BBC but one of the undeclared candidates for the job, was uncharacteristically bilious: 'I think people should ponder what Michael Grade is going to do with a Channel that was set up to cater for minority interests. Are we going to get *Terry and June*? He has no feel for the things Channel 4 does.' This vulgarizing charge was echoed in the *New Statesman* by John Ellis: 'Unlike Isaacs, Grade is always tempted to be a showman and a crowd pleaser. He is a commercial animal who still has to prove his fundamental commitment to Channel 4's brief to promote "innovation and experiment" in the form and content of programmes. His experience has been almost entirely as a bright and energetic promoter at the more popular end of the market.' And another disappointed candidate, Anthony Smith of the British Film Institute who could fairly claim to have been the source of many of the ideas which eventually produced Channel 4, castigated the appointments board for 'allowing the conduct of British TV to fall into the hands of people who play games with it'.

Yet again the ghost of the Grade song-and-dance tradition was haunting me; yet again in interviews and press statements I was required to trot out the same old mantra that I was not a populist at any price, calling in aid my record at both the BBC and LWT for promoting programmes aimed at minorities, both cultural and racial. I found insulting the imputation that I would be laying a desecrator's hands on Channel 4's sacred treasures. I bitterly resented the condescending attitude to viewers implied in the charge that one could only increase ratings at the expense of programme quality. If that were true, then there would be no point in public-service broadcasting at all, for its whole purpose is to add to the worthwhile experience of a growing number of viewers and listeners.

They said I would dumb down Channel 4, but in that very same week it put on at peak viewing time the old comedy film *Send Me No Flowers*, starring Doris Day and Rock Hudson. In his time, Jeremy Isaacs, the champion of high culture, had commissioned a shlock-buster mini-series called *A Woman of Substance* by Barbara Taylor Bradford, one episode of which achieved the largest audience in Channel 4's history, nearly fourteen million viewers. Then there was another series called *The Far Pavilions* in which Amy Irving, a white Hollywood star, actually blacked up to play an Indian princess. I can just imagine the headlines if I had agreed to such an artifice – I would have been accused of importing a version of the Black and White Minstrels on to the cultural channel. I had no problems at all with such programmes – they would have fitted comfortably within any schedule I was likely to produce – but if by happenstance they had been

transmitted after I had taken over at Charlotte Street, the critics
would have pointed to them as evidence that the reign of Grade
the Barbarian had already begun.

I was shaken by the venom of some of the élitist critics of my
appointment but I had no intention of bowing down and
worshipping Channel 4 as a cultural icon to appease them. I saw
no reason either to vandalize Channel 4's schedules or to treat
them as perfect and inviolate. As a regular viewer, my impression
was that the initial impetus of Jeremy's creative flair had spent
itself. It always happens in scheduling that over time a winning
pattern becomes rather predictable and flat. The channel's
entire programme policy was due for an overhaul, an indisputa-
ble fact that any of my critics would have to concede if they had
a modicum of programme judgement. So I entered the portals
of Channel 4 neither cowed nor complacent. And I certainly
didn't intend to skulk in Jeremy's shadow. I would do it my way,
establishing a much higher public profile for the channel,
keeping the press fully informed of my hopes and ambitions.

At the BBC, the waters closed over the transient impression
in the sand I'd left there. There was no leaving party; neither
did John Birt organize a surprise farewell trip to Paris for me. I
didn't regret my years at the BBC: it had been a privilege to
work for the greatest broadcasting organization in the world. I
was just sorry that neither Dukey nor Birt gave the slightest
impression that they shared that sense of privilege.

My first impression of Channel 4 was amazement at how small
an operation it was. The entire staff were crammed into a few
floors of an inadequate building in Charlotte Street. And a high
proportion of them at every level in the organization were
women, which was a refreshing contrast to the hierarchical,
male-dominated BBC. We worked in close proximity to one
another and there was none of that territorial demarcation –
certain floors designated for management – I'd grown used to at
the BBC. There was no way executives could distance themselves
from the rest of the staff, we bumped into one another a

hundred times a day, so there was a constant buzz about the place and something of the intimacy and mutual care of a village community. And its location near Soho was at the cosmopolitan heart of London; just round the corner was the theatreland in which I had grown up and where the Grade family had done business for decades. It was a wonderful place to work after being stuck out in the BBC Television Centre at the end of the concrete wilderness that was the Westway. Compared to the formality of the BBC with its miles of echoing corridors, Channel 4 was like a commune. There was barely a suit or frock to be seen. It was a noisy, undisciplined and immensely stimulating atmosphere in which to work. Jeremy had instilled into his staff an almost missionary zeal about Channel 4's remit to explore cultural diversity, turn exciting ideas into programmes and to take risks. If the BBC was established church, lofty, traditional and paternalistic, Channel 4 was an evangelical sect, bursting with enthusiasm, spontaneity and heretical ideas.

There was an interregnum of about two months between my taking the job and arriving at Channel 4, so I played some golf, watched a lot of Channel 4 television and at Dickie Attenborough's request attended a strategy conference at Nuneham Courtney near Oxford. All the Channel 4 commissioning editors and the management team were present. On the first evening, Jeremy made his farewell speech. He was playing on his home ground and in front of his most fervent supporters. He did a sort of final audit of his time at Channel 4. He was eloquent, passionate and funny. Listening to him, I could well understand where the channel's evangelical zeal had come from. Interestingly he defined the cornerstone of the channel's remit in terms of a number of significant programmes they had transmitted. I thought that unwise. Channel 4 must inevitably be in a state of constant flux, and if its identity were to be defined in specific programme terms, when they eventually reach the end of their natural life, it would be back to the drawing-board for a fresh identity.

The next morning I faced the audience, feeling like a lion in a den of Christians. Scepticism rather than outright hostility was etched on most of their faces. I shared with them my enthusiasm for some of their work – *Channel 4 News*, *The Tube*, *The Comic Strip Presents . . .*, *Max Headroom*, a highly inventive computer-graphics show and, of course, *Film on Four*. I also told them that in my view in contrast to these great achievements there was too much mediocre material, badly executed, which the BBC would never have transmitted. My aim, I told the by now less than enrapt audience, was to ensure that Channel 4 lost its amateur status. Because the channel commissioned programmes from independent producers rather than made its own, editorial control was at one remove from the production process and quality control didn't always seem very rigorous.

In the question-and-answer session, one commissioning editor defended his output by saying that his programmes were too serious to be interrupted by commercial breaks. That was the problem: the notion that without the advertising breaks there wouldn't be any revenue to pay for these serious programmes seemed not to have occurred to him. His comment encapsulated the problems of a channel some of whose editors pursued artistic and cultural aims so lofty that they thought it vulgar to consider such sordid matters as ratings and money. I put a question to all of them: were there any programmes transmitted they had not actually previewed? They admitted there were, explaining that they were frantically busy, their support staff was skeletal and certain producers could be trusted to deliver the goods, indeed, were so distinguished that it would be an insult to monitor their work. I asked them, could they imagine Marks and Spencer ordering a number of jumpers from a factory and putting them straight on the shelves without satisfying themselves about colour, size and quality? This was what I meant by the amateur mentality. There are amateurs who have flashes of brilliance but it is a consistently high level of performance that marks out the professional. Channel 4 had to lose its innocence; the heady early days when ratings counted for nothing and no programme idea was too far-fetched were gone. The broadcasting industry was entering a period of frantic competitiveness: media tycoons such as Murdoch didn't play games, they went for the jugular. We had to get Channel 4 on a war footing.

In a sense, the financial structure of Channel 4 tended to encourage complacency and militate against hard competitiveness. Perhaps the most dramatic difference between Channel 4 and any of the other jobs I've had in broadcasting was the feeling of absolute financial security. I wasn't involved in any battle for funds against other areas of the same organization as in the BBC, neither need I try to persuade hard-nosed boards of directors to part with more programme money, which had been the reality of my life at LWT and Embassy. At the time I joined it, Channel 4 was rather like a teenager whose rich father paid all his bills, 'Daddy' was ITV, and the only financial worry we had was to see that we didn't overspend our allowance. Our revenue was a fixed number set at the beginning of the year, and every month on the dot, Daddy handed out our pocket money.

Though this arrangement may have sounded like a charitable impulse on the part of the ITV barons, they weren't keeping Channel 4 in comfort for the good of their souls. In return, they maintained their monopoly of advertising sales by controlling Channel 4's commercial air time as well as their own. If you wanted to advertise anywhere on television, in those days, there was only one phone call you could make and that was to ITV. The standard joke ran: it's a waste of time ringing the advertising director of an ITV company on a Wednesday – his secretary will tell you that he never comes in on a Wednesday because it spoils both weekends. No one in ITV had to do any really hard selling because there was no competition.

All that was about to change. This was 1988 and the 1981 Broadcasting Act was coming to the end of its life and a white paper was promised to spell out the government's plans for the future of broadcasting. Mrs Thatcher was determined to shake things up, she hated monopolies of any kind, and those that governed broadcasting most virulently of all. We had to be ready for the deluge. I was convinced that Channel 4 could only survive on the basis of a high level of professionalism and keen competitiveness, and this informed every change I made in programmes and personnel for the first three years. There were comings and goings but no blood bath; I took my time sizing up key members of staff, especially the commissioning editors, whose job it was to sponsor programmes and supervise the independent producers who made them. If I were to single out one skill I had developed throughout my career, it was the capacity to delegate. I learned to choose good people then to trust them, to let them get on with the job without constantly peering over their shoulder or second-guessing their decisions. And that was how I tackled the Channel 4 job.

Two people were critical to my plans for the future. The first was Justin Dukes. He had been managing director of Channel 4 since 1981, working closely with Jeremy Isaacs, who took care of programmes while he ran the organization. He had joined Channel 4 from the *Financial Times* and was highly respected within the organization, though the odd television snob discounted him because he had no programme-making experience. Justin had applied for the chief executive's job and was bitterly disappointed to be pipped at the post by me, a late candidate who had not gone through the proper procedures. He also believed that the chairman, Dickie Attenborough, had given him a nod and a wink that the board smiled upon his candidature. On the other hand, Jeremy Isaacs, though aware of Justin's desire to be chief executive, conspicuously failed to recommend him for the top job. Justin was understandably disappointed and upset, particularly since finance and administration were not Jeremy's strong point – as the Royal Opera House was to discover – and but for Justin's quiet efficiency, the Channel would probably have gone bust. I gathered that one of Jeremy's more enterprising proposals to keep central administration down was to hand out Channel 4 cheque-books to all the producers. Justin scotched that one.

Justin Dukes and I worked together for about nine months before he moved on. From the moment I arrived, he made no secret of his intention to go but not by a flicker did he betray any hostility or disloyalty to me. I came to have great respect for his integrity and courtesy and enjoyed working with him. I suspect he found my high-profile approach to the job distasteful and undoubtedly missed Jeremy's cultural and intellectual weight. Before Justin moved on, I decided not to replace him and instead, on Justin's advice, proposed the appointment to the board of three extra directors drawn from among the senior executives to give the professionals a greater say in the governance of the channel.

Liz Forgan had also been a candidate for the top job, though in her case she was signalling her ambitions for the future rather than making a serious bid. Our paths had never crossed until I joined Channel 4, though I knew of her reputation as a *Guardian* journalist. She was deputy director of programmes and I had heard her described as the 'head girl' of the channel. Educated at Benenden and Oxford, she had been at Channel 4 from the beginning and was something of an acolyte of Jeremy Isaacs, whom she described in the press as 'a marvellous visionary. He'd say, "This is what we're going to do," and everyone would say, "Great!" and go away and think of things to fit into that. It was a marvellous, hugely fruitful way of doing things because he's a genius.' She was certainly a formidable figure, bustling, brisk and efficient; in so far as the channel had a quality controller, she was it. Jeremy had tried to get her appointed director of programmes before he left but the board would not agree.

I had bad news for Liz on the first occasion we met over a plate of sandwiches in her office. She had reasonable expectations that I might make her acting director of programmes while I got on with familiarizing myself with other aspects of the chief executive's job, but my most urgent priority was to bring the general standard of programmes up to scratch, and for that I needed to be closer to the production process, so I told her I wanted to be my own director of programmes for a few months and, after that, I'd make an appointment. It was obviously a blow, but she showed her character in the way she handled it, and as the weeks wore on it became clear that we had complementary skills. She was highly intelligent, hard-working, very articulate and breathtakingly well organized. And her soundness of judgement was sometimes critical when the blood rushed to my head and intense competitiveness overwhelmed my common sense. She had been at the channel from the beginning and was so imbued with the principles Jeremy had laid down that she became the Conscience of Channel 4 – a single comment from Liz, 'That's not Channel 4!' was enough to stop some programme ideas in their tracks.

Liz ran a tight ship, being especially good at hassling those commissioning editors who tended to keep projects gathering dust on their desks instead of making quick, firm decisions. And she was an architect of systems; I knew where I wanted to get and she would evolve the structure that made it possible. She and I developed an open and honest relationship and within a few months I felt confident enough to appoint her director of programmes at the head of a new editorial structure, which involved the creation of two new jobs, controller of Factual Programmes and controller of Arts and Entertainment. One of my aims was to speed up the decision-making process. In an increasingly competitive market, Channel 4 just didn't have the cash to outbid its rivals but we could offer quick decisions to independent producers who might otherwise starve to death waiting for giants such as the BBC to go through the cumbersome business of making up their minds. In April 1999, writing in the *Sunday Times*, Salman Rushdie told the story of his attempt in 1993 to turn *Midnight's Children* into a BBC television series. The whole thing fizzled out, he said, because it was impossible to get the BBC's bureaucracy to make a decision. 'I discovered that there were five layers of "suits" between the programme producer and the controller of BBC2.' Our bids might be lower but our decisions were swift and it was a great psychological as well as economic boost to a small production company to know that the next project was in the bag.

About nine months into my time at Channel 4, this endless bout of shadow-boxing with the ghost of Jeremy Isaacs reached its climax when I was interviewed at the National Film Theatre by Anthony Smith, who was director of the British Film Institute. Tony was a television theorist, and his ideas had been formative in creating Channel 4. He had also been an unsuccessful candidate when I got the job and made no secret of his outrage. My appointment he opined 'was a very depressing moment in British cultural history' – which I felt articulated an inflated view of my importance, even when expressed negatively. Hence, Tony came to our interview not entirely without preconceptions, but I've never been able to remember, let alone brood, on all the critical even insulting things said about me, so I was happy to talk publicly to him.

The interview went well until Tony asked me to describe my vision for the future of Channel 4. This was the sort of question Jeremy loved; he would launch himself into great flights of expansive rhetoric about God, civilization and the *Zeitgeist*. There was nothing phoney about Jeremy's eloquence. He had vision and tended to clothe it in metaphysics whereas any of my in-house critics at Channel 4 would have pointed out that to me Metaphysics was the name of a racehorse. But I was thrown by Tony's question, not because it was hard to answer but because for me it was meaningless. It was a trick question. I didn't think in terms of visions, I had a number of severely practical issues to tackle to sort out the channel, then to save it, since leaks from Downing Street hinted that Mrs Thatcher was on the warpath, determined to press ahead with privatization. I really couldn't afford the luxury of visions from the mountain-top. So, to Tony's question, I had virtually nothing to say, apart from a few clichés. Several press reports of the interview claimed that my reaction to this question revealed that I had been found out, the bankruptcy of my thinking exposed by Tony's searching question. One commentator felt it significant that I could not even utter one of my famous one-line cracks to joke my way out of trouble. I couldn't win. Had I responded to Tony's question with a witticism I would no doubt have been written off as a comedian.

In a *Sunday Times* profile, Brian Appleyard saw me as the victim of 'elaborate and insidious snobbery' at Channel 4. He was only inaccurate in saying that it all started when I joined Channel 4: I've always been a victim of it. For example, my angriest moment at the BBC was when two of the director general's special advisers came along to the Television Programme Review Board and one of them, an academic called Janet Morgan, opened her address by saying, 'I have been brought into the BBC to think.'

I exploded: 'What on earth do you imagine we do all day? Stick bits of video and film together?' Intellectual snobbery ran like a fault-line through the BBC. The thinkers, Oxbridge to a man and woman, philosophized about Reithian values while the rest of us, being mere mechanics, fiddled about and occasionally came up with brilliant programmes by accident.

Truth to tell, I was getting heartily sick of being constantly compared to Jeremy Isaacs. As was often pointed out to me, he was Oxbridge trained, well read, had a fine mind and was a great debater. How come, then, that Mike Grade, this oik from vaudeville, had added 3 per cent to Channel 4 ratings within months of taking over? The answer of the more supercilious critics was that I had increased audiences by dumbing down the channel. Had the ratings gone down, then that would have been because I had failed to meet the cultural aspirations of the discerning audience Jeremy and his team had attracted. Again and again, I had to insist that it was not necessary to be a towering intellectual to run Channel 4 so long as you could lay your hands on a towering intellectual when you needed one. As Bill Cotton used to say, 'I may not know the answer, but I know someone who does.'

*

Possibly because of the undertow of denigration I felt constantly during my early days at Channel 4, I had just not got back on to the wavelength of ITV after my spell at the BBC, and in March 1988, I had the novel experience of being booed at the British Academy of Film and Television Awards by my ITV colleagues. I'd been on the council of BAFTA for years and was invited to present one of the prizes at its annual awards ceremony. The sheer number of BBC voting members of BAFTA meant that every year the Corporation won most of the prizes. ITV was fragmented anyway, each company competed with the others, so there was no such thing as an ITV block vote to counterbalance the BBC's voting strength. The result was that occasionally excellent ITV programmes, which deserved to win prizes, were voted down in favour of inferior BBC entries. This particular year, Yorkshire Television had submitted an excellent documentary, *The Falklands War – The Untold Story*, which was not even nominated for an award, so in an uncharacteristic fit of petulance, they decided to boycott the BAFTA ceremony and put out a feature film in their area rather than show it on television. I thought this was a poor show and said so in my introductory remarks and got roundly booed for my pains by most of the ITV representatives present. I felt strongly that for one of the biggest companies to boycott the ceremony was an insult to all those present who had won prizes. They weren't responsible for the rules by which BAFTA operated. Being something of a regular performer at BAFTA, I was accustomed to storms of applause and laughter rather than vilification, and on reflection realized that the degree of opposition I was meeting at Channel 4 had got to me. I had lost some of my sureness of touch in handling sensitive public issues. I ought to have made my indignation at Yorkshire's actions known to the board of BAFTA privately and not chastised them in front of millions of television viewers.

My domestic situation didn't help. I was working every hour that God sent, out by six in the morning and home if I was lucky by ten o'clock at night, but even then facing a couple of hours' video-cassette viewing. Sarah spent most of her time in the States so we were perpetually in a state of 'getting to know you again'. We decided to get a London base at Clarendon Close, which was a bolt-hole in town for both of us but also an office from which Sarah could work when she was at the London end. Our lives had by now diverged to the extent that we were strangers. The closeness, camaraderie and laughter of our Hollywood days had gone, and I just hadn't the wisdom to work out what was wrong or the emotional strength to do something about it. I was lonely and unhappy and, above all, baffled by my inability to sustain a relationship. Though I often used in my work that old Yiddish joke 'If at first you don't succeed, you're fired!' it's almost as though I was saying just that to my successive partners. Once the magic and mystery left the relationship, and a sustained act of will was required to take it on to the next stage, I just cut and ran.

All my adult life, I had flung myself deep into relationships then broken them off out of boredom or thwarted expectations. There was a kind of doom-laden foreboding about each fresh encounter, the awful sense that the exciting new was destined to become the disappointing old – which is a reflection on me, not on the intelligent, attractive and understanding women I've been privileged to know who somehow thought it worthwhile to make real contact with my emotions. I expected them to change to accommodate all my quirks yet, despite my apparent self-confidence, I was unwilling to confront my own inner uncertainty.

It is amazing how long we can go on deluding ourselves. It was only as my marriage to Sarah disintegrated that I realized I had reached the end of the line. Yet again I'd gone through the familiar cycle of initial excitement in which I swore eternal fidelity and total commitment, then came the inevitable slow disintegration of a relationship that I would not permit to grow deep roots. Nothing novel about it – I guess it's the story of many marriages – but I hadn't the emotional maturity to realize that love is more a sustained act of will than an erotic spasm, so instead of trying all the harder to make it work, I ran away. I cast around for some way out and came up with a mechanism I'd used before: an affair, which didn't so much destroy the marriage as signal its end.

Everything about my life was in a state of flux. In despair, I just stopped everything, sat down and took stock. It was Lord Byron who wrote, 'I have been all my life trying to make someone love me.' Every woman I loved seemed to disappoint me or at least failed to fill some inner void, a vacuum at the core of my personality. Freudians would probably say it was a mother-shaped blank. God knows, but I seemed doomed to repeat this pattern again and again, causing great hurt to my abandoned partners and endless misery to myself.

It was one thing to acknowledge I was in a real mess but quite another to find a way out. I needed help and turned to a friend, John Cleese. A witty and highly intelligent man, John had developed almost a second vocation in psychotherapy, writing several books with his psychiatrist friend Robin Skynner. In jocular mood, I used to accuse him of boring for Britain about head-shrinking and poured scorn on what I thought was a load of quackery. Now the laugh was on me. I swallowed my pride, rang him and confessed I was desperately in need of expert help. He sounded not in the least surprised and gave me half a dozen telephone numbers.

I chose an experienced woman psychotherapist whose straightforward, non-technical approach immediately impressed and reassured me. As far as I could make out, she wasn't Freudian or Jungian or behaviourist, jargon-ridden and determined to impose her ideology on me. It was like chatting to a bank manager or solicitor. She played the role of a wise, utterly clear-eyed friend, who gently but firmly refused to allow me to take refuge in escapism or faulty thinking. She calmed me down, eased my inner panic and in a sense introduced me to the real Michael Grade. I saw her twice a week for six years and the sessions only stopped when she retired. I called it a day then, partly because I didn't want to start from scratch with another therapist but also because I felt confident that with her help I had grown up.

She enabled me to understand my childhood as superficially privileged but fundamentally deprived because of a succession of grievous personal losses, first, my mother at a most crucial time in my infant development, then my father twice – once when he set up a separate family home away from my sister and myself, and then just as I was getting physically and emotionally close to him, he died. Then there was the trauma of my estrangement from an older sister to whom I had clung as a rock in a turbulent sea. Finally, towering over our childhood was the dominant figure of Olga, whom my sister Lynda once described as a tyrant. That's not how I remember her. Her love for me was certainly intense to a point just short of overpowering, but she offered me real security. Yet no grandmother, however devoted, can fully take the place of a mother without creating emotional confusion in a child.

So one way or another, though I was calm and self-possessed on the outside, I was really a crazy, mixed-up kid, as they used to say in American movies. Over my childhood years I grew a hard shell underneath a soft and biddable exterior to protect myself against further losses and to prevent people from getting too close to me. There was a basic fracture between my deepest feelings and my behaviour. Though outwardly affectionate towards my partners, inwardly, I was chronically suspicious, looking for and expecting signs of disaffection. I was always alert and ready to reject them before they rejected me, and I took it for granted that sooner or later they *would* spurn me, for this had been the sorry experience of my childhood.

My psychotherapist helped me to realize that a genuine relationship entails a willingness to take risks. Because I had armoured myself against vulnerability, I could neither give nor receive lasting love – a hedgehog with extended spines is not a cuddlesome creature. I was no longer an anxious child casting around for a mother's unconditional love while masquerading as a successful adult. I had to learn to repudiate or at least to draw a line under the emotional history of my childhood. I realized that I could not move on towards maturity without leaving behind a lot of accumulated clutter from my past.

I slowly came to realize that most women are to be trusted; they can be relied on to give themselves utterly to creating a fulfilling permanent relationship, provided their partner is also prepared to make a similar investment and work at it. That sounds like a tedious statement of the obvious, but it has cost me much pain and loss to reach the point where I believe it.

I also learned that I have much for which to be grateful. Each of my marriages has enriched my life in some way. My first marriage to Penny produced Alison and Jonathan, two adorable children who, unlike me, have been incredibly fortunate in their mother. I enjoyed being a part of the family of my second wife, Sarah. She taught me to take more responsibility for my financial affairs, which I had rather let slip due to a lack of training and an over-generous father.

Nonetheless, my marriage was still over, though to the very end Sarah believed we should try to rescue it. But I was lonely and craved companionship, so I turned to someone else. I had met Pati Marr when I was asked by the BBC to take part in a series called *My First Job*, which was being made at Pebble Mill for daytime programmes. I found it terrific fun to be a sports reporter again and I was asked to cover a match between Arsenal and Southampton for the *Daily Mirror*. I met the camera crew at the ground, and Pati was there as director. We met up again at the old *Daily Mirror* building at Holborn, where they filmed me writing up the story of the match I'd covered. All the *Mirror* staff in the vicinity kept saying knowingly that Bob was in the building, and sure enough the then owner Robert Maxwell lumbered up to me surrounded by flunkeys – he wasn't one to miss the chance of a photo-call. 'Michael, welcome back to the *Mirror*,' he boomed.

Remembering the old days, I looked up and joked, 'Could

you sign my expenses?' All the *Mirror* journalists round me roared with laughter.

Bob was not amused, however, and his henchmen remained stone-faced. 'Things have changed around here. There are no expenses,' he said grimly. I felt like a comedian who'd died the death on stage at the Glasgow Empire on a wet Monday night.

Later, I phoned Pati, took her out to dinner and the inevitable happened. We formed a relationship, which lasted on and off for a number of years and effectively buried a marriage that had been dying on its feet. I moved out of Clarendon Close in April 1989, and when all the legal formalities had been gone through, Sarah and I were divorced. There's not much more to say about it. It is tragic that others have had to pay the price of my struggle to grow up.

My arrival at Channel 4 coincided with the final stages of the consultation process that led to the 1990 Broadcasting Act, so from the beginning I found myself drawn into the political arena. The BBC had the luxury of a whole department to handle its relations with government, which meant that the rest of the staff could get on with the business of making programmes, but at Channel 4 I was responsible in the end for everything, programmes and politics. The struggle to prevent Channel 4 being privatized became a recurrent theme of my entire career there, which is a delicious irony considering the number of critics of my appointment who were convinced I intended to sell it down the river to the highest bidder. It is equally ironic that had Channel 4 been privatized I would have ended up a very rich man. Before I left, the merchant bankers were provisionally valuing it at around £2.5 billion, so a modest 1 per cent of that would have put shoes on my children's feet. On that fateful Saturday at Dickie's house on Richmond Green, when I promised the Channel 4 appointments board that I would loyally defend the channel against the depredations of the asset-strippers, I had no idea what I was letting myself in for. The battle started a year after I joined Channel 4 when the government published a White Paper: 'Broadcasting in the 90s: Competition, Choice and Quality.' It was very complimentary about Channel 4's output and expressed its intention that it should continue to provide a distinctive voice within the independent sector. But what sort of financial structure should undergird its programme policies? The White Paper offered three alternatives: to privatize the channel and put it out to tender; to link it with a new commercial terrestrial Channel 5; or allow it to carry on as a non-profit-making body with the right to compete for advertising against ITV as a subsidiary of an Independent Television Commission, which would be set up to replace the IBA.

I had a meeting with Lady Shirley Littler, the newly appointed director general of the IBA, who had been the Home Office mandarin given much of the credit for drafting the 1981 Broadcasting Act. She asked me how I intended to position Channel 4 in the debate on the White Paper. I told her that I had started out convinced that we should fight to keep Channel 4's status unchanged but I soon came round to the view that we needed a two-pronged strategy: to fight any proposal for the privatization of Channel 4 and seek to obtain charity status or even argue for a Royal Charter like that which governs the BBC. And we could pay our own way by selling air time in competition with ITV on condition that a funding safety net was in place, which the ITC would underwrite. Such a fail-safe mechanism would not be a subsidy but a way of protecting the channel's income against an unforeseen slump in air-time sales. Shirley Littler strongly disagreed with my proposal: in her view, my original idea had been the right one – we must argue to retain the *status quo*, remaining under the wing of ITV and accepting gratefully our monthly allowance.

Lady Littler knew much more about the Whitehall machine than I did, but I was sure she was misreading Mrs Thatcher's psychology. The Prime Minister was at her most pugnacious, taking on all the entrenched institutions she believed stood in the way of a truly liberated British society, as she called it. Here was her opportunity to redesign the entire landscape of broadcasting, whose most prominent landmarks were two monopolies: the BBC, which had a monopoly of the licence fee, and ITV, which had a monopoly of advertising revenue. So, trying to hide behind the skirts of ITV, in the hope that Mrs Thatcher wouldn't notice us, did not seem to me to be an option, whereas splitting Channel 4 from ITV would be smashing the advertising monopoly and had the feel of a radical idea she might smile on.

In the end I was proved right, but my first battle was to counter all the arguments for privatizing Channel 4. At stake was not one financial structure rather than another but the essential genius of Channel 4. The choice facing the government was simple. They could have a privatized channel or one with a public service remit, but not both. No amount of regulation would preserve public-service broadcasting intact in the face of an economic downturn, lower revenues and a load of unhappy shareholders. So far as I could see, there were only four motives for privatization. The first was to promote efficiency, and Channel 4 was the most effective broadcaster in the business, with costs per hour that were remarkably low, given the quality of what was being produced. The second was to create a good pay day for the Treasury at the expense of programme budgets. Do turkeys vote for Christmas? The third motive was to create competition and widen choice, but Channel 4 was already highly competitive, giving BBC 2 and ITV a run for their money. Indeed, the privatization of Channel 4 would lessen choice by effectively creating a big ITV and a little ITV, both appealing to the same market. The fourth reason was to provide a mechanism for raising money on the capital markets. But Channel 4 was eminently bankable, as we proved when in 1993 we needed to raise money to fund the transition from being dependent on ITV to earning our own living. We borrowed and paid back £75 million with no problem at all.

I embarked on a dizzy round of interviews, lobbying and speech-making. I presented oral evidence to the Home Affairs Select Committee, arguing that Channel 4 should be a subsidiary of the ITC provided it would underwrite a safety net of about 14 per cent of terrestrial net advertising revenue in case we hit turbulent economic conditions. With this fail-safe mechanism in place, I had no doubt that Channel 4 could discharge the remit on which it was founded, 'to appeal to tastes and interests not already catered for by ITV, to innovate, experiment and pay special attention to minority interests'. ITV, fearful that they would lose their lucrative monopoly of advertising, claimed that I couldn't maintain the distinctive character of Channel 4 if we had to compete for advertising with Channels 3 and 5. Richard Dunn, chairman of the ITV Association, told the select committee that if Channel 4 went into competition with them 'they would have no option but to try to blast it out of the water'. He was convinced that Channel 4 and ITV must remain firmly yoked together if they were to compete effectively against the BBC. To pursue competitive advertising would be to sign the death warrant of Channel 4, said David Elstein, director of programmes at Thames TV, and even some of my colleagues at Charlotte Street felt I was gambling recklessly with the Channel's future. They were inclined to share ITV's gloomy though self-serving prediction that if we were cut loose from the independent sector's apron strings we would starve.

In this poker game, I was not gambling blindly. I actually had sight of some of my opponent's cards. I discovered I had a friend who worked at 10 Downing Street. This person betrayed no state secrets but was invaluable in indicating to me the general drift of Mrs Thatcher's thinking. Thus I was told that she was warming to an idea put to her by Lord Young, the secretary of state at the Department of Trade and Industry, that BBC 2 and Channel 4 should become satellite channels and our terrestrial frequencies sold off to the highest bidder, making space for as many as half a dozen land-based rival commercial channels. I asked to see Lord Young and told him I'd heard about his plan to put Channel 4 and BBC on satellite and then auction the terrestrial frequencies.

He sat bolt upright. 'Where did you get that from? It's the bloody Home Office, isn't it?' The rivalry between the

Department of Trade and Industry and the Home Office for control of broadcasting was legendary. Both claimed it fell within their terms of reference: the DTI because broadcasting had become a vast industry employing hundreds of thousands of people, and the Home Office because it had always licensed and monitored the radio and television frequencies.

Since I had no intention of betraying my mole, I neither confirmed nor denied that I had had a tip-off from the Home Office; if David Young drew that conclusion, so be it. I felt that this was a war we were engaged in and I was all for sowing confusion among the enemy. David and I then fell to animated discussion about his satellite idea. Foolishly, I began by saying, 'The first thing I have to explain to you, David, is that broadcasting is not like any other business.'

He cut in, 'Stop right there, Michael. Everyone who comes into this office starts off by saying, 'What you've got to understand, Secretary of State, is that the airline business or the hotel business or the ball-bearing business or whatever isn't like any other.'

I never used that phrase again; I expunged it from my vocabulary. But I recovered and told him that if this satellite proposal was in the Broadcasting Bill, there would be keen competition between the governors of the BBC and the board of Channel 4 to be first to get their resignations on to the Prime Minister's desk, and my resignation wouldn't be far behind. He nodded impassively and scribbled something on his notepad.

When I left the DTI, I phoned the Home Office and told them all about David's plan. They gave no indication as to whether they already knew about it but seemed delighted that I had ferreted out the information. Obviously they realized the premature publicity would almost certainly kill an idea they thought quite unworkable since it would take programmes watched on and off by 80 per cent of the population away from non-satellite households. It was an élitist proposal that would penalize the poor, who couldn't afford satellite subscriptions on top of an already punishing licence fee.

The next day the government made public 'for discussion' their satellite proposal, knowing that any chance of winning approval for the idea by quiet persuasion was out of the question now that I knew what was going on: since I was a devout believer in the power of propaganda, I would soon be talking to the tabloids. Both Michael Checkland, as director general of the BBC, and I were called to the Home Office and told by a po-faced official, who seemed to have difficulty in meeting my eye, that the announcement about the satellite proposal was about to be made. We both registered our opposition and went out to meet the press. There were a few days of fevered speculation, heated debate and mounting opposition, then things went quiet. When the Bill was published there was not a word about the proposal.

The often-repeated dictum that 'information is power' is especially relevant during the complicated process of drafting a major piece of parliamentary legislation such as a broadcasting Bill. Just before the White Paper was due to be published, my mole asked me to come to Downing Street, where he handed me a draft of it. The door was locked behind me and I was given just twenty minutes to read it, but not allowed to take notes. The document was inches thick and stiff with convoluted, legal language. I felt like a contestant on *The Generation Game* trying to memorize the array of household goods that flowed past me on a conveyor belt ... cutlery set ... cuddly toy ... washing-machine ... case of champagne ... but there was no Bruce Forsyth to urge me on.

When my time was up, I leaped into my car and said to my driver, 'Don't move or say a word or even breathe.' I sat in the back seat of the car and scribbled down all I could remember of the document. Back in my office, I summoned my White Paper campaign team – David Scott and Peter Ibbotson whom I'd brought over with me from the BBC – and went through it with them, reciting parrot-like as much as I could recall while they egged me on with encouraging noises. Those few days of advance knowledge were to prove invaluable in preparing our responses to the government's plans.

Not all my political contacts were clandestine: most were out in the open and occasionally led to bizarre adventures. During the drafting of the Broadcasting Bill I had meetings with Professor Brian Griffiths, now Lord Griffiths, who was head of Mrs Thatcher's policy unit. We seemed to get on well, sharing some convictions on the way ahead. He asked me one day in his mellifluous Welsh accent whether I would like to go to Washington to meet President George Bush. I said I'd be delighted and we arranged to meet in the US capital where he told me I was to meet the President at a prayer breakfast that took place every year and had profound political as well as spiritual significance. (It was at a prayer breakfast that Bill Clinton finally expressed deep remorse to the nation's spiritual leaders about his affair with Monica Lewinsky.)

Here I was, a nice Jewish boy from North London, sitting next to Brian Griffiths at the top table where he'd been invited to join the President at this evangelical Christian event in the ballroom of the Washington Hilton. After a few minutes, Doug Coe, the man who had organized the event, came over and asked me if I would be prepared to read a lesson from the Old Testament during the meal. I gulped.

'You have a Bible on you,' he stated, as though it was an accessory no well-dressed executive would venture out of doors without – wallet, keys, handkerchief, Bible. I didn't feel able to point out that we Jews were not in the habit of carrying a Bible, even though we had written most of it.

'Uh, er, no,' I replied, patting my pockets just to make sure.

'Well, have mine.'

He told me the passage he wanted me to read. I thought I'd better rehearse it. I had no intention of making an idiot of myself in front of the President of the United States and all the great and good of US society. I placed the Bible on my knee, put my head down and started to read it half under the table, reciting to myself quietly. Suddenly a large black gentleman tapped me on the shoulder and introduced himself as the prime minister of St Kitts.

'Are you a parson?' he asked, obviously vastly impressed by my piety.

I replied, 'Boy, have you got the wrong man!' That was the first and only time I've been mistaken for a man of the cloth.

Perhaps the Almighty, too, was impressed by my earnest recitation of Holy Scripture because when the Broadcasting Bill was published it revealed that Mrs Thatcher had not got her way: Channel 4 was not to be privatized and would be allowed to sell its own advertising in competition with ITV. We were to be insulated from the full impact of market forces by a fail-safe mechanism, but this was to be provided not by the newly formed ITC but by ITV. If our earnings did not reach a minimum level, the independent companies would have to cough up cash. The reasoning behind this was quite ingenious. If Channel 4 and ITV parted company, ITV, being much wealthier and more powerful, could decimate our audience by competitive scheduling, but if they attempted to do that, they themselves would have to make up the income we had lost through their commercial aggressiveness. Thus they had a very strong incentive not to drive Channel 4 out of the market. But there was a snag: we would be penalized if we did too well. Any surplus we earned over a magic 14 per cent had to be shared with ITV. From Daddy paying his lad an allowance, the new system required that the lad should subsidize his parent. The trouble was that someone had got their sums wrong and Channel 4 ended up paying ITV some £70–80 million a year to line the pockets of its shareholders. This funding formula was a millstone round our neck, a brake on enterprise, a disincentive to improve our audience share. It led to the ludicrous result that poor Channel 4 ended up subsidizing rich ITV. Getting rid of this funding formula and staving off further attempts to privatize Channel 4 were to occupy me until I left the television industry.

I felt only modified rapture at the result of all our lobbying. The bad news was that Channel 4 would not be made a charity or a chartered corporation but turned into a statutory corporation with the government reserving the power to appoint the directors. The very idea filled me with alarm – after all, I'd suffered like the rest of the BBC staff under the rule of Thatcher-appointed governors whose timidity and conservatism stifled the creativity of programme-makers. The spectre of a William Rees-Mogg Mark 2 dominating the Channel 4 board rose up to haunt me, so Dickie and I went off once more to lobby the home secretary, Douglas Hurd. Dickie was quite prepared to resign and take his board with him if this proposal wasn't dropped. In the end a compromise was cobbled together where the ITC would consult the Chairman of Channel 4 on any names to be recommended to the home secretary for appointment to the Channel 4 board and hence any veto would be public and no appointment would made without Channel 4's prior knowledge. Thus was the danger of a politically rigged board averted.

But damn me if another clause of the Broadcasting Bill didn't bring the noble Lord Rees-Mogg back to torment broadcasters in the role he loved best, pontificating about taste and standards and, like Nanny, wagging an admonitory finger at a child and telling him that whatever he was doing he must stop it. Rees-Mogg had never hidden his contempt for broadcasters and his lofty disdain for popular programmes.

The government announced that Lord Rees-Mogg was to chair a newly set up Broadcasting Standards Council. Personalities aside, I had long been opposed in principle to the very idea. I was not against enlightened regulation but I felt television was about to be regulated to death. What on earth were the governors of the BBC and members of the ITC for? Given the moral climate of the time, I could see the ITC and the BSC trying to outdo each other in demonstrating their toughness with broadcasters, the regulators competing to censor programmes – I vaguely recalled Jonathan Swift penning some lines about fleas having smaller fleas on their backs to bite them. What were we supposed to do if the ITC approved a programme and then the BSC gave it the thumbs down? Toss a coin?

The incident that was supposed to have triggered govern-

ment alarm at the amount of violence on TV and spawned the
BSC was the massacre at Hungerford in 1987 when Michael
Ryan ran amok, allegedly modelling himself on Sylvester Stallone
in the *Rambo* movies. In fact, *Rambo* had never been shown on
television and Ryan didn't possess a video recorder, but in an
atmosphere of semi-hysteria the Tory government reverted to
type and recruited the establishment pundit least likely to understand popular taste to head up the BSC. The average age of the
original BSC members was twenty years older than that of
Channel 4 viewers. Frankly, they were too elderly and too out of
touch to be anything other than an irritant to hard-pressed
programme-makers. They were a bunch of well-meaning, highly
respected individuals who, I was prepared to wager, had never
seen some of the more experimental programmes on any of the
channels. I doubted any of them had seen Channel 4's *Network
7*, for instance. We broadcasters well knew that these youth
programmes straddled the fuzzy boundary between the acceptable and the unacceptable, and we needed informed understanding of what we were trying to achieve, not head-shaking
incomprehension.

Rees-Mogg followed the announcement of his appointment
by giving broadcasters an ultimatum. Unless they toed the line,
he would seek statutory powers to compel them to obey the
BSC's directions. He also demanded the right to preview programmes, a proposal that made even his friend on the neigh-
bouring estate, Duke Hussey, gag. 'We have always made it clear
that the previewing of any programmes due to be broadcast by
the BBC should not be part of the council's remit,' he protested.
When asked about his viewing tastes, Lord Rees-Mogg went
so far as to confess that he actually enjoyed one BBC comedy,
'Allo 'Allo, though he also revealed that when he was a BBC
governor he had 'stopped *Rambo* being scheduled at Christmas
by saying it was a disgrace'. It was clear the broadcasters were in
for a fun time with Lord Rees-Mogg guarding the morals of the
nation.

*

In November 1988, I got a public opportunity to vent my spleen on the Broadcasting Standards Council when I was invited to speak at the Oxford Union and propose the motion, 'The government does not appreciate the strengths of British broadcasting.' On the other side of the house were Douglas Hurd, the home secretary, Professor Norman Stone and Lord Rees-Mogg's son, Jacob, who was an Oxford undergraduate. I enlisted my friend Mark Lawson, the journalist and broadcaster, to help me with the speech. Between us we composed a veritable diatribe against the new Puritans who were strangling British broadcasting.

'The Government knows that an accidental expanse of thigh, a random nipple flashed on the nation's television screens can fill the loins of the least libidinous of men with lust. The Government knows that a gun seen on the screen can lead a man to take his gun and use it. And so seeing the abhorrent torrent of well-stacked women and well-armed men which daily pours from our television sets, the Government knows that it must create a broadcasting council and that an elderly peer of the realm and sometime antiquarian bookseller, William Rees-Mogg, should be created the nation's first switch-finder general.'

I then went on to examine the Government's facile assumption that sexually explicit scenes on television must incite licentiousness and promiscuity in real life. If this thesis were true, then the viewers most likely to be influenced were the members of the BSC themselves who spent their lives peering at the screen in search of a glimpse of bare flesh or bout of bedroom acrobats in order to cry, 'Woe! Thrice Woe!' 'I fear for Lady Rees-Mogg and Mrs Richard Baker and the other spouses of the Broadcasting Standards Council watchdogs. They are in for a bruising few years. What right have we, the privileged and intelligent, to assume that we are immune to such exposure but the ordinary viewer is not?'

I had a side-swipe at the Government's fatuous ban on the voices of Sinn Fein members being heard over the airwaves, though their faces could still be shown and an actor spoke their lines. This, I suggested, was a recruiting device for lip-reading, deaf terrorists. Then I turned to the Broadcasting White Paper. 'It treats British television as just a new, fat piggy-bank for entrepreneurs. The viewer is increasingly called the consumer and the play, documentary, serial or news report is called the product. This shift in language is quite deliberate because, in application of the market argument, it aims to reduce a cultural and democratic heritage to the status of goods on a shelf. We must think deeply and carefully before changing the management of the system and undermining its capital structure. If you travel as a representative of British television in almost any country of the world you become aware that the industry in this country is regarded in quality and integrity as a touchstone, and yet we are indeed prophets without honour in Westminster.'

I concluded by appealing to the house to support the argument that the Government had over-emphasized the political, persuasive and corruptive strengths of broadcasting and totally failed to appreciate its democratic, ambassadorial and cultural strengths. 'As a result of these miscalculations, it is sending in the redevelopers' bulldozers when it ought merely to be sending in the decorators.'

We won the day by a comfortable margin, and Douglas Hurd obviously took his defeat in good part for a few months later he appointed me chairman of a Home Office working party on the fear of crime. But there was still an eleventh-hour battle to be fought to prevent more political interference with broadcasting freedom. More than a hundred Tory MPs signed a Commons motion urging the Government to introduce tighter controls on the editorial freedom of broadcasters; they urged ministers to toughen up the Broadcasting Bill that was currently before the House of Lords. This motion marked the culmination of months of Tory attacks against broadcasters for what the MPs claimed was rampant anti-government bias in the media. They cited three examples: a BBC *Timewatch* programme, *The Summer of the Bomb*, Channel 4's *Oh Superman!*, in which Harold Pinter attacked American foreign policy and Mrs Thatcher's support for it, and Granada's *World in Action* for its generally left-wing stance.

The MPs urged the home secretary to accept a series of amendments proposed by Woodrow Wyatt in the House of Lords. A *News of the World* journalist, Lord Wyatt was a model of impartiality and he teamed up with another right-wing Tory peer, Lord Orr-Ewing, to come up with a novel way of trying to ensure political impartiality in television programmes. They proposed that whenever a television programme advocated one political position, equal time should be given within the same programme for the opposing viewpoint. The two peers took it for granted that all broadcasting organizations were hot-beds of lefty propaganda and this was their wheeze for ensuring that the right wing always got its say. The effect of any such silly proposal would not have been political balance but excruciating boredom: programmes of opinion generate interest precisely because they are not exactly balanced – mix black and white in the same container and you end up with a dirty grey mish-mash.

In fact, the two peers were addressing a serious issue in a totally frivolous manner. From the days of Reith, first the BBC and then ITV, aware of the dangerous power of broadcasting, had struggled to evolve an effective working definition of impartiality. Over decades of hard experience, broadcasters have used a tried and tested rule of thumb: the impartial treatment of a controversial subject is one where a platform is offered for the widest possible range of views and opinions on it; where the listener or viewer is made aware of the weight and authority of the voices advocating each position; and where the flux or direction of the argument is clearly indicated. But Woodrow Wyatt's notion of achieving impartiality by balancing each viewpoint by its mirror image set terms that were much too restrictive. After all, the government and the opposition between them don't have a monopoly of wisdom on every issue. There may be novel insights, fresh ideas, new angles that can't be accommodated within the traditional adversarial political system. And what all broadcasters try to aim for is balance over time, ensuring that any bias in one programme is countered in another. With the exception of programmes clearly labelled as personal statements, such as the BBC's *Open Space* or Channel 4's *Comment* in which the broadcasting authority takes no editorial responsibility for the content, we try to be impartial by offering a range of significant opinions on a subject within a setting where the channel is plainly neutral – the chairman, presenter, camera operative and editor make no attempt to impose their own viewpoint – and each participant has an equal chance to state his or her case.

This stopwatch notion of political balance where each protagonist is given equal time was plainly a nonsense. Public impact can't be measured by the minute. Some personalities on the political scene are colourful, animated and given to vivid speech: they can make five minutes pass in a flash. Others make five minutes seem like a dress rehearsal for eternity: they are lacklustre, colourless and rambling. The only way to achieve political balance by mathematical equivalence would be to breed out of political life all the characters, mavericks and charismatic personalities. The result would be not enlightenment but nullity.

I attacked the McCarthyism of these Tory MPs who were trying to embroil the broadcasters in a web of litigation that would so sap our energies and bank balances that we would have no time left to make honest programmes. I felt so strongly that the Wyatt challenge had to be resisted that I organized a letter to *The Times*, signed by newspaper proprietor Conrad Black, Robert Runcie, Archbishop of Canterbury, Klaus Moser, the distinguished academic, and John Birt and myself. I also tried to get Rupert Murdoch to sign it but he declined and said he would send his own letter. He never did.

On publication day I was at the Tory Party conference, enjoying the hospitality of Jeffrey Archer's famed Krug champagne and shepherd's pie, when I was buttonholed – pinned to the wall is more accurate – by David Mellor, who as the minister at the Home Office was trying hard to mitigate the worst excesses of the Broadcasting Bill. He was bringing the light of common sense to bear on doctrinaire broadcasting ideas and had made himself very unpopular in Downing Street. Apparently our letter had infuriated Mrs Thatcher and stiffened her resolve to back Woodrow Wyatt and the Tory MPs just when David was getting her to see reason over critically important issues such as abandoning the idea of privatizing Channel 4 and writing into ITV franchises a quality threshold. I was both penitent and reassured. David Mellor proved to be a staunch champion of public-service broadcasting, not wavering even when he was booed at his own party conference for defending the BBC.

We had another friend at court in the late Willie Whitelaw. It was ironic that we should spend so much of our time at Channel 4 fighting off the threat of privatization posed by successive Tory governments because the channel was their creature – it was one of their indubitable successes. Willie Whitelaw knew this and never lost his faith in the channel he had done so much to foster; throughout, he remained our staunch friend and wise adviser. His quiet intervention undoubtedly saved us from disaster on several occasions. Whenever in desperation I approached him, he would say, 'I'm not sure I can do anything, but do keep me in touch.' He had this marvellous, absent-minded way about him, almost as if he'd wandered into the highest echelons of power by mistake but since he was there he might as well do his bit. He never made any promises or divulged any confidences but somehow things changed as a result of his influence.

In the end, David Mellor and Willie Whitelaw moved the Government away from any support for the Wyatt/Orr-Ewing motion, though they were powerless to prevent a last-minute compromise in which the Independent Television Commission was asked to impose an impartiality code of practice on all the companies it licensed. The backwoods Tory MPs had to be appeased. The ITC itself was utterly opposed to the requirement, which, it said, would be unworkable and bring the law into disrepute by provoking 'vexatious litigation'. It took particular exception to the phrase 'impartiality on individual issues', which, it insisted, could have serious effects on news programmes since the code 'would appear to require that news events on a particular day, involving, for example, the Prime Minister and the Leader of the Opposition would have to be balanced by comments on the same issue from the opposing party'.

Willie Whitelaw rounded fiercely on the Government's impartiality amendment, describing it as 'profoundly disturbing and very upsetting'. He said it was utterly wrong for the ITC to be asked to introduce an impartiality clause it did not agree with. 'I have a passionate belief that the further away government is from impartiality and anything to do with broadcasting content at all, the better for government.' He was speaking in a last-ditch lobbying meeting we organized in one of the committee rooms of the House of Lords. In one of his better speeches, John Birt, present as deputy director general of the BBC, spoke for all of us when he said, 'Impartiality is achieved by the steady exercise of good judgement at every link in the editorial chain and not by any application of a tit-for-tat formula, which would stultify programme-making and obstruct public understanding.' In the end, the Government and the ITC agreed on a formula about impartiality, which was rather more a pious hope than a set of specific requirements. We broadcasters could live with it.

In all these political struggles I was blessed in the chairmen I served under at Channel 4. Dickie supported me throughout our lobbying campaign to get a favourable position for Channel 4 in the 1990 Broadcasting Act. When he retired, his place was taken by Sir Michael Bishop, who founded and ran British Midland Airways. When we found ourselves battling to stave off privatization, he was a tower of strength, which surprised me because he was a natural Conservative: his airline had been established and flourished because of Mrs Thatcher's deregulation policy and her desire to see competition for British Airways. She had opened up the skies and the landing slots that enabled him to create a splendid business, so it was hardly surprising that he was true blue. On the final occasion that the issue of privatizing Channel 4 came up, during John Major's premiership, I asked Michael Bishop to intervene on our behalf. David Scott, the finance director of Channel 4, and I sat down and we drafted a couple of pages for the Prime Minister, over-egging the argument because we assumed that the chairman, noted for his diplomacy, would soften it. We faxed the letter up to the Midlands. Two days later his handwritten final draft arrived. He hadn't inserted any honeyed words. Instead he had made it stronger. He ended, 'You and I, Prime Minister, have sat on platforms together extolling the virtues of privatization, but in this case I have to tell you that to privatize Channel 4 would be an act of cultural vandalism.' Wonderful stuff. It took John Major three months to send a formal and noncommittal reply, but when the Red Book, which set out the Government's finance plans eventually appeared, there was no mention of Channel 4 in it.

Like a dark shadow, the threat of Channel 4 being sold off to shareholders hovered over me throughout my time there. We could never completely relax. Somewhere in the Treasury, a mandarin on the lookout to make a quick buck for his Chancellor of the Exchequer was doing his sums and weighing the odds.

All this politicking had taken an immense amount of my time and energy that would otherwise have been devoted to programme matters. Stories began to appear in the press from unnamed Channel 4 producers grumbling that I was betraying the channel's distinctive remit. They alleged that our weekly top ten contained too many quizzes, comedies and editions of *Brookside* – tastes and interests that could easily be catered for by ITV. They expressed their fear that, once Channel 4 had to pay its way by selling advertising in competition with Channels 3 and 5, it would be inexorably driven downmarket to improve its ratings. A 'Channel 4 editor' was quoted as saying, 'We need someone to fly the flag. There is a mass of marvellous programming coming out of the channel, but we need someone to focus attention on it. There is no one thinking, breathing and feeling programmes in the way that Jeremy did. You feel the channel lacks an editorial heartbeat.'

I think I had cause to feel aggrieved. I had worked day and night, with the board's blessing, to head the campaign to prevent the privatization of the channel and to get a good deal for us out of the Broadcasting Act, yet I was being taunted again with the ghost of the sainted Jeremy. It was factually untrue that I had taken the channel downmarket, and who should have known it better than one of my own editors? I had recruited outstanding senior staff: John Willis, from Yorkshire Television, as controller of Factual Programmes, Waldemar Januszczak as arts editor and Avril MacRory as the channel's first music editor. Indeed, the very week these critical articles appeared, I had cleared the entire schedule at peak viewing time on a Saturday evening to show all six hours of Peter Brook's adaptation of the Indian classic, the *Mahabharata*. If that wasn't creative risk-taking, then words have lost their meaning. I strengthened drama with series such as *The Manageress*, the award-winning *Traffik* and *A Very British Coup*. Granted, we had two daytime quiz shows, *Fifteen to One* and *Countdown*, and I saw nothing to be ashamed of in either. It's hardly dumbing down to promote general-knowledge competitions competently presented and produced. *Film on Four* was virtually sustaining the British film industry and *Dispatches*, our flagship current-affairs programme, made regular headlines. Perhaps the most noticeable change was in the number of classy American programmes I imported: *The Golden Girls*, *Roseanne* and *thirtysomething*. Having spent three years in Hollywood specializing in sit-coms, I was well qualified to recognize slick, polished plots, and I reckon we offered British viewers the pick of the crop. Channel 4 was not in bad shape, but I had a long way to go to realize the first of my aims: to sort the channel out.

Chapter Nine

FOUR WEDDINGS AND A
LOT OF GRIEF

IT WAS ON impulse that I had phoned Dickie Attenborough and offered myself to Channel 4, but once there, it dawned on me that fate or chance or whatever divinity shapes our ends had guided me to a job that was tailor-made for me. All my previous experience had been a preparation for Channel 4. I had a CV that was unique in British television. Each aspect of the chief executive's range of duties demanded a particular skill or experience I had acquired at some stage in my career. My life as an agent had made me an expert talent-spotter, and the search for new stars was the constant preoccupation of a small channel constantly being raided by our bigger competitors. Discovering potential stars then nursing them through the insecurities and neuroses of their turbulent early days on the ladder of fame was second nature to me. At LWT and the BBC I had honed my skills as a programme scheduler – I knew every trick in that book – and I'd commissioned and transmitted enough programmes, good, bad and indifferent, to be able to read, so far as anyone other than a clairvoyant can, the television tastes of the British public.

Having worked in Hollywood, I knew the American television and film scene intimately: day in and day out I had read comedy scripts, supervised the production of the best of them and then had to sell the result to the big US networks. I knew what a polished US comedy looked like and where to find one to brighten up the Channel 4 schedules.

I had run my own production company in Hollywood, handling big stars and large budget movies: Channel 4's great *Film on Four* was familiar territory to me. I'd been a journalist so I knew how to deal with the press, and in the BBC, largely through dealing with the so-called Obscenity Bill, I developed political skills, learning all about lobbying MPs, arguing with government departments and influencing public opinion on controversial issues. At a more mundane level I had commercial experience, having been a partner in one of the biggest agencies in Britain, so selling air time, reading balance sheets and juggling large sums of money held no terrors for me.

Most happily, at Channel 4 I was able to indulge that streak of showmanship I had absorbed from my uncles Lew and Bernie. Every now and then I could burst out as an impresario. In 1992 when Channel 4 launched the romantic comedy film *Hear My Song* – about a down-at-heel nightclub owner who hires a Josef Locke lookalike to attract more Irish customers – I took personal charge of the première with an enthusiasm powered by nostalgia. Josef Locke had been one of my father's more difficult clients, and as a child I can recall an exasperated Dad screaming down the phone at him. We dedicated the proceeds from the première to one of the Princess of Wales's charities and she was guest of honour. We flew Josef Locke over and arranged with Thames Television for him to be the surprise subject of *This Is Your Life*, Michael Aspel ambushing him with the big red book while Locke was taking a bow at the end of the film.

The blunt truth is that, contrary to the prognostications of doom from a handful of disaffected staff who believed that a new dark age dawned at Charlotte Street the day Jeremy Isaacs left and I replaced him, I drove up the ratings of Channel 4 and expanded the range of its programmes. It wasn't an accident of fortuitous timing, catching the industry on a roll: I brought wide, even unrivalled experience to the job. I was young and had immense energy, and my instinct for picking talented people, then trusting them to get on with the job resulted in a dynamic and highly creative management team. If it is false modesty not to take the credit that is due to me, it would be dishonest not to acknowledge that my team got less recognition than they deserved. Because I was always in the news, the fortunes of Channel 4 were personalized in me, so I got criticism I didn't deserve and plaudits I hadn't earned. I led a brilliant team and Jeremy Isaacs had given us a rocket-propelled start.

My programme judgement was soon put to the test. Every evening and at the weekends I trundled off home loaded down with cassettes so that I could make a detailed analysis of our output. Children's programmes worried me. With limited resources, Jeremy had opened up a lunchtime strand, *Just For Fun*, but he was up against the BBC, which had a tradition of making programmes for children that went back to the days of Uncle Mac at Savoy Hill. The Corporation had vast experience in this area, a large staff and adequate funding. They spent ten times as much as Channel 4 on children's programmes – I knew that because as controller of BBC 1 I had provided the money. They had moved beyond studio programmes and pioneered children's drama and documentaries. In competition with them we were on a hiding to nothing: our children's programmes were a waste of resources. I abandoned them, with the exception of those for children with special needs. I saw no point in doing badly what the BBC and ITV did supremely well. On the other hand, I felt that the teenage youth audience was neglected. We'd had success with *Network 7* and *The Chart Show*, and I wanted to put more money into programmes for this age group. This meant that I had to dispense with the services of Rosemary Shepherd, a rather fey lady who had been a Jeremy Isaacs acolyte. She put up a spirited fight for her programmes but I was adamant, and she went, protesting to the last.

Auditing children's programmes had drawn my attention to another of Channel 4's afternoon programmes, *Mavis on Four*, which was transmitted three times weekly. Mavis Nicholson was a veteran presenter, who was known as the queen of the chat-show; on one channel or another she had been interviewing people for seventeen years. I greatly respected her professionalism but felt that this particular format had come to the end of its natural life. It had the feel of an import that had strayed over the border from the ITV afternoon schedules. Mavis was understandably displeased with me and, like the hard-boiled journalist she was, used the press to great effect, hinting that it was because she was a woman of a certain age that I had taken against her. She gave a heart-rending anecdote of a viewer who was so horrified at the prospect of *Mavis on Four* being cancelled that, though she was poor, she saved up for a video recorder because she couldn't bear to miss any of the shows if she happened to be out. And, of course, out came the old 'Grade as Vulgarian' accusation: Mavis harboured deep suspicions that I intended to put a quiz show in her place. For axing *Mavis on Four*, I earned the undying enmity of Richard Ingrams, then editor of *Private Eye*. He was a friend of Mavis Nicholson and gave me a roasting in his *Observer* television column; he's had a very jaundiced view of me ever since.

Meanwhile, I'd been turning my attention to arts programmes. These were run by Michael Kustow, a most engaging and articulate man who was immensely knowledgeable across a wide range of disciplines. In a sense he was the embodiment of the spirit of Jeremy Isaacs. Among the papers he sent to me before I arrived at the channel was a report on a creative conference the commissioning editors had attended at the Barbican in the summer of 1987. Each wrote a think-piece. Michael's essay was called 'An Argument with Myself', which I found clever but self-indulgent and élitist to a degree. He was entitled to his views about art but I didn't see why he should be allowed to impose them on the viewers: he was a marked man and I watched his output with a gimlet eye.

Kustow invited me to Paris to meet the executives of La Sept, the French government's arts channel with whom we did some business. I duly arrived at the building and then had to hang around for an hour and a half until he arrived. He then compounded the offence by taking it for granted that being a song-and-dance man I would speak no French so painstakingly translated everything that was said until I disabused him with an outburst in the vernacular. Such a minor contretemps would not have mattered had we been able to agree on what constituted a true arts programme. Michael had admittedly made some distinguished programmes, but times were changing and at all costs art had to be made accessible to a small but growing public. I felt that Michael was making programmes for fellow arts producers and connoisseurs rather than the generality of the viewers. Much to his fury, I gave the thumbs down to one of his pet projects, *Ghosts in the Machine*, which was a series on experimental video. There was nothing ideological about this decision: I just didn't think the programme worked and felt that getting Brownie points from the Arts Council was no substitute for engaging with the audience. So Michael, too, left Channel 4, and I was again portrayed as a cultural illiterate obviously about to replace high art with low music hall. The fact that one of my first decisions was to expunge any trace of the hours of snooker Jeremy had filled the schedule with was never quoted in my favour.

I'm making no claims to infallibility in my programme judgements. When I was first shown the pilot of a comedy set on a small island off the west coast of Ireland, I just didn't find it funny. In fact, I couldn't even follow the plot line, which struck me as being infantile. I sent a note to Channel 4's head of Comedy, Seamus Cassidy, stating dogmatically that I didn't think it had an outside chance of working; I found it mindless and childish, and suggested we should count it as an experiment that had failed. Seamus didn't agree with me and went on doggedly developing the idea, which was just as well. *Father Ted* became one of Channel 4's greatest successes. Seamus believed in it, and I believed in him; he was right and I was wrong. In mitigation, my initial reaction to the pilot took me back to my days in Hollywood and the in-humour of ethnic comedy where you had to get inside Hispanic or Jewish culture to appreciate some of the subtleties of the plot. And, as the public's response to *Father Ted* showed, Catholics – and Irish Catholics in particular – found nuances of humour in it that went right over the head of a good Jewish boy like me. But once we started transmitting it, for half an hour a week I became an honorary papist and surrendered myself to that wonderful capacity the Irish have to laugh at themselves. Had it not been for the tragic death of its star, Dermot Morgan, *Father Ted* would still be delighting Channel 4 audiences.

Programme judgement is one of the black arts: you operate in unknown territory where you are making guesses about the most unpredictable element in the whole business – public taste. Though I bought in *Neighbours* for the BBC, I never thought it would become such a national institution. I thought it was a cheery soap that made an undemanding bridge between after-noon and evening viewing. Later I smiled modestly when con-gratulated on my far-sightedness and thanked my lucky stars that the general public had no access to my wastepaper basket where some programme ideas that might have been equally successful had died a premature death.

Talent-spotting is another of the black arts where instinct is more important than any technical skill. In 1989, Channel 4 moved into breakfast television. It is the story of the emergence, then the ascendancy of a gawky, brash young man who came to dominate the nation's television screens every morning. I had no overwhelming desire to break into breakfast television but our blank screen in the morning was an invitation to the regulators to take those hours from us. I decided to try a television version of the Radio 4 *Today* programme. *Channel 4 Daily* was the title I chose to signal our aim, which was to give the viewers authoritative, global news, city reports and arts reviews. We researched it carefully and promoted it widely. The only problem was that virtually nobody watched it, even though it had some distinguished contributors: Carol Barnes reported from London, James Mates from Tokyo and Michael Nicholson from Washington. The audience peaked at around 200,000, which was risible compared to TV-am's couple of million. One of the jokes my friends insisted on telling me was that Greta Garbo didn't need to hide in a New York apartment block: if she really wanted to be alone, she could have appeared on Channel 4 breakfast television instead, then she'd be sure nobody had seen her. 'More boring than BBC breakfast television,' said one critic, which cut me to the quick.

Under the original financial structure of Channel 4 where Uncle ITV paid our bills, we didn't need to worry too much about ratings, but one of the consequences of our hard lobbying to be cut loose from ITV's apron strings was that in 1993 we would be paying our own way. TV-am had been subsidizing us to the tune of about £13 million a year and only got about £9 million back in advertising revenue, so that £4 million shortfall meant *Channel 4 Daily* could become a serious drain on our resources. I was determined that breakfast television should stand on its own feet; I had no intention of diverting cash from peak-time output, so something had to be done. Now that the toothpaste was out of the tube, there was no way of squeezing it back and reverting to blank screens in the morning as in pre-breakfast television days. Our whole pitch to the government in discussions about the Broadcasting Act had been that Channel 4 is all about competition, choice and quality. We had a statutory obligation to provide alternative viewing, and that was what I intended to do. We changed the presenters and commissioned children's programmes to hammock the news reports. We considered then rejected the idea of cutting down *Channel 4 Daily*, virtually reducing it to a rolling news service. That wouldn't interest the advertisers and its realistic competition would be Radio 4's *Today* programme rather than TV-am: not a battle I believed we could win.

Liz Forgan and I met the editorial team and considered all the options. We wanted an original format, not a pale imitation of BBC breakfast television, TV-am, or a rejig of what we were already transmitting: we had tinkered enough with *Channel 4 Daily*. We let it be known throughout the production community that we were in the market for something fresh and different to occupy two hours every morning and excite viewers. Back came over a hundred suggestions. One was from a company that proposed presenting the show from one of Harrods' shop windows, another thought the main concourse of Waterloo station would be an ideal location for a wacky, noisy programme. Andrea Wonfor, the controller of Arts and Entertainment, passed along a proposal from Planet 24, a company part-owned by the founder and driving force behind Live Aid, Bob Geldof, for something called *The Big Breakfast*. Everyone round the table thought it sounded great fun, but of course it wouldn't work.

We whittled the ideas down from a hundred to half a dozen, and somehow Geldof's proposal survived until it was a straight choice between *The Big Breakfast* and a proposal from Central Television for a show that would be in the mould of TV-am, all sweaters and sofas. This was the safe option, a well-tried formula backed by a highly professional team, and the consensus was that we should plump for it – though there was also a sneaking feeling that if Channel 4 didn't take a risk with *The Big Breakfast*, no one else would. And it *was* different, which put it squarely within our remit.

I had 'live' pilots of both Central Television's proposal and *The Big Breakfast* fed into my office. After five minutes of the Central production my eyes glazed over, but *The Big Breakfast*, and particularly its presenter Chris Evans, a former Greater London Radio disc-jockey, transfixed me. In places it was crude, even amateurish, but it had immense energy and there was no danger that the casual viewer who switched on could mistake it for any of its competitors. Central's main aim was to be informative whereas Geldof's programme was predominantly entertainment with a quick news update every thirty minutes. The spine of the show was to be a pre-recorded interview in which Bob Geldof would quiz the kind of world-class personalities only he could get hold of – the Dalai Lama, Nelson Mandela and Paul Keating, the Australian prime minister. The company proposed to buy three Victorian lock-keepers' cottages in the East End and each segment of the show would come from a different room. Geldof's then wife, Paula Yates, presided in the boudoir, where, lounging on a double bed, she would chat in her sexy, provocative style about passion and fashion with interesting people. The role of Chris Evans and Gaby Roslin was to hold the show together and link Geldof's interviews to items such as 'The People Report' where viewers would be given the opportunity to get gripes off their chests.

Breakfast-time is obviously on the wrong side of the watershed and our aim was to attract young people, so questions of bad language might arise – Geldof, Paula Yates and Chris Evans all had a ripe turn of phrase, which meant we would be walking a tight-rope. Bob himself was phlegmatic: 'Who knows if anyone will watch?' he told the press. 'Maybe I'm crap, I don't know. All I can say is it will be worth a look.'

The pilot showed that *The Big Breakfast* was indeed worth a look. And for me the secret of its power was Chris Evans. Bob Geldof and Paula Yates were big names, so naturally the press made a great fuss of them, but I realized that before our eyes a new star was in the making. Evans, with his mop of unruly red hair, rabbit grin and horn-rimmed glasses, was only in his twenties and his media career had been turbulent. An ex-fork-lift-truck driver, his early radio career in Manchester had come to a sudden end when he told a dubious joke on air. He quit the north, moved to London and was given the chance to present his own show on GLR. Then he moved over briefly to television via BSkyB and TV-am. He was wild, anarchic and totally on the wavelength of the youth audience. Geldof himself described him as 'an extraordinary performer' and Bob knew what he was talking about: he had worked with some extraordinary performers in the pop world. I knew in my bones that Evans was going to be a major star, all my old instincts as a talent-spotting theatrical agent told me so, and I had better be right because *The Big Breakfast* would stand or fall on his performance. The chemistry between Evans and his co-presenter, Gaby Roslin, worked a treat, which was a bonus because these things are unpredictable. We were in business.

The show was a huge success. I recall Michael Green, the chairman of Carlton TV, accusing me in only a semi-jocular way of abandoning Channel 4's remit and producing a programme that was 'just blatant populism'. 'All right, Michael,' I replied. 'If I had shown you the original programme submission for *The Big Breakfast* and invited you to bet twelve million quid on its success, you would have laughed in my face.' The show was the biggest commercial risk we'd ever taken at Channel 4: we were confronting viewers with the production values of anarchy at a time when much of the population is preoccupied with the routine business of the coming day. The landscape of early-morning television was littered with the rusting wreckage of discarded breakfast shows – certainly, former presenters could hold their annual reunion in the Royal Albert Hall.

We launched *The Big Breakfast* and duly got a pasting from the press. 'Pretentious', 'unprofessional', and 'superficial' were some of the nicer things they said about it. 'In the last ten days, only John Major and Norman Lamont (in the throes of a financial crisis) have suffered a worse press than Channel 4's latest attempt at a viable breakfast programme,' wrote Steve Clarke in the *Daily Telegraph*. Not for the first time the critics were out of step with the audience. In our first week we attracted over half a million viewers, taking some from TV-am, some from the BBC and persuading others to break the habit of a lifetime and switch on television over breakfast. The early audience surveys showed that we had attracted youngsters and held on to their parents. We certainly made our competitors' programmes look safe and dull. The show had its rough edges and at times was over-frenetic but we intended to do nothing to rein back Chris Evans. He filled the screen with magic. Our critics raged against the inanity of regular spots such as 'Hunt the Sausage' and 'Celebrity Washing Line' and we laughed all the way to the bank – and on to the rostrum to collect the award for the 'best teamwork show' at the Royal Television Society nine months after *The Big Breakfast* went on air.

The Big Breakfast quadrupled our morning ratings and Chris Evans became a national figure. Sharp, cynical and totally engaging even when he was at his most outrageous, Evans took breakfast television into a new era and administered a nasty shock to the backers of GMTV, a consortium made up of LWT, Carlton, STV and the *Guardian*. They had taken the franchise away from TV-am with a sales pitch that promised the ITC they would revolutionize breakfast-time TV. By the time they went on air in January 1993, we had already done it by launching three months earlier and making their rather modest innovations look antediluvian.

The word 'genius' is thrown around loosely to describe anyone who has gifts out of the ordinary, but I came to believe that Chris Evans is truly a television genius. In some ways he was the natural successor to Kenny Everett, always pushing at the frontiers, technical and cultural, of the medium. He soon became one of the hottest properties in television – the other networks tried to smother him in banknotes to get him to work for them. Asked why he stayed at Channel 4, Chris said simply, 'It's not the money. Michael Grade believes in me. He's open to ideas and he's enthusiastic.' He soon put me to the test. After *The Big Breakfast* had been running for about a year, he rang and asked to see me. He came in and gave me the pitch for a new show to be called *Don't Forget Your Toothbrush* – the title referred to a segment in the programme where two guests each week would win a holiday abroad, provided they left as soon as the show finished. He mesmerized me as he poured out this flood of ideas, some wacky, others in dubious taste but all original. 'Let's do it,' I said, and mentally pencilled it in as one of the main props of our 1993 winter schedules, to go out at peak viewing time on Saturday evenings.

We set aside money and resources for a pilot and I sat back smugly, waiting to slaver with joy at the result. However, I was greeted one morning as I got into the office by John Willis, my director of programmes. He had a face as long as the Telecom tower. 'I've got the Chris Evans tape,' he said gloomily. 'It doesn't work.' I took a look at it. He was right: it was a shambles, the pacing was wrong, the direction was all over the place and it lacked any coherence. It was as though Chris had strolled into a studio and done the first thing that had come into his head. A genius might get away with that, once, but all the supporting cast were completely at sea. They hadn't the foggiest notion what was coming next, and although chaos was a classic Chris Evans ploy, it was always carefully contrived. This was the real thing.

We needed a show-doctor who could bring some order to the project without squeezing the life out of it. My old agency client William G. Stewart was the man I thought of. He had created the quiz shows *The Price Is Right* and *Fifteen to One* and produced *Father, Dear Father,* and *Bless This House* among others, all successful comedies. Though he was a pioneer of television entertainment, there was nothing traditional about him. He just loved showbusiness, he was an enthusiast and a professional. I was confident he would see both the potential and the weaknesses of the plot. Sure enough, hours after I sent it to him he phoned me to say he thought the idea was brilliant but that the team didn't know how to realize it. I booked him and told him to go on piloting the show until it came right. He brought his immense television experience to the project and gave it a structure that anchored a surreal idea within the conventions of television grammar and syntax without throttling it to death. His second pilot was transmittable but we did a third to make sure.

As they say, the rest is history. Though Chris Evans has been portrayed in the press as a difficult character, a prima donna, arrogant and boorish, I never found him anything other than intelligent, considerate and loyal. He could 'read' a television programme, whatever it was – drama, documentary, comedy – and would know why it did or didn't work. Perhaps he was less perceptive about his own shows, but that's understandable: he was emotionally involved in them but he was a fast learner. In general, though, his programme judgement was impeccable. He could probably have done my programming job at Channel 4 – he would certainly make a superlative channel controller, though not at the Birtian BBC, where imagination, because it cannot be quantified, is regarded, to use the jargon, as a frictional overhead.

Chris was by now in universal demand, and after a couple of series of *Don't Forget Your Toothbrush* he told me he wanted to move on. His instincts about the direction of his own career were impeccable. The show could have gone on for years, either presented by Chris or by someone else, but he wanted to go out on a high, and I thought he was right. 'What will you do?' I asked. He'd decided to move back into radio as a DJ, which I thought was a brilliant career move. He would still get mass exposure on BBC Radio 1 but the wireless wouldn't eat up his material in the way television does. He was still contractually bound to us but I mentally parked him in the pending file. A year or so later, I heard rumours that BBC Television was making approaches to him. I rang Mike Foster, his agent, and asked him what was going on. Mike gave me the kind of evasive reply which as an ex-agent I had often employed myself so I knew negotiations were under way. The rumours grew that Chris had already signed for the BBC. He asked to see me.

Chris was typically straightforward. 'I had great times at Channel 4, but I don't want people to think that's all I'm capable of. I'm well in at the BBC and I have my own production company. I want to spread my wings, so I've made a deal with the BBC for them to do *Don't Forget Your Toothbrush* with a different presenter. And I've got another idea for a show I want to try on them.'

'Chris,' I said, 'you can't do *Toothbrush* for the BBC without my permission because we jointly own the format. I'm not saying I won't give you permission but you and Mike need to go back and read what the contract says about copyright.' Then I asked him what the other show was and he described *TFI Friday*, which sounded very exciting. I wished him well and warned him to

watch himself at the BBC, which, under Birt, was no longer
geared to take the kind of risks he relished.

'You're taking this very well, Michael,' he said.

'What can I do?' I replied. 'You've signed a contract with the
BBC and that's that. We can still be friends.'

'Oh,' he said. 'We haven't actually signed anything.'

'Ah,' I said. 'Shut that door!'

An hour later we had a deal. Channel 4 would make *TFI
Friday* and I agreed that he could sell the *Toothbrush* format to
the BBC, on condition that he himself did not present it. The
lawyers turned the contract round overnight, and I rang Alan
Yentob at the BBC to tell him I was the bearer of good and bad
news. The good news was that I would license the BBC to
produce *Toothbrush* without Chris Evans on condition that the
Corporation paid a royalty and ran a credit on the closing titles,
'By arrangement with Channel 4'. The bad news, for him, was
that we had contracted to make Chris Evans's new show, *TFI
Friday*. Alan felt I was trying to humiliate him, but there was
nothing personal in it. We were a small channel, the BBC was
a giant, so we were entitled to drive the toughest bargain we
could get.

Channel 4 had never been far from political controversy and I
had been there less than a year when I found myself embroiled
in one. The issue was *Fire Raiser*, a drama-documentary about Air
Chief Marshal Arthur Harris and his alleged carpet-bombing of
Dresden on the night of 13 February 1945, which flattened the
historic city and burned to death over a hundred thousand
citizens and refugees. It had been commissioned before my time
from an independent production company called Barefoot
Video, and I was told that Jeremy Isaacs had reservations about
it. The programme was due to be screened forty years to the day
after the event and blended drama with archive footage. When
the Bomber Command Association learned that it was to be
made and heard rumours about its contents, they complained to
the IBA and to 10 Downing Street. Soon letters began to arrive

on my desk from Air Force types claiming that we intended to desecrate the memory of a great war-time leader. I thought: Here we go again, *Monocled Mutineer* round two. I decided I had better view rough-cuts of the programme to equip myself to come out fighting in defence of free speech and Channel 4's duty to state minority viewpoint. To my astonishment, as I watched the programme, I felt more and more strongly that it was unfair to Harris. Quotations from his speeches were put into his mouth, which, I suppose, was barely permissible though people don't normally talk in private with the vehemence they use in public orations. What worried me more were the passages of scripted dialogue which were intercut with eye-witness testimonies from survivors of the Dresden firestorm. The result was a damning indictment of Harris because the criticisms of him were drawn from real life while some of his side of the argument was fictional. It seemed that *Fire Raiser* was agitprop television, which had no place on a public-service broadcasting channel. It was also a meretricious piece of work, which didn't meet our professional standards. I decided we wouldn't screen it.

The programme's producer, Kim Longinotto, said that I had bowed to political pressure and allowed myself to be influenced by people who had not seen the film, to wit: the officials of the Bomber Command Association. 'Censorship is being applied to prevent us re-examining controversial historical figures because it challenges some of the myths which are held by people.' Alan Sapper, the general secretary of the ACCT, accused me of 'blatant political censorship' as my first act on taking over from Jeremy Isaacs and warned that his union would make the strongest representations. All kinds of allegations were levelled against me, but no one would believe I had banned the film strictly on professional grounds. It did not meet the exacting standards of accuracy and balance required of public-service broadcasting. We were under no obligation to buy the film so we didn't

My decision incensed the pro-Isaacs faction among the staff, reinforcing their dark suspicions that I intended to sell the pass on Channel 4's precious heritage. In fact, such attitudes revealed a worryingly amateur approach to programme-making: if they couldn't tell the difference between professional and political judgements then we were in trouble. The film was indefensible and that was all there was to it.

Freedom of expression is too precious a democratic value to be restricted without grave cause, and in all my years at Channel 4, other than *Fire Raiser* and a crass documentary which purported to psychoanalyse the Princess of Wales, of which more anon, I banned only one series – or, rather, blackballed its star – and that was in 1996. I have a fairly thick skin but I developed serious sense-of-humour failure with Chris Morris over a series called *Brass Eye*. Morris's speciality is the satirical humiliation of celebrities. He was a veteran of brushes with the regulators and channel controllers. In 1994 the BBC took him off the airwaves when he told Radio 1 listeners that Michael Heseltine had died, then tricked MPs into paying tribute to him. He once filled a studio with helium gas so that a newsreader had to report a motorway pile-up in tones that sounded like Donald Duck, and at GLR he re-edited the Queen's Speech, splicing together two separate sentences to produce a snide reference to George VI. I thought a series he had recently done for BBC 2, *The Day Today*, in which he had aped presenters such as Jeremy Paxman and Michael Buerk introducing news items that could almost have been true was certainly very funny. There was a serious point to his japes: he was exposing the voracious appetite of some celebrities to appear on television at any price. But why on earth was I keen to buy trouble by giving him a slot on Channel 4? Why do people become lion-tamers or swallow razor-blades for a living? I recognized a rare talent and felt that Channel 4 had a libertarian tradition that ought to be able to accommodate Chris Morris's satire – though, as with lion-taming, the cardinal rule would have to be: never take your eye off the beast.

We put in a lot of work to get *Brass Eye* ready for transmission. I took personal responsibility for monitoring its content and had to postpone its initial transmission date by a couple of months because I was unhappy about a hoax Morris had perpetrated on a couple of government ministers. He persuaded MPs to ask them questions about the misuse of a recreational drug popularly known as 'cake', which apparently was not controlled under the various acts and conventions. The minister duly replied that the drug in question, which Noel Edmonds had been hoodwinked into condemning on television, was under consideration by a government sub-committee. 'Cake', of course, did not exist. I wasn't bothered about making ministers look a little foolish, but I worried that the subject of the hoax, dangerous drugs, might breach the rules on taste and standards.

Chris Morris responded to the postponement in a typically robust way. He wrote to President Mandela explaining that his series had been banned by Michael Grade, who had led a campaign to keep the President in prison. He also urged Oliver North, the former Marine colonel and Pentagon official, to intervene on his behalf because I had used my power in the media to smear him. The series was duly transmitted to screams of outrage from the *Daily Mail* about yet another example of Channel 4's 'tasteless and publicity-seeking stunts'. Some of Chris Morris's jokes worked, some didn't, and I was prepared for the inevitable public backlash. But in the final programme Morris went too far. He managed to doctor the final transmission tape so that the subliminal message 'Grade is a cunt' was broadcast, though it was only detectable if you had a video-recorder and knew which frame to freeze.

That was it. What upset me was not the insult, though I thought it base ingratitude after the hammering I'd taken to get the series on air and defend it from its critics. It was the breach of the oldest convention in broadcasting: the editor or producer trusts the presenter not to speak or act unilaterally on air in breach of the agreement they've made together about the content of the programme. In any case, subliminal messages are illegal. The editor carries the can for everything that is said and done in a programme and a presenter who cannot be trusted not to play games with a transmission tape could be putting the whole channel at risk of legal or other sanctions from the ITC.

So far as I was concerned, Chris Morris was not to be trusted and therefore unemployable. The tabloids who had attacked my defence of *Brass Eye* as another aberration by Britain's pornographer-in-chief duly reviled me for acting as censor-in-chief in banishing him from Channel 4.

Two other programmes took up much of my time in my early years at Channel 4. The first was *Brookside*, which had been made for Channel 4 by Mersey Television since 1982. It was created at Jeremy Isaacs's initiative by Phil Redmond, who had produced *Grange Hill*. It was tough, gritty and a good antidote to that more folksy view of the North-west, *Coronation Street*. It tackled sensitive issues without compromise. In its first year, to the distaste of the more sensitive souls in middle England, it had dealt with rape, race and suicide.

I loved *Brookside*, but the ITC hated it. I was on the receiving end of a constant stream of grumbles and the occasional outright warning that the programme's content was too explicit for its scheduled time on the wrong side of the watershed. The ITC had plenty to get its teeth into: the death of a mother and toddler through a fall from scaffolding, a lesbian kiss and a case of incest. But the issue that led to a full-scale confrontation with the ITC occurred in an episode when one of the characters threatened his wife with a kitchen knife. We were told that the incident transgressed the programme code forbidding the use of domestic implements as weapons before the nine o'clock watershed. I reviewed the scene frame by frame, and although a kitchen knife was shown in the hand of the assailant, there was no shot of it being used. The ITC considered the issue and finally found against us: they declared a breach of the code, but then proceeded to tighten the rules still further.

Before the dust had settled on *Brookside*, the ITC took against *The Word*, an anarchic, late-night youth show whose items ranged from the quirky to the totally outrageous. It was not aimed at the generations represented by the members of the ITC, though I'd be prepared to put money on the fact that their children were fans. Channel 4 was always on the lookout for youthful talent and new formats. But if we were to give innovative youthful newcomers a platform, we had to adjust our taste threshold. Anarchy, a certain lusty crudeness and exhibitionism were all part of the student milieu and to reach it we had to push back frontiers drawn by more conformist, conservative generations.

The Word was originally created and produced by 24 Hour Productions, then by Planet 24, the same team who gave us *The Big Breakfast*, but it had a much greater shock quotient. It was the programme you wouldn't want your mother to watch, fronted by Terry Christian, an untried Northern lad you might not want your daughter to marry. It might almost have been designed to offend white, Puritan, middle-aged, middle-class middle England. Eventually the programme was pre-recorded, so we were able to edit out some of its more egregious excesses, and those regulators and viewers who complained about its contents should have seen what we cut out. Every edition was watched by the tabloids for juicy copy, by the ITC to have chapter and verse for the complaints they directed at me, and by Channel 4's compliance lawyers to see where the next assault would come from.

ITC pressure to kill the show intensified week by week. I felt it was time to involve the board of Channel 4. I sent each of them tapes of twelve programmes as 'homework'. Wading through them must have numbed their sensitivities so that they were rendered incapable of distinguishing between the outrageous, the appalling and the merely disgusting. The clip in which a naked man with a ring through his penis lifted two stone of sausages would stand out as the epitome of bad taste in a single show but when it was merely one of a succession of similar japes, all the benchmarks were obliterated. I often cringed at what I saw but had to remind myself that *The Word* was not aimed at my generation, let alone the tribal elders who made up the ITC. It was university rag material, crude, anarchic and noisy, a rite of passage into adulthood from an adolescence soon to be left behind. The Channel 4 board had reservations about some items but accepted my horses-for-courses arguments.

The Word had a number of elements that the ITC and senior generations found baffling. The presenters were the antithesis of the laid-back, estuary-English-speaking, besuited or befrocked personalities who usually fronted studio programmes on the BBC and ITV. The standard joke was that the programme had been called *The Word* because the title represented the total vocabulary of its famously inarticulate main presenter, Terry Christian. One of his co-presenters was Amanda de Cadenet dressed in rainbow-hued gear that assaulted the human retina. She was followed by Huffty, a loud-mouthed, shaven-headed Geordie woman not at all out of the same stable as the average bland BBC presenter. Then there were the studio stunts, some of which I frankly found distasteful – eating worms, drinking vomit and throwing colostomy bags around the place is not my idea of entertainment – but I had always to remember that Channel 4 was not my private preserve, to reflect my tastes and please my sensibilities.

I had learned the hard way that one of the toughest tasks of a channel controller is to meet the legitimate needs of viewers whose world is alien to one's own. The point I made to the ITC was that Channel 4 alone catered for late-night youth audiences and *The Word* was only one of a range of distinguished programmes we aimed at them, some of which had a strong social message about the dangers of drug abuse and so on.

In 1995, after 104 episodes over five years, we finally laid *The Word* to rest. It had run longer than any youth programme except *The Tube*. Given the opposition it generated and the perpetual sniping of regulatory bodies such as the Broadcasting Standards Council and the ITC, its survival was remarkable. It wasn't so much killed as died a natural death, as innovatory programmes tend to do when the supply of imaginative energy runs out and what was once shocking becomes ever so slightly predictable. But yet again Channel 4 inspired inventiveness elsewhere as BBC 2 unveiled its version, *The Sunday Show*, employing a former *Word* presenter, Katie Puckrik, and offering the same mix of items, though much tamer – the canteen being the only place at the BBC where anyone was likely to eat worms. My desk soon seemed empty without the huge pile of letters of protest and copies of the minutes of ITC meetings where *The Word* took its ritual battering.

Youth programmes were not the only area of output to get me into trouble at Channel 4. Our documentary series *Dispatches* had a reputation for exploring highly sensitive subjects, one of which landed us in court in 1991. A programme called *The Committee* made by Box Productions alleged that members of the security forces, loyalist paramilitaries and local businessmen had formed a committee in Northern Ireland's Protestant community to plan the killing of Catholics. From the moment the project was mooted we knew we were handling a highly contentious issue. The producer, who also did the investigative reporting, was an Irish Catholic called Sean McPhilemy. I knew him slightly, as he had worked for me at LWT. David Lloyd, our commissioning editor for News and Current Affairs, referred the idea upwards in the very early stages, first to Liz Forgan and then to me. We laid down rules of engagement – the tests of evidence, who might be asked to appear on camera and who could not – and we barred absolutely any suggestion that money should change hands in return for evidence.

I warned the Channel 4 board that we were working on the programme, though it might well be abandoned unless a credible case for the committee's existence could be established. The programme's principal source claimed to be a member of the committee who was prepared to appear only on condition that his identity was protected, otherwise his life and that of his family might be in danger. Step by painstaking step the evidence was accumulated and I became convinced that this was an important and responsible contribution to a most important political debate. As the time for transmission got nearer, things turned nasty. Sean McPhilemy suspected that his home was being watched and he started to receive death threats. I was so worried that I went to see Special Branch at Scotland Yard, told them about the programme and the death threats that more than one of the production staff had by then received. They came along to Channel 4 and took us through the standard anti-terrorist procedures. Our lawyers went over the programme word by word and picture by picture and, after demanding all kinds of minor changes, cleared it. I took a deep breath and gave final approval for its transmission.

The outrage, especially from Unionist MPs such as David Trimble and the Reverend Ian Paisley, was predictable. The producer was accused of being a secret IRA sympathizer and Channel 4 was traduced for undermining the morale of the security forces. Then we were visited again by the Special Branch, invoking the Prevention of Terrorism Act to get us to reveal our sources, especially the identity of the programme's main witness. I had no idea who he was, though I had been assured he was not a terrorist. I was not prepared to reveal any sources we had that might lead to his exposure, though we handed over an eighty-page dossier containing documents and other material relating to the programme. No chief executive could have asked for greater support than I received from the board of Channel 4; I cannot imagine the BBC governors being as staunch.

It is one of the great traditions of a free press and media that journalists do not reveal their sources, but since the Special Branch were acting on an order issued by a judge, we were charged with contempt of court and could not run a public-interest defence because national security was involved. This was the first time that the Prevention of Terrorism Act had been used to force journalists to reveal their sources. We were hauled before a magistrates' court where we again refused to name our sources, whereupon the Director of Public Prosecutions sought leave from a High Court judge to seek fines or sequestration of Channel 4's assets. A *Daily Mail* headline announced triumphantly that I might be sent to gaol. Indeed, if they'd got their way I would have been given a public flogging. This was a case of spite distorting professional judgement for it was as much on behalf of *Daily Mail* journalists as any others that we defied the law, and in no spirit of cocky defiance. We realized the gravity of what we were doing. We had been put in the invidious position of either breaking the law or putting someone's life at risk.

We engaged as counsel Gareth Williams QC, since ennobled and now a member of the Government. The hearing was very much a matter of technical legal argument between the Crown and counsel for the defence; there were no witnesses and no presentation of evidence because the facts were not in dispute. I went to a final pre-trial conference in Gareth Williams's chambers. At the end of the meeting he asked me whether Dickie Attenborough and I intended to be present in court. I confirmed that we had both cleared our diaries. Since he and I were both high-profile figures, Gareth felt that if we were to be present at all we should stay put; the commotion caused by any comings and goings would be noticed by the judges. He also suggested, with due diffidence, that it would be best if we did not react visibly to anything we heard. Since Dickie was a noted thespian and I had a reputation for being a bit of an exhibitionist, presumably Gareth was afraid we might pantomime our joy or despair. I swore we would not move a muscle nor expel an audible breath.

For two days, Dickie and Michael Bishop, at that time his deputy chairman, and I sat like paralysed rabbits under the eye of Lord Justice Woolf and Mr Justice Pill in the well of the court, afraid to blink. My great fear was that we might be given an incremental fine of, say, £100,000 a day until we either revealed the name of our source or went bankrupt. Gareth thought that unlikely: judges were not without political awareness and would not want to be seen to close down a national television network on what boiled down to an issue of free speech. In his judgement, Lord Woolf acknowledged that both Channel 4 and Box Productions had found themselves in a moral dilemma. In his view our mistake had been to give an unqualified undertaking to our source that we would not reveal his name, though the judge accepted that without this guarantee the source would never have agreed to appear in the film. He ruled that we were wrong not to have borne in mind that our programme would inevitably undermine both the reputation of the RUC and also the rule of law. As to punishment, he noted that the DPP had requested a sequestration order, but the only effect of this would be the destruction of both Channel 4 and Box Productions; it would not change our moral stance. We were fined £75,000 plus costs.

After the case had been heard, the board of Channel 4 called in Michael Beloff QC to do a compliance audit of *The Committee*, checking every aspect of the production process and interviewing everyone involved. He tested the safeguards we had applied to see whether any of the ITC's or Channel 4's rules had been broken. To my relief, we were given a clean bill of health.

But the saga was not yet over. Six months later, the *Sunday Times* ran a story in which it claimed to have tracked down our anonymous source and got him to admit that the whole thing was a hoax. Jim Sands, a former youth worker who ran a women's football team in Portadown, alleged he had been promised £5,000 to appear masked on screen to recite a prepared script. He would claim to have personal knowledge of events he had only heard as rumours in the pubs around Belfast or had got from a Dublin journalist, Martin O'Hagan, who was writing about the existence of the Inner Force, a clandestine group that arranged murders in the province. The police uncovered Sands's identity after they found documents at the home of Ben Hamilton, who had been the programme's researcher. Sands claimed that he and others had been tricked into appearing in the programme.

I stood by the documentary, insisting that it had been made to the highest journalistic standards after a lengthy and scrupulous investigation. I was sure of my ground. To no single programme in my entire career had I and my senior editorial and legal staff dedicated so much time and effort at every stage in its making; there was not a word or a picture in it I hadn't scrutinized, tested for accuracy and approved. It seemed to me the only way to settle the issue was to have an independent public inquiry into the allegations made in *The Committee*, then let the chips fall where they may. I made repeated requests for the RUC to conduct such an inquiry but no one would discuss the idea with me let alone do anything about it. The tabloid press was much more interested in my discomfiture at the hoaxer allegations and the £1 million cost of the court case than in the awful possibility that there might be a secret Protestant organization in Northern Ireland responsible for nineteen sectarian murders.

Because I knew the American TV scene very well, I was able to introduce some of its best shows to British television. I was a great admirer of *The Phil Donahue Show*. He invented the formula that combines a studio audience with guests facing moral dilemmas or telling human-interest stories. It was transmitted out of Chicago and I'd been one of his guests a couple of times, once to defend my decision at the BBC to drop beauty contests and the other to justify the famous bare-bottomed bonking scene in Dennis Potter's *The Singing Detective*. For years he had been a lone pioneer in the studio chat-show, then up popped Oprah Winfrey, who launched her own version of Phil's show and eventually became a serious challenger to his supremacy. She had style, a crusading spirit and that Southern warmth which made guests feel welcome and able to open their hearts to her. I had kept in touch with a number of my old colleagues at Embassy and one who had worked on *The Phil Donahue Show*, and therefore knew what she was talking about, insisted that the next time I was in the States I should watch Oprah in action.

I was in the States for the NATPE Convention, which is a kind of vast market where you can watch and buy television shows. At the Disney Television International stand I came across the head of its London operation, Étienne de Villiers, who was a friend of mine. He said he had a show he was keen for me to see. It was *Oprah* – Disney International were her distributors, though I didn't know that. It was pure coincidence that I had gone over to the States determined to keep an eye open for

Oprah, then met her distributors who were keen to get her on Channel 4. I sat down in their screening room, watched a number of tapes and decided immediately to buy the show. I had the day-time audience in mind and took account of the fact that to appeal to British viewers, it would need editing to weed out the segments that were of strictly American domestic interest.

We ran *Oprah* two or three times a week and didn't just slap it on the air, we were discriminating about the episodes we showed, nursing it with care and at considerable expense. We got a British company to repackage it and they employed an experienced producer, Susan Fleischer, who although American had worked in British television long enough to understand the audience's tastes. Eventually *Oprah* changed distributors, away from Disney to Kingworld. I was sailing in the Mediterranean when I heard that Kingworld had sold it to BSkyB without consulting us or giving us the opportunity to bid against them. I have rarely been angrier.

The *Oprah* saga did nothing to improve my opinion of BSkyB, who had already established a reputation as cherry-pickers, raiding the output of channels such as ours, trying to persuade the independent producers who supplied some of our best programmes to sell to them. Apart from provoking my natural combativeness, I felt they were undermining the whole point and purpose of Channel 4, which was to show programmes that would otherwise not be seen on British television. I laid down the law to my colleagues. We would sell nothing to BSkyB and we would share nothing with them. So far as I was concerned, we were deadly competitors.

Then one day I got a phone call from Sam Chisholm, BSkyB's chief executive. He had Elisabeth Murdoch, Rupert Murdoch's daughter and general manager of BSkyB, with him in the office and she was badgering him to improve Sky One.

'Why don't you share *Friends* and *ER* with us?' These were two of the brightest jewels in our crown obtained because of my Hollywood contacts and knowledge of the US industry. I said I

neither wanted nor needed to share the two series with BSkyB.
'Anyway,' I added, ever the Grade scenting a deal, 'what's in it
for me?'

'What do you want?' he asked.

'*The Simpsons*,' I said, disingenuously.

'I can't do it,' he said, regretfully. 'We've sold it to the BBC.'

We had several conversations that came to nothing, but my
instinct told me that BSkyB wouldn't easily give up. The next
thing I knew was that a representative of Warner Brothers, who
distributed *Friends* and *ER*, asked to see me to tell me that they
would not be renewing their contract with us; they had sold both
series 'elsewhere'. Eventually they admitted that the deal had
been done with BSkyB and Channel 5. This was war and I knew
where the soft underbelly of the enemy was to be found. I used
my Hollywood contacts to get the names of the agents and
lawyers of the key personalities of both series and sent them all
a fax. I explained that Warner Brothers intended to abandon an
arrangement that had done well for them in order to sell their
shows in a huge package together with old films and assorted
dross. This meant setting a price for *Friends* and *ER* that was way
below their market value. I was prepared to double whatever
nominal price was set against their shows.

Three days later, Warner Brothers made contact offering a
compromise. They were prepared to renew the deal with Channel 4 on condition that we shared the shows with BSkyB. I know
when I've got the best deal I'm likely to get so I signed up. I can
imagine the fireworks at Warner Brothers HQ when the
immensely powerful lawyers and agents of *Friends* and *ER* stars
and producers began hammering on the door. I hated having to
end up in bed with BSkyB but it was *force majeure*. There could
only have been one worse fate – to have lost the shows, and a lot
of advertisers with them, to the new Channel 5.

In my time, working at the BBC was like being in a guarded
fortress. Trying to get to see the BBC's director general was an
obstacle course where you'd collapse with exhaustion long

before you cleared the last hurdle. His press conferences and public appearances were strictly controlled, and he had an army of aides, advisers and colleagues to shield him from public scrutiny except on his own terms. Channel 4 was literally a goldfish bowl – even my office had glass walls and I was only a hop and step from the entrance. The PA's standard prevarication, 'He's not in the office, he's out at a meeting,' would not wash, neither would I wish it to. I was happy enough to be occupying a goldfish bowl and saw anyone who wanted to see me. Channel 4's provocative programmes, which regularly created public controversy, combined with my own outgoing personality were an inflammatory mix that attracted the press as moths to a flame. I was rarely out of the news or gossip columns; some of the stories were far-fetched, they were occasionally unfair, but by and large I had no complaint. The press have a job to do and I believe I have more to gain by co-operating with them than in trying to obstruct them.

But there are limits. In October 1991, my PA, Ros, got a message asking her to phone Corinna Honan, a reporter on the *Daily Mail*, who wished to interview me about a personal matter. I thought it was probably about the collapse of my marriage to Sarah. We were going through a bad time arguing about money and property, as couples do when they are getting divorced. But when Ros came into my office after calling Corinna Honan she was as white as a sheet. 'It's not Sarah,' she said. 'It's about your mother.' I was poleaxed. Ros said afterwards that I shrank back in my chair like a terrified child. It was almost half a century since my mother had left us and almost as long since I'd given her any thought. I had coped with the catastrophe by shutting her out of my life completely; it was as though she had never been. This was one door in my psyche I hadn't opened because God knows what ghosts were hidden behind it. Now the *Mail* intended to dredge it all up. I was distraught, not because of any public embarrassment the story might cause me but for a more profound reason: I was going to be made to relive a very painful experience.

I consulted my sister Anita's husband, Brook Land, who is a lawyer with lots of experience in dealing with the media. We agreed that to refuse to meet the *Daily Mail* would be a mistake since they could then write any old rubbish about me without the possibility of redress unless they grossly libelled me, and they were much too experienced to do that. Brook phoned the *Daily Mail* and asked for a meeting with some senior editorial figure and their lawyer so we could find out exactly what the story was and what ground rules should apply to any co-operation we might offer. Brook and I duly met a senior editor and Dennis Cheetal, the *Daily Mail* lawyer. What exactly was the story about? I asked. The editor hummed and hawed about a new series the *Daily Mail* was launching about the background of public figures; the intention was to begin with me. He seemed almost put out that I wasn't flattered. Precisely what about my background? I persisted. My hobbies? My time at the *Daily Mirror*? My support for Charlton Athletic Football Club? Eventually he admitted that they had tracked down my mother. That was it. I swept out of the room followed by Brook. The next day, full of foreboding, I went off to Newcastle to a conference on disability and television.

On Friday morning, 18 October 1991, I bought a copy of the *Daily Mail* at Newcastle station to read on the train back to London. I had dreaded reading the story and it was worse than I could have imagined. Under a banner headline 'MOTHER LOVE: The Strange Story of Why Michael Grade Hasn't Spoken To His Mother For 45 Years' there were three pages of poisonous innuendo laced with a few facts. No one close to me was spared: photographs of my grandmother, Olga, and my twenty-year-old daughter Alison were plastered across the pages alongside my ex-wives, my then partner Pati, a wedding picture of my father and mother, and Kent Walton, the Canadian wrestling commentator, with whom, so the paper alleged, my mother had run off. The reporters had tracked her down and described her as 'a fragile, still pretty woman in her seventies who leans heavily on a stick and lives in a £300,000 mock Tudor mansion in Haslemere.' Apparently, she was 'a suburban granny who might have been the mainstay of the Haslemere Bridge Club.' The *Mail* had obviously got her to talk to their reporters. 'Her powdery blue eyes momentarily filled with tears,' they commented touchingly, as she protested that she couldn't talk about me. I suspect her distress was more likely to have been caused by the way the *Mail* was hectoring her than any affection for me. She had chosen to cut herself off from all the Grade family and that was her right. It was appalling that the *Mail* should have dragged her into the limelight in her old age after decades in obscurity.

I was subjected to paragraphs of crude psychoanalysis. The general drift was summarized in the banner headlines across the second and third pages – 'Poor Michael, He Likes Strong Women. He's Tried Three Mother Figures and None Has Been Right' – this insight was attributed to a 'close friend'. My 'drive for success' compensated for the fact that I never felt loved as a child. Apparently I grew up with the Yiddish word *kurva* ringing in my ears. 'It means "loose woman" and it is the term Michael's grandmother uses to refer to her errant former daughter-in-law. She also cruelly mimics his mother's limp, losing no chance to portray her as a flighty Gentile of doubtful morals.' Having got its teeth into my grandmother, the article went on to do a thorough demolition job on her, obviously drawing on my sister Lynda's unhappy memories and their frequent quarrels.

The piece ended by asking whether my sister Lynda having been told (by the ever-considerate *Daily Mail*) that her mother lived only a few minutes' car drive away was curious meet her. 'The Grade in her says, "I don't want her phone number. I'm not interested. It's too far in the past." Then her voice breaks. "What does she look like?" It is a question Michael Grade must have asked himself often.' For the record, I haven't.

I was travelling on the train down from Newcastle with Channel 4's general manager, Frank McGettigan – it was the day before my daughter Alison's twenty-first birthday party. Frank was astounded to see me burst into tears as I reached the end of the *Mail* article. I sobbed my heart out, and the poor man didn't know what to do. Passengers near us in the dining car looked across curiously, and any of them who happened to know who we were must have concluded that Frank was one hell of a tough cookie to be able to reduce his boss to floods of tears. That had to be one of the lowest points of my public life.

That *Daily Mail* article was the opening shot in a guerrilla war Associated Newspapers waged against me for years. I was often in the gossip columns of other tabloids and some of the snippets were mischievous, but it was bearable. The *Daily Mail*'s stories about me were different: they were vitriolic, vindictive, almost hate-filled, and they pounded at me relentlessly as though an order had gone out from someone on high: 'Get Grade!' I recall a friend of mine, John Whale, a former *Sunday Times* journalist who was head of Religious Television when I was at the BBC, once saying to me when I was complaining bitterly about yet another *Daily Mail* hatchet job, 'Remember, Michael, the *Daily Mail* is the enemy of all good works.'

I suppose I personified everything detested by the white, middle-class, reactionary constituency the *Daily Mail* served. I was a flamboyant, ex-showbiz type with a colourful personal life who headed a channel whose programmes gave a platform to blacks, gays and lesbians, extrovert young people, the disabled and political radicals. When we won the Bertlesmann Prize for Social Responsibility in Broadcasting, the citation said, 'Channel 4 has committed itself to a pro-active pluralism not just the passive mirroring or toleration of social differences. It brings real generosity of spirit to its dealings with outside groups.' During the Gulf war we were accused of treachery for putting Arab voices on the screen and challenging the official line in documentaries such as *Hell No, We Won't Go* and *The Gulf Between Us.* Our Poverty Season was deliberately crusading, aimed at indicting politicians for their timidity. In December 1993, when the BBC and ITV were unpacking their Christmas parcels bursting with jolly seasonal fayre – oodles of comedies, light entertainment and family movies – Channel 4 launched the second series in six months about the war in Bosnia.

These themes, attitudes and qualities were the antithesis of the *Daily Mail*'s publishing philosophy. And I am Jewish.

The *Daily Mail* went ballistic when in 1994 I got into a row with the ITC about a 'grossly offensive remark', a crude joke about incest made by the American actor Alexis Arquette in an episode of *The Word*. The ITC claimed that Channel 4 ought to have apologized while the show was actually on air. We accepted that Arquette's remarks were quite out of order and we edited them out of the repeat but disagreed with the ITC's judgement that we should have apologized there and then. We felt this would only have inflamed the situation and drawn even more attention to what had been said.

Of course, television programmes with live inserts could be dangerous, especially on a minority-interest channel where we were exploring the boundaries of taste and would occasionally stumble over them, but this very tightrope-walking quality gave the programme energy and edge. The Arquette incident was a sort of third-strike offence, which in the crime world sends you to the electric chair. The year before, another moral busybody, the Broadcasting Standards Council, had upheld a complaint against *The Word* about a jocular comment that homosexuals should be crucified, and there had been a fuss a few weeks before when in the programme's phone-in segment, a viewer rang up and punctuated his comments with a liberal sprinkling of the F-word.

To defend the honour and purity of the nation's viewers, Paul Johnson, known in Fleet Street as 'Rent-a-Rant', rode into the fray astride his sturdy hobby-horse, armed with generous space by the *Daily Mail*, whose banner headline ran: 'Time to Sack Britain's Pornographer-in-Chief.' I had made Channel 4 a haven for filth and either Channel 4 ought to lose its licence or I should be sacked for giving the ITC a 'characteristic two-fingered gesture of defiance'. After cataloguing some of the excesses of *The Word*, he went on to point out, 'Visual jokes about vomit, excrement, penises, vaginas and anuses are staple fare for Channel 4. As Grade says, puffing his giant cigar, itself a symbol of where the channel's interests lie, "That's showbusiness, folks!"' Obviously not having read the Broadcasting Act, he ridiculed my claim that Channel 4 is required to cater for minorities. 'Lesbians,' he declaimed, 'homosexuals and sex perverts, necrophiliacs, fanatical anti-papists, students of scatology and animal cruelty, people who like watching other people being grossly humiliated and abused and who want to see the man whose penis was cut off by an angry wife – these minorities, if that is the word for them, are well catered for by Channel 4.' Apparently, the minorities I ignored were those who 'go to church regularly, who love their country, who are faithful to their spouses, who bring up their children to be truthful, honest and law-abiding and whose lives are models of usefulness and decency – these are contemptuously ignored by Grade and his myrmidons'. I treated such decent citizens as 'non-persons with no more rights than the worms eaten in his programme sandwiches'.

On and on Johnson raged. As invective it was highly entertaining, but as a fair account of my policies and motives it was a grotesque distortion and was treated as such by most people in the business. A Fleet Street editor told me, 'Don't worry about Paul, he's a dancing bear. When the crowd's there we open the cage, let him out for a bit of a pirouette and put him back. He's absolutely barking but he's also a first-class writer who will tackle any subject at very short notice and turn in a well-crafted, controversial piece.' I wasn't disposed to be magnanimous about Johnson's literary virtues because the title of his article, 'Pornographer-in-Chief', stuck to me like glue, and that made me blazing angry. Peddling pornography is illegal, so he was accusing me of criminal activity. I thought briefly of suing him, but what was the point? He was the licensed jester of Fleet Street: what verdict could a court render other than guilty but insane? He was a sort of journalistic Vicar of Bray notorious for switching his allegiances according to whoever happened to be residing in Downing Street. He has been a 'myrmidon' – to use a word he taught me – of Harold Wilson, then Margaret Thatcher and now

Tony Blair. And when his Fleet Street mates gave him a dose of the treatment he's been handing out to others for years, it turned out that he was partial to the English vice, discipline at the hands of a mistress – truly a worthy champion of that minority he alleged I treated like worms, church-going, faithful, decent and upright citizens.

Curiously, just before Johnson's *Mail* article was published I had been at a party in honour of John Freeman's eightieth birthday. Paul Johnson had been Freeman's contemporary at the *New Statesman* and was present with his wife, who at one point told me that her daughter was working in the drama department at LWT, but big changes were afoot and she was uncertain about the future. Would I be prepared to see and advise her? I said I'd be delighted and it was arranged that she would ring me. Throughout this conversation, Paul Johnson was at his wife's elbow.

The morning the 'Pornographer-in-Chief' attack appeared in the *Mail*, I went to a breakfast at the Festival Hall and found myself sitting next to the *Daily Mail*'s editor, the late David English, and Stewart Steven, who was then editor of the *Evening Standard*, which is part of the same Associated Newspapers group. David chuckled: 'I see Paul's had a go at you this morning.' I nodded and then said I was struck with the irony of it. 'I was at a dinner party recently for John Freeman and Paul Johnson's wife asked me to give her daughter a job. It was well within Paul's hearing and he said nothing.' Stewart Steven said, 'That's a good story, can I have it for the Diary?' Within minutes of the paper hitting the streets Paul Johnson was on the phone to the *Evening Standard* claiming it was defamatory, that I'd made the whole story up. When the *Standard*'s lawyer asked me about the incident I gave him chapter and verse, including half a dozen witnesses, one of whom was Paul Johnson.

Johnson didn't let up and I almost became inured to his attacks on me. My crimes gradually escalated from trying to swamp Britain with tidal waves of filth to inciting the masses to revolution. In June 1995, he warned *Mail* readers: 'Behind this coarse-grained, self-obsessed cultural élite, setting our standards are the emerging forces of anarchy, the helpless, hopeless single mothers, the drug addicts and Aids victims who are the true children of sixties culture. So long as Michael Grade can give the rest of us a two-fingered salute and smirk all the way to the bank, we know that Britain is a sick, sick society.'

In yet another article Johnson accused me of engaging in a crusade against the Christian faith – now, where have Jews heard that before? 'Spitting on God and religion is another fashionable activity these days. It is not clear whether Grade's vast salary is primarily related to successful sexploitation or his attacks on the beliefs of ordinary people – to undermine the nation's morals or to sneer at our religious beliefs?'

Then, having watched an edition of Channel 4's *Girlie Show* about shoplifting, Johnson detected a conspiracy on my part to encourage outright criminality. I was, he wrote in the *Mail*, 'a millionaire allowed a licence to incite theft'. Johnson just couldn't refrain from banging on about my salary and seemed to spend hours watching programmes with a sexual content aimed at viewers a third his age, so it was hard to decide whether he was motivated more by voyeurism, envy or snobbery. He charged that my 'brash, shameless, arrogant and vulgar persona epitomizes everything that is morally repugnant in the materialistic Britain of the nineties' while the accents of the teenagers who took part in the show were 'so impenetrable that it was not always possible to comprehend what was being said'. Which makes me wonder how Paul could be so sure they were 'uttering expressions rarely heard outside a brothel or the lowest type of Soho strip joint'. How would he know about such things?

I began to get the impression that Mr Johnson's dislike of me amounted almost to an unhealthy fixation, but he didn't rile me too much until he turned his fire on Michael Bishop, who had taken Dickie Attenborough's place as chairman of Channel 4's board. Then I was beside myself with fury. It was one thing to have a go at me, I regarded a certain amount of public calumny as an occupational hazard, but Michael Bishop was a civilian. Writing this time in the *Sunday Telegraph*, Johnson called for the public to boycott Michael Bishop's airline, British Midland, 'Since Chairman Bishop has so ostentatiously placed himself on the side of the pornographers and against Christianity, he and his works are an obvious target for consumer protest . . . Aircraft are fragile things and an awful lot can go wrong with them. And Almighty God is not mocked with impunity. Personally I would not travel on an airline run by a man who also chairs a pornography channel notorious for its anti-Christian cynicism.'

Michael Bishop was surprisingly unfazed by the article. He felt that Johnson, in calling down the wrath of God on British Midland jets, was in the same bracket as the religious maniacs who insisted that God had deliberately aimed the lightning bolt at York Minster because the radical Bishop of Durham was installed there. What amazed me was that a reputable British newspaper could actually print such ravings, so I took the editor of the *Sunday Telegraph*, Charles Moore, out to lunch to find out why. He agreed with me that the article was utterly outrageous but he had been away from the office when it was submitted. His paper, though not a natural fan of Channel 4, certainly moderated its attacks after that.

But the *Daily Mail* was unremitting. During our Gay and Lesbian Season, the paper set about making the life of its commissioning editor, Caroline Spry, miserable. She made it no secret that she was lesbian, but just to be sure that no one she loved should be spared, the *Mail* phoned her parents politely enquiring whether they knew their daughter was living with another woman? Apparently, the fact that she lived in Haringey was also deeply significant as everyone knows it is the very heart of loony left country.

Anything, even my actions of which the *Daily Mail* could be expected to approve, was contorted into an attack on me. At the beginning of May 1996, the *Mail*'s headline ran: 'Diana "Sick" TV Show is Axed.' It reported, accurately, that I had pulled the plug on a programme in the *Without Walls* series called 'Psychoanalysing Diana' in which psychotherapist Dylan Evans questioned a Diana lookalike, Nicky Lilley, about her failed marriage, her bulimia and traumatic incidents from her childhood. The *Sun* got advance notice of the programme and unleashed a storm of protest, most notably from Diana herself, who had not been consulted. Her press secretary called me and asked if I knew about the programme. I told her I didn't, but this wasn't unusual since under the delegated system I ran at Channel 4, a director of programmes and a commissioning editor kept an eye on productions in the pipeline. They would tell me if they were worried about a project; the programme obviously hadn't got that far along the production process.

I insisted on a preview and hated what I saw. It was a meretricious piece of work, which demeaned the Princess and gave psychoanalysis a bad name. It was a parody of a serious therapeutic method and put into the actress's mouth sensational revelations, mostly derived from Andrew Morton's recently published book, in the guise of confessions wrung out of Diana after careful probing. There was no way I could defend the programme in public so I banned it, and overnight in anti-Grade circles I mutated from 'Pornographer-in-Chief' to 'Censor-in-Chief'. Never lost for a way of turning good into evil, the *Mail*, in the same edition that reported that I had banned the Diana programme, ran an article asking, 'Who's Really On the Couch?' Some *Mail* hack purported to psychoanalyse me, declaring triumphantly, 'Here are some questions guaranteed to make Michael Grade squirm: "Do you think you are dangerously obsessed with sex? Why have you never sustained a successful and lasting relationship with any woman? What is the significance of your unmistakably phallic cigars?"'

All my career I have fought for the freedom of the press, and I fully accept that those of us who choose to live in the public eye have few claims to privacy. But no one has the right to reduce us to a bunch of headlines and a collection of glossy pictures, violating that God-given right to an inner sanctum of privacy everyone possesses by virtue of being human. I can live with gossip about my private life, it's usually harmless and entertaining, but the *Mail*'s campaign against me was sinister and malignant: it was an ideological campaign mounted by a reactionary and bigoted newspaper, which hated everything that I and Channel 4 stood for.

In 1991, the ITV franchises were up for auction. I described the process at the time as 'a government-sponsored nervous breakdown'. The fifteen companies already running TV stations had everything to lose, the challengers everything to play for, and the ITC was destined to spend the summer poring over thousands of pages of exam papers submitted by the applicants. This was the third franchise round since ITV came into existence in 1955, and the whole arrangement was barmy. All kinds of things had to be taken into account, the amount of the bid, a so-called quality threshold to prevent an applicant offering wall-to-wall game-shows, and something called 'exceptional circumstances', a get-out clause that enabled the ITC to blackball any undesirable character who managed to leap over all the other hurdles. This chaos of requirements was to be boiled down to a great, fat document put together by the best brains in the City and polished by the lawyers. The ITC then had to plough through this mountain of documents, their task being to ensure that the Treasury got a good rake-off, the regional ITV service retained its character and ITV was financially and managerially capable of remaining the nation's most popular quality channel and not be destroyed by too much change too soon.

In the scramble for these franchises, alliances were being formed between business and media moguls to make bids. One requirement for a serious offer was a detailed account of the programme policy the new company would implement. But exciting programme policies were just pie in the sky or rather papers in a file unless there was a team of experienced television professionals to make them work. Hence, a franchise submission would be greatly strengthened if it could list the names of respected television executives and producers prepared to join the new company.

The frenetic atmosphere of franchise bids opened up a fault-line in my personality. Indeed, I freely confess I'm schizoid. I have been a salaried employee since I was thirty years old; I've never made any capital and what savings I accumulated were wiped out by two divorces. By their own efforts, my father and uncles had made a great deal of money. Through shrewd dealing, hard work and a certain amount of luck they ended up owning valuable assets. I earned enough to support an affluent lifestyle but there was no possibility of my making a leap into their wealth bracket without capital appreciation. I suppose once a Grade always a Grade, I was on my mettle to prove that I was worthy of the name, and to be a Grade meant not only gaining social and professional recognition but also having money in the bank. The one thing I was good at was television; there was a franchise round coming up and the successful bidders would obviously end up very rich. I decided to dip a toe in the water and see what the temperature was like. I rang Richard Branson, who I knew was keen to get into television.

He was reasonably interested. I proposed, as a likely target, the franchise at that time held by Television South and Richard asked for a paper setting out a strategy for making a bid. I was confident I could handle the programme side of an application but I needed a partner who could support me on the organizational and financial side, and lighted on Bob Phillis, who had been joint managing director of Carlton Communications and was then chief executive of Independent Television News. Bob has one of the best business brains in the industry and was prepared to explore possibilities. The snag from Richard's point of view was that Bob and I would need to work full time on the project for a couple of years leading up to the bid, and that meant him carrying two very highly paid executives – we were both prepared to back our skill and judgement by taking the gamble of quitting secure jobs, but we had family commitments. Richard added up the sums and decided that though he was keen to get into television he wasn't that keen, so we parted amicably.

In spite of a certain understandable disappointment that an exciting and risky venture had come to nothing, I consoled myself that at least I had tried. I abandoned any franchise-owning ambitions there and then. I wasn't unhappy about reverting to my Channel 4 job, which I found totally absorbing and challenging. Then, out of the blue, I got a phone call from Michael Green, the chairman of Carlton Communications. He was putting together a team to bid for a franchise and was curious to know whether I was prepared to lead it. Michael walked me round his garden a few times and talked serious money. I asked for time to think about it. Pacing the bedroom floor in the small hours I realized what a dual personality I became when money was involved. I had tried hard to persuade Richard Branson to back a franchise bid which, if successful, would make me very rich, then when the opportunity came unbidden, I hesitated. I had no doubt that I could work with Michael Green and that any franchise bid he put forward had to have a better than even chance of being successful.

My nerve failed me. When it came to the crunch, money alone was not a good enough reason to quit Channel 4 with the job half finished; almost, but not quite. Given the stark choice, I found that public-service broadcasting was precious to me. It gave me not only a job but also a world-view. I could have remained a song-and-dance man, mega-rich but culturally unformed, but the BBC and Channel 4 educated me, taught me about world affairs, introduced me to politics, opera, drama and music. I thanked Michael for his confidence in me and tendered my regets; I recommended that he approach Nigel Walmsley, who ran Capital Radio. They got on well together and Nigel ended up chief executive of Carlton Television. Given that Michael had paid headhunters a huge fee to find someone to take my place, he owes me a box of cigars for my inspired suggestion.

In a roundabout way, the franchise bids almost led to my dropping *Brookside*. Its founder and executive producer Phil Redmond was also after a franchise and fancied his chances of dispossessing Granada. The manic energy he had devoted to masterminding *Brookside* and ensuring that its plots were up to standard was diverted into drawing up a submission and putting together a team to bid for the north-west region franchise. He remained executive producer but was never in the office when we tried to get in touch with him. *Brookside*'s ratings began to fall, its storylines lost their edge and even the actors seemed bored. I summoned my commissioning editor for drama, Peter Ansorge, who told me that *Brookside* was a rudderless ship and he despaired of getting Phil Redmond's attention. 'Right,' I said, 'I'll give you some money and you can start developing two or three ideas for a soap to replace *Brookside*. Invite offers from the market generally, and don't keep it a secret.'

Phil appeared in my office smartish once he had heard that Channel 4 was considering replacing *Brookside*. I read him his horoscope. He had two choices: he could either get back to producing the show or appoint a competent producer to replace him, but I was making no promises about its future. I wanted to see what appeared on the screen over the next few months. Phil's face drained of colour. He had got the point and proved himself a good talent-spotter. He appointed Mal Young, who revitalized *Brookside*. Soon it was in the news with unsparing and controversial storylines. I knew it was out of the doldrums when I started getting complaints from the ITC again. Their silent approval had been an ominous indicator that *Brookside* had lost its edge.

I wasn't the only target of the franchise bidders: members of my management group began to get beguiling invitations to go out to lunch with merchant bankers, tycoons or media heavy-weights who were building teams to work on submissions to the ITC. For my money David Scott was the best finance director in British television, working with a superb general manager, Frank McGettigan. Colin Leventhal as director of acquisitions was responsible for the business end of *Film on Four* and the driving force behind all our commercial activities. Then there was Liz Forgan, who held the editorial team together and had firm, clear convictions about the channel's general direction. I knew that these extremely talented young people were bound to be targeted by franchise-bidders who wanted impressive names on their letter-heads.

I confided my fears to the Channel 4 board and they asked me to come up with a scheme to deter defections. I consulted the experts who know about such things and proposed an arrangement which ensured that if Channel 4's senior managers signed contracts to stay with the company until two years after the franchise round was over, they would get a substantial bonus. This would make poaching an expensive business since any marauders would not only have to better Channel 4's salaries but also buy out the loyalty payment of any senior staff member they had targeted.

Why duck it? I would also benefit from this arrangement, though I took no part in the discussions of the remuneration committee that finally adopted it. If the ballpark figures waved before my eyes by franchise bidders courting me were anything to go by, I was a valuable commodity. The feeding frenzy for talent unleashed by a crazy franchise system drove up salaries at the top of the television industry and I was worth the going rate. That's business; I had nothing to apologize about. Much as I admired Mother Theresa, I'd taken no vow of poverty when I joined Channel 4.

Inevitably the press got wind of the scheme, the bonus payments being described as 'golden handcuffs'. The *Sun* asked in an editorial whether I found it hard to look myself in the eye as I shaved. It attacked the £500,000 I was being paid not to join another company and the new five-year contract I'd signed. 'Rich, isn't it, that the man who presides over a TV channel which invades our living rooms with blasphemy, profanity and homosexuality should be deemed so valuable?' It concluded that I wore colourful braces because my wallet was weighing me down. I had to withstand the press onslaught alone, and therefore defend my own salary, without Dickie Attenborough, because he was up a mountain somewhere, shooting his latest movie, *Chaplin*.

My old nemesis, Anthony Smith, by then president of Magdalen College, Oxford, wrote to the *Independent* protesting at the very principle of 'golden handcuffs'. Tony having been one of the group which evolved the concept that eventually became Channel 4 seemed to take any deviation from his original blueprint as a personal affront. Once again, he failed to declare that he had been an unsuccessful rival for my job. Top executives at Channel 4 were not meant to stay for long, he argued. They should do four-year stints and then move on. It was clear he had never had to run a complex organization where continuity and experience in management were essential to efficiency. Dickie answered Tony's criticism in a letter to the *Independent* in which he pointed out that Channel 4's top management team, without exception, had been made tempting offers by franchise bidders. 'Experience has shown us that if one senior figure leaves he or she tends to take other key people with them, thus increasing the disruption. We therefore judged it prudent to minimize the risk of losing a whole generation of expertise in one fell swoop.'

I felt uncomfortable about the whole business though not apologetic. Given the state of the market, I could have earned a fortune had I quit Channel 4, so my mind was at peace about the golden handcuffs deal. The staff of Channel 4 saw things differently and a strong head of steam built up. There was no point in sitting tight and hoping the whole thing would blow over, so I met the commissioning editors and other groups of staff and listened to their strong views. Given their salary levels, the figures quoted in the press, often inaccurately, sounded grossly inflated, but the harsh reality was that if Channel 4 lost its whole senior management team, their jobs would be in real jeopardy. They weren't convinced and we had to agree to differ.

The golden handcuffs affair led to my one and only row with Liz Forgan. In her role, which we valued, as the conscience of the channel she expressed misgivings about the golden-handcuffs scheme and had predicted accurately that there would be an almighty stink when the matter became public. But once the remuneration committee had done the figures, she went along with the arrangement and banked her bonus.

In fact, the story broke while we were both attending a conference of the Royal Television Society in Cambridge. The public interest was so enormous that I agreed to speak and answer questions at an emergency session of the conference. I had nothing to hide, I spelled out the reasoning behind the decision then endured some aggressive questions, particularly from some of the independent producers present who were understandably aggrieved because theirs was an insecure occupation where they had to survive from one project to the next. I had great sympathy with their position but they had chosen it; many of them were talented enough to hold down senior posts in a big TV company but opted for the dangerous freedom of the independent sector, where there were many satisfactions and some risks.

Liz Forgan was in the audience and said nothing. I felt she might at least have got to her feet and pointed out that the decision had been made by the board; I had not been present when the issue was discussed. But she left me twisting in the wind. Strange, that. I'm sure it was coincidental, but around this time rumours began to circulate that she intended to go off and work for John Birt at the BBC. I didn't take them very seriously, but I was about to go on holiday and needed to be reassured that she wouldn't jump ship while I was away. I put it to her plainly that this rumour persisted and that if there was any truth in it I much preferred to deal with it before I left on holiday. She looked me straight in the eye and assured me that she had received no offer from John Birt at the BBC.

When I got back from sailing the Atlantic with some mates, a letter was waiting for me which Liz, who was at her holiday home in Scotland, had dictated to her secretary. It said that she was resigning from Channel 4 and would be joining the BBC. I could only conjecture that the ethos of the new-style BBC was congenial to her; after all, she had once been nicknamed 'Birt in a skirt'. But there was the question of the golden handcuff she had been paid by Channel 4 as a loyalty incentive – it obviously hadn't been very effective. She asked if we would be prepared to accept repayment of her bonus free of tax, then if the BBC was prepared to cover the gross sum, the resulting loss to her would be more modest. I shook my head in disbelief and had to remind myself that this was the same Liz who, when the idea of golden handcuffs was proposed, had written me a two-page memo listing all the reasons why she thought it wrong in principle.

I spoke to her and asked if I was to take this unsigned letter as formal notice of resignation. She agreed that it was and I told her that the amount of bonus repayment was a matter for the chairman, who was in Hong Kong. Sir Michael Bishop, now in the chair, was adamant that the bonus should be repaid in full. Liz felt that this was shabby treatment after all the years she had served Channel 4, and I had to remind her that she was breaking her contract. I wanted the matter settled quickly as all the rumours about her were bad for the channel; I intended to make an early announcement of her departure. She said that this would ruin her negotiating position with the BBC – which puzzled me because I had assumed the deal had already been done; I suspected the Corporation was digging in its heels on the question of the bonus. No sooner had I told the staff that she was leaving than she phoned me and said she had changed her mind, she was staying put. When I pointed out that I was holding her letter of resignation, she claimed it had no legal force because it had only been signed by her secretary. I'd had enough. She was no use to us if she was looking over her shoulder all the time for a better offer. Then the BBC agreed to buy out her bonus payment and she joined them shortly afterwards.

Before she left us, Liz had to endure a grossly unfair attack in the House of Lords from Lord Wyatt, who described her as a 'fearsome lady who is not fit to be in charge of any programmes anywhere which have any bearing on matters political or industrial'. Wyatt, taking advantage of parliamentary privilege, said, 'She has broken the law, is breaking the law and will continue to break the law.' He then added superciliously, 'She might do well on gardening programmes, although the flowers featured would be mostly red, a few yellow and none blue.' The Channel 4 chairman, Sir Michael Bishop, defended her robustly, which was pretty magnanimous of him given that she had misled me and was in the process of secret negotiations with the BBC. 'The board is well content that its journalism is under the stewardship of such a senior and universally respected journalist as Liz Forgan' – which was true. I had no problem with her considerable ability, it was what I saw as her lack of loyalty that disappointed me.

It was widely predicted that Liz would be appointed deputy director general of the BBC. In fact, that job went to Bob Phillis, the chief executive of ITN, whom I had approached about a franchise bid. She ended up as number three in the pecking order as managing director, radio, and left the BBC prematurely – no doubt on a matter of principle.

I greatly admired the firmness with which Michael Bishop handled the Forgan business. In fact, I had become a fan of his while he was still deputy chairman. We were summoned to meet the ITC because Liz Forgan had made a speech rightly criticizing the high cost of regulating bodies of one kind or another. She compounded the offence by approving a programme in which one of the officers of ITC was given a grilling. At the ITC we were confronted by the chairman, Sir George Russell, the deputy chairman Jocelyn Stevens, and David Glencross, ITC's chief executive. We were berated for an hour about the indiscipline and irresponsibility of Channel 4. Jocelyn Stevens was particularly strident and virtually screamed that we were totally out of control – he certainly was. Michael Bishop said nothing until George Russell invited him to speak. Quietly and firmly, he put our case, demolishing Jocelyn Stevens's hyperbole. As we left the ITC, he asked me whether regulators usually behaved like that. I shrugged philosophically. 'Well,' he said, 'I'm used to dealing with regulators in the airline business where we're dealing with life and death, literally, and we never get that kind of abuse from them. Television is only an art form, for goodness' sake, it isn't a substitute for real life.' I've never forgotten that shrewd appraisal of our business, and I was devoted to him from that moment on.

Channel 4 was the only television station prepared to give air time to some alternative comedies that were later taken over by the BBC and ITV – *The Comic Strip Presents . . .*, which won the Golden Rose at Montreux, *Who Dares Wins*, and *Saturday Live*. Our channel was all about being innovative and taking risks so it was inevitable that many of these shows in their early days should stub their toes against the ITC's rule book. We took a regular kicking from the regulators while other channels collected the plaudits later. We saw them through growing pains and adolescent excesses: the BBC and ITV got the benefit of their maturity.

I had no hard feelings about this. It was part of Channel 4's remit to seek out talent then smile philosophically as it moved on to a larger stage – Ben Elton, Stephen Fry, French and Saunders, Reeves and Mortimer, Julian Clary, Jack Dee, Paul Whitehouse, Lily Savage, Gaby Roslin, Clive Anderson, Paul Merton and many more got their first chance on Channel 4. It was understandable that they would want to go off in search of bigger audiences and this was one of the most dramatic, though little noticed, ways in which Channel 4 influenced the BBC and ITV. These alternative comedians became such big stars that they gave a different 'feel' to the schedules they were to dominate. On the other hand, their departure made room for the next generation of talent and we developed quite a sophisticated scouting system. A select few, notably perhaps Rory Bremner with his sparring partners John Bird and John Fortune, have chosen to stay with Channel 4 because it offers them a unique degree of freedom. The public expects Channel 4 to be slightly subversive and anti-establishment, so Bremner and Co. can push biting political satire to the limit.

The flow of talent wasn't all one-way between Channel 4 and the BBC and ITV. We lost to them some outstanding young stars, but we also offered a congenial environment for established writers who relished freedom and innovation. Shortly after I joined Channel 4, I persuaded the incomparable Alan Bleasdale, who wrote *Boys From the Black Stuff*, to let us produce his next series, *GBH*, which he described as 'one caring, liberal madman's odyssey through the vagaries of life in Great Britain in the early nineties, trying to make some sense of the place'. Alan had appreciated the robust defence I mounted at the BBC of his drama *Monocled Mutineer* and felt uncomfortable with the Birtian regime, so he was delighted to sign up with me. My other drama scoop was to entice Dennis Potter to write a series for Channel 4 in the aftermath of the critical mauling he received for *Blackeyes*, made for the BBC after I had left.

Blackeyes was widely felt to be exploitative of women and Dennis found himself saddled with the insulting epithet 'Dirty Den' after the *EastEnders* character; he was shocked and insulted, believing himself to be a moralist merely chronicling not approving the sexually ambiguous even degrading situations women found themselves in. But in *Blackeyes*, he cast himself as the first-person narrator, which I thought a mistake: his tone was obviously intended to be playful but came across as lubricious and he sounded like the standard dirty old man obsessed with a beautiful young girl. I suppose the state of his health influenced his performance: it must be hellish hard to sound light and carefree when you are in pain or deeply depressed or drugged to the eyeballs. He also directed *Blackeyes* with an almost obsessive attention to detail, and because he was the writer, he played around with the script to fit the technical requirements of a particular scene, which was disastrous. Members of the cast afterwards confessed that they often had to ask each other what the scene was about and what their lines meant.

Blackeyes was badly received by the critics and the public. One critic wrote cruelly that Potter 'was now not only crippled in his body but also in his mind'. I sent him a personal note, commiserating with him about the hostile reception his drama had received and assuring him that even on an off-day his work was still better than 99 per cent of what passed for drama on the television screen. But I felt I owed him honesty: he was too great an artist to be flattered with weasel words. I drew his attention to the list of credits – produced by . . . directed by . . . written by . . . additional dialogue by . . . It was a one-man band. There was no one on the set able to step back and judge what was going on objectively, then tell Dennis frankly what they thought. He had become too proprietorial about his work, and that section of the press always hostile to what they don't understand took one look at his name appearing again and again in the list of credits and decided he had now moved beyond pornography into megalomania.

I got no reply to my note, but some months later he rang me, we had a drink and he sketched out an outline plot for *Lipstick On Your Collar*. It was to be a semi-autobiographical six-part musical drama set in the War Office during the Suez crisis in 1956 where a young man doing his national service is pitched into the intelligence service. He stays with a long-suffering aunt and puritanical uncle, and his fellow lodger is a voluptuous beauty married to the brutal corporal who is his superior. Meanwhile his workmate is smitten by the niece of an American colonel attached to the War Office. The two young men pursue their romances, one of them to end tragically, while their officers do nothing much except get drunk and philosophize about the changing state of Britain.

The underlying theme of *Lipstick On Your Collar* was the plight of young people, giddily suspended between the end of the old world order, the decay of empire and the shrinking of Britain's international power – all signalled by the Suez crisis, and a new permissive age, the sixties, promising lashings of sex and rock and roll. Even the songs that punctuate the drama spelt out the gulf between old and new: ballads such as 'Green Door' and 'The

Garden of Eden' contrasted with Elvis and Bill Haley numbers. It was not, however, an uncritical rant at the old by the rebellious young. One of the most sympathetically drawn characters is a colonel, who eventually cracks up because he sees crumbling away all the values that for him meant the old England.

I assured Dennis that, of course, Channel 4 would produce it, but I had one worry. The moral of *Blackeyes* was that Dennis's attempt to control every aspect of the production as well as write it had backfired disastrously. I wasn't averse to him having an executive producer credit for *Lipstick On Your Collar* but I felt strongly that there should be a strong director to counterbalance him. However, this was a matter for my head of Drama, Peter Ansorge, to sort out. I told him I would back him either way. Potter told the *Observer* media correspondent Richard Brooks what happened next. 'I was summoned to see drama executive Peter Ansorge, who politely wondered whether I wanted to direct *Lipstick*. I suddenly realized the little bugger was inviting me to stand down. I called for Michael Grade. Cigar in hand, he came in and suggested that I should make myself a smaller target for criticism. I relented and it was directed by Renny Rye. I'd probably be dead if I'd done it. The strain would have killed me. I'll never direct again.'

We transmitted *Lipstick On Your Collar* in February 1993. I thought it a seriously underrated series that will some day be recognized as a great piece of television drama, and I looked forward eagerly to Dennis's next script. But some months later, his agent, Judy Daish, rang and said that Dennis wanted to come and see me. I was delighted, but her next words stunned me. 'It's very sad. He's been diagnosed with cancer. He's not got long and he wants to come and say goodbye.' I offered to go to his home but Judy assured me he wanted to come to my office. We met at five thirty one evening at Charlotte Street. I knew Dennis well, so I laid on a bottle of red wine, lots of cigarettes, matches and ashtrays around the room. He poured out his heart to me. We talked about the BBC, his family and his work, and he moved me to tears by the warmth of his appreciation for the support I'd given him. It was a strange occasion. It ought to have been desperately sad, listening to a wonderful man describing how he was coming to terms with the fact that, in a few weeks or months at most, he would be dead. Yet the atmosphere wasn't morbid, it was oddly uplifting and life-enhancing. He deployed that same luminous intelligence, stunning power of language and mordant wit he had brought to his dramatic writing to sum up his life and speculate about death.

I walked with him to the front door. I said goodbye and then purely on impulse added, 'You know Dennis, if you want any of this on film, I'd be more than happy to fix it.' As I pottered around my office afterwards mulling over our conversation, I suddenly thought he might have misunderstood me and assumed I was talking about his obituary. Immediately I rang Judy and explained that what I had in mind was a filmed interview in which he talked at will and we would turn it round rapidly so that he and his family could see it together. She phoned me back to say that Dennis would do the interview but warned me that he would need lots of money since he wanted his family well cared for. I wasn't going to haggle; we agreed a fee and then settled on Melvyn Bragg as the interviewer. We decided to put it out as a *Without Walls* special.

Melvyn made an editorial decision I thought risky but which turned out to be brilliant. It would be a straight studio interview not interspersed with any clips from Dennis's works. Could Melvyn and Dennis hold the viewers' attention on a serious even solemn conversation for an hour without relieving the tension from time to time with drama inserts? Melvyn thought they could and he was right. He abandoned the conventions of studio programmes where the cameras and microphones are invisible and the fiction is created that people are chatting in their sitting room. The programme showed all the mechanics of the film crew setting up their gear, the sound and lighting engineers going about their work; all the hubbub and activity that was television behind the scenes, the world Dennis had loved and made his own.

Dennis smoked, joking about the possible damage to his health, drank wine and sipped pain-killing morphine from a hip flask. He'd struck a deal with his doctor, which would enable him to go on writing to the end; his GP worked out exactly how much morphine he would need to take daily to numb the pain without addling his brain. He talked frankly about his cancer, describing it as a 'little kiss or a little gift from somebody' because it had been diagnosed on St Valentine's Day. He had shed no tears though he grieved for his family. Indeed, in some ways, the cancer was a reprieve from the terrible skin disease that had blighted his life. He felt almost affectionate towards it and had given it a pet name, 'Rupert', to signify his contempt for Rupert Murdoch whom he accused of polluting the British press. There was a kind of triumphant grin on his face as he said it as though he was taunting the Murdoch lawyers to try to get him before his pancreatic cancer did.

Life, he said, can only be defined in the present tense, nowness, and he felt almost serene, able to celebrate life. He had lost the crippling shyness that made him seem belligerent and angry; he even felt benevolent towards his old sparring partner, God, who was not a 'nasty old sod' but the giver of creativity who inspired us to make love and art. But he wouldn't turn to God for comfort because as he said in a flashing epigram, 'religion is the wound, not the bandage.'

He discussed his television career, his passionately held political beliefs, his fears for the future of both British society and British television. Watching the programme at home, I held out until Dennis recited a hymn he had sung as a child, 'When I wake with the blessed, in the mansion of rest, will there be any stars in my crown?' That broke me up. Melvyn's questions were brief and infrequent. He had judged the whole thing to perfection. With a talker like Dennis Potter on a theme as momentous as life and death, it was a case of lighting the touch-paper and stepping back, and Melvyn did just that. In contrast to some TV interviewers who think they are not earning their money unless they interrupt every second sentence their subject utters, Melvyn knew when to react by saying absolutely nothing and so allow Dennis to develop his ideas.

Dennis was cunning to the last. At the end of the interview he made a public appeal to Alan Yentob, who was controller of BBC2, and myself to collaborate in transmitting the two series, *Cold Lazarus* and *Karaoke*, he was working against time to complete. How could the last wishes of a condemned man be ignored? Six months after Dennis's death, at a special charity tribute in his local theatre, the Everyman in Cheltenham, Alan Yentob and I publicly committed ourselves to work together and fund Dennis's last plays, to be made by his own company Whistling Gypsy and produced by his long-time collaborator Kenith Trodd.

At Channel 4 we had thousands of letters in response to Dennis's interview. Without doubt it was one of the most significant interviews ever to have been transmitted on British television. The only word for its impact was 'spiritual': it had brought the public up short against the crunch issues of life. We put together an excellent team to work on the two plays Dennis had struggled to finish. *Karaoke* was fine, but *Cold Lazarus*, which he had been writing until hours before his death, was two or three revisions short of his best. Who cared? It was a tremendous testimony to the courage and pertinacity of a great dramatist I am proud to have known.

Having been a lifelong devotee of soccer and a sports writer on the *Daily Mirror*, I took a particular interest in our sports programmes at Channel 4. Our coverage of horse-racing was too seasonal. We had all the summer classic events but little in the winter. The two great events were the Grand National at Aintree and the big Festival at Cheltenham. The BBC had the rights to both of them. I knew we had no chance of dispossessing them of the Grand National but Cheltenham was a fair target. The man who mattered at Cheltenham was Tommy Wallace, whom I'd met several times socially, so I took him out to lunch and told him I knew the BBC contract was coming up for renewal shortly: Channel 4 would like to bid for it. He choked on his soup. They had worked for the BBC for years and it would be an acute embarrassment if I put in a bid. He wasn't to be budged so I left it and we parted amicably. The quaintness of his refusal to hold an auction was endearing but totally unworldly in an increasingly competitive field.

Meanwhile Channel 4 had been strengthening its coverage of horse-racing generally and I decided to play it long and wait until next time the Cheltenham contract approached renewal. Then I went to see some friends of mine who were members of the Jockey Club, Lord Hartington, Lord Swaythling and several others. I told them about my encounter with Tommy Wallace and said that though I admired his loyalty to the BBC, the truth was that Channel 4 was now the main player in the horse-racing stakes. We covered the Derby, the other four classics and eighty further days of racing at ten British racecourses. Without us, the industry would be the poorer. Televised racing provided the essential visual information for betting shops and the sponsorship that paid most of the bills. They might also like to reflect that more and more sporting events were being sold to satellite for paying subscribers only. Horse-racing may have been described as the sport of kings but there was nothing élitist about it, as those famous Alfred Munnings paintings of the crowds picnicking around the great courses proved. Now satellite threatened to divide the sporting community into payers and non-payers. For all these reasons I felt we had earned the right to bid for Cheltenham even if we lost.

Notice was taken of these points and a competition was set up between the BBC and ourselves to bid for the Cheltenham National Hunt Festival, which included the Gold Cup. We did a big sales pitch and beat the BBC fair and square, winning a five-year contract that added seventeen days of racing to Channel 4's calendar. I realized that had I made a big fuss first time round, I would not only have lost any chance to bid but probably made enough enemies to frustrate my attempt second time round. I bided my time.

Golf was the other sport I felt Channel 4 needed to break into. Internationally there was a lot of dissatisfaction with the BBC's coverage of the Open golf championship. I discussed it with Mark McCormack, the highly influential head of IMG, the agency that handled most of the big stars. He in turn talked to Sir Michael Bonallack, the secretary of the Royal and Ancient Golf Club, which governed the sport. All kinds of encouraging messages reached me and I began to get excited at the prospect of meeting the committee and making a big pitch. Again it was to be a run-off between the BBC and ourselves. The committee members would spend the morning at the Television Centre then retire to Brown's Hotel in the West End where we would have an opportunity to present our bid.

I went along to Brown's Hotel, buoyed by a phone call I'd had from Mark McCormack assuring me that the deal was in the bag. He'd been at the BBC presentation and reported that our bid topped theirs by £5 million. It was a shoe-in. I strolled confidently into the room. Confronting me were twenty or thirty dour, dull grey men, identically dressed in blue blazers, grey slacks and R and A ties: the *crème de la crème* of British golf. It was a wet Monday evening at the Glasgow Empire time again – row upon row of sullen citizens defying a performer to interest or entertain them. And I was there to pay these royal and ancient gentlemen a fortune, for God's sake. I died the death. I opened with a gentle joke that went down about as well as the church choir singing 'Sheep May Safely Graze' at the butcher's funeral. They made it obvious they didn't like me, they didn't want to be subjected to this ordeal in which they had to sit quietly and listen to someone else's voice. Mark McCormack got so exasperated that at one point he stood up and started berating them which, while I appreciated his support, didn't help my case. He misread the mood completely. The issue wasn't about money, and therefore not something Mark would understand.

I duly went through the motions of finishing my pitch. Quite apart from topping the BBC's bid by a mile, Channel 4 was offering to cover junior tournaments, putting money aside for golf scholarships and guaranteeing peak-time highlights. I gave up. 'Gentlemen,' I said, looking at my watch, 'thank you for your time. It's now just after twelve thirty. I don't know about you but I'm dying for a gin and tonic.' Suddenly, the odd crack appeared in their granite visages at the mention of gin and some actually smiled. Mike Bonallack rang me later in the day to tell me that the BBC had won the contract. As I said to him, if I'd known that the lowest bidder would win, I'd have offered nothing.

Almost all my life I have been a film buff and had grown up listening to Lew talking about the movies his company had made. My father represented a number of Hollywood stars and occasionally I got to meet one, gazing goggle-eyed at some sumptuous beauty or dashing hero. My Los Angeles production company had made a number of movies so my past experience of the film world was another asset I brought to Channel 4. And the first test of my taste and judgement was sitting waiting for me on the shelves of our film library when I arrived – the satirical film *Monty Python's Life of Brian*. It's a comedy about a lad in first-century Palestine who, because of a series of ludicrous misunderstandings, is mistaken for the Messiah. It parodies Gospel incidents, bursts at the seams with episodes and language in excruciatingly bad taste and ends with Brian, crucified in the company of an assorted collection of criminals, joining them in the rendition of a chorus beginning, 'Always Look on the Bright Side of Life!'.

The film is a farcical commentary on what probably happened again and again in a first-century Palestine awash with nationalist fervour and Messianic expectations. As a Jew myself I found this whole subject fascinating. For centuries the Jews had kept alive their belief that the Messiah would appear one day; we had been trained since childhood to be on the lookout for him. So first-century Messiah-spotters must have lighted on any number of Brians, or whatever their Jewish names were. The crowd having already talked themselves into believing Brian is the Messiah, ask him for a sign, and from then onwards they seize eagerly upon anything associated with him, however trivial or ludicrous, as confirmation of what they believe. In fleeing their attention, he loses a sandal, so the wearing of a single sandal becomes a symbol of Messiahship. And the more vehemently Brian denies he is the Messiah, the more passionately the crowd believe he is, for by definition only the true Messiah would deny his divinity.

I don't think *Life of Brian* was sending up Jesus at all, though to be fair to its critics, much of the humour came from the resonances in their minds with his story. I suppose a comic Messiah is funny only because there could be a serious one. It is the shadow-image of the true Messiah flitting in and out of viewers' minds that supplied the sense of incongruity that fuels much of the humour in *Life of Brian*. But I was convinced that it was emphatically not disrespectful of Jesus or the Christian faith. I wrote to John Cleese, who was one of the producers and stars of the film, and asked him what he thought it was about. He confirmed that *Life of Brian* was meant to be a parody on human gullibility. Fearful and desperate people are frantic to follow someone somewhere, even if it's over the edge of the nearest cliff. There is never any shortage of true believers searching anxiously for someone to believe in. 'Give us a sign!' they cry, and whatever is given becomes a sign, even if it is intended as a brush-off.

Armed with John Cleese's letter, I tackled the Channel 4 board. Jeremy Isaacs had bought the film but he had been unable to persuade the board to allow him to show it because one of its members, Tony Pragnell, a nice man, was a devout Catholic and thought *Life of Brian* blasphemous. There were a couple of protracted discussions against the background of some press-inspired righteous indignation from the odd bishop and religious groups. Eventually, in April 1991, the film was transmitted and was received with less than half a dozen protesting phone calls.

The Last Temptation of Christ raised much more serious issues than the *Life of Brian*. Martin Scorsese's film was an adaptation of Nikos Kazantzakis' classic novel of the same title. The theme was a fictional exploration of the perpetual battle between spirit and flesh, done with sensitivity and without salaciousness. The BBC had bought the film but the governors, strenuously lobbied by church groups, refused to allow it to be shown. I thought that decision outrageous. This wasn't cheap pornography, but a serious piece of work that in my opinion could be classified as art. And the cavalier way in which the BBC governors dismissed it with a handful of self-righteous clichés seemed to me an appalling dereliction of duty. Every serious work, whatever its subject, deserves respectful analysis before any decision is made to reject it, otherwise we are pandering to the book-burning mentality. However, the governors had made up their minds, and that was that.

I bided my time and when the BBC's licence to show *The Last Temptation of Christ* ran out, I bought it. Whereupon the hounds of heaven took their teeth out of the BBC governors and set about savaging me. Channel 4 had received thousands of letters of protest, hundreds in batches from the same postal district, so it was an organized claque. I was denounced from pulpits and in church newsletters; Christian businessmen's groups threatened a boycott of advertising on Channel 4. Mrs Mary Whitehouse's National Viewers' and Listeners' Association, who had threatened to prosecute Martin Scorsese for blasphemy in 1988 when the film was made, showed formidable powers of organization; their members rang Channel 4's duty office in droves, most when challenged confessing that they had never seen the film but were registering opposition solely on the strength of what they had been told about it.

I was summoned to meet an all-party committee of MPs and peers at Westminster. One peer prefaced his attack by saying, 'We who are religious . . .'

I cut in, 'Hold it right there. That "we who are religious" includes me. I have a strong faith too, one that was resisting blasphemy long before Christianity came into being, so let's not turn this into holy war between Christians and barbarians. The argument is about an artist's freedom of expression, and my conviction that the viewers on a minority channel have a right to see this work of art and judge for themselves what it is worth without an army of religious nannies telling them what's good for them.'

Michael Allison, a former Tory minister and Church of England spokesman in the Commons, told me that the showing of the film broke regulations in the 1990 Broadcasting Act.

Why, then, I asked him, had the film already been shown on BSkyB several times without the ITC complaining? And why was it on general release in cinemas with the approval of the British Board of Film Classification?

It was not for me, a Jew, to trespass on Christian territory or pretend to be a theologian, but I read all I could and tried to put myself in the place of the protestors, and for the life of me I really couldn't understand the cause for offence. Far from the idea being blasphemous, I should have thought it self-evident that if Jesus of Nazareth was truly a man, as Christians claim, then he must have felt the contrary pull, as all human beings do, of the spiritual and the fleshly. The scenes that are purported to give greatest offence are those when Jesus, in anguish on the cross, hallucinates and is tempted to abandon his divine destiny for the delights of the life of a normal husband and father. A fictional Jesus was portrayed fantasizing: which human being doesn't?

Scorsese's film was intelligent, beautifully made and gave a faithful rendering of the novel on which it was based. With the backing of the Channel 4 board we transmitted it in April 1995. The morning after, the ITC announced that it had received a record 1,500 complaints about *The Last Temptation of Christ* before it was shown and only five afterwards. Our duty office even had some calls thanking us for showing the film from viewers who had earlier called to protest. It was Macauley who wrote, 'We know of no spectacle so ridiculous as the British public in one of its periodical fits of morality.' I wouldn't presume to put it like that but I know what he meant.

It's a pity that critics such as Paul Johnson who from positions

of invincible ignorance contemptuously dismiss Channel 4 producers as pornographers and degenerates don't take the trouble
to find out just how much careful analysis and anguished debate
takes place in the building before we screen any controversial or
challenging movie. Take Quentin Tarantino's *Reservoir Dogs*,
possibly the ultimate gangster movie about a robbery that goes
wrong. Far from glorifying violence for its own sake, the film has
the inexorable logic of a morality play as, one after another, the
villains are undermined then destroyed by the flaws in their
characters. When I first saw it, I was struck not by its violence
but by the exercise of that prime artistic virtue, reticence, which
is the ability to communicate experience without spelling it out,
to coax the imagination along without battering it into submission with specific imagery. This quality is the exact opposite
of the urge that governs pornography – which is usually
described as 'explicit', leaving nothing to the imagination. The
true artist, whatever his or her medium, knows how to use the
allusive, the oblique, the metaphorical to emphasize what is not
made manifest. Two immortal examples: the shower-room murder in Hitchcock's *Psycho* – you don't actually see the knife strike,
you only think you do; and the tavern scene in *Tom Jones*, where
frenzied eating hints at the orgy to come, but the consummation
is not shown.

In *Reservoir Dogs*, Tarantino shows himself to be not a purveyor of mindless violence but a master of reticence. In the most
talked-about scene where one of the villains approaches a tied-
up cop to cut off his ear, you see the flashing knife then a bloody
object but no explicit action. Unlike the sanitized but wanton
violence of a *Rambo* film where the hero sprays bullets around as
though from a hosepipe, dozens die but no one gets hurt,
Reservoir Dogs hints at just how obnoxious and terrifying the real
thing is. Indeed, with cynical wit, Tarantino satirizes the blood-
and-guts gangster movie.

Our editorial group previewed it and a heated debate followed. The degree of responsibility, even gravity, with which we
approached the decision whether or not to transmit it is well

illustrated by a memo I got from Clare Kitson, one of the commissioning editors, who accepted that the film was a serious work of cinematic art which in the cinema would be watched closely and then thought about; television is not often watched in that way – people zap channels, get distracted, miss beginnings and endings. She was concerned that volatile people might be watching at night, certainly our duty log revealed that a tiny minority of our viewers seemed to be violent, drunken racists and homophobes, if the views they expressed were anything to go by. Who knows whether what they see on television might trigger their violent instincts?

Clare was articulating the conundrum I had faced again and again during my years at LWT, the BBC and Channel 4: what is the relationship between television violence and violence in real life? The cry 'There is too much violence on TV' has now become as much a part of contemporary folk wisdom as 'Britain is swamped by black immigrants' or 'The BBC is run by trendy left-wingers'. The lack of evidence for such opinions has no effect on the tenacity with which they are held. In the case of television violence, mountains of research reports warning against simplistic conclusions are blown away in gusts of fury by those appalled by the state of our society and casting around for the source of the depravity. Lo and behold, they discern its glassy eye staring at them from the corner of their living rooms.

The residents of one of those crumbling tower-blocks in our inner cities, overcrowded and under-policed, have no problem in identifying the real causes of the daily violence they endure, and television is nowhere on the list. A much bigger influence on their thinking than the two-dimensional image of a villain on the TV screen is the three-dimensional thug hanging about at the bottom of the ill-lit lift shaft. The nearer you get to the sewer of social decay, the more accurately you can pinpoint the source of the bad smell.

When used by the general public, I suspect that the sentence 'There's too much violence on TV' has become a form of shorthand for a whole welter of anxieties felt by some viewers about the power of television, its ability to seduce them, take over the imagination of their children and alter their own life-patterns. They may be greatly overestimating television's influence but this is how they feel. And one way of expressing this anxiety and resentment is by focusing on television's more disturbing images. I am in no way suggesting that public concern about television's impact on society ought not to be taken with the utmost seriousness by broadcasters. There clearly *is* a problem here but it is much more complex than some of our critics will allow. I should have thought, for instance, that common sense rather than any social theory suggests society is such an infinitely elaborate system of interlocking forces, pressures and relationships that there is no single cause of any social ill. Television will inevitably attract a disproportionate amount of attention not simply because it is all pervasive but because it is a mystery medium. Public television is, after all, only half a century old and in spite of thousands of research reports, relatively little is known about its effects on human behaviour. This is an issue that needs to be subjected to cool and careful analysis; we will get nowhere by moralistic knee-jerk reactions.

There is also the drip-drip argument, which charges that the sheer volume and frequency of violence on television desensitizes viewers to the point where they take brutality for granted so a barrier of abhorrence, which acts as a deterrent to real-life violence, is broken down. Of course, it is beyond argument that sustained doses of any stimulus will have a numbing effect on the human system so it takes a greater quantity to produce the same effect. But because viewers may become desensitized to violence on the screen, which is certainly a problem for the writer and producer, it doesn't follow that they will become equally blasé about violence in real life. Anyone who has been in war-time combat will confirm that a regular diet of John Wayne or Errol Flynn death-or-glory movies in no way prepared them for what they were about to experience on the battlefield. We may see innumerable car crashes on the television screen, but the horror is in no way mitigated when we first encounter those mangled bodies in a real-life car wreck.

The point is that television engages only two of our senses: sight and hearing. We can see and hear a violent act but not feel the pain of it. If we ever got round to marketing the 'feelies' of Aldous Huxley's *Brave New World* where television viewers experienced the full sensuous impact of what they saw, the smell, taste and feel as well as the sight and sound of it, the chances are that nine-tenths of the violence would vanish from the TV screen overnight. Who would want to pay that price for realism?

I have long been conscious of this paradox. One danger in controlling too rigorously the depiction of violence on television is that what remains may not be violent enough: it may mislead viewers about the true horror of violence and seduce them into believing that people can be shot, slashed and beaten neatly, painlessly, almost forensically. Far from the shock of the real thing being lessened by its televisual representation, it may be all the more traumatic because the violence they have seen on the small screen has been distorted and sanitized.

I felt the critical question to address when we were thinking of showing *Reservoir Dogs* was not 'Will it provoke some lunatic to homicidal behaviour?'. If we made that the benchmark it would rule out of court every war film and most news bulletins. For me, the key question was 'Is this a serious piece of work or exploitative?'. Since I had no doubt what the answer was, I approved the transmission of *Reservoir Dogs*.

Film on Four operated with almost complete independence within the organization. It had been founded and was run by David Rose, who had a safe pair of hands, he knew what he was doing. I signed the cheques, let the production team get on with it then sat back smugly and received plaudits I'd done little to deserve as one film after another was a hit – two of my favourites from Jeremy Isaacs's time were *Letter to Brezhnev* and *My Beautiful Laundrette*. When David Rose retired we looked around for a suitable replacement and eventually Liz Forgan made a suggestion. She had met David Aukin, who was second in command at the National Theatre. He was a theatre man and knew nothing about the technicalities of film-making, but I met him and was impressed that he had the one quality I prize above all others: taste. I appointed him and was soon content to let him get on with things without interference.

I have a low violence threshold and find some perfectly acceptable films impossible to watch. My timidity almost led to my rejecting what proved to be one of our most successful films, Danny Boyle's *Shallow Grave*, a story about the efforts of three young people to dispose of the body of a flatmate who had died of a fatal overdose, leaving behind a fortune in banknotes. Inevitably the friends fall out as greed takes over and the result is bloody mayhem. *Film on Four* operated with a great deal of independence and I had only vague memories of approving the budget of *Shallow Grave*. I never asked to see scripts or the rough-cut of any of our productions unless they had been specifically referred to me because they raised questions of taste and standards.

So one morning I slipped into our viewing theatre with a real sense of anticipation to preview the final version of *Shallow Grave*. I thought the first twenty minutes of the film were exceptional. It was witty, beautifully shot and crackling with suspense, then I felt it descended into *grand guignol*, got much blacker and made my flesh creep. The dismembering of the body was accomplished with such gut-wrenching realism I could hardly bear to watch the screen and the sound of a saw rasping on human bones set my teeth on edge. When the film ended and the lights came on, I was asked by the producer, in tones that anticipated congratulation, how I had enjoyed it?

'I don't know what to say,' I ventured. 'It began brilliantly and then for me it was utterly destroyed by those graphic torture scenes. I thought it was shaping up into a wonderful black comedy and then it turned into something unwatchable. Not only that, but I doubt if it is even transmittable.'

I left the theatre to an embarrassed silence. In retrospect, I realize that I had made a poor programme judgement. However uncongenial I personally might find the film, I had missed its point and am now vastly relieved that I had the sense not to bury it. *Shallow Grave* became a great hit and at the 1994 Dinard Festival picked up the Golden Hitchcock award for best film and best acting. At BAFTA in 1995, it achieved the Alexander Korda Award for Best British Film.

The degree of confidence I had in the *Film on Four* team is shown by the fact that the first I heard of *Four Weddings and a Funeral*, destined to be one of our greatest hits ever, was when I walked into the office one morning to a discernible buzz among the staff. I asked what the fuss was about. Excitedly they told me they'd been to a screening of *Four Weddings and a Funeral*, which they said was the best film they'd seen in years. This was one of the nice things about Channel 4: we were more than an organization; we were a family where everyone, whatever their job, shared in the common delight if we had a great success and were downcast when we failed. And what successes we had to celebrate! In 1993 we received nine Oscar nominations for *Howards End* and six for *The Crying Game*. Two years later, *The Madness of King George* was nominated for five Oscars and *Four Weddings and a Funeral* for two.

Movies were in my blood and I felt surefooted, though not infallible, in the programme areas of Channel 4, but the endless politicking began to get me down. December 1992 was Channel 4's last month on Daddy ITV's allowance before we had to go out into the cold, hard world and fend for ourselves. There were some nervous people around as the time drew nearer to when we would have to exist on the advertising we could sell. As I left for my Christmas holidays, we had about a million pounds of revenue promised out of the £300 million we needed for the first year. Sure, I was worried. If I got this calculation wrong, Channel 4 was finished. I knew I had a great team and could prove that ITV's monopoly of air-time sales had worked to our detriment. In the last year that ITV sold the air time on our behalf, those sales amounted to 13.9 per cent of total commercial revenue. In our first year of financial independence we got it up to 18 per cent, and it has kept on growing since.

The threat of privatization hovered over us from 1988 for the entire life of Conservative rule. In June 1996, the heritage minister said in the House of Commons that though the government was not considering immediate privatization he did not rule out the possibility for the future. This statement fuelled speculation that the proposal might appear in the Conservative Party's manifesto for the 1997 general election, raising at least £1.5 billion to finance tax cuts. The Channel 4 board issued a strong statement saying, yet again, that it was implacably opposed to any such move since it would turn the Channel into a cheap ITV clone. Gerald Kaufman, the Labour MP, came to our defence in the *Evening Standard*, arguing that whereas Channel 4 was not accountable to the taxpayers, who didn't contribute a penny piece towards it, the BBC certainly was paid for by the public and ought to be made much more accountable by getting rid of the Great and the Good who are the board of governors and either find a cash-rich partner such as British Telecom or raise serious money on the market. Pithily his case was summarized in the headline, 'Memo to Labour: save Grade, sell Birt.'

I began to bore even myself as I had to keep on repeating the mantra, 'You can have a privatized Channel 4 or one with a public-service remit, but not both.' Some city analysts used my own efforts against me. The very success of Channel 4 in recent years, they argued, was adequate justification for privatization. I'd turned it into a desirable property by increasing audience ratings and fighting to be rid of the controversial payments we had to make to ITV. To counter that ploy I had one trump card: since I was identified so closely with Channel 4's success, they had to consider the possibility that if privatization went ahead, I would go. I did nothing to disabuse them, though I had now become sufficiently politically astute to realize that a deterrent is only effective so long as it isn't used. I carefully avoided even hinting at resignation; instead, I embarked on another endless round of public meetings, letter campaigns and the lobbying of

MPs. In the event, the Tories lost the 1997 election, which meant that we had to switch targets and lobby strenuously to make sure the newly elected Blair administration didn't take privatization over as one of the previous government's policies it intended to honour.

The other threat, not just to Channel 4 but to the entire British public broadcasting system, came from Rupert Murdoch's News International conglomerate. I first encountered Murdoch when I was still a sports reporter on the *Daily Mirror*. Our boss, Hugh Cudlipp, had bought Odhams Press and with the package came the *Daily Herald*, a fading Labour-supporting downmarket newspaper. Hugh was indisputably a newspaper genius, but his decision to rename the *Herald* and relaunch it as a broadsheet called the *Sun* proved disastrous. In the *Mirror* office we perused the first edition and knew that it wouldn't work. It was suspended in a circulation limbo: broadsheets such as *The Times* and the *Daily Telegraph* did the serious stuff much better, while the *Sun* was too high-minded and dense to appeal to the masses. We were all vastly relieved when Hugh found this mug, a wetback from the outback, to buy it.

Hugh couldn't have known that in selling the *Sun* to Rupert Murdoch he was accelerating the end of the *Mirror*'s dominance of the tabloid market. He did what many people have done since, to their great cost: underestimated Rupert. That is the recurrent theme of the Rupert Murdoch story. Besides the *Mirror*, the BBC underestimated him, so did BSB, and the Carr family, owners of the *News of the World*, who went into partnership with him, like the gentle jungle folk in the fairy-tale who thought they could dine with a lion and found themselves the main course. I had some fellow feeling with Murdoch: we were both outsiders, patronized and resented by the establishment, which made us grimly determined to beat them at their own game.

Rupert's special skill is to parley newspaper power into political advantage, then use this political clout to gain even more commercial leverage. He did it first in Australia, then in the UK and tried it, to slightly less effect, in the United States. It is easy to demonize him, as the opposition press are bound to do. But though we locked horns on a number of broadcasting issues, I have no personal animus against him. It's spineless politicians I despise, the ones who underestimate Rupert, begin by patronizing him and end up terrified of his power. That mock semi-literate banner headline, 'Its the Sun Wot Won It!', is not just braggadocio. Murdoch really believes that by the power of his newspapers he can win elections, and he's managed to mesmerize the politicians into believing it too. It is a scandal that a foreigner has been able to amass so much media real-estate in Britain without any real political challenge. He's like Moses crossing the Red Sea: the waves always mysteriously part to allow him through.

I was very vocally critical in 1994 when Murdoch's BSkyB proposed a deal with the Premier Football League to show its games on satellite TV. This meant that *Match of the Day*, a national institution, might be lost to terrestrial television viewers and be available only to satellite subscribers. The Football Association realized that such a move would have made them unpopular with ordinary fans and created political waves, and they were on the point of turning Murdoch down when the BBC came to their rescue by offering to take back *Match of the Day*.

I called in what favours I had and rang my old friend Bob Phillis, by now deputy director general of the BBC, begging him not to agree to the deal. He obviously thought my warning that the BBC was making a pact with the devil was either hysteria or sour grapes. 'You are conniving at the creation of a monster that will devour us all,' I told him. He was polite but dismissive: the BBC, he told me, were excited at the prospect of this new commercial venture. I should have known that a Birtian BBC would relish a deal with Murdoch, which might bring as a bonus favourable treatment from the hitherto critical *Times* and *Sunday Times*.

All right, if the Murdoch deal had gone ahead without the BBC, the Corporation might not have regained *Match of the Day*, but it's a racing certainty they would have hung on to a whole series of great sporting events, such as the Ryder Cup, that BSkyB are now snapping up. John Birt may fancy himself as a business brain, but compared to Rupert Murdoch he's an amateur, and with that cocksureness that vitiates his real abilities, John, like almost everybody else, underestimated his antagonist.

In 1995, I flew to Nelson Mandela's new South Africa to give evidence to a Commission of Inquiry that had been set up to consider the feasibility of establishing the equivalent of a Channel 4 there. I took my friend and colleague Peter Ibbotson with me and for long hours on the flight we discussed the implications of the advertisements the government had placed in national newspapers inviting bids for a new terrestrial channel, Channel 5. We speculated on what would happen if Murdoch, who already had a satellite monopoly, should gain control of the only unallocated terrestrial channel. Channel 4 would then be the nut between the nutcrackers: Murdoch could starve us of all kinds of imported material, including, for instance, American movies – he controlled access to the entire library of 20th Century Fox.

I decided to go public. I was due to give a speech for the British Journalism Review in April 1995, so I tore up the script I had already written and sketched out a nightmare scenario in which a consortium dominated by Murdoch won the bid for Channel 5. It would be the final chapter in a saga of government incompetence and weakness dating back to the 1980s when the tax breaks promised to cable companies were rescinded and BT was forbidden to take part in the provision of entertainment services, even though the whole country was wired to receive them. Then there was the satellite débâcle. The odds were loaded against BSB, which had to use 'Rolls-Royce' technology while Rupert Murdoch was allowed to compete against them from his Luxembourg-based channel using the Astra satellite, which had been designed for telecommunications. The more expensive British service was undercut and Murdoch's Sky was able to destroy it by a merger that absorbed it. By a remarkable coincidence the whole deal was done just a few days before the 1990 Broadcasting Act came into force, which would have given the ITC power to intervene. This was Murdoch demonstrating his legendary powers to walk through regulatory and legislative barriers as though they didn't exist.

Then there was the central feature of the 1990 Act, the auctioning of ITV franchises, which turned into farce. The winning bids ranged from £2,000 to £34 million for immensely valuable assets. And, of course, as I reminded my audience, the government forced Channel 4 to pay nearly £100 million to ITV in the first two years as the price of its having the right to sell its own advertising. Now Murdoch's tentacles were attaching them-selves to a national terrestrial network, giving him an unbreak-able stranglehold on our entire broadcasting system. So while the BBC had been wrestling with government over its future, and ITV was distracted by the auction process and the problem of mergers within a tired federal structure and Channel 4 was battling against the absurdity of the funding formula, Murdoch had gone on remorselessly exploiting his special advantage. Add Channel 5 to his seven satellite TV channels and his 36 per cent ownership of the British press, and he would be the most powerful man in Britain.

I ended by spelling out the only option open to the govern-ment facing this fearsome cross-media dynasty: pass an urgent one-line Bill giving the ITC wider discretion to ignore the highest bid – which was bound to be Murdoch's – in awarding the Channel 5 licence, or instruct the ITC to delay the Channel 5 bidding process until new ownership rules are in place.

'Judging by press reports this week, MPs of all parties are beginning to stir uncomfortably at the prospect of further terres-trial media advances by Mr Murdoch. The politicians cannot say they have not been warned.'

So desperate was I to get my warning across to the British public that I played fast and loose with journalistic ethics and offered my speech to the *Guardian*, the *Daily Telegraph* and the *Independent*, telling each of them they could have it as an exclusive story. I ended up with massive coverage and the ill-will of the editors I had duped. But a few weeks later, when the bids were revealed, alarmed by the political pressure building up against it, the Murdoch consortium, which was an immensely powerful combination of News International, Polygram, Granada Television and the American cable giant TCI, did a tactical withdrawal and instead of the rumoured £25–6 million offered only £2 million.

It was all very exciting but I began to get sick of political campaigning. Broadcasting Bills are like the Circle Line, they just keep coming round: same arguments, same vested interests, same struggle to keep the politicians off our backs. I had been forced to move further and further away from the production process; the Channel's schedule was virtually being run by John Willis, who did it so brilliantly as to raise increasingly in my mind the question: assuming that our political and financial base is secure, does the Channel really need me any longer?

Epilogue

OUT OF THE BOX

O N 28 JANUARY 1997, I resigned from Channel 4. According to the *Guardian*,

> It was a routine board meeting. No one working at Channel 4's hi-tech glass tower had given it a second thought. But just after 6.30 p.m. the meeting broke up and the news began to seep out: Michael Grade was leaving not just his beloved channel but the television industry ... Last night there was shock and bewilderment among staff working late at the channel's Richard Rogers-designed headquarters. In a notoriously leaky business, there had been no advance warning. Mr Grade was regarded by his staff as an inspirational creative leader with an instinctive flair for television as show business.

That evening the chairman of the board, Sir Michael Bishop, informed the press, 'Michael Grade has told me he wishes to leave the television industry and pursue his other interests.' He went on to say that there were two conditions attached to the board's agreement to release me: I had to make a compensatory payment to buy out my contract and also give a legally binding undertaking that I wouldn't go into direct competition with Channel 4.

The press were taken by surprise, and their punning headline writers ran riot. According to the *Daily Express*, I was 'The Mogul Who Put the Ogle into our TV'. I should be called, they said, in a pathetic play on my uncle's name, Lewd Grade, though on an inside page, Martin Vander Weyer wrote that I had been 'loud, aggressive, arrogant – just right for the job. Grey men will never be successful risk-takers. So we should cheer, not mock, the likes of Michael Grade.' The *Star* reported my departure as 'The King of Telly Sleaze's Grade Escape.' The *Daily Mail* said, 'The Abominable Showman Is On the Move' – though they did wish me well. It was, thought *The Times*, a 'Grade A resignation with knobs on'.

The *Evening Standard* was judicious: 'Grade has sometimes shown lack of judgement – or indeed, mistaken his role as chief of an avowedly liberal channel, by seeming to deny a responsibility to exercise any judgement at all. Yet overall, he has been a shrewd, benign, highly skilful TV impresario who has deservedly become one of the most popular and respected figures in British television.' *Broadcast*, the trade journal of the television and radio industry, asked, 'Can it really be true? Television without Michael Grade is going to be like meat without salt or *King Lear* without Cordelia. A little more bland, a little less passionate. It just won't be the same when he's gone.' The *Sun*, ever the guardian of public morals, was less laudatory. It declared, 'This was the man who took TV into the sewers. He gave us a gay Christmas, lesbian nights, Europorn and four-letter filth. Decent people will not mourn his passing. Let's hope the airwaves smell a little sweeter.'

Mary Whitehouse's successor as head of the self-styled National Viewers' and Listeners' Association, the Reverend Graham Stevens, echoed the *Sun* and heaved a sigh of relief at the news of my departure. 'We are not sad to see him go. He made decisions which indicated he wished to push back the boundaries of broadcasting', and Valerie Riches, chairman of the lobby group Family and Youth Concern said, 'He overstepped the mark on a number of occasions. I would like to see someone in his place who pays regard to the total health of society rather than pushing back barriers.'

There were expressions of regret, Virginia Bottomley, the

National Heritage Secretary, paid tribute to the 'formidable contribution' I'd made to British television, and wished me well. A number of my colleagues in the industry, ranging from Michael Green, chairman of Carlton, David Elstein, Channel 5's chief executive, and Michael Jackson at the BBC made public statements lamenting my departure, though some were laced with the competitive spirit that made my job so challenging. Greg Dyke, chairman of Channel 5 said, 'I believe Michael has run C4 with a combination of political acumen, financial astuteness, scheduling flair and programming independence. C4 will miss him greatly but for C5 it's got to be good news.' Dawn Airey, Channel 5's director of programmes, commented tersely, 'One less critic of Channel 5 has to be a good thing.'

After the ritual expressions of sorrow or satisfaction came the post-mortems. *Broadcast* magazine thought that my three great achievements at Channel 4 were to persuade the government to phase out the funding formula so that money could be ploughed back into programmes, my key role in the fight to stave off the attempt to privatize the channel, and the renaissance of the UK film industry through hits such as *Four Weddings and a Funeral* and *Trainspotting*. However, in the *Guardian*, Maggie Brown wondered whether I'd decided to go because I was losing my touch. She thought my departure was

> by no means a tragedy for the station or for viewers. Michael Grade has charisma (enhanced by frequent top-up tans from trips on his ocean-going yacht) charm and more sensitivity than his cigar-chomping image suggests . . . And he's got an awful lot right at the channel . . . but the suspicion has recently mounted that the man at the top didn't quite understand what his commissioning editors were up to. 'I think Grade is a prime example of the trendy ageing syndrome,' said one critic yesterday.

After a catalogue of what she regarded as my programme errors, Maggie Brown concluded that in twenty-three years of television, my greatest contribution had been in the middle eighties when I transformed the BBC 1 schedules.

Raymond Snoddy in *The Times* was more magnanimous. I was, he concluded, leaving Channel 4 in good shape; it was still recognizable as a place where new ideas and talents could flourish. He felt I had demonstrated both broadcasting skills such as scheduling and an understanding of business and airtime sales. *Marketing Week* was also flattering.

> Not many television chief executives come to personify the channels they head. But in Michael Grade's case, the man was the brand. The outsize cigar stubbed in an ashtray outside his office was like a flag over Windsor Castle, denoting the chief was in. The ubiquitous red braces signalled Flamboyance in a world of grey suits. Braces and cigar were apt symbols of a rare combination of talents: creative thinking and business nous. They will be exceptionally difficult to replace in one person . . . but quit while you're ahead is a good maxim.

There was considerable comment on the fact that I had bought out my contract. In the financial section of *The Times*, Jon Ashworth wrote,

> Imagine that. Michael Grade writes out a cheque for £105,000, lights up a cigar and walks away from one of the best-paid jobs in British broadcasting. So inconsiderate. How can we write about fat-cat indulgence, when the moggies start handing the spoils back? It is apparent that Mr Grade has given up more than a token £105,000. In extricating himself from a five-year contract, he has given up the right to an unquantifiable sum in salary and bonuses, let alone the rest.

Then there was the question of what I would do next. According to the *Independent*, 'London's media village was alive with speculation that Mr Grade (a Charlton Athletic fanatic) plans to become chief executive of the Premier League.' A month after I resigned from Channel 4, I did in fact join the board of Charlton Athletic club, but as a non-executive director – no money, serious or otherwise, there. I also became chairman of the National Theatre Development Council, responsible for drumming up cash to supplement the NT's annual income, but that wasn't a day job, either. The *Guardian* said that unconfirmed rumours in the city linked me to a bid with Michael Green for the Rank Organization or to the full-time chairmanship of the video-distribution firm VCI, of which I was already non-executive chairman.

A couple of days later the punters had another field day when the board of First Leisure Corporation announced that I would become executive chairman before the end of the year. 'C4 Chief Excited by Life of Leisure'; 'A Leisurely Way to Make the Grade'; 'Blackpool and Bingo Lures Grade from TV'; 'Grade Seeks Fresh Opportunities for Leisure'. Eric Reguly in *The Times* summarized First Leisure's activities:

> It has a large portfolio of bars and nightclubs, including the Equinox in London's Leicester Square and the Brannigan's Music Bars, a mixed bag of bowling alleys, marinas jointly owned by British Aerospace and an indoor ski slope. There are bingo clubs, two West End theatres, a health and fitness division that is growing strongly, and seaside resorts. Blackpool, where it owns the Blackpool Tower, the Winter Gardens, three piers and two hotels, seems to be its private domain.

Reguly offered three reasons for my move: my fear of getting stale at Channel 4, an emotional attachment to First Leisure, which was founded by my uncle, Bernie Delfont, and the possibility of earning serious money because 'Channel 4 could not give him share options, the source of any top executive's real earnings power'.

Reguly's analysis was shrewd. I had been happy to renew my contract with Channel 4 in 1995 but the battle over the funding formula rumbled on interminably, and even when we won, the legislation was delayed so we had to keep up the momentum of our campaign to ensure that the government didn't stumble at the last fence. The process began to exhaust me. I had moved further and further away from programme-making, so I missed the creative buzz – there is little to get the adrenaline flowing in regular appearances before Select Committees and the study of endless Green Papers. I had become a political lobbyist, a perfectly honourable profession, but this was not why I had gone into the television industry.

In other words, I was getting bored. Channel 4 was financially sound with an impressive 11 per cent share of the viewing audience, and with our range of programmes we had effectively stolen the BBC's clothes – setting the agenda for minority programming as commentators talked about BBC 2 beginning to look more and more like Channel 4. And my director of programmes, John Willis, effectively ran the show, winning prizes right across the board – documentary, drama, comedy and films. He was superb at his job and didn't really need me. All I was required to do was pay the bills and take the flak, and I was happy to do both, but my heart sank at the thought of spending my best years fighting off further attempts at privatization and battling to influence the next Broadcasting Bill – and the one after that.

My frustration came to a head at the 1996 annual performance review by the ITC. The 1990 Broadcasting Act had removed from the ITC its legal power to be Independent Television's publisher with the right to preview any programmes, but because it licensed Channel 4 as well as ITV, Channel 5, TVam and GMTV, the ITC could impose a performance review on us, which it did. This became for me an annual martyrdom. Every year we dutifully trooped into the ITC headquarters and had to listen to a litany of second-guessing about our programmes. 'We' didn't like this, that or the other, 'we' thought the camera work on that documentary was poor, 'we' felt this joke in poor taste – on and on *ad nauseam*. This almighty, anonymous 'we' was an amalgam of personal prejudices, gleanings from television critics, what the ITC members' cleaning staff thought, and general scuttlebutt in the industry. The ITC had a full-time staff, a sort of civil service, some of whom had been BBC and ITV producers. Their comments rarely showed the depth of perception to be found in, say, the BBC's programme review board where highly experienced professionals analysed their colleagues' work with utter frankness tempered by an understanding of the technical problems involved.

On this particular occasion, it was a series of dramas by new writers we'd asked Alan Bleasdale to produce that came under the hammer. We were talent-spotting and Alan had read thousands of scripts before selecting half a dozen. As might be expected with new writing, the results were mixed, but in all six Alan had recognized potential and we at Channel 4 were delighted to sponsor them for, in the end, good writing is the scarcest commodity in television. One of the ITC's junior officials launched into a mincing, nit-picking critique, pronouncing, 'We thought the series was below par.' I was aghast that the ITC should put their authority behind the ill-informed opinion of an inexperienced bureaucrat pitting his judgement against that of one of television's most distinguished playwrights, Alan Bleasdale, and Peter Ansorge, Channel 4's head of drama.

I had no quarrel with the ITC doing its job as a regulatory body, seeing to it that we observed the conditions of our licence and provided the range of programmes we had promised when we applied for it. They had a legal duty to police their own programme codes, but their general judgements about programme quality were as subjective as anyone else's. Of course, they were entitled to them, but when these sometimes amateurish opinions were set down in the official minutes of their meetings and made public, they could be destructive of the morale of programme makers.

I kept my temper with great difficulty, but as I left the meeting, I thought, I've had enough of this. I was weary of being lectured, preached at, threatened and tut-tutted at by MPs, newspaper editorials, standards councils, viewers' associations and broadcasting commissions, all claiming to know what is best for the public. They alone have the delicate conscience, the higher moral sense that enables them to oversee the people's viewing habits. As a matter of stern duty, they watch television by the hour and remain unaffected by the tidal waves of filth and obscenity they are convinced programme makers are directing at ordinary viewers in order to corrupt the nation. I believe in intelligent legal regulation but not when it degenerates into creative strangulation. There is no more depressing sight than the wagging admonitory fingers and quivering noses of professional moralists conveying lofty disapproval at the artistry of people far more talented than they are. I was fed up with the lot of them – not a healthy state of mind.

So after the most fulfilling nine years, I decided to call it a day. Professionally, the channel was in excellent hands, protected and nurtured by a board presided over by a great chairman, Sir Michael Bishop, who had succeeded another, Dickie (Lord) Attenborough. A television channel which is set up to be experimental and to concentrate on minority programming needs to re-invent itself every so often to combat the effects of that inertia which is the price of success – the tendency to go on doing the same things in the same way because they work. Fans of Jeremy Isaacs were appalled at the changes I made at Channel 4, and some have frowned, no doubt, on changes my successor Michael Jackson has made, but as I told him when he was appointed, I expected him to turn the place upside down. He could rely on my support, whatever changes he made, because I knew full well that the policies and programme formats established during my time as chief executive would need a massive overhaul. I would be disappointed if the impress of his personality did not result in radical change.

My management team at Channel 4 was running smoothly but I knew the time was rapidly approaching when I would have to shake it up before competence shaded into complacency. These were not just colleagues but friends, and I hated the thought of having to cull some of them. As my encounters with John Birt had taught me, I am not a great one for personal confrontation. I have no problem in dealing firmly with incompetence or dishonesty, but to dispense with excellent colleagues because the overall mix of skills and experience must be changed to refresh the channel was a prospect I found distasteful. Better to let my successor size up his/her team and flesh out his/her vision for the future accordingly.

The board of First Leisure had approached me on a number of occasions to see whether I was interested in becoming an executive chairman and in the end they wore me down. And I had an emotional stake in the company my late uncle Bernie had created by some very nifty and courageous financial footwork. Though he was in his seventies, he masterminded a management buy-out of some assorted leisure assets from Charles Forte in 1983 to create First Leisure. For years Bernie had made no secret of his desire that I should succeed him. When I was in Hollywood, he invited me to join him as understudy right at the outset of the creation of First Leisure. So it was all unfinished business for me. I became non-executive chairman of First Leisure in 1991 but in that role my power to shape policy was strictly limited. When I took over as executive chairman I was a Grade again.

I settled down in Uncle Bernie's old chair at First Leisure. For the first year and a half, I didn't do a press interview and, surprisingly, suffered no withdrawal symptoms. When my name appeared in a newspaper, it wasn't on the front page but way back in the business section, no lurid story to do with sex and violence on television but some technical adjustment in company structure. My press exposure value shrank from a couple of columns to a couple of inches, and I loved it. I had got my life back. And I didn't *have* to watch television: it became a matter of choice, not necessity. For years, I had arrived home each evening with a pile of cassettes I needed to view and assess before programme meetings the following day. I love television, but it was necessary to discover that I could live without it in order to prevent it from taking over my new life with Francesca.

The company was solid and well founded but unexciting; its momentum had flagged, it needed to be jolted into growth again. It was just too conservative in a fast-moving industry. In its time, First Leisure had been the darling of the city but was underperforming in the stock market, so I was faced with the kind of challenge I love: to re-invent an institution with a great history and real potential but temporarily on a plateau. That's what I'm best at, what I did with BBC 1 and with Channel 4. I soon discovered that any restructuring that put First Leisure in good shape for the future would have to be much more radical than I had first thought. I proposed a drastic slimming down of its activities, which had become too disparate and lacked focus. We decided to offload our seaside pleasure concerns, such as Blackpool Tower, and our bingo halls to concentrate on the rapidly burgeoning health and leisure industry.

I have found it all immensely hard work, requiring intense mental concentration and considerable nerve – analysing the market, predicting which way competitors will jump, buying and selling, investing and safeguarding shareholders' money. The job is tough, but in contrast to the broadcasting industry, I only have one master to serve. I don't need to satisfy a whole array of constituencies – viewers, independent producers, advertisers, boards of governors, regulatory bodies and the government. The shareholders alone are my master. My loyalties are not fragmented and my concentration span has narrowed so I can give my whole mind to one overarching task.

Because I started out as a journalist, my relationship with the press had always been relaxed, but here in the city it is a much more formal and arm's-length matter. When I was in television I'd spend hours gossiping with journalists and we had a pretty clear idea of what was on or off the record. The newspapers were bursting with speculation and rumour about the entertainment business, but even the wildest inaccuracies usually did little harm. However, financial journalism is much more serious: millions of pounds can be wiped off the value of shares on the strength of newspaper rumours, which may or may not be well founded. And financial journalists can exercise a kind of summary judgement I found it hard to get used to. We'd spend months planning our future policies, consulting the experts, working all the hours that God sends, incorporating our findings in very precisely phrased reports, which the financial press would skim through and then approve or rubbish in a couple of paragraphs. Millions of pounds and hundreds of jobs might hang on a casual thumbs up or down.

Once I decided that First Leisure would have to slim down by disposing of many of its traditional assets, I realized that I was like someone busy sawing away at the branch on which he is sitting – the more effective the operation, the sooner I will work myself out of a job. Within months I might well be unemployed. I have no grand plan. What spare time I have has been spent working as a non-executive director of the New Millennium Experience Company, helping to manage the creative process, delivering the contents which, I believe, will make a visit to the Millennium Dome an unforgettable experience. In one sense, the Dome is the greatest circus ring in the world, and as an old song-and-dance man, I'm in my element helping to stage-manage the show. After all, that was where the Grade dynasty began – to the smell of greasepaint, the roar of the crowd and, of course, bums on seats.

An announcement that John Birt was leaving the BBC in April 2000 and the governors were about to advertise for a replacement as director general gave me cause to think seriously. Once, it had been my ambition to run the greatest broadcasting organization in the world. When the advertisement appeared, should I throw my hat into the ring? A number of my friends and former BBC colleagues urged me to put my name forward, and I was almost, but not quite, tempted to apply. The more I thought about it, the more I realized that I had undergone what amounted to a character-change. Five years previously I would have battered down the door of the chairman's office for an application form, but I found that my insatiable obsession about the BBC had moderated. Even were I to be acceptable to a board of governors about whom I'd been pretty scathing, I could no longer summon up that almost obsessive energy to do this one thing above all else and to the exclusion of all else. I had become a more rounded, less hyperactive personality. Now in my middle fifties with a new marriage and a young family, I was no longer prepared or able to narrow the focus of my existence to make the BBC the be-all and end-all of my life. It was long past time when I should put my wife and family first.

At the finale of Beethoven's opera *Fidelio*, prisoners grope their way out of the depths of Pizarro's fortress dungeon, blinded by the unaccustomed sunlight, their years of incarceration behind them. That seems to me to be an apt image for the BBC staff when they emerge from the dark ages of the Birtian era. And the next director general will require immense energy and single-minded dedication to reverse twelve years of creative restriction and bureaucratic muddle. And that's not me, not any longer. My friend Bill Cotton has a saying about the BBC. It is, he says, a lucky organization: in its moment of greatest need, when all seems lost, something or someone always turns up. And that is precisely what has happened with the appointment of Greg Dyke to succeed John Birt.

Once I knew that Greg Dyke's hat was in the ring, any lingering thoughts of applying for the job myself vanished. I could not have been happier. I know him well as a colleague and friend. There is a touch of the Grades about him in his respect for creative people, his managerial style, his openness to new ideas and his grasp of business. When in the 1960s Hugh Carleton Greene was appointed director general he said that his intention was to open the windows of the BBC and let in some fresh air. And he did precisely that. His was a libertarian spirit, defending and encouraging anarchic comedy series such as *Till Death Us Do Part* (with Alf Garnett lurching from expletive to expletive), and late-night satire shows such as *That Was the Week That Was* (which attacked targets like the Royal Family and the Church of England that had been previously sacrosanct) and tough drama documentaries such as *Cathy Come Home* and *Up the Junction*, which dealt head-on with previously unmentionable subjects like homelessness, schizophrenia and abortion. I truly believe Greg will be a DG squarely in the Hugh Greene tradition.

After all the harsh things I've said and thought about the BBC's board of governors, the least I can do is to admit that this time they got it spectacularly right, though it is an awful commentary on the Birt years that it was impossible to muster a slate of outstanding candidates from within the organization. The cleverest, most imaginative and enterprising personalities have been driven out or quit in despair. I exempt Alan Yentob from that stricture, he is an outstandingly creative executive and the BBC is lucky to have him, but the DG's job was not for him; he needs as few administrative and political responsibilities as possible in order to concentrate on programme quality and talent.

To my way of thinking, an added bonus of Greg's appointment is that the systematic campaign by *The Times* to undermine his candidature indicates that Rupert Murdoch must respect or even fear him greatly. Rupert doesn't like independent-minded, effective competition. The BBC is the biggest bulwark against a News International takeover of the airwaves, especially if it is run by a DG capable of rugged independence, even bloody-mindedness, and Greg's the man.

I suppose most is owed to Sir Christopher Bland for sticking to his conviction that Greg Dyke was the best man for the job against a barrage of counter-propaganda, but quite a lot is owed to William Hague too. You could say that Greg was Hague's first appointment since the Tory leader's cack-handed public declaration of Greg's unacceptability undoubtedly stiffened the sinews of the governors, who plainly could not be seen to be browbeaten by any politician. This is not to say that Greg Dyke's financial link to the Labour Party was not a legitimate issue to raise. The row that resulted from this revelation has had the beneficial effect of underlining the centrality of political impartiality as one of the BBC's fundamental principles. Newspapers are neither required nor expected to be impartial; they can jump on any party bandwagon or openly support any political cause or personality they please. The BBC has never been given or sought such freedom. From the outset it was decreed that the

Corporation should be denied any political opinions of its own; it should not be able to editorialize on its own behalf.

There were originally two reasons for this. Throughout the early decades of its existence the BBC had the sole use of a scarce resource – the airwaves, which, unlike the printing presses, were controlled by Parliament. It was felt inappropriate that a body enjoying such a unique privilege should adopt partisan positions on issues of the day. And there was the financial argument. It was decided that the BBC should be funded by licence fee, which is, in effect, a covenant with the whole of the British people to supply them with education, entertainment and information in return for financial security. And since the public have a wide range of party-political loyalties, they can reasonably expect that the BBC will not use their money to take up an entrenched position against them.

So the governors were absolutely right to satisfy themselves that any candidate for the BBC's top job should leave behind his political allegiances at the entrance to Broadcasting House. In Greg's case the issue was clear cut and could be dealt with head on because his financial contributions to the Labour Party were open and a matter of public record. The politics of previous director generals were shrouded in mystery. For example, earlier in his career Sir Ian Trethowan had been a Tory activist; this was never publicly declared. However, there is not the slightest evidence that as director general he showed politicial bias or tried to influence the Corporation to favour the Tory Party. Indeed, were the director general – who is shut away on the third floor of Broadcasting House, cut off from the programme-makers by about ten layers of management – to move a muscle in the direction of influencing the content of a programme, the fact would be splashed across the front pages of the press the next day. The BBC is the leakiest organization in the world.

The Tory party's announcement, in the wake of Greg's appointment, that it would set aside £100,000 to pay a monitoring organization to watch BBC programmes for signs of anti-Tory bias is a crude attempt at political intimidation, trying to frighten programme-makers into giving the Party an easy ride. It is also cloud-cuckoo economics. The BBC produces thousands of hours of programmes on radio and television every year and it would take an army of researchers working round the clock to monitor them. The problem they face was comically illustrated in the *Today* programme on the day the setting up of this monitoring operation was announced. A down-the-line interview with Michael Heseltine about the Tory Party's policy on the euro was lost through technical trouble – or was it an act of sabotage by a raving leftie sound engineer? And should the loss of the interview be marked down as anti-Tory sabotage? After all, Heseltine is, in fact, at odds with his party's euro policy; hence, denying him air-time might please the Conservative Party Central Office. Tick or cross?

Mr Hague's advisers should know that this mechanical approach to impartiality has been tried throughout the BBC's long history and it doesn't work. There have been demands that each party should be given the same amount of air-time in news and current-affairs programmes. But public impact cannot be measured by the minute. There are personalities who are colourful, animated, articulate, who can make five minutes pass in a flash; others make five minutes seem like a dress rehearsal for death, they are so lacklustre and rambling. The only way you could achieve stopwatch impartiality is to breed out of public life the characters, the mavericks and charismatic personalities. The result would be not political balance but paralytic boredom.

I learned a lot about impartiality during my time at the BBC. I would call a programme politically impartial if a balance of significant opinions on the subject is offered, within a setting where the BBC, represented by the presenter, the camera operative or the editor, makes no attempt to impose its own viewpoint, where the subject is treated objectively with no descent into personalities or unworthy argument, and each participant has an equal chance to state his or her case; in other words, they are treated fairly.

Over the decades, through a thousand bruising encounters with politicians of all parties, the BBC has built up an impressive body of case law to guard against programme-makers imposing their private political convictions on the general public. But let's be realistic. Like absolute truth or perfect justice, total impartiality is an ideal no flesh-and-blood human being can attain. The result is bound to be a matter of more or less, and this is not because broadcasters are left-wing subversives or closet fascists but because they are not infallible. There are limits to their wisdom, knowledge and capacity to be open-minded. And they wouldn't be working as broadcasters if they weren't highly opinionated and bursting with ideas.

As I have often said, no matter what rules and guidelines, checks and balances are set in place to guard against political partisanship, they can only act as a safety-net for those walking this particular tightrope. In the end, it is the programme-makers' grasp of what constitutes truth, decency and fairness that really matters. And these moral qualities are nurtured long before broadcasters sign their first employment contract: they are nourished in the wider community. Our society gets the broadcasting and the broadcasters it deserves and, as Greg will discover, the BBC, in spite of the stultifying impact of the last decade, is still well blessed with programme-makers who have both creativity and conscience.

I have confessed my admiration for Hugh Carleton Greene; I think the present-day broadcasters can learn a lot from him. Libertarian though he was, he made it clear that there are limits to impartiality. He declared that the BBC was not impartial between good and evil. He had no intention of allowing the BBC to provide a platform for opinions and ideas that might undermine democracy. He had been the *Daily Telegraph's* correspondent in Germany before the Second World War and had a ringside view of the rise of Nazism; he had never forgotten the lessons he learned. The BBC could not be impartial about such issues as racism, fascism or anti-Semitism. Greene had a vision of the BBC not just as an organization or an institution but as a moral being, dedicated to enhancing the worthwhile experience of its viewers and listeners. I passionately believe Greg will inspire a rediscovery of this high view of the Corporation after a decade when management rhetoric has made it sound like a high-tech factory, producing conformity.

The buzzword of the moment is 'digital'. Billions of pounds are being invested throughout the world to take advantage of the commercial opportunities offered by this new technology. In essence it means almost unlimited TV channels, convergence of telephony, computers and traditional broadcasting on to one TV screen with one set-top box. John Birt has been evangelical in promoting the BBC's position in this brave new world, and to his great credit, he personally led the Corporation's push into providing the first public service on the Internet. The BBC's website is the most frequently visited domestic site, and this inspired legacy is perhaps his only unarguable achievement.

What will the digital revolution mean for viewers? Cheaper phone calls, home shopping, easy communication and access to knowledge through the Internet are on their way. But those who still look to their TV set for some cultural stimulation, for high-quality home-produced fare, for programmes that stimulate and provoke, or offer some sense of community, should not hold their breath. Digital is simply a means of distribution, a new way of selling goods, a way of repackaging existing programming, like movies and sport, then charging viewers more for it. I see no signs of any great programming innovation from the new digital channels. It is left to the BBC, ITV and Channel 4 to maintain the cultural dimension that has for fifty years been the hallmark of British broadcasting, the envy of the world. The recent disgraceful 'faking' of guests on talk-shows is just one example of commercial pressures lowering ethical standards in programme-making.

As governments seek to create a legislative framework to encourage digital developments over the next few years, they must do so with one eye carefully fixed on the BBC and other key terrestrial services to ensure a secure funding environment. In essence this means preserving the BBC licence fee at a sufficient level. Those who argue that the licence fee is an anachronism in this exciting age of consumer choice may have a theoretically unarguable position. But as the marketplace takes over and TV becomes more and more of a commodity, I believe the BBC's public-service role will become more and more important, and the case for the licence fee stronger, not weaker. Only the BBC can be relied on to deliver programme services with more on its mind than making money. Since the arrival of ITV in 1955 television in Britain has been a carefully managed enterprise, balancing the two conflicting imperatives: commerce and culture. The new digital world of plenty shifts the emphasis overwhelmingly to commerce. Only the BBC (and a non-privatized Channel 4) can stop television surrendering entirely to market economics and supply the programming that the market has already shown itself unwilling or unable to provide – education, original arts, high-cost contemporary drama, experimental comedy, high-risk formats and so on. The British public will not forgive any government that allows the BBC and Channel 4 to give up this high ground for the sake of political dogma or a one-off pay-day for the Treasury.

It wasn't just my career that took a dramatic new turn when I quit the television industry for First Leisure: my personal life achieved a new focus and fulfilment. I discovered that very ordinary but very precious thing, peace of mind. For all my adult life I had been in a hurry, desperate to repeat the Grade family success and get to the top in the television business. Because I hadn't developed the maturity of judgement to distinguish between what is important and what isn't in life, I allowed my relationships, however passionately I entered into them, to become ornaments to or diversions from my real goal, which was emulating the Grade brothers. At the first sign of a problem in my personal life, I backed off and dived into my work with even greater intensity and hoped things would just come right at home. They never did. For lack of loving attention, one relationship after another withered on the vine.

After my marriage to Sarah ended, I had a couple of serious, high-profile relationships that just fizzled out. So I concluded that I was one of those people not destined to enjoy a lifelong partnership. I totted up my assets and felt grateful for what I possessed – my health, two wonderful children, a decent living in a high-profile job, a yacht and plenty of friends. I concluded that living permanently with a partner was one of those skills, like juggling, that are inborn: if they don't come naturally, you can try as hard as you like but you'll never really master them.

Then I met Francesca at a Royal Television Society event in 1996. She was twenty years younger than me and had worked as deputy director for the Edinburgh Television Festival management. She came from a large, secure and loving family. We had a drink together and I gave her a lift to the station. I couldn't get her out of my mind. I rang her the next day and embarked upon a relationship that turned out to be quite different from any that preceded it. Because I lived in a goldfish bowl, nothing I did escaped press scrutiny, and Nigel Dempster in his *Mail on Sunday* column naturally reported that there was a new love in my life. Francesca is, according to his headline, a 'Grade One Sailor' and shares my love of opera. 'Darkly attractive and in her early thirties, Francesca works in the film and television rights department of HarperCollins.'

No quarrel with any of that, for once the press got it right. What no newspaper could reasonably understand was that I just knew, as we got closer, that where it matters most, in my heart and in my soul, we could make each other happier than we had ever been. Francesca was the first person ever capable of persuading me to convey my innermost feelings. This was a totally new experience for me and I bless her every day for her gift. The long struggle to find my true soulmate was finally over, just at the moment when I had given up. My mission in life is now to make her just as happy in return.

For our Christmas holidays in 1997 Francesca and I went sailing around the Caribbean on my boat *Laphroaig*, and on 5 January 1998 we got married on the Island of Mustique. It was quite a maritime operation. The only minister licensed to conduct the marriage service was based in St Vincent in the Grenadines, so we picked up the licence from there, sailed across to Mustique and in a bamboo hut, which was a non-denominational chapel, we were married by a charming but very serious Methodist preacher. There was a wild party at Basil's Bar, where regulars and guests alike toasted our health. Then the four friends who had stood as legal witnesses at the ceremony left us and we sailed away into the sunset on honeymoon. Magical!

On 7 December 1998 another Charlton Athletic supporter joined the family. I wasn't in the delivery room when my two children by Penny, my first wife, were born. At the time, it had not yet become customary for the father to witness the birth of a child – one paced the waiting room, sweating out the hours – so I did not see Alison and Jonathan come into the world. I only realized what I had missed as I sat in the operating theatre, stroking Francesca's head as the doctors performed an emergency Caesarian section. The surgeon called me, I looked over in time to see him, like a conjuror, producing a rabbit out of a hat, dangling from his hand this little blue creature. That was a defining moment in my life. I think that's when I finally grew up.

One week after Samuel's birth, Uncle Lew died. The final curtain had come down on a saga that began in Tsarist Russia and stretched to encompass the British entertainment industry for most of this century. One by one, the three brothers, Leslie, Bernie and Lew, had taken their bow and left the stage. In honour of Lew, our wonderful baby became Samuel Milo Lewis Grade. Who knows? Perhaps another Grade empire is in the making. When and if he reaches for a big cigar the entertainment industry had better watch out.

I have found peace and contentment in a secure, equal marriage. There is nothing left to prove, no raging ambitions unfulfilled, no empty hours to fill with frantic activity. Its good to get home at the end of the day to my wife and family. Marrying Francesca seemed a good idea at the time. It has turned out to be the very best idea I've ever had.

On 31 January 2000, I completed the restructuring of First Leisure, doing myself out of a job in the process. The shareholders, with one notable exception, approved of the radical action I took in selling off all our many businesses at full value, returning the cash and leaving them with shares in one, fast-growing high-quality business: health and fitness clubs.

The one exception was my very vocal aunt, Lady (Carol) Delfont, widow of my uncle Bernie, who started the company. She disapproved of the board's actions and feels very let down. I can understand her feelings, but the markets are not sentimental. First Leisure needed reinventing. All great businesses have to change, some have to reinvent themselves. You only have to look at great names like Marks and Spencer, who are changing from the inside, and Rover, who are being changed from the outside. Standing still is not an option. I doubt she will ever forgive me, which makes me sad, but what was done was in the best interests of the shareholders.

To fill the work vacuum, I have established a portfolio of interests – no full-time executive job, but lots of different responsibilities. I did put together a consortium to try to buy the Stoll Moss Theatre group when it was put up for sale. We bid some 15 million pounds less than Andrew Lloyd Webber's group, who won the auction at around 81 million. Again, I am sad that the theatres, where once my uncles Lew and Bernie appeared as dancers and which Lew once owned through his ATV group, didn't come back to the family.

The experience of this process proved to me that I could raise money in the city for the right opportunity. Soon after the theatres deal collapsed, an old friend, Ivan Dunleavy, came to me with the idea of buying Pinewood Studios. It took three months from the first idea to signing on the dotted line in February to buy the 100-acre site from the Rank Group, who had owned it for over sixty years. It is a thrill to turn up there for work, to the studios where I used to go with Billy Marsh in my talent-agent days to see Eric and Ernie and Norman Wisdom making their movies.

In addition, I have three non-executive positions, one of them with Camelot, who are bidding to run the next stage of the National Lottery. Life is good – so long as you keep your health, as my dad used to say. For once in my life I seem to have it all: the happiest home life with Francesca and baby Samuel; Alison and Jonathan nearby and thriving; and now a career that allows me total fulfilment.

Even Charlton Athletic has come good and won the First Division championship. Jonathan and I can't wait to take Samuel to his first game when we grace the Premiership next season. As my late grandmother used to say, 'Mustn't grumble!'

INDEX